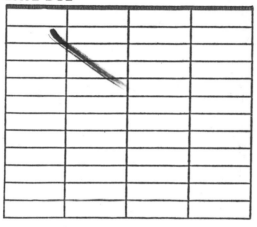

YALE HISTORICAL PUBLICATIONS
MISCELLANY, 110

THE GODLY MAN

IN STUART ENGLAND

Anglicans, Puritans, and the Two Tables, 1620–1670

J. Sears McGee

New Haven and London
Yale University Press
1976

Published under the direction
of the Department of History of Yale University
with assistance from the income of the
Frederick John Kingsbury Memorial Fund.
Library of Congress catalog card number: 75–43325
International standard book number: 0–300–01637–9

Designed by Sally Sullivan
and set in Baskerville type.
Printed in the United States of America by
The Vail-Ballou Press, Inc., Binghamton, New York.

Published in Great Britain, Europe, Africa, and Asia
(except Japan) by Yale University Press, Ltd., London.
Distributed in Latin America by Kaiman & Polon,
Inc., New York City; in Australia and New Zealand by
Book & Film Services, Artarmon, N.S.W., Australia;
in Japan by John Weatherhill, Inc., Tokyo.

TO MY WIFE

CONTENTS

PREFACE

Have you indeed seized the moment "which God hath fashioned and prepared by his own hand, for the accomplishing of the great work of reformation, wherewith God hath entrusted and honored you?" What specifically have you done both as individuals and as "Parliament-men . . . in reference to the First Table" and "to the Second Table?" These challenging questions recorded in the printed version of the sermon were addressed to the members of the House of Commons by Thomas Case on May 26, 1647. He then added that those members who had been guided by the Two Tables were godly men who had, like "so many Joshuas gone about the work in God's strength, in God's methods, and to God's ends."[1] Case, a famous London preacher and lecturer and a prominent figure in the Westminster Assembly of Divines, confidently and correctly assumed that his hearers and readers would not think that he was asking them about pieces of furniture. Moses had originally written the Ten Commandments on two stone tablets or "tables." Although the accounts in the Old Testament do not say which laws were on which tablets, tradition dictated that the first four (which express man's duties to God) appeared on the First Table. The latter six (which describe man's duties to other men) were engraved on the Second Table. The distinction between the two was a widely used device in catechisms and summaries of Christian doctrine. The Two Tables of the Decalogue provided, as the greatly respected theologian and scholar Archbishop James Ussher wrote, a means by which Christians might "the better remember our whole duty

1. *Spirituall Whordome Discovered* (1647), sigs. A3 (verso), A4 (recto). In the footnotes, the place of publication is London unless otherwise indicated. A staunch partisan, Case was said to issue the invitation to receive communion as follows: "You that have freely and liberally contributed to the Parliament for the defense of God's cause and the Gospel, draw near." *DNB*, s.v. Thomas Case. Several medieval examples of the use of "table" as "a tablet bearing or intended for an inscription" can be found in the *OED*. Our modern use of the word came somewhat later.

both to God and man; it being as a card or map of a country easily
carried about with us."[2]

Scholars who have studied the English Revolution have disagreed
in their answers to a basic question regarding whether the labels
"Anglican" and "Puritan" are useful and meaningful in our continuing discussion of the causes of that complex struggle. It is my
purpose to argue that the terms are useful, and that the Two Tables
provide a handy "card or map" to the definition of these terms in
the period from about 1620 to about 1670. This is a study of two
ideal types of the individual Christian man, one Anglican and the
other Puritan, and of the way in which interpretations of the duties
of the Two Tables serve as trustworthy guides to the important
points of difference between the two models in the period before,
during, and immediately after the Revolution itself. These conceptions of "the true Israelite," the truly converted godly man, are by
no means mutually exclusive; Anglicans and Puritans extolled many
of the same traits and held many assumptions in common. Yet the
ideal types were still distinct in certain important ways. These
types help us to understand the conflict between Anglicans and
Puritans, not because every man fitted one or the other of them in
every detail, but because believers attempted to gain assurance of
salvation by emulating the ideals, and by it comfort in distress, and
thus took different approaches to the outstanding issues of the day.
Public figures, such as the Duke of Buckingham, Archbishop Laud,
the Earl of Strafford, John Pym, Oliver Cromwell, and King
Charles himself, were evaluated, their authority and influence
strengthened or weakened, by the extent to which they could be
seen to be promoting or hindering the achievement of such ideal
goals in English life and worship.

2. James Ussher, *The Principles of Christian Religion*, 7th ed. (1678), p. 170. For
examples of the use of the "Two Tables" distinction, see Hammond, *Catechism*, pp.
189–90; Perkins, 2:10 and 3:32ff. Patrick Collinson found that there was "increased attention paid to the Ten Commandments both in catechisms and sermons,
a trend discernible equally on the continent" and in England toward the end of the
sixteenth century. *SCH* 1:208. The article by L. W. Batten in the *Encyclopedia of
Religion and Ethics* (Edinburgh: T. and T. Clark, 1911), 4:513–17, has a discussion
of the variation between the two Old Testament versions of the Decalogue. It
should also be noted that the Roman Catholic method of enumerating the commandments differs slightly from that used in the Anglican and Reformed traditions. *ODCC*, p. 319.

My method is in a sense comparable to that suggested by Professor J. G. A. Pocock's brilliant analysis of a "common-law language of politics" in which at different times different "conceptual vocabularies . . . heavy with assumptions" are in use.[3] I have attempted to describe and analyze what might be called a divine-law language of politics in which certain terms and phrases were equally "heavy with assumptions." The extent to which I fail to demonstrate that such terms as "idolatry," "charity," "brethren," "morality," "obedience," and "peace" were employed in ways which helped like-minded men and women to tell friend from foe is my own. The extent to which I succeed owes more than I can repay to the many people who have advised and assisted me before and during the years that this book, originally my doctoral dissertation, was in the making. My interest in early modern European history began during an undergraduate year at Trinity College, Cambridge, thanks to the generosity of the Abraham Foundation of Houston, Texas. My supervisors at Trinity, Mr. Peter Laslett and Dr. John H. Elliott, corrected my blunders, introduced me to the serious study of history with great patience, and retained an interest in my progress with great kindness. During my senior year at Rice University, Louis Galambos and Leonard Marsak taught me much and nominated me for the Woodrow Wilson Fellowship which enabled me to begin graduate study. At Yale the instruction and friendship I received from F. L. Baumer, Howard Lamar, and Ian Siggins was as needed as it was welcome. My dissertation committee included Edmund S. Morgan and Martin Griffin, and their advice was always valuable.

Those who know my dissertation adviser, J. H. Hexter, will understand my gratitude to him. He demanded the rigor, insight, intelligence, and industry which characterizes his own scholarship. Though I cannot match him, I can no more fail to try than he can fail to be fertile in suggestion and generous in encouragement and support when I do. A kind letter from the great authority on Stuart Puritanism, the late William Haller, provided suggestions that I very much appreciated. I hope that this book will be considered a worthy supplement to his tradition of scholarship. A number of

3. J. G. A. Pocock, "Working on Ideas in Time," in L. P. Curtis, ed., *The Historian's Workshop* (New York: Alfred Knopf, 1970), p. 158.

historians have read one or another of the versions of my manuscript in whole or in part: Jerald C. Brauer, Patrick Collinson, Abraham Friesen, Steven W. Haas, Warren Hollister, G. H. Joiner, Laura O'Connell, John Phillips, Kenneth Shipps, Don Smith, and Jack Talbott. For their many contributions and for their interest I am very grateful—no less so in those places where I decided not to follow their advice.

Circumstances have constrained me to modernize spelling, capitalization, and punctuation in quotations. Contractions and abbreviations have generally been expanded. The impracticality of searching out the original versions of works I used in their nineteenth-century editions has made this necessary. The original forms of the titles of seventeenth-century sources have, however, been preserved. Dates are Old Style but the year has been taken to begin on January 1.

Most of the research for this book was done in the North Library of the British Museum, and I am happy to express my sincere thanks for the unfailing courtesy of its staff. For occasional help I am also grateful to the staffs of the Sterling Memorial Library and the Beinecke Rare Book Library at Yale, Dr. Williams's Library in London, the Henry E. Huntington Library in San Marino, California, the Miriam L. Stark Library at the University of Texas in Austin, and the Library of the University of California at Santa Barbara. Grants from the University of California and the National Endowment for the Humanities have helped me pursue this work in its later stages. Kenneth Shipps kindly allowed me to use his notes on the lectures given by James Harrison to the Sir Thomas Barrington family between 1626 and 1643 (from a transcription made by Miss Mary Bohannon at Cornell of the MSS in the Essex Record Office). While in London I benefited greatly from two seminars at the Institute of Historical Research, one given by A. G. Dickens and Patrick Collinson on the Reformation and the other conducted by Roger Lockyer, Henry Roseveare, and Ian Roy on seventeenth-century England (where I read an early draft of part of chapter 5 and received criticism). In addition to his warm friendship, John Chandos gave me countless references and interesting ideas, and shared with me his boundless enthusiasm for discussing them. I owe much to the vigilant and perceptive editing of Nancy Paxton.

My greatest debt is to my wife, Mary Arnall McGee. Both a student of theology and a writer, she has suggested innumerable improvements in style, syntax, and sense. Her patience with my absorption in the seventeenth century has never given out, though sorely tested. No "yoke-fellow" could have done more to lighten my burden, nor shared it more willingly and more gracefully.

Santa Barbara, California   J. Sears McGee
May 1975

ABBREVIATIONS AND SHORT TITLES

Abbott	W. C. Abbott, ed. *The Writings and Speeches of Oliver Cromwell.*
AHR	*American Historical Review.*
AR	*Archiv für Reformationsgeschichte.*
An Account	*An Account given to the Parliament by the Ministers sent by them to Oxford.* 1647.
Baker	Sir Richard Baker. *Meditations and Disquisitions Upon the First Psalm; the Penitential Psalms; and Seven Consolatory Psalms.* 1639–40.
Benbrigge, *Christ*	John Benbrigge. *Christ Above All Exalted.* 1645.
Benbrigge, *Gods Fury*	John Benbrigge. *Gods Fury, Englands Fire.* 1646.
Bosher	R. S. Bosher. *The Making of the Restoration Settlement.*
Bramhall	John Bramhall. *Works.* vol. 5.
Brooks	Thomas Brooks. *Works.* 4 vols.
Byam	Henry Byam. *XIII Sermons.* 1675.
Caryl, *Job*	Joseph Caryl. *An Exposition with Practicall Observations upon the Book of Job.* 12 vols. 1647–71. See the bibliography for publishing dates of the individual volumes. Citations in the footnotes give the chapters treated in parentheses.
Caryl, *Prayer*	Joseph Caryl. *Davids Prayer for Solomon.* 1643.
Case, *Correction*	Thomas Case. *Correction, Instruction; Or, a Treatise of Afflictions.* 1652.
Case, *Two Sermons*	Thomas Case. *Two Sermons Lately Preached at Westminster.* 1642.
CD	Samuel Rawson Gardiner, ed. *Constitu-*

	tional Documents of the Puritan Revolution, 1625–1660.
CH	*Church History.*
Chillingworth	William Chillingworth. *Works.* 3 vols.
Collinson	Patrick Collinson. *The Elizabethan Puritan Movement.*
Coolidge	John S. Coolidge. *The Pauline Renaissance in England.*
CR	A. G. Matthews. *Calamy Revised.*
Cragg	Gerald R. Cragg, ed. *The Cambridge Platonists.*
CSPD	*Calendar of State Papers, Domestic.*
Contemplations	Sir Edward Hyde, Earl of Clarendon. "Contemplations and Reflections Upon the Psalms of David." In *A Collection of Several Tracts of the Right Honorable Earl of Clarendon.* 1727.
Cudworth	Ralph Cudworth. *A Sermon Preached Before the House of Commons, March 31, 1647.*
DNB	*Dictionary of National Biography.*
Doolittle, *Antidote*	Thomas Doolittle. *A Spiritual Antidote Against Sinful Contagion.* 1667.
Doolittle, *Rebukes*	Thomas Doolittle. *Rebukes for Sin By God's Burning Anger.* 1667.
EHR	*English Historical Review.*
Eikon	Charles I. *Eikon Basilike.*
Falkland	Viscount Falkland (Sir Lucius Cary). *His Discourse of Infallibility.* 1651.
Farindon	Anthony Farindon. *The Sermons of Anthony Farindon.* 4 vols. References to vol. 1 are from a collection first published in 1657.
Fenner, *Affections*	William Fenner. *A Treatise of the Affections.* 1642.
Fenner, *Looking-Glasse*	William Fenner. *The Souls Looking-Glasse.* 1643.
Gardiner, *History*	Samuel Rawson Gardiner. *History of England . . . 1603–1642.* 10 vols.

Gardiner, *War*	Samuel Rawson Gardiner. *History of the Great Civil War, 1642–1649.* 4 vols.
T. Goodwin	Thomas Goodwin. *The Works of Thomas Goodwin.* 9 vols.
Hales	John Hales. *The Works of the Ever Memorable Mr. John Hales of Eaton.*
Hall	Joseph Hall. *The Works.* 10 vols.
Haller	William Haller. *The Rise of Puritanism.*
Hammond	Henry Hammond. *Miscellaneous Theological Works.* Vol. 3 (sermons).
Hammond, *Catechism*	Henry Hammond. *A Practical Catechism.* 14th ed. 1700.
Harrison	Notes taken by members of Sir Thomas Barrington's family on lectures given by the suspended Puritan, James Harrison, between 1626 and 1643. Essex Record Office, Barrington MSS/D/DBa/F5/2.
HJ	*The Historical Journal*
T. Hooker, *Lessons*	Thomas Hooker. *The Christians Two Chiefe Lessons.* 1640.
Hyde, *Legacy*	Edward Hyde. *A Christian Legacy.* 1657.
JBS	*Journal of British Studies.*
JEH	*Journal of Ecclesiastical History.*
Mocket	Thomas Mocket. *The Churches Troubles and Deliverance.* 1642.
ODCC	F. L. Cross and E. A. Livingstone, eds. *The Oxford Dictionary of the Christian Church.* 2d ed.
Owen	John Owen. *The Works.* vol. 8 (sermons).
Pearl	Valerie Pearl. *London and the Outbreak of the Puritan Revolution.*
Perkins	William Perkins, *Works.* 3 vols. 1613.
Pierce	Thomas Pierce. *A Collection of Sermons Upon Several Occasions.* 1671.
PP	*Past and Present.*
Preston, *Breast-Plate*	John Preston. *The Breast-Plate of Faith and Love.* 1631.
Preston, *Cuppe*	John Preston. *Cuppe of Blessing.* 1633.
Preston, *Life*	John Preston. *Life Eternall.* 1632.

Preston, *Sermons*   John Preston. *Sermons Preached Before his Majestie.* 1631.

Sanderson   Robert Sanderson. *Sermons.* 2 vols.

SCH   *Studies in Church History.*

Sheldon   Gilbert Sheldon. *Davids Deliverance and Thanksgiving.* 1660.

Sibbes, *Cordialls*   Richard Sibbes. *The Saints Cordialls.* 1637.

Sibbes, *Works*   Richard Sibbes. *The Complete Works.* Vol. 7.

Sibbes, *Letter*   Richard Sibbes. *A Consolatory Letter To An Afflicted Conscience.* 1641.

Skippon   Philip Skippon. *A Salve For Every Sore.* 1643.

Speeches and Prayers   *The Speeches and Prayers of Some of the late King's Judges.* 1660.

Sydenham, *Sermons*   Humphrey Sydenham. *Five Sermons.* 1637.

Sydenham, *Occasions*   Humphrey Sydenham. *Sermons upon Solemne Occasions.* 1637.

Taylor   Jeremy Taylor. *The Whole Works.* 15 vols.

VCH   *Victoria County History.*

Walzer   Michael Walzer. *The Revolution of the Saints.*

WP   *Winthrop Papers.* Vols. 1 and 2.

WR   A. G. Matthews. *Walker Revised.*

Watson   Thomas Watson. *A Body of Divinity.*

Whichcote   Benjamin Whichcote. *Works.* 4 vols.

Wormald   Brian H. G. Wormald. *Clarendon.*

Zagorin   Perez Zagorin. *The Court and the Country.*

THE GODLY MAN IN STUART ENGLAND

1

THE ENGLISH
PROTESTANT MINDS

The Mohammedans who worship a cursed imposter; the pagans, who worship the sun, moon and stars; the Egyptians, who worship onions, leeks, cats and dogs, never had such divisions amongst them as the worshippers of Jesus Christ have had, and have at this day amongst ourselves.

Jeremiah Burroughs, Irenicum (1646)

I tell you, Major, what Cortés did turned out to be one of the shrewdest mistakes ever made by the military mind. He reasoned into Aztec theocracy, which he would not have understood if he had lived an additional five hundred years. In Mexico the gods ruled, the priests interpreted and interposed, and the people obeyed. In Spain, the priests ruled, the king interpreted and interposed, and the gods obeyed. A nuance in an ideological difference is a wide chasm.

Richard Condon, A Talent for Loving (1967)

Professor J. H. Plumb has written that although historians have been confused by the apparent chaos of English politics in the quarter century after the Glorious Revolution of 1688, "contemporaries were less distracted and they rarely had difficulty, at least after the middle 1690s, in distinguishing Whig from Tory."[1] An analogous confusion has existed among historians writing about Anglicans and Puritans in early Stuart England. Then as now, however, people more or less formally associate themselves with each other to work toward certain goals, and their groups and coalitions of groups undergo changes in membership, in priorities,

---

1. *The Growth of Political Stability in England, 1675–1725*, p. 134.

and in means to their ends. Means acceptable to some may come to be in the course of events unacceptable to others, and the differences about means are often related to the ways in which priorities among the goals have been ranked. These very priorities may be reordered. One of the historian's most challenging tasks is the selection of a nomenclature which promotes rather than impedes progress toward an understanding of people and their actions. A terminology must be firm enough to allow us to get a grip on why people did what they did—but it must not be so rigid as to obscure the subtlety, multiplicity, and changeability of human motivation. Categories— capacious ones—we must have, but they must be delicate tools and not unwieldy bludgeons. The difficulty of finding such categories increases at the same rate as the need for them when we are dealing with an age of revolutionary upheaval in ideas, politics, and society.

An Anglican could recognize a Puritan when he met one and vice-versa because each viewed the other from behind lenses strongly tinted by a particular ideal conception of true Christianity. Indeed, in terms of the spectrum of religious politics before the Civil War, Puritans saw in Anglicanism not "English Protestantism" but Arminianism and Roman Catholicism; Anglicans saw in Puritanism not "English Protestantism" but Anabaptism and Antinomianism. Therefore these terms, like Whig and Tory, can meet our demanding specifications for trustworthy nomenclature if properly understood. To say this is to take a stand on one side of a current historiographical controversy. There are many studies of Puritans and Puritanism.[2] There are fewer, but still many, studies of Anglicans and Anglicanism. But comparative studies of Anglicans and Puritans are curiously scarce. An unfortunate result has been the tendency of the students of one group or the other to allow the antipathy their subjects felt for the opposition to creep unbidden into their own thinking. Comparative studies by J. F. H. New[3] and Charles and Katherine George have recently sought to fill the gap, but their books and articles contain quite different conclusions. The Georges

2. Paul Seaver has noted that Puritanism has become "a minor scholarly industry" in the last few years. *The Puritan Lectureships*, p. vii. See the bibliographical note for further discussion.

3. John F. H. New, *Anglican and Puritan*. On pp. 104–06 New refers to the Georges' conclusions. He reiterates his view that there were basic theological differences in "The Whitgift-Cartwright Controversy," *AR* 59 (1968):203–11.

categorically deny that it is possible to find significant ideological distinctions between Anglicans and Puritans, while New maintains that differences between them were not only deeply ingrained at the outset, but that they became both more profound and more ingrained in the decades leading up to the Civil War. The Georges conclude that historians have operated on the basis of hindsight provided by the events of 1640–60 and thus have observed a serious religious division which did not really exist. Religious differences did exist but not seriously enough to be considered a factor in the causation of the Civil War.[4]

The contribution of the Georges' work to our understanding of religion, society, and politics in Stuart England is valuable in many ways. It has forced us to recognize that there was a religious consensus in early seventeenth-century England, that there was an "English Protestant mind" founded upon a widespread agreement about many of the most fundamental and important doctrines of the Christian religion.[5] Not the least of the virtues of this approach is that it adds a dimension of depth to our understanding of such figures as John Gauden, Richard Baxter, and Edward Reynolds.[6]

4. Charles H. and Katherine George, *The Protestant Mind of the English Reformation, 1570–1640*, p. 398. George vigorously supports his view in "Puritanism as History and Historiography," *PP* 41 (1968):77–104. William M. Lamont's critical response is in *PP* 44 (1969):133–46. There is a brief but careful survey of the matter in Patrick McGrath, *Papists and Puritans under Elizabeth I*, pp. 31–46. McGrath's footnotes and (more fully) those in George's article in *PP* provide a good bibliography of the controversy. Especially important items include Basil Hall's article, "Puritanism: The Problem of Definition," *SCH* 2 (1965):283–96; Christopher Hill, *Society and Puritanism in Pre-Revolutionary England*, chap. 1. Also see Basil Hall's discussion of the use of the terms "Calvinist" and "Reformed" in "The Genevan Tradition," *JEH* 20 (1969):111–16. F. Smith Fussner, *Tudor History and Historians*, pp. 121–23, also compares the arguments of New and the Georges.
5. Charles F. Allison has also said that we "sometimes overlook how much agreement existed among Christians at the beginning of the seventeenth century." *The Rise of Moralism*, p. 1. For a good brief discussion of what Perry Miller and Thomas Johnson called "the vast substratum of agreement which actually underlay the disagreement between Puritans and Anglicans," see their introduction to *The Puritans*, 1:5–11.
6. Gauden seemed to oppose Laudianism in a sermon delivered before the House of Commons in November, 1641. For an analysis of it, see John F. Wilson, *Pulpit in Parliament*, pp. 42–43. But he ended his career as a bishop and was probably the compiler/author of Charles I's *Eikon Basilike*. *DNB* and *Eikon*, pp. xxvii–xxxii. Baxter was a chaplain in the parliamentary army and was among the ejected ministers in 1662, yet he appears as an exemplar in Paul Elmer More and Frank

It reminds us that all "puritan" attitudes and ideas were not necessarily the exclusive property of Puritans. The famous "plain style" of preaching, for example, was by no means used only by Puritans. Nor was the desire to eradicate abuses of ecclesiastical finances and judicature exclusively a puritan concern. The Georges have helped to foster a healthy emphasis upon the variations of Puritanism and a healthy reluctance to generalize too broadly about it.[7]

Despite these merits, the Georges' view that religious differences cannot have contributed significantly to the mid-century conflict is open to some grave objections. It requires us to take matters of religion off our list of causes for the Civil War despite the certainty of contemporaries that religion was an issue of overriding importance. It imputes to the membership of the Long Parliament in the early stages of the conflict a degree and a depth of cynicism which is hard to imagine. While we had better not take entirely at face value the religious concern expressed by Members of Parliament in countless resolutions, ordinances, protestations, speeches, and letters, neither should we go to the opposite extreme and assume them all to be hypocritical. Doubtless many were happy to seize the opportunity to cut the bishops down a notch in order to build up (or, as they would have preferred it, to restore) their own authority. But a good case can be made for the sincere desire of many to see a different kind of church established, a church with a godly ministry preaching the kinds of sermons which Archbishop Laud and his bishops had suppressed, a church stressing a style of worship and behavior radically different from the Laudian ideal in certain vital respects.

Quite aside from the question of whether there were substantial doctrinal differences between Anglicans and Puritans, the Georges' view badly underestimates the importance of differences in degrees

Leslie Cross, eds. *Anglicanism.* Joan Webber decided that "he finally belongs with the Puritans rather than the Anglicans" but "provides a dividing line and a rule-proving exception." *The Eloquent "I"*, p. 7. Reynolds took the Covenant in March, 1644, but became Bishop of Norwich in 1661. *DNB.*

7. Everett H. Emerson, for example, states that "it is questionable whether one can make sound generalizations about puritan economic attitudes or puritan social theory" or about "puritan style." *English Puritanism from John Hooper to John Milton*, p. 46. See also Timothy H. Breen, "The Non-Existent Controversy: Puritan and Anglican Attitudes on Work and Wealth, 1600–1640," *CH* 35 (1966):273–87.

of adherence to doctrines and in weight of emphasis upon doctrines. As Edmund S. Morgan has written, "the most hotly contested religious differences have often been differences of degree: the shift from orthodoxy to heresy may be no more than a shift of emphasis."[8] The absence of doctrinal disagreement on a number of important matters cannot in itself be regarded as proof that differences of emphasis did not fuel the fires of conflict. It is arguable that the converse is true because, as Richard Sibbes put it, "Opposition is bitterest betwixt those that are nearest; as betwixt the flesh and spirit in the same soul, between hypocrites and true-hearted Christians in the same womb of the church." Sibbes was the master of Saint Catherine's Hall, Cambridge, which produced many puritan preachers. He was himself the lecturer to a generation of lawyers at Gray's Inn. If he was not a Puritan, then there were indeed no Puritans.[9] Clarendon, for the anglican side, expressed the same notion with partisan zeal. Never in the history of the Christian church, he wrote, had religion ever received "so desperate wounds, or hath been nearer expiring, by any the most bloody persecution it hath sustained, as by the loose tongues and dissolute language and behavior of those who pretend to be Christians [in] this most profane and licentious age in which we live."[10]

That Charles and Katherine George fail to appreciate the importance of differences of emphasis is demonstrated by reviewing one of the doctrines upon which they found broad agreement among English Protestants. The Georges found that on the volatile issue of the validity of the Roman Catholic Church, the only differences that could be found across the whole spectrum of English Protestant opinion were differences of degree. They note that the "puritan" Sibbes granted "that the Papists hold all the positive points of true

8. *Roger Williams: The Church and the State*, p. 11. Austin Woolrych makes much the same point. See his essay, "Puritans, Politics and Society" in E. W. Ives, ed., *The English Revolution, 1600–1660*, pp. 87–100.

9. Sibbes, *Cordialls*, p. 142. Cf. Hammond, p. 15 and Jeremiah Burroughs, *Irenicum* (1646), pp. 240–42. On Sibbes, see Haller, pp. 65–67 and Wilbur Kitchener Jordan, *The Development of Religious Toleration in England*, 2:358–61.

10. *Contemplations*, p. 545. All references to this work are to the part written between 1647 and 1651. Although Sir Edward Hyde did not become the Earl of Clarendon until after the Restoration, I shall refer to him as Clarendon throughout in order to distinguish him from his cousin, Edward Hyde, D.D.

religion," and thus the fundamentals of Christianity might still be found in some members of the Roman Church.[11] But if one looks more closely at Sibbes's sermons, this apparent moderation on the subject of Rome is seen to be ephemeral. Sibbes agreed that there was some truth to be found at Rome, but he was extremely critical of anyone who attempted to use that fact as an argument to peaceful relations between the Churches of England and Rome. Because the Romanists joined faith and works, Sibbes said that the "Roman Church is an apostate church and may well be styled an adulteress and a whore, for she is fallen from her husband Jesus Christ." What is even more interesting in terms of anglican-puritan tensions in England is Sibbes's application of this statement. Because the Romanists err in a matter pertaining to salvation, he held that they "err in the foundation; the very life and soul of religion consists in this." Therefore, he asked rhetorically, "What may we think of those that would bring light and darkness, Christ and Antichrist, the ark and Dagon together, that would reconcile us as if it were no such great matter?"[12]

It is clear that "the gentle Sibbes" was vigorously opposed to any such union. So was his friend John Preston, in many respects the leader of the "puritan faction" from about 1622 until his death in 1628. In a sermon preached before the king at court in 1627, he denounced "those Cassanders that think by wit and policy to reconcile us, . . . a thing impossible." True doctrine and errors, "whether Popish or Arminian," could no more be mixed together "than oil with water, iron and steel with clay, . . . or as the elements when once they are mingled in a compound, both do lose their proper forms and cease to be religions in God's account."[13] These

---

11. Charles and Katherine George, *Protestant Mind*, p. 389.

12. Sibbes, *Cordialls*, pp. 230–31. See T. Goodwin, 7:546–48, for a statement that differs only in that the indictment of the "Arminians" is more pointed. See also William Gouge, *Gods Three Arrowes* (1631), pp. 46–47. For more of Sibbes's fire on this subject, see Christopher Hill, *Antichrist in Seventeenth-century England*, pp. 67–68. For impressive evidence that many English Protestants believed that the Pope was the Antichrist, see Hill, chap. 1, and William M. Lamont, *Godly Rule*, pp. 20, 23, 28–52. On the origins of this notion, see Norman Cohn, *The Pursuit of the Millennium*, p. 80.

13. Preston, *Sermons*, pp. 15, 24. George Cassander (1513–66), a Roman Catholic theologian, had argued that "abuses were no sufficient reason for leaving the Catholic Church." *ODCC*, p. 245. Preston's biographer, Irvonwy Morgan, sug-

sermons by Sibbes and Preston appeared in print at a time when many Englishmen were deeply concerned that the churchmen led by Archbishop Laud were at least considering just such a linking of "light and darkness, Christ and Antichrist." Even the Georges noticed that in the 1630s, the more "conservative" (vis-à-vis the Puritans) English clerics were, with "greater frequency and boldness," pointing up the "validly Christian, though imperfect, nature of the Roman Catholic Church."[14] They were indeed. In the course of a series of private conferences with a papal emissary in 1636 Richard Montagu, the Bishop of Chichester, said that reunion with Rome could be easily accomplished. When the Pope's man expressed doubt, the reply was: "Had you been acquainted with this nation ten years ago, you might have observed such an alteration in the language and inclinations of the people, that it would not only put you in hopes of a union, but you would conclude it was near at hand." Montagu dismissed "the aversion [to Rome] we discover in printed books and sermons" as "things of form, chiefly to humor the populace, and not much to be regarded."[15] Events were to demonstrate that Montagu seriously underestimated the strength of "the aversion" in his countrymen. It was precisely a growing fear of the direction being taken by Laud and his colleagues that helped raise tensions to the flashpoint late in the 1630s. The Georges compare Roman Catholicism with Protestantism in order to show that the doctrinal differences between them were greater than those among Protestants—which is true and important. But it does not necessarily mean that smaller doctrinal differences (or merely differences in emphasis and interpretation) within English Protestantism were unimportant in England. Even small changes of direction were important partly because of the religious analogue of the "phenomenon of political foreshortening" which J. H. Hexter has described. It is the tendency of men of right-wing views to see in men of the center, not moderation but left-wing radicalism (and

gests that this sermon was a reaction against the appearance of Cosin's *Devotions* in 1628. *Prince Charles's Puritan Chaplain*, p. 187.

14. *Protestant Mind*, pp. 387–88.

15. *The Memoirs of Gregorio Panzani*, Joseph Berington, ed., p. 248. On the meetings with Panzani, see pp. 237–48 and Gardiner, *History*, 8:138–39, 143–44. On Montagu's earlier clash with the Puritans, see the section entitled "Puritans and the 'Idol of our Godly Brethren,' " in chap. 5 below.

vice-versa). It is one of the things which makes the way of the peacemaker hard.[16] As we shall see, Puritans accused their opposition of preaching salvation by the good works of obedience and charity, while Anglicans accused Puritans of preaching salvation by faith without its necessary complement of good Christian behavior. A careful reading of sermons from both sides shows that neither accusation was fair but also shows that each side clearly perceived where the other placed its heaviest emphasis. Each side caricatured the other, and caricatures can be very accurate.

In the full context of the religious politics of Western Europe in the seventeenth century, the change of direction taken by Laud was small enough. But close at hand, relatively minor changes of emphasis and direction looked much larger. For Puritans who had been expecting progress toward "reformation" and "purification" of the Church of England, any retrograde step was ominous in the extreme. Sibbes and his fellow Feoffees for Impropriations did not have our broad perspective on the matter. They were struggling to fill English pulpits with "godly preachers," and they were forced by the authorities to desist. Perhaps they knew that, in 1625, Laud had given King Charles a list of divines identified as "O" for Orthodox or "P" for Puritan. If they did not know of the list, they quickly saw the results in ecclesiastical appointments. At the level of practical politics, an administrator's priorities appeared soon enough. No amount of broad doctrinal agreement could make a preaching ministry Laud's first priority. His concern for what he called "the external decent worship of God" was idolatry to the Puritans. No attempt to fathom the anglican-puritan controversy can stop with the study of dogma. Differences of emphasis, direction, and interpretation could widen a tiny fissure of disagreement between divines who breathed the lofty atmosphere of theology into an enormous chasm when translated into terms comprehensible to those who inhabited the broad, humble, heavily-populated plain where people sought to understand, believe, and practice the true faith. As Dr. Henry Hammond, the royalist chaplain, put it in 1640, "The

16. J. H. Hexter, *The Reign of King Pym*, pp. 52–53. See also his brief but highly suggestive argument about the place of Puritanism in the complex matrix of causes of the English Revolution in "The English Aristocracy, Its Crises, and the English Revolution, 1558–1660," *JBS* 8 (1968):52–70.

doctrine raised from any Scripture is easily digested, but all the demur is about the practical inference."[17] In a particular political context, and especially in periods of rapid change, the apparent direction of a man's thinking and the arrangement of his priorities (and thereby the degree of his imitation of an ideal) might have been more important than his doctrinal position. A full understanding of the religious dimension of the Civil War conflict requires careful attention to these vital matters of direction and emphasis. We must not fall victim to a phenomenon of historical foreshortening in which we compare such major entities as Protestantism and Roman Catholicism and use the differences between them to belittle the differences among subgroups. Each set of differences is a proper object of study within its proper context and its proper perspective. When viewed from a sufficiently remote altitude, there are doubtless many similarities between Christianity and Hinduism—but that does not invalidate the study of differences within branches of Christianity and Hinduism for their impact upon the histories of Western European and Asiatic civilizations.

Patrick Collinson has written that Puritanism "should be defined with respect to the Puritans, and not vice versa." This excellent dictum should also be applied to Anglicanism in the seventeenth century. For the purposes of this study, Puritans were those whose highest priority was the dissemination of "godly preaching" throughout England. It was their vision that England could then move toward complete "reformation" in their sense, meaning the establishment of "a piety and moral order" which was distinctive.[18]

17. Hammond, p. 226. Laud made his statement about worship in censuring Bastwick, Burton, and Prynne in 1637. It is reprinted in Stuart E. Prall, ed., *The Puritan Revolution*, p. 84. The story about his list of friends and enemies is in Gardiner, *History*, 5:364. On the Feoffees, see I. M. Calder, *Activities of the Puritan Faction of the Church of England, 1625–1633*; Seaver, *Puritan Lectureships*, pp. 88–89, 236–38; I. Morgan, *Prince Charles's Puritan Chaplain*, pp. 174ff.

18. Collinson, pp. 13, 465. My definition is therefore similar to New's, *Anglican and Puritan*, pp. 2–3. I also agree with New's argument that, despite many shared assumptions and ideas, the various sectarians to the "left" of the Puritans are best called Separatists. Separatists withdrew from the Church of England in order to achieve a purity which Puritans sought within it. Several recent studies have spoken of the latter as "mainstream Puritans": Zagorin, pp. 158–59; Walzer, pp. viii, 21; Seaver, *Puritan Lectureships*, p. 30. Similarly, Collinson characterizes Elizabethan Puritans as those seeking " 'a further reformation', the logical completion of the process of reconstituting the national Church, which in their view had been

By the late 1620s it was obvious to them that there could be no real progress without changes in the ritual and leadership of the Caroline Church of England. Anglicans were those more or less content with the episcopal organization and liturgy of the Church of England. Some enthusiastically welcomed Archbishop Laud's program and his methods of enforcing it and some did not, but even those who became critical of Laud made their highest priority the maintenance of a domestic peace within which they could work for a distinctively anglican "piety and moral order." The circularity of these definitions is unavoidable because the ideals at which each group aimed require the fuller descriptions they will receive in subsequent chapters. This is to subsume within puritan ranks those who protested against the rise of what they called "Arminianism" in the Church of England beginning in the 1620s, the Presbyterians and Independents of the 1640s and 1650s, and most of the Nonconformists after the Restoration. Under the anglican rubric there are the Laudians and their successors, the High Churchmen of the 1650s and 1660s. There are also several varieties of "moderate Episcopalians" such as the members of Lord Falkland's Great Tew circle, the Cambridge Platonists, and the Latitudinarians.[19] There are difficulties in the use of both terms. "Anglicanism" is an anachronism and "Puritanism" has been so stretched as to lose most of its shape. But they are the best we have, and they do correspond, in a rough way, to the political divisions present in the early stages of the Civil War. Although there are many objections to these terms, all the other possibilities entail even more problems. It is best simply to recognize that in the aftermath of the Protestant Reformation, all the churches, all the splinters, large and small, of Western Christendom, were moving through a long, complex, and difficult period of transition toward some measure of doctrinal and organizational stability. In the kaleidoscopic confusion, no nomenclature can be unexceptionable. The story of religious, social, and political

arrested halfway" (p. 12). See also pp. 25–28 and 36–37. Among others, Everett H. Emerson has noted that "Puritans did differ from the conformists in their attitude towards the importance of the sermon." *English Puritanism*, p. 44.

19. On the moderates, see *n.* 20 below. I am using "Arminianism" in its English rather than its Dutch sense—see T. M. Parker, "Arminianism and Laudianism in Seventeenth-century England," *SCH* 1 (1964):20–34. On the anti-Erastian character of this Arminianism, see Lamont, *Godly Rule*, p. 64.

conflict in Stuart England is not a Homeric epic in which captains were designated and hosts marshaled neatly and thoroughly into serried ranks at the blast of the first trumpet. The perfect set of clear, orderly terms is not likely to be found for application to a situation in which clarity and order were in terribly short supply.

Thus the term "Anglican" may be used to describe those who, under a series of labels (each with its own validity and nuances), associated themselves with the Elizabethan Settlement in ecclesiastical policy as interpreted and enforced by Archbishops Whitgift, Bancroft, Laud, and Sheldon and who defended the special relationship between the monarchy and the episcopacy for which Charles I fought and died. Some of them, often thought of as "Laudians" or "High Churchmen," advocated a relatively harsh set of measures against Nonconformity. Others, who might be considered "moderate Episcopalians," felt that the Church of England's purposes would be better served by mildness and accommodation. Certainly William Chillingworth and John Hales of the Great Tew circle fall into this latter category—they were hardly uncritical admirers of Laudianism. Too, such Restoration High Churchmen as Sheldon and Thomas Pierce can be distinguished from Latitudinarians like Benjamin Whichcote. Henry Hammond and Robert Sanderson fall in between the extremes. But all these men can be described as Anglicans as long as we remember that there are valid distinctions to be made between them. We must not assume that they represent a monolithic or fully homogeneous school of thought and practice.[20] The distinctions between different groups of Anglicans are varied and important, as are those between different groups of Puritans. But when all such distinctions have been recognized, these two broader terms still have meaning, and this meaning, rightly under-

20. The best guide to anglican groupings presently available is, fortunately, a good one, and one which covers more ground than the title indicates—R. S. Bosher, *The Making of this Restoration Settlement*. Bosher distinguishes between the Laudians and a "moderate wing of the Episcopalians" during the Interregnum (pp. 120–21) and shows how the latter, though certainly more numerous, had little to do with the ecclesiastical settlement. But on Clarendon's "Laudianism" see Lamont, *Godly Rule*, pp. 154–58, and Wormald, pp. 1–13, 37–40, who opposes the notion that Clarendon's goal in 1641 was to save the church. On the difficulties involved in using the term "Cambridge Platonist" see Robert A. Greene and Hugh MacCullum, eds., *An Elegant and Learned Discourse of the Light of Nature* by Nathanael Culverwell, p. xlviii.

stood and carefully applied, can illuminate the central conflict of seventeenth-century England.

In the pages which follow, the reader will hear many different voices. Some will be familiar enough even to the general reader; who does not know of Oliver Cromwell and the Earl of Clarendon? Some will be familiar only to the specialists and some perhaps to no one at all. On the anglican side the fact of hierarchy within the Church of England lends some authority to the words of Laud and other prelates (such as John Bramhall, Joseph Hall, Richard Montagu). Others will be cited who were active in the anglican cause before the "troubles" and rose to high places soon after the Restoration (Jeremy Taylor, Robert Sanderson, George Hall, Thomas Pierce). Still others would probably have gained notable preferment had they lived longer (Henry Hammond, Anthony Farindon). Some were royal chaplains (Henry Byam, Richard Harwood) or were well known for the quality of their thought (William Chillingworth, Benjamin Whichcote). The Puritans lacked an obvious hierarchy, and it is difficult to evaluate spokesmen in terms of their influence. Some (John Preston, Richard Sibbes, William Gouge) were leaders of the Feoffees for Impropriations, an organization which sought to spread puritan preaching throughout the realm. Some received the accolade of invitations to preach before one of the Houses of Parliament and to join the Westminster Assembly (Joseph Caryl, Thomas Goodwin, John Owen, Thomas Case, Jeremiah Burroughs, Thomas Hill, Cornelius Burges). Beyond this, it is difficult to rank them except by what we can discover of their reputations. Many were parish clergy or lecturers who were proud to style themselves as "preachers of God's Word."

The river of time, proceeding on its own unsystematic course of erosion, has worn away some reputations more than others. It is likely that some divines of whom we know little were more influential than others of whom we know much. Little-known writers, both lay and clerical, have been cited precisely because they were followers rather than leaders. In a study of this sort, it seemed desirable to demonstrate that the attitudes discussed were to be found not only in the cathedral chapter, the royal chapel, the pulpits of big London churches, the universities, and the Inns of Court —but also in such out of the way places as Rye, Sussex, and adjacent

Ashburnham (where John Benbrigge preached) or in Puckington, Somerset, and nearby Chard (where Humphrey Sydenham preached). What follows is a study of priorities, emphases, and loyalties expressed by the rank and file as well as by the leaders. It proceeds from the conviction that "out of the abundance of the heart the mouth speaketh" (Matt. 12:34), and therefore historians must pay as much attention to ideas and attitudes which seem to recur and drive men's thoughts and actions as they do to the place of these things in entire systems of thought.

Clerics and laymen, leaders and followers, had many descriptions for the century in which they lived: "the brokenness and distraction of minds and times," "these degenerate days . . . these tympanous and swelling times of ours," "the dregs of time," "this profane and wretched age," "this brain-sick age of ours."[21] Many would have agreed with the royalist preacher who said that "we are fallen, I do not only say, into an iron age, but into an age whose very iron hath gathered rust too, wherein the most do so live, as if they should never die."[22] They addressed each other about the times and troubles in thousands of sermons, tracts, and letters, many of which can now be read only in their original editions. This book is based on a survey of writings almost all of which were in some sense exhortatory.[23] The writers were anxious to explain God's plan for man's worship and his behavior among men. They used an extensive "rhetoric of suffering" as a means to point to the paradigmatic "true Israelite." Men suffer afflictions either because they have sinned and God punishes them in order to urge them to repentance, conversion, and a new life—or because He is testing the strength of the armor they have put on against sin by their conversions. Either way, they must compare their lives to the pattern of perfection which all sermons and treatises utilized. As chapter 2

21. John Gauden, *Three Sermons Preached upon Several Public Occasions* (1642), p. 2; Sydenham, *Sermons*, pp. 130, 182; George Hall, *God's Appearing for the Tribe of Levi* (1655), p. 23; T. Hooker, *Lessons*, p. 230; Hyde, *Legacy*, p. 100.

22. Pierce, p. 436. The metaphor, a famous one from Hesiod, was also used by Farindon, 1:96. On Bullinger's use of it, see Ernest Lee Tuveson, *Millennium and Utopia*, pp. 40–41.

23. A recent, substantial, and beautifully edited sampling which contains selections from a number of the writers I have used is by John Chandos, *In God's Name: Examples of Preaching in England from the Act of Supremacy to the Act of Uniformity, 1534–1662.*

will show, seventeenth-century Englishmen did not differ with each other about some quite fundamental matters. That God has a plan for his creatures, that He teaches men not only by scriptural revelation but through events, that most men are unlikely to learn from Scripture alone but must be instructed through sufferings as well as through hearing and reading, that assurance of salvation is the only valid defense against affliction—on these points, among others, there was indeed an "English Protestant mind."

It is possible, however, to be of (at least) two minds. Despite consensus on some fundamentals, there were differences about the details and even about some of the main aspects of God's plan. These differences (treated in chapters 3–5) appear in the answers to some important questions. How should men worship God? How does God expect his followers to behave? To what extent should they obey the established authorities? For what should they yearn and whom should they spurn? Which sins are the most heinous and which virtues the most desirable? The answers to these questions, when taken all together, form partially overlapping but partially distinct value systems which correspond to anglican and puritan versions of the ideal Christian or "true Israelite." Theology may be systematic but people rarely are. They pick and choose among possible courses of action. In the midst of what one divine called "the daily bruise of his manifold affliction,"[24] each individual was powerfully urged to act so as to emulate as fully as possible one or the other of these ideals of true, saving Christian discipleship.

24. Humphrey Sydenham, *The Royall Passing-Bell* (1630), p. 4.

2

THE RHETORIC
OF SUFFERING

Assuredly we bring not innocence into the world, we bring impurity . . . that which purifies us is trial, and trial is by what is contrary.

John Milton, *Areopagitica* (1644)

Thus by his gracious demeanor in tribulation appeared it that all troubles that even chanced unto him, by his patient sufferance thereof, were to him no painful punishments but [as a consequence of] his patience, profitable exercises.

Roper's *Life of More* (ca. 1556)

My dear sister, I fear we both are laying too much to heart our troubles and dwelling too much on secondary causes and human agents, and clinging too much to a race [of Negro slaves] who are more than willing to let us go, and to a property which has never been very profitable, . . . However we may be able to prove the wickedness of our enemies, we must acknowledge that the providence of God has decided against us in the tremendous struggle we have just made for property rights and country. The hand of the Lord is upon us! Oh for the grace to be humble and behave aright before him until these calamities be overpass!

Rev. John Jones, August 21, 1865
(in R. M. Myers, ed., *The Children of Pride*)

In London in December, 1628, John Winthrop (soon to become the Governor of the Massachusetts Bay Colony) fell ill of what he called "a dangerous hot malignant fever." He and his friends feared that he was "under the sentence of death," but he concluded that God showed him great mercy in several ways. God "sanctified" the illness to Winthrop by showing him a number of corruptions into which he had drifted. One of these was the "immoderate use and love of tobacco," and Winthrop gave it up entirely. "But the greatest of all was the assurance He gave me of my salvation. . . . I never had more sweet communion with him, than in that affliction." Writing thus in his diary, Winthrop displayed assumptions about and attitudes toward his tribulations which appear frequently in the writings of seventeenth-century Englishmen. Although the terminology he used is sometimes thought of as having a "puritan" air, the basic attitudes he expressed differ in no important way from those of his contemporaries, Anglicans as well as fellow Puritans. "Never was there any man in any moment of life entirely happy," said the anglican John Hales, "either in body, goods, or good name; every man hath some part of affliction." Human life was necessarily a life of trouble, pain, and sorrow. Triumph occurred by responding to suffering in the way God intended; it came through suffering, not in spite of it.[1]

The problem of suffering is perpetual, and it is therefore a continuing preoccupation of religion. Men have thought and written about it ever since they were able to think and to write. It is, after all, the problem of evil in another guise. All religions and philosophies may be viewed as responses to the problem of human suffering.[2] All of them provide explanations for and defenses against the pain, fear, and misery we feel when things go wrong. It is precisely because the problem of suffering is a perennial one that it gives us access to thoughts and feelings of men and women in Stuart England, an age in many ways quite different from our own. Winthrop's "dangerous hot malignant fever" was one of many ailments which snuffed out human lives at a terrifying rate. Lady Ann Clifford, for example, lost all five of her male babies; among her Compton grandchildren, four of five died young; among her Coventry great-grandchildren, three of five died as babies.[3] Perhaps

1. *WP*, 1:412–13; Hales, 2:273.
2. Max Weber in fact did this by construing "the world religions as variant interpretations of senseless suffering." H. H. Gerth and C. Wright Mills, eds., *From Max Weber*, p. 59. See also an introduction to the subject of ideal types (discussed below) in Weber's essay, "The Social Psychology of the World Religions," chap. 11.
3. *The Diary of the Lady Anne Clifford*, Vita Sackville-West, ed., p. xlviii. See Keith Thomas, *Religion and the Decline of Magic*, pp. 5–21, on the conditions of life in our period. His chap. 4 contains much that is relevant to the "rhetoric of suffering."

even more disturbing to modern minds than the high mortality rate
is an awareness of how agonizing mere survival must have been.
Physical pains now considered minor were excruciating when no
painkillers were available. Dame Veronica Wedgwood has written
that "familiarity with pain bred, in all classes, a certain stoicism, a
deep acceptance of suffering as a part of the necessary order of the
world."[4] Most upper-class Englishmen from the sixteenth through
the eighteenth centuries were assaulted by the battery of diseases
which troubled the Elizabethan courtier, Sir Horatio Palavicino.
He was tortured by the gout, rheumatoid arthritis, kidney stones
and various disorders of the digestive system. His biographer notes
that "this chronic ill-health was the norm" for gentlemen of the age,
due to the utter lack of any knowledge of the principles of medicine,
hygiene, nutrition, and protection against cold.[5]

Hobbes's famous description of life in the state of nature seems a
fair picture of life in the seventeenth century: "solitary, poor, nasty,
brutish and short." One could argue that for the affluent and even
for the not so affluent residents of industrialized nations today, life
is solitary, poor, nasty, brutish, and long. But the rise of modern
science and of the industrialization which rests upon it has changed
the quality and structure of human life and experience much more
radically than most of us realize. Many of the agonies to which
flesh and even spirit are heir can be alleviated (if not cured) by one
or more of the branches of modern medicine. The success of modern
science has been so striking and its growth so rapid in the last three
centuries that we have come to rely upon technical innovations for
the solution of all our problems. We still suffer, but our defenses
against suffering are so different from Winthrop's that he seems almost to be speaking another language in his retrospective assessment
of his affliction. In Winthrop's time theology was not only a science
—it was the queen of the sciences. Universities existed primarily to
provide divines to fill the pulpits of the land. The questions which
were asked were phrased in theological terms and required theological answers. An answer is nothing more than a statement which
satisfies the questioner. If Winthrop had asked why he suffered and

4. *The King's Peace*, p. 40. Cf. A. G. Dickens, *Thomas Cromwell and the English
Reformation*, p. 92.
5. Lawrence Stone, *An Elizabethan: Sir Horatio Palavicino*, pp. 34–36.

had been told that it was because his temperature was rising while his body struggled with a viral infection, he would hardly have regarded that as a satisfactory answer. Lacking the power to manipulate nature with antibiotics or appendectomies, Winthrop looked beyond nature and decided that God was purging his soul of such corruptions as his immoderate love of tobacco.

Thus, though we suffer still, we have lost contact with an important requisite for an understanding of the way seventeenth-century Englishmen looked upon suffering. Because we think in terms, not of theological, but of technical solutions to our problems, it is difficult for us to believe that theological answers could ever have satisfied anyone. As Dr. Bryan Wilson has recently stated, "Theology remains an essentially rhetorical subject," and we are suspicious of it because we rely on technical rather than verbal solutions. The purpose of rhetoric is to persuade, convert, and convince one's opponents while it comforts, supports, and reassures one's self and one's friends. In the seventeenth century it was used to evoke faith in God and in his plan for individual men and for men in groups. In a century wracked by plague, fires, and in the middle decades, civil war, suffering was, as we shall see, firmly believed to be an integral part of God's plan. There was, of course, nothing new about the need for methods of dealing with the omnipresence of physical suffering, the absence of effective means to alleviate it, and the universal awareness of the nearness of death. As Garrett Mattingly wrote, "The Judaeo-Christian tradition is rich in resources for explaining apparently irrational behavior on the part of the Deity." This chapter presents a brief description of the prominent themes in the rhetoric of suffering which seventeenth-century writers added to the mountain of such material built up in preceding centuries, a mountain from which they quarried many of their ideas. The themes appear in statements about the cause, message, use, and cure of suffering. The value of such a description is that it helps us to understand the nature of the force which drove men and women to seek out and to attempt to live up to ideal modes of conduct. If, as J. H. Hexter has written, we are concerned with "what individuals or groups of men have done," then we must also concern ourselves with what they were like and with "what it . . . was like to be them."[6]

6. Wilson, in *Observer Review*, 2 March 1969; Mattingly, *The Armada*, p. 391;

The period from 1620 to 1670 was rich not only in the usual and ordinary sorts of troubles (such as Winthrop's fever) but in great public calamities as well. In the 1640s and 1650s the supporters of the king and the established church suffered heavily. Before 1640 and after 1660 many who opposed the policies of the king and his advisers underwent persecution of various kinds. The complex amalgams of "factions," "parties," and "interests" which made up the parliamentarian and royalist sides each had their own sets of reasons for acting as they did, and each had a flexible rhetoric of suffering in order to explain defeats and boost morale. At first glance, these rhetorics of the warring parties appear to be little more than copies of each other, more or less subtle explanations of why "God is on our side." When, for example, puritan attempts to "reform" the Church of England from within ran up against the solid wall of episcopal opposition in the 1630s, Puritans proudly proclaimed that the truth (i.e., what they were being persecuted for) had always been persecuted: Christ and his apostles had been persecuted; therefore, the bishops were worse than Nero and their victims were the true believers. The fiery puritan lecturer, Simeon Ash, exclaimed as much to the members of the House of Commons in 1642: "How hell and earth are combined against us, because we endeavor reformation." Even as he spoke, the tide was turning, and it was the Anglicans who were experiencing expropriation and banishment. William Stampe, a vicar who had been imprisoned for thirty-four weeks for "malignancy" toward the Parliament, fled to Oxford and later to The Hague. In a vigorous attack on his enemies written in exile, he sadly recounted the troubles of the Church of England and its supporters. But he comforted himself with the thought that "the severest persecution is not the weakest argument of the Gospel's profession in its greatest candor and sincerity." When the tide turned again in 1660, John Cooke, the regicide who had prosecuted Charles I, was himself condemned to die a traitor's death. He wrote to a friend shortly before his execution that the highest honor God could confer upon one of his saints was to call him to a martyr's death, "suffering for Christ being a strong argument of his electing love, . . . and a greater matter of rejoicing."[7]

J. H. Hexter, *Doing History*, p. 131.

7. Simeon Ash, *The Best Refuge for the Most Oppressed* (1642), p. 15; William Stampe, *A Treatise of Spiritual Infatuation* (The Hague, 1650), sig. A (recto); Cooke,

At this level, for Anglicans no less than for Puritans, the rhetoric of suffering seems at best a simple and soon repetitive litany of self-congratulation. It is a kind of rhetoric heavily used in our own time by fanatics of one stripe or another. We discount it as automatically as we do the inflated claims of advertisers of cold remedies and carbonated beverages on television.

We must not, however, dismiss the use of such patterns of language and thought as unimportant in a religious age because of their connotations in our secular age. To do so would be to deny ourselves access to rich sources for understanding the relationship of religion and politics in seventeenth-century England. Each new faith in human history has made claims about its power to improve the quality of human life, either by gaining more things in this life or assuring bliss in the next, or both. These faiths, whether religious or secular (as science, nationalism, and liberalism) have gained enough adherents to shape lives, institutions, and events. Each drew its power from the hope that its methods would lead toward the good life, however that might be conceived, and away from suffering and pain, however that was being experienced.

THE CAUSE OF SUFFERING

The son of a great classical scholar, Meric Casaubon was also a classical scholar, a protégé of Lancelot Andrewes, a beneficiary of Laud's patronage, and an Oxford doctor of divinity by order of Charles I. In 1644, however, he joined the swelling ranks of Anglicans who had been stripped of their preferments on the orders of the Long Parliament. He was abused, fined, and imprisoned because some of his Kentish parishioners objected that both he and his curate had been "zealous for ceremonies." Perhaps it was this

in *Speeches and Prayers*, p. 42. For Stampe, see *WR*. He went on to add that in "an age so miserably corrupted and depraved, . . . he that designs himself always to the strongest side will certainly be involved in the broad way which leadeth to destruction" (sig. B10 [recto]). Similarly, Henry Ferne, *Certain Considerations of present Concernment* (1653), sig. A2 (recto and verso): "And it is no new thing for the enemies of God's truth to scoff at the afflicted condition of the professors of it." Ferne was a royalist chaplain and later bishop of Chester. For more samples of anglican rhetoric during Cromwell's hegemony, see Bosher, chaps. 1 and 2, and *Contemplations*, p. 392.

experience that led him to begin work on a treatise on divine providence. In it he said that biblical doctrine is so clear as to the cause
of suffering that he who draws any other conclusion besides the
correct one "sees not the sun in the firmament at noon day." Casaubon did not doubt, nor could he imagine how anyone could doubt,
that "all evil of sin is from man, by the instigation of the devil,"
and that "all evil of punishment is from God, for the amendment
of sinners." Man's sin and God's punishment for man's sins are
"the two springs, from whence . . . *omnes lachrymae*, whatsoever
Adam's wretched posterity groaneth under."[8] Casaubon did not
exert himself to give reasons for this dogma, though clerics (like
lawyers) were trained to give many reasons for everything they
said, no matter how self-evident. He gave no reasons because no
one in England at the time would have disputed it with him. He
stated it as a fact, as plain as the light of day, as plain as noses on
faces. William Chillingworth, a leading member of Lord Falkland's
circle at Great Tew, the author of a famous defense of Protestantism
against Roman Catholicism, and a well-known preacher in the
royalist stronghold of Oxford during the Civil War, was equally
dogmatic. Throughout the whole "history of God's providence,
ever since the foundation of the world," God had held to a "constant, unaltered course of revenging himself upon sin, in whatever
persons he finds it."[9]

Casaubon and Chillingworth were Anglicans, but the doctrine
that sin brings suffering knew no party lines among divines. John
Benbrigge, a Sussex Puritan with a preference for a Presbyterian
system of church government, condemned the hypocrite who is
"outwardly with us for God's cause" but actually by his sin and
hypocrisy "pulls at the rope of God's consuming vengeance."
William Gouge, who was a famous puritan preacher in London and
one of the clerical Feoffees for Impropriations, told his congregation

8. *The Originall Cause of Temporall Evils* (1645), sig. A3 (recto). This is a small
tract prefatory to the larger work which was never published. For Casaubon, see
DNB and *WR*. On the tradition into which this tract fits, see Tuveson, *Millennium
and Utopia*, p. 158ff.
9. Chillingworth, 3:253. For a good brief description of the Tew Circle, see
Wormald, pp. 240–61. On Chillingworth, the most recent study is by Robert R.
Orr, *Reason and Authority: The Thought of William Chillingworth* (the sermons are
discussed in chap. 8).

at Blackfriars to "take a view of the judgments recorded in Scripture, and you may easily find sin to be the cause of all." A younger contemporary of Gouge's (who later became one of Laud's most enthusiastic supporters in Somerset) was Humphrey Sydenham. At Oxford he had been nicknamed "Silver-Tongued" Sydenham and was celebrated for his ability to preach lucid sermons on the most complex theological problems. It was perhaps as such a "popularizer" that he was asked to preach at Paul's Cross in London in 1622. His subject was the vexed pair of questions as to why some men are elected to eternal life and others to damnation and how it could nevertheless be that God was not responsible for men's sins. The question of responsibility for sin was, he said, "the pith and the kernel" of the controversy, and all else was but "the bark and the skin." There were two extreme answers which had been given by heretics: either God was responsible or He was only "a bare and idle spectator" with no responsibility. But the truth lay in another answer which "runs in a midway and ever directs to safety." The truth, said Sydenham, is that although God is the author of the punishment of sin, He is not the author of the sin itself: "although it be by his permission that we can do evil, yet it is not by his inspiration that we will do evil."[10]

10. Benbrigge, *Gods Fury*, p. 57; Gouge, *Gods Three Arrowes: Plague, Famine, Sword*, p. 5; Sydenham, *Sermons*, pp. 79–81. On Gouge, see Haller, pp. 67–69, and Seaver, *Puritan Lectureships*, pp. 255–56; on Sydenham, see *DNB* and G. F. Sydenham, *The History of the Sydenham Family*. John Benbrigge does not appear in the *DNB* or in Foster's *Alumni Oxoniensis*, but he may be the "John Bembrick" who was admitted as a pensioner at Emmanuel in 1623 and proceeded B. A. (1627) and M.A. (1634) in Venn's *Alumni Cantabrigiensis*. At some time before 1645 he received the benefice of Ashburnham, near Rye, Sussex. Rye was his native town, as he mentioned in the dedication of his tract, *Usura Accommodata* (1646). A "Joseph Bentrick" was granted the freedom of Rye in 1612, possibly the same "Joseph Benbricke" who was the mayor of the town in 1628–29. On "Bentrick," see William Holloway, *History and Antiquities of the Ancient Town and Port of Rye* (1847), p. 209; on "Benbricke," see L. A. Vidler, *A New History of Rye* (1934), p. 160. It seems safe to assume that the preacher was a relative (perhaps a son or a nephew) of the mayor, especially when we find that "Joseph Bembricke, gent." was presented before the archidiaconal court at Lewes in 1629 " for not bowing at the name of Jesus when the Gospel is reading." There was also a complaint that he held many private conventicles in 1624. On these incidents, see Walter C. Roushaw, "Notes from the Act Books of the Archdeaconry Court of Lewes," *Sussex Archaeological Collections*, 49 (1906): 59, 63. Joseph Bembricke was a "chief supporter" of a puritan lecturer who was active in Rye without leave from Canterbury in the early 1620s, according to Charles Thomas-Stanford, *Sussex in the Great Civil War and the Interregnum, 1642–1660*, pp.

The notion that man's sins brought down both physical and spiritual afflictions from God was not held solely by divines, the experts in theological mysteries. It was a piece of the conventional wisdom—a conviction held by laymen as well. Sir Richard Baker wrote during his long imprisonment as a debtor that the primary and original cause of all human misery is sin. "God's anger, like the house that Samson pulled upon his own head, falls upon us but when we pull it upon ourselves by sin."[11] A group of Roundhead

---

26–28. Rye was, it should be noted, the major town of the strongly puritan eastern half of Sussex (see Mary Frear Keeler, *The Long Parliament*, p. 66, and *VCH, Sussex,* vol. 2). The evidence for John Benbrigge's Puritanism does not, however, rest on his presumed connection with the puritanical mayor. He can be directly connected with William Hay, who sat for Rye in the Long Parliament and remained in the Rump and was returned in 1656, 1658, 1660, and 1661 (according to Vidler, pp. 216–17). Keeler states that Hay was "a member of a local puritan and parliamentary family, and a brother-in-law of a Rye resident" (pp. 77, 209). He was a ringleader among the puritan justices of the peace in Sussex (*CSPD Charles I,* 442:37), and Benbrigge's *Usura Accommodata* is warmly dedicated to "the religious and grave senator William Hay." Benbrigge's three publications appeared in 1645 and 1646 and all contain strong exhortations for support of the parliamentary side. *Gods Fury, Englands Fire* (1646) was dedicated to "Captain Thomas Collines, one of the Committee for Sussex." Nowhere in his tracts does Benbrigge discuss forms of church government, but there are indications that he preferred a presbyterian system. *Gods Fury* contains a strong plea for unity among the godly in England and for adhering to the Covenant at just about the time that the Independents were beginning to put a dangerous strain on that unity (pp. 115–17). He also argued against the "schismatical Separatists" in terms which suggest that he thought of the church as having a national rather than a congregational structure (p. 7). In any case, by far the heaviest emphasis in these sermons falls upon the establishment of the puritan piety and moral order. Benbrigge certainly did not hesitate to accept the name "Puritan" because he insisted that God "owns them for his children, calls them his holy ones. But the world which had named them Puritans, turned Anabaptist, hath repatized [rebaptized] them, and calls them now Roundheads. But howsoever the world despiseth them, yet are they the flower of his people" (p. 57).
    11. Baker, p. 151. Cf. p. 417: "We cannot so justly say that crosses and afflictions are cast upon us by God, as that they are drawn upon us by our own sins." For Baker's biography, see *DNB* and A. B. Grosart's introduction to his collection of Baker's devotional writings. Baker's plight seems to have arisen from the fact that, at the time of his marriage, he committed himself to guaranteeing payment of the debts of certain members of his wife's family. Their bankruptcies led to his. That he had puritan leanings is indicated by his contribution of £50 to a fund for preparing forces to recover the Palatinate by force of arms after the collapse of the Spanish marriage negotiations. See his *Chronicle of the Kings of England* (1679), p. 419. His account of the Hampton Court Conference emphasizes the minor puritan gains there (*Chronicle,* pp. 421–23). He was highly critical of Arminius—see his *Apologie For Lay-Mens Writing in Divinity* (1641), sig. B8 (recto and verso). He died in the Fleet in 1644.

officers which included Oliver Cromwell expressed the same view when the "blessed cause" for which they were struggling seemed to be faltering in 1647. They decided "to go solemnly to search out our own iniquities . . . which, we were persuaded, had provoked the Lord against us, to bring such sad perplexities upon us at that day." Lord Willoughby, who had begun as a supporter of the Parliament but lost all when he went over to the king, wrote to his wife from Barbados in 1651: "Though God is at present pleased to afflict us, and that justly for my sins, yet so long as he gives us health, let us not despair." John Winthrop's brother-in-law, Thomas Fones, wrote upon the death of his wife that he had "drunk a bitter potion of God's judgments which my sins have long called for." Clarendon, in his exile, wrote that when "the godly man finds himself in great tribulation, . . . he is first to procure a pardon for his own sins, which were the forerunners of his punishment."[12]

It is hardly necessary (although it would be easy enough) to multiply examples of seventeenth-century Englishmen, laymen and clerics, Anglicans and Puritans, making similar statements about the cause of human suffering. It is fundamental Christian doctrine that sin destroyed Eden and made the life of every man born of woman a life full of trouble. It is the purpose of this chapter to explore the major doctrines which were drawn from this elemental verity by all of the writers, regardless of position or party. It will be shown that anglican and puritan attitudes toward tribulation shared three basic doctrines, each of which had certain significant corollaries. The first was that God afflicts his chosen children in love rather than in wrath and does so in such a way as to speak to them through chastisements. The second was that these elect children should make use of what God tells them through affliction by repenting their sins, reforming their conduct, and taking comfort and support from this evidence of his concern for their salvation. The third was that the vital thing for any particular man to know was whether or not he were among the godly. This is to say that he had to know whether his conversion to Christianity was truly

12. Thomas Carlyle, ed., *Oliver Cromwell's Letters and Speeches*, 4 vols. (London: Chapman and Hall, 1897), 1:315–16; Willoughby in Henry Cary, ed., *Memorials of the Great Civil War*, 2:317; Fones in *WP*, 1:238; *Contemplations*, pp. 436–37. For similar statements, see *WP*, 1:279, 285, 286, 345 and 2:99, 129, 240, 309, 312; *Contemplations*, pp. 396, 448, 513–14, 519.

sincere because, without this knowledge, he could not know whether the intentions behind his troubles were malign or benign. He could not otherwise tell whether the divine judgments which troubled either his body or his soul were the result of God's love or God's anger.

THE MESSAGE OF SUFFERING

The seventeenth century witnessed a proliferation of devotional handbooks intended for lay use, and some of them were written by laymen. One of the most popular was a tiny duodecimo volume entitled *Crumms of Comfort*. Its author was Michael Sparke, the puritan bookseller and publisher who was fined and pilloried for publishing William Prynne's *Histrio-mastix*. Sparke said in 1652 that there had been forty printings of *Crumms of Comfort* and over sixty thousand copies had been sold from his shop under the sign of the Blue Bible near the Old Bailey. Sparke stated quite simply the doctrine which underlay and supported much of what he had to offer in the way of "comfortable" thoughts when he wrote that "crosses to the godly reclaim them, crosses to the wicked consume them."[13] This doctrine—that God afflicted his children in love and his enemies in anger—was expounded upon innumerable occasions by leading members of the "spiritual brotherhood" of puritan preachers. Richard Sibbes told his audience of lawyers at Gray's Inn that God's judgments upon the wicked had to be distinguished from those upon the godly. In the former, there was "not the least taste of his love," whereas the latter were "moderate corrections" rather than punishments meted out in wrath. Sibbes's colleague, John Preston, concurred, saying that although the same calamities befell both the

13. *Crumms of Comfort* (1632), sigs. C2 (verso), C3 (recto). The earliest edition in the British Museum is the seventh of 1623 and the last one is in 1708. Sparke was the son of an Oxfordshire husbandman; he took up his freedom in 1610. Like Prynne, he despised Laud and hated with equal venom the antinomian doctrines which surfaced late in the 1640s. See his preface and *A Second Beacon Fired by Scintilla* (1652, reprinted in Edward Arber, ed., *Transcripts of the Stationer's Company*, 4:35–8). For Sparke's biography, see Henry R. Plomer, *A Dictionary of the Booksellers and Printers Who Were at Work in England, Scotland and Ireland from 1641 to 1667*, p. 169. The figures about the number of editions and copies sold of the *Crumms* are from Sparke's introduction to *Crumms of Comfort: The Second Part to the Grones of the Spirit in Prayers Meditations Consolations and Preparation for Death* (1652), sig. ¶5 (verso).

servants of God and evildoers, "yet He doth it to the one for love, to the other He doth the same act for destruction." William Gouge demonstrated this with the example of Job. Even saintly Job was not so free of sin as to be free of all judgments, and Gouge concluded that "saints in their afflictions have confessed their sins, for which they knew they were deservedly and justly humbled." He added that some afflictions were intended partly to provide "evidence, proof, and exercise of such graces" as God had given to his chosen ones.[14] But this was no real modification of the basic doctrine. Godly men were tested and purged of sins by afflictions, and men who were destined to be godly were driven to repentance and conversion by them. Only in the case of hardened and unrepenting reprobates were afflictions sent purely for vengeance, unmixed with divine love.

Puritans, however, held no monopoly on the doctrine that the purpose of affliction varied according to the spiritual condition of the sufferer. While Puritans were carrying Sparke's little *Crumms* around with them and were hearing and taking notes on the sermons of Sibbes, Preston, and others, Anglicans were making precisely the same distinction. Dr. Robert Sanderson was perhaps the leading casuist of the age. Charles I thought so highly of him that he never missed his sermons, saying, "I carry my ears to hear other preachers, but I carry my conscience to hear Mr. Sanderson, and to act accordingly." In a fast-day sermon preached before the court at Whitehall on July 8, 1640, Sanderson once again explained the distinction between the two different kinds of divine judgments upon sinful men. He applied the distinction to such public disasters as plagues, famines, and wars as well as to such more selective "private afflictions that light upon particular families or persons, as sickness, poverty, disgraces, injuries, death of friends, and the like." All of these things are, he said, results of God's "heavy displeasure, . . . upon his enemies, intending therein their destruction . . . or they are laid by Almighty God as gentle corrections upon his own children."[15] During Cromwell's protectorate, Sanderson was one of the

14. Sibbes, *Cordialls*, p. 225; Preston, *Breast-Plate*, pt. 2, p. 195; Gouge, *Gods Three Arrowes*, pp. 5–6. Cf. Henry Burton, *The Seven Vials* (1628), p. 93.
15. Sanderson, 1:229–30. Charles's remark is quoted in Izaak Walton's "Life" of Sanderson, p. 4.

Anglicans who attended the services conducted by Anthony Farindon at Saint Mary Magdalen in Milk Street, London. He may have
been there when Farindon restated this same doctrine, a doctrine
which could only have become more and more reassuring to Anglicans since 1640. He said that even if "the righteous do taste of the
same cup of bitterness with the wicked, yet it hath not the same taste
and relish to them both." This distinction between God's purpose
for good men and bad was a recurrent theme in Clarendon's
thoughts. "Though thy rebukes and chastisements are for our many
sins," he prayed "that they proceed from thy fatherly care and
tenderness for our reformation, and not out of thy anger and hot
displeasure for our destruction."[16]

Anglicans and Puritans agreed not only that God afflicted his
children in love, but, paradoxically, that He was more angered by
their sins than He was by those of the ungodly. That is to say, God
was more angered by the disobedience of the godly, but He punished
them not in anger but rather chastised them with affection. Their
sins were the more grievous to God precisely because He expected
more of them. All men were bound to sin and Christians, even good
Christians, were men. God, however, foreknew which men had or
would at some time in their lives truly convert from the broad way
of sin into the narrow way of salvation because it was He who had
written their names into the Book of Life. When his elect slipped
from that path and turned, however momentarily, out of the right
way, God was deeply angered and his judgments rained down upon
them. Dr. Gilbert Sheldon, preaching a sermon of thanksgiving
"for the happy return of his majesty" before Charles II at Whitehall
in 1660, explained the matter quite briefly: "All saints are sinners
and sin will be punished in God's children soonest of all; he least
endures it in them." Sibbes had earlier explained the reason for this
in some detail. He said that God's judgments begin in his own
house. He afflicts his own people more than others because "they are
of his own family, . . . the disorders of the family tend to the
disgrace of the governor of it." Among other things, he added, "their
sins are idolatry, for they are not only the house of God, but the
spouse of God," and their sins are the worse for the same reason that

16. Farindon, 1:456; *Contemplations*, p. 394. Cf. pp. 392, 439.

adultery is more reprehensible than fornication. The anglican polemicist, Dr. Thomas Pierce, gave the same explanation in 1665. God, he said, not only sees "sin in his children" sooner; "He hates, and will punish it much more in them, than in those that are strangers and aliens to him. . . . He is very much offended with the adulteries of the harlot, but more with the whoredoms of an obliged spouse."[17]

The logical conclusion which had to be drawn from these premises was that when judgments came, the sufferer had no one to blame but himself. Any man who had any reason to hope that he was a child of God could not blame the sins of his enemies for his troubles. The godly man's enemies were God's instruments chastising him for his failure to live up to his profession of faith in God—or, at the best, a testing of the truth and sincerity of that profession. To blame one's enemies for judgments was to murmur against God's justice, especially if a mote or two remained in one's own eyes. When London was heavily beset by the plague, the puritan William Gouge listed various means by which the public sins that had brought down the pestilence could be searched out. But he concluded by saying, "Especially, let every one examine himself and search out his own sins. . . . Every one ought most to suspect himself and to fear lest his sins among and above others have incensed the fire of God's wrath." Joseph Caryl spoke of both "public and national rods" and "private and personal rods" and reminded each of his City parishioners that when God used one of these, "yourselves by your sins are the procurers of it." Thomas Doolittle told his noncon- formist flock that wicked men "cannot harm you without the permission of your Father; they must have leave from God before they can touch one hair of your head."[18] Like most of their con-

17. Sheldon, p. 3; Sibbes, *Cordialls*, p. 218; Pierce, pp. 128, 139. Sheldon was dean of the Chapel Royal and soon succeeded Juxon as Archbishop of Canterbury, Pierce was a chaplain to Charles II and was famous and controversial as a lecturer early in the 1660s. He was elected president of Magdalen College, Oxford, but resigned in 1672, later to become dean of Salisbury. *DNB*. He is prominent among Bosher's "Laudians."

18. Gouge, *Gods Three Arrowes*, p. 7; Caryl, *Job* (chaps. 22–26), p. 444; Doolittle, *Rebukes*, p. 563. Caryl spent nearly thirty years (ca. 1640–1670) lecturing almost exclusively on Job. The twelve closely printed volumes he published form certainly the lengthiest commentary on Job ever written. He was a moderate Independent, a member of the Westminster Assembly, and a Trier. *DNB* and *CR*. For Doolittle, see *DNB* and *CR*. He owed his conversion to Baxter's *Saint's Everlasting Rest*.

temporaries, the Puritans believed in the governance of even the minutest details of life by the providence of God. Those who were or would be the children of God did not need to fear anything other than sin in themselves. They were bound to work against evil in all forms, and the failure to do so was as much a sin as any positive act. The primary responsibility for God's judgments was therefore within one's person and one's party. Reformation of public life had to begin with reformation of private lives. Thus Cornelius Burges told the members of the Long Parliament in 1645 that each should "begin with a personal reformation . . . then shall you be better able to carry on and advance the great work of reformation of others." John Benbrigge had the same message for his listeners in Sussex: he urged that each man "ransack every corner of his heart, the mansion house of sin. . . . For except a thorough examination go before, a thorough reformation will not, nay, cannot follow." Sibbes put it in another way, saying that if "men would search and plough up their own hearts, they would not need the plowing of God's enemies; we should not need God's judgments, if we would judge ourselves."[19] Thus the Puritans believed that judgments would be lifted, and godly men would be more successful in their work against the public enemies of God's truth and righteousness when they achieved the greatest measure of victory over sin within themselves.

The Anglicans were equally ready when judgments came to ask, with Jeremiah, "Hast thou not procured this unto thyself (2:17)?" Charles I himself, if he was indeed the author of the *Eikon Basilike*, was thinking in these terms. In the prayer which follows his reflections on the subject of reformation, he wrote, "Our greatest deformities are within; make us the severest censurers and reformers of our own souls." Sanderson said in 1632 that we should not make the error of blaming our sufferings entirely on the iniquity of others. To blame them would be to accuse the Lord of injustice because it was often He who had directed them "to chasten us for some sinful error, neglect or lust in part still remaining in us unsubdued." In a sermon prepared for delivery before the king in 1648, Hammond too maintained that his auditory should "take special notice of

19. Cornelius Burges, *Two Sermons* (1645), p. 37; Benbrigge, *Gods Fury*, p. 60; Sibbes, *Cordialls*, p. 223. Cf. pp. 146–47 and Brooks, 2:9.

every the softest degree of smiting that ever befalls them in their
lives." He wrote that the odds were long, "a thousand to one it is an
application of God's to some special distemper of thine." Hammond admitted that sometimes smitings were intended by God
"for the exercise of many Christian virtues, . . . yet believe me,
thou hast so much reason to suspect thyself, that it will be worth
thy pains to examine, upon every stroke on the body, thy estate."[20]

The modern reader, exercising proper skepticism, cannot help
wondering about the extent to which this sort of *mea culpa* represented nothing more than an attempt to appear holier than one's
enemies. Some of the practical applications of this doctrine were,
however, more specific and more self-critical than might be expected
of partisans in a bitter struggle. George Morley, a member of the
Great Tew circle and later a bishop, wrote against the replacement
of the episcopal system of church government with a presbyterian
one in 1641. But he admitted that the "general and constant
clamor" against abuses in the existing system was not without cause
"in some few particulars." "It would be a sin in us not to hearken"
to the complaints, "and I fear it is one cause of our chastisements,
that we have been deaf to it so long." The proud Clarendon privately reflected in exile that royalists would do best not to gloat
over God's judgments upon their enemies. They should instead give
more consideration to "the justice and goodness of God, and more
to apprehend his anger than the rage of our enemies." Clarendon
admitted that "many of our actions, endeavors and councils,
though right and justifiable in themselves, have therefore been
checked, and proved unprosperous because our ends have not been
direct, and more out of despite to satisfy our own vanity or ambition
or revenge upon those who have been faulty, than out of the conscience of our duty." It was, he thought, a certainty that the "shame
and reproach and sorrow" which lay heavy upon the royalist
cause had been pulled down upon it by its own adherents.[21]

Clarendon's meditations upon this theme were private, but the

20. *Eikon*, p. 128; Sanderson, 2:66 (cf. p. 236); Hammond, pp. 203–04. The
question of the authorship of the *Eikon Basilike* is surveyed in the introduction by
P. A. Knachel.

21. George Morley, *A Modest Advertisement* (1641), p. 19; *Contemplations*, p. 396
(cf. pp. 404–05, 409, 422, 439, 448, 470–71, 519–20). On Morley, see *DNB* and
Bosher. He led the delegation of bishops at the Savoy Conference in 1662.

same ideas were stated with full publicity during the Civil War itself. In a sermon that was preached in the spring after Edgehill and ordered into print by the king, William Stampe lambasted not only the king's parliamentarian enemies but a good many of his supporters as well. Royalists could, he said, advance against the Roundheads confidently only if "our drunkenness, our profaneness and the poison of the whorish woman [were] banished [from] our quarters. . . . Are the hazards of war so far from startling the military man, that as if (together with his commission) he had a dispensation to be more desperate and daring in his sins than any other man?" Stampe finished his harangue in the best of his form by warning his audience against sullying their cause with the stain of their sins, "lest whilst you appear for your sovereign . . . by your purses and your persons, ye plait thorns in his crown some other secret way." One of the king's chaplains, Richard Harwood, had a similar message for the royalist parliament members soon after the terrible defeat at Naseby. He told them that to compare their present afflictions to their past sins was to compare a child to a monster, a David to a Goliath. "O our impenitency is our greatest calamity! This hath spun out the moment into so many years already." The war would have ended before had not "our many crimes" detained it in "so long an assize with us." Job compared his sins to the sands of the sea, said Harwood, and the sins which caused the war are as the Alps in relation to the sufferings they caused. The chaplain spared them nothing: "Boast not to me, what a good subject thou art, when thou dost recruit the king with thy money and rout him with thy sins."[22]

Both Anglicans and Puritans believed that God afflicts his children in love in order to turn them toward salvation and to keep them walking toward that ultimate goal. But they saw in suffering an even more explicit meaning than this. God's judgments were

22. Stampe, *A Sermon Preached before His Majestie at Christ-Church* (Oxford, 1643), pp. 22–24; Harwood, *The Loyall Subject's Retiring-Roome* (Oxford, 1645), pp. 34–35. On Harwood, see *WR* and Wood, *Fasti,* 2:240. For an eloquent and bitter statement of this theme, also preached before the king at Oxford during the war, see Chillingworth, 3:11–14. He found all the "publicans and sinners on the side, against scribes and Pharisees on the other." As the quotations from Stampe and Harwood show, this was a conventional admonition. It seems unlikely that Chillingworth's audience would have been shocked by it.

regarded as a means of communication between God and his chosen saints. As Joseph Caryl put it, "Every affliction is a messenger from God, it hath somewhat to say to us from heaven."[23] Afflictions to the godly carried not only the general message that they were doing something wrong, but also often contained very specific instructions as to what they were doing wrong, and as to how they should go about putting it right. Later in the seventeenth and in the eighteenth centuries, a new school of divines would extol nature as "God's Second Book." It is no exaggeration to contrast with this the earlier theology which regarded suffering as "God's Second Book." There were, as everyone recognized, various means by which God spoke to men. Most directly, He spoke by way of the revealed Word in the Scriptures. God had also made himself known through miraculous revocations of natural laws, though never in such a way as to contradict the Word but only to confirm it. Few Stuart Englishmen expected either more Scriptures or miracles (perhaps in part because Roman Catholics set such great store by the latter). Anglicans and Puritans usually thought of God as working in their lives through natural means—through providences rather than through miracles.[24] He manipulated not only forces of nature but human beings and institutions for his own long range purposes. We are familiar with the more positive results of this kind of thinking. For example, in 1533 Henry VIII's propaganda machine produced a justification of the royal break with Rome which cited good harvests, the absence of plague, and Queen Anne's delivery of a child as indications of divine approval. Englishmen and even Spaniards believed God had sent the wind which dispersed the Armada in 1588. The discovery of gunpowder barrels under the parliament in 1605 was long after commemorated as a providential deliverance. Cromwell's famous letters to the House of Commons attribute the parliamentary victories to the way (as at Tredah) that "God was pleased to animate" the soldiers. Royalists such as Clarendon and John Evelyn were no less certain that the restoration of the Stuart

23. Caryl, *Job* (chaps. 4–7), p. 325.
24. See, for example, one of Winthrop's arguments for a colony in New England. "Though miracles be ceased, yet we may expect a more than ordinary blessing from God upon all lawful means, . . . for it is usual with him to increase the strength of the means or to weaken them as He is pleased or displeased with the instruments and the actions; and yet both without miracle." *WP*, 2:137.

monarchy in 1660 was God's work. All would have agreed with Benjamin Whichcote that "the affairs of mankind are the choice piece of the administration of providence."[25]

We are less familiar, however, with the other side of the providential coin. In a civil conflict, a benevolent providence on one side is necessarily a judgment upon the other. Private and public setbacks and sufferings of all kinds were interpreted as providences in which God's hand could be seen, his voice heard, and his presence felt. Thomas Case, a presbyterian preacher who had been imprisoned for his complicity in Christopher Love's plot against Cromwell, used the privacy of his cell to compose his *Correction, Instruction: or, A Treatise of Afflictions* (1652). One of its themes is that "by affliction God maketh himself known unto his people. . . . We get more by one practical discovery of God, than by many sermons. . . . In the Word we do but hear of God, in affliction we see him."[26] Sir Nathaniel Bernardiston applied this doctrine to his own experience in a letter to John Winthrop. He wrote that "it pleased the Lord to visit me with a great and long sickness," but prayers for his recovery had been granted, and the Lord had been pleased to "lend me (most unworthy) some longer time the better to fit myself for him, and to try how far that correction would work my unruly and polluted heart to better obedience." Puritans such as Case and Bernardiston looked upon judgments as God's way of frightening men into the repentance required for their souls. Hearing and reading of the Word were thus reinforced by heavy afflictions which were more tangible and much harder to ignore. When judgments stripped a man of such inessentials as wealth, honor, health, and liberty, he was forced to fall back on the knowledge of religion that he had

25. J. J. Scarisbrick, *Henry VIII*, p. 323; Mattingly, *The Armada*, pp. 390–91; Abbott, 2:126 (cf. 1:360, 377, 387); *Contemplations*, pp. 370–71; *Diary and Correspondence of John Evelyn*, William Bray, ed., p. 233; Whichcote, 1:125. William Cecil, an astute politician aware of the danger of allowing enemies to appear to have the aid of providence, urged Elizabeth not to delay the execution of the ineptly treacherous Duke of Norfolk. Otherwise, some might suspect a "lack of power in her hand, by God's ordinance; yea, some to the Scottish queen's prayers and fasting." Quoted in Wallace MacCaffrey, *The Shaping of the Elizabethan Regime*, p. 428.

26. Case, *Correction*, p. 78. Cf. p. 91: "In the school of affliction God reads lectures upon his attributes, visible lectures, and expounds himself unto his people; so that many times they come to know more of God or more experimentally by half a year's sufferings, than by many years' sermons."

gained but had never been required to act upon. As Case put it, God sends us "into the school of affliction: because we will not hear the Word, we force God to turn over to a severer discipline." God thus spoke loudly to his children when they failed to learn that fear of him which they professed but did not exhibit in their behavior. Another Puritan, Thomas Hodges, said as much in a fast-day sermon before the members of the House of Commons on September 28, 1642: "Tis a sad case my brethren, that nothing but blows will make us fear; when God falls a plaguing, then usually men a fearing." Thomas Doolittle described the Great Plague of 1665 as "a speaking judgment. The word that signifies the 'plague' comes from a word that signifies to 'speak'. God in lesser judgments whispereth to a sin, but in a plague he speaketh out."[27]

Throughout these statements there is an awareness of sin and retribution as a dialogue between God and man. Men, especially godly men, anger God with the sins that are referred to as "crying sins" and "provoking sins." The sins cry out for and provoke divine vengeance, but in the case of the children of God, the retribution is tempered with love and aims at conversion and reformation of life in the believer. When the child of God does begin to behave as he should, God either lifts the judgment or gives the spiritual support necessary to shoulder the burden. The judgment is itself a word spoken in due season for the spiritual benefit of the hearer. Sibbes defined judgment as "correction moderated to God's children." God's laws, he said, were judgments that gave directions for the Christian life, and "when we do not that men should He is forced to judge us with real judgments." Anglicans also interpreted afflictions in terms of just such a dialogue between God and man. The Cambridge Platonist, Benjamin Whichcote, referred to the way that "sometimes God doth visit us by some cross, providence" as "sickness, diseases and pains and these are to be looked on as God's awakening of us." William Laud wrote to his close friend, Lord Scudamore, in an attempt to comfort him upon the death of his infant son in 1624. The comfort, however, had an ominous sound. Laud told the peer that such tragedies were the "greater and louder callings of God upon us" and that even when there is a measure of

27. WP, 4:217; Case, Correction, p. 216; Thomas Hodges, A Glimpse of Gods Glory (1642), p. 11; Doolittle, Antidote, p. 49.

mercy in them, they still have "the nature of punishment." Jeremy
Taylor, after receiving news from John Evelyn of the losses of two
sons to smallpox, commended his friend for looking upon their loss
"as a rod of God; and he that so smites here will spare hereafter."
Thomas Pierce employed the same oft-used metaphor in a sermon
preached before Charles II in 1665. London was in the throes of the
last great visitation of the plague, and England was at war with the
French and the Dutch as well. Such sore afflictions were, said
Pierce, God's means of calling his people to repentance. His usual
method was first to move the "public preachers of his Word" to give
appropriate warnings. If the prophetic utterances failed to frighten
men into repentance, then "the rod comes in with its sermon" and
all must hear it.[28]

Anglicans, like Puritans, applied the notion that judgments are
one of God's most important means of communication with man to
both private and public disasters. They also agreed that God spoke
through such judgments in order to chastise the godly for their
backsliding, convert the unconverted, and destroy the wicked. There
remained, however, a tricky problem in the understanding of God's
message to sufferers. There was, as Whichcote put it, "a great
danger of making false interpretations of providence." How was the
godly man to discern just where he had gone wrong? How could he
know God's particular and specific aim? Thomas Case had stated
that it was the duty of the afflicted soul "seriously to enquire what it
is which God calls for under the present dispensation." Thus in every
new trouble, he was "to mind what new duty God expects, what new
grace he is to exert and exercise." The divines, for obvious reasons,
held the view that it was part of their duty to act as interpreters and
analyzers of these messages. William Gouge said that it "is the part
of ministers of God's Word, out of his Word to declare what he
intendeth and expecteth when he smileth or frowneth on his
people." As we have just seen, the anglican Dr. Pierce referred to
preachers as one of the "two sorts of voices" used by God to urge
repentance from judgment-provoking sins. All the ministers and
most laymen as well agreed that an important part of the ministerial

28. Sibbes, *Cordialls*, p. 225; Whichcote, 1:46–47; Hugh R. Trevor-Roper,
Archbishop Laud, p. 411; Taylor, 1:lxxviii; Pierce, p. 126. For other Anglicans on
"provoking sins," see *Contemplations*, pp. 437, 439; Whichcote, 1:86.

function was careful scrutiny of the runes of tribulation for signs as
to which sins were causing them. The care and thought that went
into the analysis of God's intentions in his threatenings and judgments were enormous.[29] We must resist the temptation to dismiss
this analysis as mere sacerdotal thaumaturgy. These were intelligent
men deeply concerned to find satisfying answers to the eternal riddle
of human suffering in the only way open to them—the searching of
God's Word for the principles upon which the universe operated and
the application of these to the discrete units of human agony which
they daily confronted. In a time when natural science lay in its
swaddling clothes, ministers, as devotees of theology, the queen of
the sciences, were expected to have answers.

One of the ways that divines sought to arrive at God's meaning
and aim in his judgments was to reason from the doctrine that God
was a god of method and order. The correspondence between
afflictions and sins was not merely one of severity and heinousness.
The particular kind of affliction was often an indication from God
of the particular nature of the offense. Sibbes put it this way: "God
is methodical in his corrections, and doth (many times) so suit the
cross to the sin, that you may read the sin in the cross." Another
Puritan, Joseph Caryl, used the same theory in one of his sermons on
the book of Job. "Punishment," he said, "often bears the image and
superscription of sin upon it. . . . God often returns the sin of man
upon him; sin comes to him in its own likeness, and he may read
the name of it stamped upon the affliction." One of the examples
Caryl cited is one which the Puritans were especially concerned
about. It is recounted in Leviticus 10:1 that Nadab and Abihu
sought to worship the Lord in a way which He had not commanded.
More specifically, they offered "strange fire" in the form of incense
burning in the censers they carried as sons of Aaron. Caryl para-

29. Case, *Correction*, pp. 91–92; Whichcote, 1:128; Gouge, *Gods Three Arrowes*,
sig. A4 (recto); Pierce, p. 125. Gouge provided an interesting example of the
statistical approach to the problem of suffering. He gave figures to show that the
plague began slowly and increased only because the warnings of the ministers were
not heeded. In the week beginning January 13, 1625, only one plague death was
reported; in successive weeks the toll was three, then five, three, one, two, eight,
six, eight, eighteen, eighteen. It continued to increase thereafter until the August 18
toll was 4,463. This was proof of God's mercy in beginning "this judgment of the
plague by degrees, that so like wise men we might foresee the uttermost peril and
answerably prepare ourselves." *Gods Three Arrowes*, p. 31.

phrased verse two as follows: as they had offered strange fire, "they reaped the same, God by fire from heaven, in a strange manner, slew them in a moment." Clarendon used an image which always sprang quickly into anglican minds. God, he said, "commonly punishes men by the same vices which they have practised to the prejudice and damage of others; him who is disobedient to his father, by the disobedience of a son of his own, and the like." This variation in the choice of examples has a significance which will be discussed in subsequent chapters. What should be noted here is the agreement as to God's methods and general aims in his judgments. The key point was, as Whichcote explained it, that "no man's afflictions are wholly casual or contingent but are directed by an intelligent agent: of which he may make a certain interpretation to his own advantage." This was a "great point of divinity."[30]

Thus both Anglicans and Puritans used what may be called the boomerang principle as a device for understanding the correspondence between man's provoking sins and God's speaking judgments. When the boomerang theorem is placed in its context of God's concern for the sins of godly men, it is clear that the rhetoric of suffering employed by both Anglicans and Puritans placed a tremendous responsibility upon the saint or would-be saint. He was not and could not, in this life, be perfect in his obedience to God's commandments. Nevertheless, the sins which he, as a son of Adam, would of necessity commit, enraged God much more than the sins of the obstinately wicked. Although he was in duty bound to oppose evil and evil men and would make enemies in the process, he could not blame them for his troubles. They were merely instruments of God's wrath and were the more to be pitied because all knew what God did with his rods when he had finished using them. He threw them into the fire.[31] The godly man had to look into himself for the sins which pulled upon the rope of God's vengeance, repent them sincerely, and repeat them no more. Then and only then would the judgments cease or—if they did not cease—could the saint look upon

30. Sibbes, *Letter*, p. 3; Caryl, *Job* (chaps. 4–7), pp. 51–52; *Contemplations*, p. 479. Cf. Sibbes, *Cordialls*, p. 220; *Contemplations*, pp. 519–20; Whichcote, 1:125. For a slightly different but equally puritan reading of the Nadab and Abihu story, see T. Goodwin, 3:345–47 (see also *WP*, 2:193).

31. See Case, *Correction*, p. 212; Sibbes, *Cordialls*, p. 145; Lionel Gatford, *Englands Complaint* (1648), p. 41.

them as tests and exercises of his faith rather than as clarion calls for repentance. This was the message of suffering and it spoke directly to the behavior of the believer. This, at any rate, was God's intention for it. We must next consider more fully the implications of this principle for the believer. How could these doctrines be of use to him? Despite the burden which they placed upon him, the comfort which could be derived from them was great.

THE USE OF SUFFERING

Sir John Tyndal, Master of Chancery, was shot to death on November 12, 1616, by the deranged loser of a lawsuit which had been tried in his court. Sir John's son, Arthur Tyndal, described the ensuing days as "bitter times of trial" for the Tyndal family, a family forced to face not only a father's brutal slaying but a great deal of malicious gossip prompted by the murderer's claim that Sir John had been guilty of wrongdoing in the case. Ten days after the murder, Arthur said in a letter, "Good mother, comfort yourself in the Lord, . . . if we make right use of this [He will] restore us again to comfort." Arthur's sister, Margaret, who had married John Winthrop, was facing a different time of trial in 1630 while separated from her husband during his initial journey to Massachusetts. She wrote that her hope was that the Lord "will sanctify it to me and give me a right use of it." In desiring to "sanctify" God's messages in the form of afflictions, these lay Puritans were acting upon the counsel of many puritan preachers. Richard Sibbes, for example, said that every saint, knowing that God's "main aim is at our melioration and sanctification" must ask himself, "How shall we carry and behave ourselves under this cross, that our souls may reap profit by it?" Anglicans preached and urged practice of the same doctrine. Thomas Pierce said that afflictions "help to make us happy even in this present world if we have but the grace to use them rightly; else they will make us the unhappier in that world which is to come." Clarendon reminded himself of the imperative need to "make the right use of our afflictions, improve ourselves, and grow the better by them."[32]

32. *WP*, 1:182; 2:209; Sibbes, *Letter*, p. 2; Pierce, p. 159; *Contemplations*, p. 468. Cf. Mocket, p. 34: "Afflictions and troubles, wisely managed, help to make a

Insofar as they were able to make the proper use of afflictions, Stuart Englishmen who hoped for salvation made themselves eligible for a number of valuable benefits. God's purpose in afflicting them was to drive them to repentance of sin and reformation of life. That, as we have seen, was the message of suffering from God's point of view. The performance of repentance (if sincere) and reformation (if maintained) was the "right use" or "sanctification" of affliction which God wanted. A man signified that he had heard and understood the message when he revised and re-ordered his life by eschewing the sins which had caused his suffering. A continuance in sin was evidence of continuing reprobation. It was a spurning of the God's love because, for all the true children of God, the message of suffering was a message of love. "When a sin is committed," wrote Sir Richard Baker, "a shower of God's anger rains presently down upon the sinner, and continues raining till there be repentance." To defer repentance was to provoke a flood of divine anger which would end in destruction by drowning unless, Baker said, the sinner "like Noah, begins to make his ark, betimes, and returns to God with a speedy repentance."[33] Once the initial step of repentance was taken (and even though a good many more would have to follow it), the believer could begin to avail himself of the cabinet of comforts which was suddenly opened up to him. His first "right use" of affliction made it possible for him to avail himself of a series of further uses, all of which would afford comfort in the tribulations to come.

One benefit of affliction for which the truly repentant sinner could hope was deliverance from his temporal troubles. John Owen treated the fall of the royalist stronghold of Colchester and the release of the members of the parliamentary committee of Essex who had been imprisoned there as just such a merciful deliverance in a pair of sermons preached at thanksgiving services in the autumn

---

man a complete Christian." Perkins, 2:31: "Afflictions and chastisements that seize upon God's children, do leave after them amendment of life, as the needle passeth through the cloth and leaveth the thread behind it." For other examples of the need for the "sanctification" or "right use" of afflictions, see *WP*, 1:191–92, 240, 412–13, 333, 385; 2:58, 321, 330, 338; Caryl, *Job* (chaps. 1–3), pp. 214, 219; Case, *Correction*, p. 4. See E. S. Morgan, *Roger Williams*, pp. 107–14, for a lucid discussion of this subject of the "improvement" of afflictions.
33. Baker, p. 139. Cf. Chillingworth, 3:256.

of 1648. "The great physician of his church," said Owen, "knows how to give his sin-sick people potions that shall work by degrees," and when the proper time came "all their iniquity" would be taken away. "When sin is taken away from within, trouble must depart from without." Early in the spring of 1647, the king and the parliamentary commissioners at Newcastle had heard a similar message from one of the odder characters of the day. Samuel Kem, who dedicated this sermon to the Earl of Pembroke, was a chaplain in the Roundhead army. He preached in military garb with a pistol on a cushion nearby. He defended his long hair by saying that it was a wig, since the biblical prohibition was not against wearing long hair but against growing long hair. Kem's sermon belied his eccentricities—it was a bland appeal for prayers for peace. He did, however, express his hope "that God will by all our evils refine us, not ruin us, correct us, not destruct us; and bring us all a precious and refined people out of all our devouring flames."[34]

It is doubtful that the king had any more liking for Kem than he did for Pembroke, a peer who had opposed him all through the troubles, but he heard the same doctrine preached by his loyal chaplain, Dr. Henry Ferne, on November 29, 1648. It was the last sermon Charles I heard. Ferne told his royal master and the small group of servants and courtiers at Newport that God "apportioneth the weight of affliction, and the length of time, with respect to our continuance in sin." There would be "a continuance of calamities so long as ye are not what ye should be." Suffering would go on "till we learned what it is to order our ways aright, and so are made fit for a deliverance," and the deliverance would only come with "true inward repentance and amendment of evil ways." The tone of Ferne's sermon was, quite understandably, pessimistic about the imminence of deliverance for the royalist cause. Royalism was approaching its nadir. Within three days, the king was stripped of his chosen attendants and removed to the army's custody at grim

34. Owen, p. 85; Samuel Kem, *An Olive Branch Found after A Storme in the Northerne Seas* (1647), p. 15. For Kem, see *DNB*. He also spent some time as a chaplain in the parliamentary navy. He says in the dedication of this sermon that he had intended to write it in peace, "which my floating condition denied me the happiness to enjoy, having my intellectuals so searummaged that they returned to me but dark and unrefined notions" (sig. A5 [verso]). His argument on hair must have been an odd one too as 1 Cor. 11:14–5 seems unequivocal.

Hurst Castle. A more optimistic mood pervades one of Clarendon's applications of the same doctrine. He was reflecting upon Psalm 30 when news came of Charles II's alliance with the Scots in 1650. He took the return of the Scots to their allegiance to the Stuart monarchy as a repentance of their former disobedience. His hopes soared as he wrote: "Our night of affliction and calamity can last no longer than our night of sin and rebellion, . . . any glimmering of repentance and godly sorrow for what we have done and of godly purpose for the time to come, shall no sooner appear, than that night of sin and suffering will vanish away." Anglicans and Puritans urged themselves and each other in this way—they besought all Englishmen to heed God's voice in afflictions and repent so that the judgments might be lifted. We are tempted to dismiss all this as mere empty posturing. But the sheer volume of such appeals should remind us that in an age which was largely prescientific, men were much more disposed to take seriously the possibility that God was, somehow or other, behind ordinary and extraordinary occurrences. It was, as Bishop McAdoo has written, a world "in which the arbitrary always seemed present." Without fear of contradiction or even dispute from biologists, geologists, physicists, economists, historians, or other "experts," a divine could say that repentance would lead to the lifting of judgments. Quite aside from the theological reasons which he could adduce, he could say, as did John Benbrigge preaching in Sussex in 1646, that "experience proves this enough by many examples."[35]

In the event that the children of God were not rewarded for the repentance of judgment-provoking sins by a lifting of those judgments, the right use or sanctification of affliction still had a reward in this world. It was an axiom of anglican and puritan thinking that godly men were never afflicted beyond the powers of their resistance to suffering. They would never be so troubled that they would ever be driven to use unlawful and unwarrantable means to escape the judgment because God would always give them the grace to keep themselves on the narrow path to salvation. They would, in other words, never sin in order to avoid the just consequences of

35. Ferne, *A Sermon Preached Before His Majesty at Newport in the Isle of Wight* (1649), pp. 2, 14, 15; *Contemplations*, pp. 447–48; H. R. McAdoo, *The Spirit of Anglicanism*, p. 5; Benbrigge, *Gods Fury*, pp. 28–29.

their sins, and they would have divine assistance as they sought to put affliction to the use intended for it. Dr. Sanderson informed Charles I and his court at Whitehall in July, 1640, of God's methods in this respect. God ministered to his servants by proportioning "our sufferings to our strength." He considered, like the good physician, "as well the malignity of the disease, the strength of the patient, and prescribeth for him accordingly, both for the ingredients and the dose." In the same way, continued Sanderson, God supported his servants by proportioning "comforts suitable to our afflictions, every whit as large as they, and more effectual, to preserve us from drooping, and to sustain our souls in the midst of our greatest sufferings." General Philip Skippon, the leader of the London militia, had the same comfort for his fellow soldiers in a tract called *A Salve for Every Sore* (1644). He paraphrased 1 Corinthians 10:13 to say, "God is faithful, who will not suffer you to be tempted above that you are able." Joseph Caryl, preaching on this theme to his puritan flock in London, said that "it is well with the righteous in their worst outward condition because God is with them." Thus, although God is certainly present in fires, storms, and earthquakes, yet Caryl maintained that "his presence makes the fire but as a warm sun, the stormy wind, a refreshing gale and the earthquake, but a pleasant dance."[36]

The assurance that suffering would never be insufferable for the godly was infinitely more valuable than temporal deliverance or worldly rewards for the same reason that these were of the world and therefore merely temporal. For both Anglicans and Puritans in the seventeenth century, Christian life was a sojourn, a pilgrimage, a wayfaring between this world and the next, a warfaring between the forces of good and evil which buffeted the soul trapped in its coffin of flesh. Professor Haller has demonstrated this attitude so effective-

36. Sanderson, 2:247–48; Skippon, p. 103; Caryl, *Job* (chaps. 4–7), p. 103. Other anglican examples: Sydenham, *The Rich Mans Warning-peece* (1630), p. 21; Hall, 5:561–63; Archbishop Robert Leighton, *The Works* (1840), p. 380; Hales, 3:45–46. Other puritan examples: T. Goodwin, 2:lxi; Sibbes, *Cordialls*, p. 164; Doolittle, *Rebukes*, p. 187; Case, *Correction*, pp. 85–87; Mocket, pp. 45–46. The Marian martyrs had used a similar argument to reassure one another: "Our common enemy shall do no more than God will permit him. God is faithful, which will not suffer us to be tempted above our strength." Latimer to Ridley, quoted in A. G. Dickens, *The English Reformation*, p. 272. Doubtless the victims of Nero, Domitian, and Diocletian used it too.

ly for the Puritans that it is easy to forget that Anglicans used this imagery frequently too. That vigorous Laudian, Humphrey Sydenham, did so in a sermon entitled "The Christian Duell," preached before the assize in Somerset in 1634. In this world, he said, all Christians live not in the "church triumphant," but in the "church militant." They cannot, therefore, rest idly in tents and garrisons, but must undertake a "daily marching against the enemy, a continual skirmishing with the flesh." In Oxford eight years before, Sydenham had defined "the life of a true Christian" as "a continual warfare," and more, the "life of the true apostle . . . a continual martyrdom." Clarendon's imagery was equally combative: "A good Christian's life in this world is a continual warfare, subject to all the skirmishes and assaults and ambushes that a dextrous and a vigilant enemy can subject us to."[37]

Traveler, pilgrim, voyager, soldier—the Christian was all of these and only one matter ultimately concerned him—his final destination. The world could not be an abiding city because it was composed of earthly things which all pass away. The godly man could be sure that his troubles in this life were trivial next to the inheritance which awaited him in his Father's house. So long as he had assurance that he was a child of God, all things could be endured. Without that assurance, no inner peace was possible. The assumption which underlay the extensive calculus of correspondence between sin and judgment in the seventeenth century was that the only source of real comfort in affliction was improvement of the sufferer's relationship with God. "All pains spring from one, that we have so little of God: all pains and cares therefore should be turned into one," said Nicholas Lockyer, "What have I of God? how might I have more? more of his love, more of his power working in my soul?" Sir Richard Baker, who had his full share of temporal troubles, was equally quick to dismiss their importance. We are all,

37. Haller, pp. 140–72; Sydenham, *Occasions*, p. 72, and *Sermons*, p. 1; *Contemplations*, p. 432. For other puritan examples, see Mocket, pp. 35–37; Doolittle, *Antidote*, p. 60; Benbrigge, *Christ*, pp. 8–9; Sibbes, *Cordialls*, pp. 174, 217; Walzer, pp. 277–80, 283. Sydenham's friend, the royal chaplain Henry Byam, used the pilgrim-traveller image to conclude a sermon preached before Charles II in exile: *XIII Sermons* (1675), p. 59. For other anglican examples, see Hyde, *Legacy*, p. 162; Hall, 5:646; Stampe, *Spiritual Infatuation*, pp. 55, 68; Pierce, pp. 463–64; Farindon, 2:191–93.

he wrote, like Martha, "troubled about many things when but one is needful. . . . That which properly troubles the soul is the proper trouble of the soul, and is only in matters between God and us." In heaven lies what Baker called "the soul's freehold; and if that inheritance be once questioned," then in that question lies "the soul of trouble."[38] This principle—that only one's relationship with God would yield real comfort—is so simple and so central to all aspects of the rhetoric of suffering in the seventeenth century that we must make a special effort to grasp it. We know that Laud, Pym, Cromwell, Clarendon, and their contemporaries took much more seriously than most of us can the notion that God manipulated men and things for his purposes. So long as the believer could have assurance that his earthly troubles were loving chastisements and not wrathful judgments, he could keep them in a perspective which made them not only bearable but, in most circumstances, welcome signs of God's concern for the good of his soul.

The one "needful thing" for man, whatever befell him, was knowledge of God's disposition toward him. Man's proper and only trouble was in matters between God and him. We must remember this because, as Dame Veronica Wedgwood wrote of another basic fact about seventeenth-century life, "It is easy to say it; it is not so easy to remember it."[39] It is easy for us to forget, or at least underestimate, the importance of this conviction because we have moved on to different theories about the causes of human troubles. All that has been learned about social and economic origins of conflict in Stuart England, though undeniably important, must not obscure the fact that most Englishmen were more concerned about the states of their souls in relation to eternal life than we are. For better or for worse, we have come a long way from the time when the most crucial relationship in the lives of a great many people was not with their spouses, their analysts, their tax attorneys, their bookies,

38. Lockyer, *Baulme For Bleeding England and Ireland*, p. 33; Baker, pp. 109–10. Lockyer was later a fast-day preacher before the House of Commons and a chaplain to Cromwell. *DNB*.
39. C. V. Wedgwood, "Charles I: the Case for the Execution," in *Charles I*, p. 5. She was referring to the fact that the "English Civil War occurred a long time before Tom Paine proclaimed the Rights of Man, a long time before the French Revolution, and a very long time before manhood suffrage was introduced in any European country."

their dissertation advisers, or their gurus—but with their God. The distance is extended by the tendency of modern observers to look upon anyone who does concern himself seriously with the state of his soul as simple, eccentric, irrational, or mad, depending upon the nature of the outward manifestation of his concern. Even the more sympathetic among us, influenced as we are by the very multiplicity and variety of modern thought and experience, may have difficulty putting aside the notion that a fervent and frequently expressed hope of heaven is not a sign of religious mania or hypocrisy or both. One of the best antidotes to this suspicion is to be found in the diaries and letters of John Winthrop, a practical, solid man of affairs—no eccentric or recluse but a busy lawyer and estate manager. In 1612 he wrote, "I have resolved by the grace of God, . . . not to suffer my heart to delight more in anything than in the comfort of my salvation." This continued to be a constant theme in his meditations. Early in 1621 he wrote to his wife, praising her as "the chiefest of all comforts under the hope of salvation, which hope cannot be valued." He urged her to heed the Lord's advice by first seeking "the kingdom of God" and remembering that "one thing is needful, and so as without it the gain of the whole world is nothing." This was, he thought, infinitely preferable to "the frothy wisdom of this world and the foolishness" of those who mistook "outward prosperity for true felicity."[40]

The Winthrops were, however, prototypical Puritans, and one is not surprised to find in them a deep concern for salvation. Anglicans could be quite as serious about it as Puritans, although perhaps somewhat less openly so. The worldly-wise Jacobean courtier and diplomat, Sir Henry Wotton (1568–1639), spent the last sixteen years of his life as Provost of Eton College. In his will he bequeathed his soul to his Maker, saying that Christ's atonement was "sole sufficient satisfaction for the sins of the whole world, and efficient for his elect." Of his election to bliss, Wotton was certain, saying "in the number of whom I am one by his mere grace, and thereof most unremoveably assured by his Holy Spirit, the true eternal comforter." Although such statements were rather conventional in wills, Wotton had expressed similar thoughts elsewhere. Upon receiving a copy of Sir Richard Baker's *Meditations on the Lord's*

40. *WP*, 1:167, 260–61.

Prayer (1637), he wrote to the author, praising the work and saying, "I see your worldly troubles have been but pressing-irons to your heavenly cogitations." Shortly before his last illness, Wotton said that he had in his "passage to the grave . . . not always floated upon the calm sea of content, but have often met with cross winds and storms and with many troubles of mind and temptations to evil." Yet as he approached his "harbor of death," he told John Hales that "Almighty God hath by his grace prevented me from making shipwreck of faith and a good conscience; the thought of which is the joy of my heart." Wotton ended his stay in those years which he had called "the suburbs of oblivion" by dying in 1639. The timing of his death was fortunate for had he lived a few years longer he would, in all likelihood, have been ejected from Eton as his friend John Hales was, thence to die in poverty. This treatment of the good man's life as a journey between two worlds in which a well-founded hope of heaven is the best defense against tribulation is a prominent theme in the thoughts of another great Anglican, the Earl of Clarendon. During his first exile, for example, he described "the pious and godly man" as one who "looks upon this world but as a passage to a better or a worse, and himself as a probationer in it." The steady doing of God's will led "the pious and the faithful man" to the attainment of a "good conscience" and thereby a claim "to God's protection; from the confidence wherein he finds a more real and substantial joy of heart, than the worldly man can find from the access and accumulation of all earthly additions and felicities."[41]

Those Stuart Englishmen, whether Anglican or Puritan, who could find some basis for believing themselves among the children of God had a vast array of rhetorical and metaphorical aids to the understanding and "improvement" of their troubles. As we have seen, both anglican and puritan preachers maintained that God's judgments began in his own family. His chastising charity began at home as a means of preparing the seed of His spirit for eternal

41. Sir Henry Wotton, *The Life and Letters of Sir Henry Wotton*, ed. Logan Pearsall Smith, 1:215; 2:370, 406 (to Sir Edmund Bacon); *Contemplations*, pp. 387, 389. Wotton's statement to Hales is quoted in Izaak Walton, ed., *Reliquiae Wottonianae* (3rd ed., 1672), sig. e4 (recto). Hales sold part of his excellent library in order to help his friend Anthony Farindon, who had a large family. *DNB*, s.v. "Anthony Farindon."

residence in his house of many mansions. Thus the anglican chaplain, Richard Harwood, said in his post-Naseby sermon that although every sin merits damnation of the sinner, yet God mercifully afflicts us so that "by a pre-libation of this bitter cup, we may prevent the drinking of the very dregs in hell." Hammond prepared a similar message for Charles I at Carisbrook in 1648:

the design of God's rod, his smitings, his punishments, [is] to give us a little of that hell beforehand, . . . to help us to some disrelish of sin at the present, . . . of the odiousness and bitterness of it, in the very mouth, that we may not have any joy in chewing or swallowing down so abhorred a mixture, which hath such a certain arrear of horror and bitterness in the stomach; to rain down some fire and brimstone into our throats whensoever we are gaping after that forbidden tree; thus to discourage, if not to allay our hydropic thirst, to encumber and trash us in our violent furious marches, to pluck off the wheels of our Egyptian chariots that they may drive more heavily.[42]

The changes that were rung upon this theme in the seventeenth century by lay and clerical writers range from the homeliest of aphorisms to the most eloquent of Ciceronian elaborations. All aimed to help the godly sufferer make the right use of his sufferings by understanding them as a purging of remaining sins and a testing of developing graces in order to prepare him for everlasting bliss. The great Independent divine, Thomas Goodwin, wrote in *The Tryall of a Christians Growth* that God purges us because he wishes to purify us for his bed; He can take no delight in us as we are, "no more than a husband can with a wife, who hath an unsavoury breath, or a loathsome disease." Samuel Clarke, the martyrologist of Puritanism, wrote in *The Saints Nosegay* that "Grace is hid in nature here, as sweet-water in rose leaves, the fire of affliction must be put under it to distill it out."[43] The anglican chaplain and later

42. Harwood, *Loyall Subjects Retiring Roome*, pp. 34–35; Hammond, p. 201. Cf. Whichcote, 1:24.
43. T. Goodwin, *The Tryall of a Christians Growth* (1649), p. 79. This treatise depends upon an extended horticultural metaphor in which afflictions arc God's means of pruning away sins while virtues grow stronger. For other examples of the use of this metaphor, see Sibbes, *Cordialls*, p. 225; Mocket, pp. 9–10; Preston,

Primate of Ireland, John Bramhall, was thinking in similar terms of
the royalists banished during the Interregnum: "Spices being
brayed in a mortar smell more sweetly; so these servants of Christ,
being beaten and bruised by persecutors, do yield a more fragrant
odor in the nostrils of God and man." Nathaniel Ward, of both Old
and New England, used precisely the same olfactory comparison and
then followed it with another which appealed to God's ear instead
of his nose. Ward compared "a sound heart" with "a sounding
harp, the more the strings whereof are stretched and wracked, the
finer the melody they make." The godly soul, he said, when it is beset
with calamities, "rather laughs than repines, as if it were rather
tickled than tortured; the reason is, because it looks beyond the
instrument unto the hand that moves it, and says, this is the finger
of God."[44]

As the foregoing examples indicate, the catalogue of comforting
metaphors available for the use of suffering Christians was rich and
varied. Indeed, it was so varied that it could be the subject of a
sizable study in its own right. Of the value of afflictions, Sanderson
said in 1640, "In the whole course of divinity I find not a field of
larger scope than that is." He was forced to restrict himself to only a
part of it on that fast day, and we too will narrow our scope by
concentrating on two "similitudes"—God as master of the refining
fire and God as a chastising father. Both occurred frequently in the
thoughts of Anglicans and Puritans. The notion of God as a master
founder, heating mixtures of metals so as to refine out all baseness
and leave only the rarest and most valuable of metals appears
several times in the Old Testament. Thomas Case was among the
Puritans who used this metaphor. "The hot furnace," he said, "is
Christ's workhouse, the most excellent vessels of honor are formed
therein." God is "the master-founder" whose judgments stoke the
furnace of affliction; those who do not sanctify the judgments by

Breast-Plate, pt. 2, pp. 195–96; Baker, p. 375; Case, _Correction_, pp. 201–02: "The
Almond tree is made fruitful by driving nails into it, letting out a noxious gum that
hindereth the fruitfulness thereof." E. S. Morgan gives examples of the use of the
marital image by New England Puritans in _The Puritan Family_, chap. 7. He also
explores the comfortable uses of the fatherhood imagery discussed below.
    44. Samuel Clarke, _The Saints Nose-gay_ (1642), p. 147; Bramhall, p. 124; Theo-
dore de la Guarden [Nathaniel Ward], _Mercurius Anti-mechanicus. Or The Simple
Coblers Boy_ (1648), pp. 3–4. See Perry Miller and Thomas H. Johnson, eds., _The
Puritans_, 1:225–36 for more on Ward and another sample of his writing.

purging out sin are wicked and, as Case put it, "God hath cast them out as the founder casts out his dross to the dunghill, and they shall never stand among vessels of honor." The royalist chaplain, Gilbert Sheldon, used it to explain the suffering of Charles I to Charles II and his court immediately after the Restoration. He said that to God's children, the saints, "afflictions are their physic; and by them, 'like gold in the furnace,' they gain lustre and lose no weight, are mended here, that they may be saved hereafter." No one, Sheldon added, should be surprised when "a saint" was afflicted, "especially if a king, if a saint-royal."[45]

The single most widely used "comfortable" metaphor was that of God as a loving yet chastising Father. This is not to say that it was invented in our period; on the contrary, it was perhaps the oldest antique in the household of Christian rhetoric, a theme central to the entire Judeo-Christian tradition. The anglican or puritan sermon, treatise, or letter which treats of affliction without reference to God's fatherly manner of proceeding to judgment is rare. If the sufferer could consider himself a legitimate child of God and not a bastard, then his troubles were fatherly corrections and not damning judgments. William Pierse, the Bishop of Bath and Wells who was hated by the Puritans of the west country, did just this on February 20, 1642, in the Tower of London. He and nine of his fellow prelates had been impeached and imprisoned by the Long Parliament on December 30, and there they languished. Pierse took as his text Paul's prayer while troubled by a thorn in the flesh. The bishop thought that the thorn had probably been "some internal and spiritual affliction in his soul," but regardless of the tangibility of the thorn, all afflictions of all kinds were "the

45. Sanderson, 2:243; Case, *Correction*, p. 162, 198–99; Sheldon, p. 3. For the refining metaphor in the Old Testament, see Prov. 25:4, 26:23, 27:21; Ps. 12:6; Isa. 1:25, 48:10; Ezek. 22:19–22; Mal. 3:2, 3. Other examples: Skippon, p. 103; Cudworth, pp. 31, 82; Doolittle, *Rebukes*, p. 53; Sibbes, *Cordialls*, p. 162; T. Hooker, *Lessons*, p. 87; Ferne, *Sermon Preached at Newport*, p. 15; Mocket, pp. 11, 12. Mocket also used the analogy of running water to describe the refining and purifying of the godly by affliction. Running water is pure, stagnant water putrefies; so "the way to refine [the godly] is to drive them from vessel to vessel, from one trouble to another." Joseph Caryl said that "affliction is a cleanser. Christ is the only lavatory" and only his blood can wash away the guilt of sin—but "God hath other fountains and lavatories to wash away the pollution of sin," i.e., "the water or fires of affliction." *Job* (chaps. 4–7), p. 117.

loving corrections of a merciful Father." Another of the imprisoned
bishops was the prolific Joseph Hall of Norwich. In a tract called
The Balm of Gilead (1646), he sought to comfort "all the distressed
members of Jesus Christ" by asking them whether they, as parents
of earthly children, had ever taken pleasure in using the rod when
it was necessary for the child's good? "Didst thou not suffer more
than thou inflictedst?" The godly, he continued, had to remember
that "if we that are evil know how to give loving and beneficial
correction unto our children, how much more shall our Father
which is in heaven know how to beat us to our advantage!" Clarendon's cousin, Dr. Edward Hyde, pointed to another comforting
aspect of the similitude whe he wrote that though earthly fathers
chasten as "after their own pleasure, . . . both unjustly and un-
measurably . . . yet surely our Father in heaven doth not so."
Thomas Pierce, explaining to the House of Lords the reasons for
the destructively heavy rains in the summer of 1665, described
them as God's threats sent to save his children from sin. "How
indulgent a Father must He be thought, who when his prodigal
children are running from him, sets a lion in their way, to fright
them back to his embraces?"[46]

Puritans were also quick to grasp at the analogy between their
earthly fathers and their heavenly Father—each had to punish his
children for their own good. It "is a truth as clear as the sun," said
Sibbes, "that God suffereth his children to fall into the mouth of
lions, . . . The history of the church in all ages shows as much."
He argued in his last sermon (preached June 28, 1635) that this
was a source of great comfort. The godly man knew that "God
dealeth with him as a correcting Father . . . a Father in covenant
with him." The pain of suffering thereby lost its sting, for "what
can come from a father but what is sweet?" Simeon Ash, the popular
puritan lecturer in London, used the metaphor of the paternal rod
to explain the sore oppressions, heavy impositions, and violent
persecutions which God's children had undergone during Charles
I's Personal Rule. Ash implied that the good people who had withstood all these tribulations were the equivalents of Job, who was

46. Pierse, *A Sermon Preached at the Tower* (1642), p. 6; Hall, 7:7; Hyde, *Legacy*,
p. 115; Pierce, p. 105 (cf. p. 116). Other anglican examples: Sanderson, 2:67,
147–48, 238–40; Farindon, 1:456–57; *Eikon*, pp. 5–6; Sydenham, *Occasions*, p. 177.

grievously afflicted. That the good men of the world should suffer so was, said Ash, a terrifying proof of the heinousness of sin; if we were to see "a wise, patient and a loving father cast his child to the ground, bruise his flesh and break his bones by blows, we would be confident the offense was foul; such a Father is God unto his people." Thomas Case in similar terms described chastisement as God's means of making himself heard above the din which surrounds and deafens a man in the midst of worldly prosperity. He wrote: "God is forced to deal with man as a father with his child playing in the market-place, and will not hear or mind his father's call. He comes and takes him out of the noise of the tumult, carries him into his counting-house, lays him upon his knee with the rod in his hand, and then the father can be heard." Rachel Huntley, the widow of a London merchant, was a lay Puritan who had fully understood the preachers in this matter. She said in a letter to John Winthrop that all of God's blessings, whether in the form of temporal prosperity or affliction, are "sanctified unto us through [Jesus Christ] for in him all our afflictions proceed from God as from a most loving God and so as fatherly chastisements."[47]

As all the metaphors imply and as both Anglicans and Puritans agreed, chastisement of sin and refinement of graces were necessary parts of the salvation process. God's true children, the gold in the midst of a world of dross, knew and understood this. They knew how to put it to use, both for amendment of conduct and for comfort in tribulation. They knew that as true sons of a heavenly Father, they had to suffer as had the Son of God during his brief sojourn upon earth. Suffering was to be welcomed, in a spiritual sense, because if it were used as it should be, it made the Christian ever more holy, more pure—more like Christ. It became a means of having, as the puritan Thomas Goodwin put it, "more fellowship with Christ in his death and sufferings by the death of sin."[48] The

47. Sibbes, *Cordialls*, p. 161; *Works*, p. 356; Ash, *Best Refuge*, p. 9; Case, *Correction*, p. 166; *WP*, 1:240. Other puritan examples: Doolittle, *Rebukes*, pp. 55, 102; Baker, pp. 100–01; *An Account*, p. 8.
48. *The Tryall of a Christians Growth*, p. 88. Cf. Thomas Hooker, *Heautonaparnumenos* (1646), p. 10. The phrase, "fellowship in his sufferings," is Saint Paul's (Phil. 3:10). For Cromwell's use of it, see his letter to his son, Richard, in Abbott, 2:236. This is the closest Puritans came to urging the "imitation of Christ," a matter to be treated further in chap. 3, below.

anglican Dr. Edward Hyde wrote that "affliction makes us conformable to Christ our Savior. . . . It makes a man here on earth
conformable to him who is the very beauty of heaven." His colleague, Anthony Farindon, stated the point quite bluntly: "It
cannot consist with the wisdom of God, that Christ should suffer
and die, and that we might live as we please, and then reign with
him." All of the agonies Christ endured, the Christian should
recognize, said Farindon, as a "heavenly science, by which our
best Master learned to succor us in our sufferings, to lift us up out
of our graves and to raise us from the dead. There is life in his death,
and comfort in his sufferings."[49] Affliction was necessary because
men continued to sin. Christ had come to remove not sin itself,
but the guilt of sin from the shoulders of the elect of God. The
purging of sin from those chosen children made them like the Son,
and they therefore knew to kiss the rod of affliction.

Although there was no way that the saints could welcome physical pain or material want in a bodily way, yet they were to welcome
it with joy of spirit. They were not to go out of their way to seek
affliction—English Protestants of all kinds were wary of Roman
Catholic asceticism. There was, in any case, more than enough
suffering to go around in the seventeenth century without hairshirts
on bare backs or pilgrimages on bare knees. The proper course was
to go one's way in one's calling, using all legitimate means to avoid
tribulation. The important thing was to be ready to face affliction
when it came, as it certainly would in some form. Joseph Caryl
described affliction as the "trial and touchstone of sincerity. . . .
Trouble makes the great trial; bring professors [of Christianity]
to the fire, and then they show their metal."[50] It was easy to profess Christianity in times of material prosperity and physical health.
The test came when God's providences so arranged things that the
right way became unprofitable and even painful. God, and only
God, knew which men professing belief were true believers and

49. Hyde, *Legacy*, pp. 107, 109; Farindon, 1:82–84.
50. Caryl, *Job* (chaps. 1–3), p. 135. As Caryl here pointed out, prosperity could
be a judgment upon a wicked man, for his misuse of his wealth would demonstrate
his wickedness. Cf. Sibbes, *Cordialls*, p. 162, 188; Sanderson, 2:359–60. For an
interesting survey of means used by Nonconformists to evade persecution under
the Clarendon Code, see G. R. Cragg, *Puritanism in the Period of the Great Persecution:
1660–1688*, pp. 37ff.

which were hypocrites. But it was necessary that the perfection of God's justice be manifest to all. The great danger facing any man who hoped for heaven was not so much affliction itself as a failure of the test of affliction. The danger was not the chastening, but the absence of it. All of the great servants of God—Moses, Job, Daniel, David, Christ Himself—had borne great pains and heavy crosses. Bishop Pierse reminded his colleagues in the Tower of what they and all their countrymen knew when he said that the Israelites had had to go through the wilderness before they arrived in Canaan: "This was a type that we must pass through afflictions to that heavenly Canaan; and therefore one that was without afflictions, said to God, 'what Lord, am I out of thy favor? am I not worthy to be afflicted?' "[51]

The central feature of all the doctrines concerning affliction and the metaphors used to express them was that only true children of God could avail themselves of the benefits which arose from a deep understanding of God's purpose in his judgments. For those who were truly converted to the Christian faith, the troubles and trials which accompanied their passage through this life were deserved chastenings for their sins or necessary tests of their graces. Affliction was a foundry which required ore containing some gold, a flock in which the sheep were cared for but not the goats, and a family in which legitimate children and not bastards received loving correction. For each metaphor, the underlying doctrine was the same: although afflictions would appear to worldly eyes to harm the righteous as well as the wicked, yet their effect differed in the soul of the sufferer. Indeed, both Anglicans and Puritans frequently said that it was likely that the godly would receive even harsher temporal treatment than the wicked, especially in times of great public and national calamities. Nevertheless, it was the inward effect that really mattered. As Joseph Caryl said near the beginning of his long series of sermons on Job, he and his contemporaries needed to understand the workings of God's justice, especially

51. Pierse, *A Sermon Preached At the Tower*, p. 6. Edward Hyde recounted the story of the "most reverend and most religious and most learned Bishop Davenant" who, on his deathbed was troubled by Heb. 12:6 because he could not remember "his own chastenings." Hyde's comment was that it was a pity Davenant had died before "the late overflowings of ungodliness," i.e., the Puritan Rebellion, could take care of his doubts on the point. *Legacy*, pp. 110–12. Cf. Baker, p. 314.

"considering the times we live in threaten us with a common de-
luge, or an overflowing scourge, which may sweep away both the
good and the bad together." As the Civil War took its sanguinary
course, Caryl told his parishioners at Saint Magnus the Martyr
near London Bridge that the troubles of the godly were trials. He
asked, "Now is there any hurt in a trial or perturbation in a pro-
bation? Trouble tries grace that it may be honored and corruption
that it may be mortified. There is no hurt in all this; rather it is a
most happy condition which makes grace conspicuous, whereby
a man's best side, his inside (wherein his glory lies) . . . is turned
outward."[52] And when a man was turned inside out by affliction,
what did he look like? That is the great difficulty with all theories
of human motivation based on the supposition that men have souls
or any sort of "inner man." The nature of a man's soul, like the
nature of his superego or his id, can only be guessed at on the basis
of what the outward man does and says he thinks. In the seventeenth-century rhetoric of suffering, all comfort rested upon the
estate of the soul. The next question for us must be, how did the
sufferer go about deciding whether his troubles were correcting
chastisements from a loving Father or wrathful judgments by an
angry Judge? What was the process of conversion to saving faith,
and how did the saved behave?

THE CURE OF SUFFERING

"My soul is with the congregation of the firstborn, my body rests
in hope; and if here I may honor my God either by doing or by suffering, I shall be most glad." When Oliver Cromwell wrote these
lines in the autumn of 1638, he was an obscure East Anglian gentleman. When he died almost twenty years later, the things he had
suffered and the things he had done had ensured his fame for centuries to come. Cromwell besought his cousin in this same letter to
"pray for me, that He who hath begun a good work would perfect
it in the day of Christ." On his deathbed the Lord Protector
remained confident that the salvation begun so long before was to
be completed. He prayed, "Lord, though I am a miserable and

52. Caryl, *Job* (chaps. 4–7), p. 116. His preface to this volume, the first in the
series, was dated November 8, 1643.

wretched creature, I am in covenant with thee through grace."[53] Cromwell was convinced that he enjoyed the kind of relationship with God that was the basis of comfort in all kinds of travail. All the biblical texts "divided" and all the doctrines adduced and applied in practically all the sermons preached and all the devotional tracts written by Cromwell's clerical contemporaries were intended to help each hearer and each reader to know how to attain a comparable measure of confidence about his entry into Canaan. This letter of Cromwell's is one of many indications that the words of the preachers did not fall on deaf ears.

But if the goal, the final end, was universally agreed upon, the means to that end were not. One had to be a true Christian, a godly man—and the first step on the way to heavenly bliss was conversion. Once that step had been taken, there were many more to follow. The way to heaven was narrow, and it was easy to take a false step. Too many little wrong steps or one or two big ones could cast doubt upon the validity of one's original conversion. It is the purpose of this section to consider the anglican and puritan understandings of the means of conversion to sincere faith in God and thus to comfort in the promises made through Christ. The three chapters which follow will consider the manner of assaying the truth and sincerity of one's conversion. The two are inextricably yoked together; they can be separated in theory for purposes of analysis, but in practice they had to remain together. The proof of the conversion ultimately lay in the "carriage" and the "conversation" of the converted professor of faith.

As to the process of conversion, both Anglicans and Puritans insisted that an "effectual turning" away from sin and toward Christ was necessary. There were various ways that this could occur. It could be sudden and dramatic, as Saint Paul's famous experience on the road to Damascus had been. He had been changed from the most vigorous of the persecutors of Christ into the most vigorous of the proclaimers of Christ's gospel. There could be no doubt that his turning had been effectual; his conduct after the event provided abundant evidence. Although Cromwell did not claim a Pauline

53. Abbott, 1:97, 4:872. See R. S. Paul's analysis of Cromwell's famous 1638 letter. The letter is a compendium of scriptural excerpts woven together. *The Lord Protector*, pp. 399–400.

conversion experience, he regarded his radical change of direction
as comparable to the apostle's when he wrote, "I was a chief, the
chief of sinners. This is true; I hated godliness, yet God had mercy
on me." A turning away from darkness and toward light, away from
sin and toward godliness, these were essential to the conversion
process. But the very use of the word "process" implies that it did
not have to be a single event. Indeed, the most general expectation
seems to have been that the Spirit worked gradually and thus, as
Cromwell hoped, continued a process which it had at some point
"begun." The safest course lay in striving as much as possible for a
good conscience and against any kind of sin because the seed of the
Spirit was usually sown in prepared ground. Most Puritans would
have agreed with the king's favorite preacher, Dr. Henry Hammond, when he urged his unregenerate listeners to prepare for conversion by way of "integrity and honesty of heart, a sober moral
life, and chiefly humility and tenderness of spirit." These and other
virtues and the good deeds which grew out of the practice of them
would "naturally incline the subject for the receiving of grace when
it comes, and by fitting, as it were, and organizing the subject,
facilitate its entrance." This was, Hammond said, because "God's
ordinary course, as far as by events we can judge of it, is to call and
save such as are thus prepared." Neither Hammond nor any of the
Puritans who opposed him expected that a dramatic conversion of
a hardened, aggressively evil and profane man was anything other
than "a most rare and extraordinary work of God's power and
mercy, not an every day's work, like to be bestowed on every habit-
uate sinner."[54]

English Protestants agreed not only that Pauline conversions
were unlikely and that the safest course was to do one's best to prepare for conversion, but also that one's best could never be good
enough to bring about conversion unaided by divine grace. No man
could effectually turn away from sin without help in the form of
some measure of God's grace. Humphrey Sydenham, paraphrasing

54. Abbott, 1:97; Hammond, pp. 457–59. Farindon said of such events, "I will
not say it is impossible, but it carrieth little show of probability." Farindon, 1:305.
Hammond was described as "a pattern-flower of loyalty, one of his majesty's
favorite chaplains," by Thomas Carlyle, ed., *Oliver Cromwell's Letters and Speeches*,
1:296. On him, see John William Packer, *The Transformation of Anglicanism, 1643–
1660: With Special Reference to Henry Hammond.*

Saint Augustine, explained it simply enough: "Grace is given to the faithful, but it is first given that he should be faithful."[55] Thus no man could do it all on his own, but he had better do something and the more he did the better his chances. All were agreed too that no man could in any way merit or earn grace. He had to realize that he had sinned heinously and had to offer heartfelt repentance to God. If he did so, God "justified" him (i.e., forgave his past sins by imputing Christ's righteousness to him), and he was thence to sin no more. But since he was still human and still had a body of flesh, he would sin more. He then had to be helped to "sanctify" himself; he had to be given the ability (more grace) to obey God's commandments faithfully and to repent his lapses sincerely. There would definitely be lapses. Only a few aberrant souls maintained the much feared antinomian doctrine that the justified man was not bound by the moral law and could do no wrong.

In terms of doctrine, there is no divergence between Anglicans and Puritans up to this point, but there are distinctions to be made in terms of emphasis. Puritans placed a great deal more emphasis upon the urgency of a sincere conviction of sin and repentance than Anglicans did. They took up the topic more frequently and urged it more vigorously. They had to because they had a more radical sense of the distance between man and God, nature, and grace. Adam's original sin had so catastrophically separated the things of the world from the things of God that only massive infusions of grace could bring them together. No Puritan could have written, as Dr. Edward Hyde did, against importunate attempts to stir up the Spirit to reveal its presence in the soul: "Wait, wait, till he is pleased to make known himself within you." Of no Puritan could Canon Stranks have said, as he did of Jeremy Taylor, that in all his vast output of devotional and theological writing little was said about conversion.

55. Sydenham, *Sermons*, p. 53. This sketch of anglican and puritan treatments of conversion is brief for two reasons. First, good studies of the puritan approach are available: Edmund S. Morgan, *Visible Saints*, pp. 65–75; Norman Pettit, *The Heart Prepared*, chaps. 1–3; Perry Miller, *The New England Mind: The Seventeenth Century*, esp. chap. 10; and Geoffrey F. Nuttall, *The Holy Spirit in Puritan Faith and Experience*, chaps. 1–2. On the Anglicans, see the bibliographical note. Secondly, because of the theological and psychological complexity of the matter, I had to choose between a brief, impressionistic survey and an extended one. I chose the former, since a full treatment would have taken a disproportionate space within the framework of this study.

The puritan approach was anything but patient. Sir Richard Baker struck a familiar puritan chord when he ransacked the Scriptures for examples of men who had assaulted God with prayers for justification and been rewarded. He concluded, "Never, therefore, fear to be importunate with God, but fear rather thou canst never be importunate enough." William Fenner, a puritan preacher in Essex, was equally insistent that a man had to inquire "whether he be in Christ or not; whether he have true grace yea, or no." The reason was that "we can never have comfort until we have put this out of question, and therefore this is a question which all questions must give way unto."[56]

Although all were agreed that God's grace was the basis of conversion, there were different diagnoses of the amount and kind of grace needed. Many puritan "physicians of the soul" made a distinction between "saving grace" and ordinary grace which Anglicans either placed little emphasis upon or did not make at all.[57] Thus Thomas Goodwin, the great Independent, thought that his youthful regrets for his sins and joys at his "thought of the things of God" were evidences of true grace in his soul; but he later realized that these experiences merely showed "how far goodness of nature might go, as well in myself as others, to whom yet true sanctifying grace never comes." Thomas Watson, the presbyterian rector of Saint Stephen's, Walbrook in London, said in the course of his sermons on the Westminster Assembly's catechism that one of the counterfeits of sanctification was "common grace, which is a slight, transient work of the Spirit, but does not amount to conversion." Only "true sanctifying grace"—something much stronger than "common grace"—could make true, sanctified Christians, capable of undergoing all afflictions with a joyful heart. Thomas Doolittle reminded his nonconformist flock of this during the great plague of 1665–66. He urged them to examine their faith carefully and

56. C. J. Stranks, *Anglican Devotion*, p. 72; Hyde, *The Mystery of Christ in Us* (1651), p. 19; Baker, p. 150 (cf. pp. 114–15, 237); Fenner, *Looking-Glasse*, pp. 1, 20. See New, *Anglican and Puritan*, chap. 1, on the Puritans' radical separation of nature and grace.

57. There were some Anglicans of the "old school," such as Bishop Hall, who did regularly ask their readers and listeners whether they had "saving grace" or not. Nevertheless, in comparison to the Puritans, they tended to emphasize the freehandedness of God in dispensing such grace and the ease of obtaining it. See, for example, Hall's *Balm of Gilead*, chaps. 2, 4 (in *The Works*, vol. 7).

critically; many souls in hell had once been confident of their salvation because "of the near resemblance, betwixt the highest degree of common grace, and lowest degree of saving grace."[58] It is just this sort of elaboration which Anglicans criticized. Anthony Farindon, for example, ruefully shook his head at the notion of "a 'first conversion,' and a second; and I know not what cycles and epicycles we have found out to salve our irregular motion in our ways to bliss."[59]

In many ways the most striking difference of emphasis between the anglican and puritan explications of the doctrine of justification is also the most relative. Simply stated, it is that Puritans made it sound hard, and Anglicans made it sound easy. Stated another way, Puritans were closer to the absolute and uncompromising predestinarianism which orthodox Dutch Calvinists had maintained at the Synod of Dort (1619); whereas, like the Arminians at the synod, Anglicans sought to soften that austere, forbidding dogma. If, as Arminius himself had said, "God foreknew, but did not foreordain, who would be saved and who would be damned,"[60] then a much more optimistic view of the ability of the human will to choose be-

58. T. Goodwin, 2:lii; Watson, p. 244; Doolittle, *Antidote*, p. 7. Cf. T. Hooker, *Lessons*, pp. 211–14: "Every one that lives in the church is bound seriously and with great diligence to try and examine his estate, how it stands betwixt God and himself in respect of the work of saving grace wrought in his soul." And further "what be the false shadows of the state of grace." In the 1593 edition of the *Institutes*, Calvin had insisted that such "free will" as man has "is not sufficient to enable man to do good works, unless he be helped by grace, indeed by special grace, which only the elect receive through regeneration." In the 1555 edition he added a sentence which distinguished between "the effective giving of grace to the elect and the 'inferior operation of the Spirit' in the reprobate." John T. McNeill, ed., and Ford Lewis Battles, trans., *Institutes of the Christian Religion*, p. 262. Cf. William Perkins, in H. C. Porter, *Reformation and Reaction in Tudor Cambridge*, pp. 300–01.

59. Farindon, 1:100. Bishop Hall was also careful to assure the "sick soul" that he need not doubt his election because he could not cite its time, place, and manner. 7:27.

60. Quoted in W. K. Jordan, *The Development of Religious Toleration in England*, 2:325. For a brief account of the controversy which led to the calling of the Synod of Dort and of its relation to English thought, see 2: 320–51. This is not to say that the Puritans did not have their own rather different means of softening the rigors of the "final decrees." A fuller account of Dort is in A. W. Harrison, *Arminianism*, pp. 48–96. See also Carl Bangs, *Arminius*; Philip Schaff, ed., *The Creeds of Christendom*, 1:508–23, 3:550–97; Douglas Nobbs, *Theocracy and Toleration*; Rosalie L. Colie, *Light and Enlightenment*, chap. 1; Robert Peters, "John Hales and the Synod of Dort," *SCH* 7 (1971); 277–88.

lief, good works, and salvation over unbelief, evil works, and damnation could be taken. The English disputants were fully aware of
this difference between them at the time. Sibbes's polemical intention was perfectly plain when he condemned the "base men, that
live in the church," but "turn over all religion to a 'Lord, have
mercy upon us, and Christ died for us,' and 'we hope we have souls
to God-ward.'" He condemned those who made the way to true
religion "wide and broad, and complain of preachers that straiten
the way to heaven." For Puritans the way to heaven was "strait"
because human corruption was so complete. "There is a very vast
gulf between the state of sin and the state of grace," said William
Fenner, "and it is marvellous hard to pass it." Sin was so pervasive
that it cried out for denunciation, and the preachers were quick to
take up the task. When sinners saw the depth of their iniquity, it
could only have been God who began their conversion from the
unregenerate to the regenerate state. They could hardly have willed
such an unnatural reversal of the courses of their lives without substantial assistance from a force outside of nature. As Sibbes and John
Davenport put it in a preface to one of John Preston's books, "before our conversion, we were of no strength: since our conversion,
we are not sufficient of ourselves to think a good thought."[61]

But if Sibbes could criticize the Anglicans for making the way to
heaven too broad, he and his puritan brethren were charged with
overemphasizing its narrowness. Humphrey Sydenham, for example, denounced those preachers who "by continual thundering
of judgments, so shake the foundations of a weak-built faith, that
they sometimes destroy the temple they should build up." He argued
that the divine who seeks to frighten his hearers into conversion
violates the principles of nature because it is against human nature
to accept compulsion; further, it is against the principle of grace
because grace is gentle and sweet. Against the "rough dialect of the
law; horror, blood and death," he pleaded for "the sweet language of
the Gospel, brethren, and beseeching, and mercies of God." Harshness, rigor, and constraint subtracted from what Sydenham called
"the prerogative and freedom of human will."[62] Farindon, after

61. Sibbes, *Works*, 7:12; Fenner, *Looking-glasse*, p. 13; Preston, *Breast-Plate*, sig.
¶ 3 (recto and verso).
62. Sydenham, *Waters of Marah, and Meribah: or The Source of Bitterness and Strife*.

rejecting puritan notions about the complexity and difficulty of
conversion, implied a similarly optimistic view of the power of the
human will by saying, "if we could once have compassion on ourselves, the work were done . . . for I may be sure I am converted,
if I be sure that I truly pity myself." And he leaves no doubt that
true repentance is within man's power: God "hath given us his
Spirit, and filleth us with his grace, if we will receive it." It is a
matter for the human will, and it is not difficult to do if we really
want to do it: "For if thou wilt, thou mayest," said Farindon.[63]

Moderate Episcopalians (such as Farindon) of the Great Tew and
Cambridge Platonist varieties were emphatic in their assertion that
God had given men the power to turn away from sin and that the
free will he had endowed them with made harsh methods oppro-
brious. According to William Chillingworth, "Our God is a gracious
God, and requires of us no more than we are able to do." Although
"many learned men can delight themselves in discoursing of the
weakness of men's nature," said John Hales, "it is not so much our
impotency and weakness as our sloth and carelessness" which holds
us back and defeats us. "Beloved," he said in another sermon, it is
"the error of most Christians, we do not know of what strength we
are." Clarendon denounced those who "make such a fence about
their religion of laws and oaths and obligations, instead of inviting
and alluring men to the practice and profession of it." Whichcote
said that "God hath made us of natures to be . . . dealt with . . .
[by] persuasion and instruction," and that "God should force,
agrees neither with the nature of God nor with the nature of man."
In 1647, his fellow Cambridge Platonist, Ralph Cudworth, argued
that as Christ himself had presented the Gospel "gently and softly"
and yet with great effect, so this was "still the most effectual way to
promote it. . . . Sweetness and ingenuity will more powerfully

_Sweetned and Allayed: By Way of Advice, Refutation, Censure Against the Pseudo-Zelots of
our Age_ (1630), p. 1, 11–12. Cf. p. 5, where he describes the gospel method as one of
"compassionate persuasion" rather than harshness. This sermon was dedicated to
two of Sydenham's relatives, both of them courtiers.

63. Farindon, 1:100, 72, 536. The Holy Ghost imprints "saving knowledge . . .
not forcing or drawing by violence, but sweetly leading and guiding us into all
faith" (p. 104). God will help us "with his assistance (which is ready, if we refuse it
not)" (p. 191). Further, "the ground of all despair is not . . . that we cannot, but
that we will not, turn" (p. 527).

command men's minds than passion, sourness and severity." Therefore he regretted that it was "the distemper of our times to scare and
fright men only with opinions" the holding of which "will not render
them anything the better in their lives or the liker unto God."[64]

Many Puritans criticized such reasoning as worse than misguided.
John Benbrigge called the presumption that true repentance was
"an easy work" one of Satan's favorite stratagems, a device that
"murders many thousands daily." Thomas Brooks took seven pages
in his popular tract, *Precious Remedies Against Satan's Devices* (eight
editions within the thirty years after the first of 1652), to provide
remedies against the "sixth device that Satan hath to draw the soul
to sin . . . persuading the soul that the work of repentance is an
easy work." The soteriological strategy which Sibbes, Benbrigge,
and Brooks so vigorously condemned, that of drawing men toward
repentance and conversion by emphasizing its simplicity and ease,
was employed by the Laudian Henry Hammond. He explained in a
sermon on Matt. 11:30 ("My yoke is easy, and my burden is light.")
that men were put off from Christ's service by fears of "the hard
tasks, unmerciful burdens that He lays on his disciples." But the
only hard part was the initial step, "the instant of putting on the
yoke, of entering into the traces." According to Hammond, once
that simple "act of spiritual daring" had been done, the believer
would enter a life of joy indescribable; he would desire nothing more
than the "intimate embraces of Christ in the regenerate heart." The
performance of any part of the Christian duty of "well-doing in
general" yields delight superior to "the daintiest dish and most
animating, emboldening award in nature."[65]

The distinction between anglican and puritan answers to these
questions about the difficulty of salvation and the role of the human
will in the process appears in a comparison of some lay views.
B. H. G. Wormald has described Lucius Cary, Viscount Falkland,
as "the outstanding partisan of the episcopalian interest" in 1641.

64. Chillingworth, 2:167; Hales, 3:195 and 2:215, 241; *Contemplations*, p. 538;
Whichcote, 1:26–7 and in Cragg, p. 428; Cudworth, pp. 62, 15. Cf. Morley, *A
Modest Advertisement* (1641), p. 13.

65. Benbrigge, *Gods Fury*, p. 122; Brooks, 1:31; Hammond, pp. 29, 32–34. Cf.
Sanderson, 2:386. Brooks was ejected from his City parish in 1662. See Trevor-
Roper, *Crisis of the Seventeenth Century*, pp. 333–34, for an account of his bloodthirsty
sermon before the Rump on the eve of the king's trial.

He had entertained generously for years at his estate at Great Tew near Oxford, and in Gardiner's phrase, his "mind was as hospitable as his house." Falkland's *Discourse of Infallibility* shows how. He admitted that there was a sense in which God had "elected those who shall persevere in faith and obedience." Nevertheless "all men (especially Christians) I believe have, and always shall have means enough to perform those conditions . . . as shall by God be required." If they "fall from necessary truths," it is because they "willfully . . . neglect Christ's instructions or commands and make themselves deaf against his voice, charm He never so wisely." Clarendon, himself a visitor at Great Tew, clearly agreed with his host. God, he wrote, "requires nothing of us but what is in our power to do and offers us a habitation in his own holy city" upon terms which are no more difficult to perform than those required "to make our residence in every ordinary corporation."[66] We need merely to decide to obey God's law, and it is in our power to do it—just as it is in our power to move from Bristol to Norwich. The agonizing sense of human impotence in the face of the corruptions of the flesh which characterizes puritan treatments of this subject is altogether absent. In them, "common grace" is not enough. Puritans were deeply concerned to find in themselves the signs of that special and substantial activity of the Holy Spirit which was needed to rebuild their inward selves so they could begin to savor "the things of God." The phrase is John Winthrop's in a letter to his fiancée in 1618. He carefully distinguishes her from "our common protestants" who think they have "an easier way to heaven than other men."[67]

The discussion of distinctions between anglican and puritan conceptions of repentance and conversion is necessarily conducted in relative, subjective terms because the process involved occurs, if it occurs at all, within the soul of the believer. It is an inward change and is therefore difficult to pin down, define, and evaluate. Because it is a spiritual phenomenon, it can only be seen with the eye of the

66. Wormald, p. 3; Gardiner, *History*, 8:255; Falkland, pp. 143–44; *Contemplations*, p. 411. Clarendon added that it is inexcusable "if we are disappointed of so inestimable a purchase, for the not payment of so easy a consideration." Cf. Chillingworth, 3:246–48, 260; Whichcote, 1:46.

67. *WP*, 1:222–23. The term, "common Protestants," is applied to Arminians in the Grand Remonstrance. *CD*, p. 207. Cf. Collinson, pp. 24, 37.

spirit. Its truth or falsity can really be judged only by God and, perhaps, by the believer himself. But if he becomes too certain of his salvation, he is guilty of spiritual pride, a dangerous and perhaps damning sin which casts doubt on the validity of his original profession of faith. The "constant message of the Puritan preachers," writes E. S. Morgan, was that "in order to be sure one must be unsure." The Puritans were especially prone to concern about this danger largely because of their heavy emphasis upon the great difficulty of true repentance and conversion. Regardless of the method of inward conversion preached, there was wide agreement that a true conversion would produce a certain pattern of behavior in the converted man. As one of Cromwell's chaplains put it, a man's life foretells what awaits him at the end. The profane man, for example, speaks the language of eternal death as surely as a Spaniard speaks Spanish. "God doth lively shadow out to man here, his condition hereafter." Here is the link between anglican and puritan rhetorics of suffering and their conceptions of the ideal Christian man. All agreed that sin caused suffering and that the cure for sin and suffering was conversion to a life of righteousness. Whether conversion came by the kind of "holy violence" which seized Saint Paul or whether it came gradually, it always produced results. It did not make men perfect, but it set them on the course of sanctification which would lead to perfection after death. Thomas Watson briefly summed up many theological tomes when he said that "election is the cause of our salvation, sanctification is our evidence. Sanctification is the earmark of Christ's elect sheep." The sanctified life consisted of obedience to God's commands and repentance of the lapses from that obedience. The truth of the inner commitment to such a life could not be ascertained with absolute certainty by any man on the face of the earth. Men could judge it only by its results, its "fruits." The proof of a true and saving conversion was a life of action directed toward the glorification of God. Truth of profession was proved, said John Preston, "Not by your desires or good meanings, but by your actions, these are the things that men see and feel."[68]

68. Morgan, *Visible Saints*, p. 70; Nicholas Lockyer (Cromwell's chaplain), *Baulme for Bleeding England and Ireland*, pp. 204, 269; Watson, p. 245; Preston, *Breast-Plate*, pt. 2, p. 207. See Trevor-Roper, *Crisis of the Seventeenth Century*, pp.

God was angered by sins and He chastised men and nations for them—that much was agreed. But how was a man to know which transgressions were the cause of God's anger? How was he to know whether the rod which was chastising him was the rod of punishment or of correction? If he knew himself to be living at least an approximation of the true Christian life, he knew that the rod was that of a loving Father. If he knew what the fruits of a true conversion were, he could undergo affliction with a glad heart. Rare was the product of the cleric's pen which did not add to or reinforce the conception of the ideal Christian life. Rare was the sermon which did not explicitly or implicitly ask all who professed Christianity to compare themselves with that conception in order to ascertain their likeness to it. Religion placed before its adherents a mirror of righteousness, a "glass of godliness," and told them to liken themselves to it. They would have comfort in tribulation in direct proportion to their success in that endeavor. Each new adversity should have led to examination of the Christian's assurance of his estate with God. And his estate and interest in God could be subjectively assessed only with the eye of the soul, a tricky and deceptive survey. Objective assessment was possible as well, and both Anglicans and Puritans went to great lengths to promulgate touchstones by which a true profession could be tested.

Laymen, who (then as now) tended to be more pragmatic than the divines, demanded these touchstones. Some were capable of the kind of regular inward fence-mending that the divines called for, but many were uneasy with it. Most, in any case, sought both. They wanted to know the outward signs and marks by which a true profession of faith could be known. John Preston pronounced fundamental Protestant doctrine when he said that "we are to be judged not only by our faith and love but also by our works; that no man hath faith and love, that none are new creatures, that none have sincerity, but works will follow."[69] The divines were happy to pro-

---

334–35, for an account of Watson's sermon before the Rump following the one by Brooks (mentioned above, n. 65). He calls Watson's attack on Pride's Purge in this sermon "one of the boldest sermons that was ever uttered in the Long Parliament."

69. Preston, *Breast-Plate*, pt. 2, p. 186. Further, "If a man have a treasure within, there will be silver in his speeches and actions; but if his heart be nothing worth, his words and actions will be but mere dross" (p. 187). Sanderson, 2:84: "Of which inward affection [love], the outward deed is the best discoverer. . . . Good

vide the standards by which sincerity could be tested so long as it was understood that they were not preaching a doctrine of "popish merit." The good works of worship, obedience, charity, mercy, and justice which all desired could not be thought of as, in any sense, meriting or earning God's grace. They were, on the contrary, evidences of the presence of a saving faith in the professor of belief. With that important and often reiterated caveat in mind, anglican and puritan divines defined good works and bad works in every aspect of relations between God and man and between man and man. They prescribed virtues and proscribed sins in response to the universal demand for a pattern of Christian life which would ward off God's judgments and bring forth his blessings. In troubled times, the question all men were asking was, "What should we *do*?" They wanted concrete, practical answers as to what their conduct ought to be. Clarendon, for example, wrote that "it is not our being in adversity, but behaving ourselves well under it, that will hasten our deliverance."[70] The question for the statesman and his contemporaries was, how do we act so as to gain God's favor and support? What particular acts are particularly pleasing to him? What, specifically, is a godly man's "carriage" and "conversation" while he is in the world?

Clarendon's private contemplations reflect throughout his confidence that his religion had given him a coherent, connected vision of the truth, a conception of an ideal standard of behavior against which he could measure his own actions and everyone else's. The same might be said of the letters, speeches, and papers of such laymen as John Winthrop, Oliver Cromwell, Sir Richard Baker, Sir Henry Wotton, and Lord Falkland. It is by comparing such writings with the sermons and devotional writings of divines that we can approach the lines of intersection between theology and politics. We can perceive the links between the activities of the practitioners of the latter and the theories of the students of the former.[71] The

---

works are the best demonstrations, as of true faith, so of true love." Cf. also pp. 222, 380.

70. *Contemplations*, p. 486.

71. But it must be said that there was nothing simple or direct about this relationship. I do not suggest that more than a handful of the preachers set out purposefully to influence political decision-making as a primary and overriding aim. They were largely interested in what Collinson (citing Haller and Porter) has called

preacher who condemned some activities as sinful and lauded others as virtuous did so largely upon the basis of his understanding of the Scriptures. The Scriptures were the omnicompetent and authoritative source of that knowledge which all desired, knowledge of the way to salvation. Humphrey Sydenham clearly expressed that attitude which was widely taken toward this knowledge when he asked what has our Savior to do with the man who knows of him but does not believe in him, or who believes in him, "but believes him not as he should?"[72]

True saving faith expressed itself in sanctified behavior. To believe as one should was to attempt to act as one should, to do the things which ought to be done and not to do the things which ought not to be done. It was to fulfill God's plan for man by obeying his instructions. Failures of obedience would, sooner or later, be punished in the ungodly and chastised in the godly. It was therefore of the highest importance to know about sin in a practical, concrete way. When temporal or spiritual adversity came, it was absolutely vital to know which sins were being reprehended by God. This was especially true because of the human tendency to pick and choose from the vast array of potential sins and virtues which the Bible catalogued. The next chapter begins a survey of puritan and anglican catalogues of sins and virtues and thus begins to paint the portraits of ideal Christians as they appear in sermons, tracts, and other sources in the literature of suffering. Chapters 4 and 5 complete the portraits by examining the major themes of "obedience to the higher powers" and "love to the brethren." In their painful and bitter experiences of persecution, banishment, and deprivation, both Anglicans and Puritans inveighed against those sins which were calling down God's wrath and admired those graces which would be rewarded with his favor. All were agreed that such evils as idolatry and rebellion were reprehensible, and such virtues as obedience and charity were good. But the connotations attached to these defects and virtues and the degrees of emphasis placed upon them varied considerably in the boiling cauldron of revolutionary England.

"practical godliness" (pp. 128–29). See my discussion of Stoeffler in the bibliographical note.
72. Sydenham, *Occasions*, p. 199.

3

THE TWO TABLES

And where the mass is used, there is true worship; even though there be no other form, with singing, organ playing, bell ringing, vestments, ornaments and gestures. For everything of this sort is an addition invented by men. When Christ himself first instituted this sacrament, . . . there was . . . no pageantry, but only thanksgiving to God and the use of the sacrament. . . . And now it has finally come to this: the chief thing in the mass has been forgotten, and nothing is remembered except the additions of men!

> Martin Luther, *A Treatise on the New Testament* (1519)

By his reasoning . . . it were idolatry for the servant to make courtesy to his master, wherein he should bow his knee, or the good man to kiss his wife; but to kneel and to kiss his superiors' hands were by him foul and filthy abomination, . . . they would have all in talking, they speak so much of preaching, so as all the gates of our senses and ways to man's understanding should be shut up, saving the ear alone.

> Stephen Gardiner, Bishop of Winchester (ca. 1544)

I have, I think, always been a Puritan in my attitude towards Art. I am as fond of fine music and handsome buildings as Milton was, or Cromwell, or Bunyan; but if I found that they were becoming the instruments of a systematic idolatry of sensuousness, I would hold it good statesmanship to blow every cathedral in the world to pieces with dynamite, organ and all. . . .

> George Bernard Shaw (1900)

The Lutheran cathedral was surprising; Gothic lines and scale had been wedded to clear glass and an austerity of decoration, noble and mournful, that left one, Bech felt, much too alone with God. He felt the Reformation here as a desolating wind, four hundred years ago.

> John Updike, *Bech: A Book* (1970)

You are to "strive against particular vices and adorn yourselves with particular graces," said the famous puritan preacher and courtier, John Preston. A full list of the particular vices and particular graces appropriate for Christians compiled from the sermons of Preston and his puritan brethren would, in many instances, overlap a similar list compiled from anglican sources. This is to say simply that the idealized versions of anglican and puritan saints would share many of the same traits. Like good Christians in all ages of the church (and like good men in most of the world's great religions), they would deal honestly one with another and would not covet each other's spouses or estates. They would eschew adultery, fornication, murder, malice, theft, drunkenness, idleness, tyranny, oppression, cruelty, idolatry, pride, rebellion, and all other offenses against God's commandments. They would cultivate all the graces which would, as Oliver Cromwell said, result in "giving Him glory by holiness of life and conversation," thereby fortifying themselves against all the suffering they would experience in this life.[1]

Despite this broad agreement among Anglicans and Puritans about the sinfulness of many sins and the graciousness of many graces, they accused each other of being "carvers." John Bramhall, a Laudian (and Primate of Ireland after the Restoration), used the term in a sermon before the Duke of Newcastle's royalist army in 1643; "Men never prosper, who deal too majestically and will needs be their own carvers with God." "Beloved," said Richard Sibbes, "here is the bane of men's souls, they will be their own carvers and take of the Gospel what they list." This would not do because truly converted men strove to obey God fully; they dared not, as Farindon put it, obey "in that text which seemeth to comply with their humor," but ignore it in others. They knew, as Sibbes insisted, that "partial obedience is indeed no obedience at all." He who hates sin hates all sins. Sanderson summed it up before the king at Newport in October, 1648. The man whose soul has been renewed by the Divine Spirit is "a kind of new creature" disposed to "true obedience," and true obedience, in turn, "submitteth to the commander's will entirely, it doth not pick and choose."[2]

1. Preston, *Breast-Plate*, pt. 2, p. 70; Abbott, 2:173.
2. Bramhall, p. 103; Sibbes, *Cordialls*, pp. 233, 168; Farindon, 1:109; Sanderson, 2:388. Cf. Preston, *Sermons*, p. 18.

Each side in fact did its own "carving." Each preached a set of virtues and denounced a set of corresponding vices which, regardless of the method of inner conversion, demonstrated outwardly the regenerate or unregenerate state. It is analysis of the various marks, signs, and touchstones of true conversion which provides the firmest ground on which to build a viable set of distinctions between different groups of English Protestants in the seventeenth century. For them and for us, the most convenient guide is the Decalogue, considered in its two parts, the Two Tables. As we have seen, the First Table (Commandments I–IV) concerned man's duties toward God while the Second (Commandments V–X) concerned his duties toward his neighbors. This chapter will demonstrate that Puritans tended to emphasize the duties of the First Table, whereas Anglicans tended to emphasize those of the Second. Further, the Puritans insisted upon an interpretation of the requirements of the First Table which the Anglicans rejected in favor of their own. These contrasting emphases and interpretations provide a key to the "bosom sins" which each set of partisans accused the other of committing, thereby demonstrating the falsity of their conversions and the unsoundness of their hopes of salvation.

The Two Tables may be further characterized by noting that the second group consisted entirely of rules which could be deduced by the use of natural reason. They described behavior which could be known and even practiced by reprobates and heathens. The prohibitions of murder, adultery, theft, lying, covetousness, and the injunction to honor parents were clear and evident natural principles which did not require direct revelation by God (as did those concerning his worship by his particular people, the Israelites). Most Anglicans had a more optimistic opinion of the potential of human nature and reason, and therefore they gave much more attention to these duties of the Second Table. Thomas Pierce said as much in a funeral sermon preached in 1659; "Give me leave to tell you, what is not every day considered. The most material part of godliness is moral honesty. . . . The Second Table is the touchstone to our obedience to the First." Because the deceased had been "so sober and so righteous," Pierce inferred that he had been "so godly too, as to have lived in opposition to those 'professors of

Christianity,' who, having a 'form only of godliness, deny the power of it. ' "3

PURITANS AND THE FIRST TABLE

The sort of people whom Pierce's anglican saint had opposed was the puritan sort. Both sides charged each other with the hypocrisy of appearing religious without performing the duties pertaining to their profession of faith. Although Puritans did, as we have noted, insist upon obedience to all God's regulations for man, it is not an exaggeration to say that the most prominent theme in their exhortations was the fundamental necessity of scrupulous obedience to the First Table. Sibbes, neatly reversing Pierce's priorities, said that the "rise of all sin against man is our sinning against God first. . . . The breach of the First Commandment is the ground of the breach of all the rest." His argument was that if God were accorded his proper place in the heart of the Christian, to the exclusion of all false gods and improper desires, then sins of all kinds would be avoided in consequence. The term which summed up all those iniquities which the First Table proscribed was "idolatry." The puritan definition of idolatry could be so broad as to include all of the sins which they considered the most heinous and therefore the most provoking of God's judgments. Indeed, William Perkins had gone so far as to say that "the ground of the nine later commandments is the first. 'Thou shalt have no other gods before me. ' " John Winthrop, after reciting a long list of worldly temptations, summed up his resolution by saying, "I will never be reconciled unto them, . . . for I know that if I enter into friendship with them, they will cause me to eat of their sacrifices, and so withdraw my heart from my God to run roaming after them and to commit idolatry with them."4 This comprehensive sense of the term

3. Pierce, p. 487. 2 Tim. 3:5.
4. Sibbes, *Cordialls*, p. 141; Perkins, 3:698; *WP*, 1:195. Winthrop had earlier condemned himself for undervaluing his justification by Christ's free grace and, as he put it, "setting up idols in mine own heart" (1:160). Also, note this attitude in the Grand Remonstrance: "We desire to unburden the consciences of men of needless and superstitious ceremonies, suppress innovations, and take away the monuments of idolatry." *CD*, p. 229.

idolatry was widely used to condemn the placing of anything at all above religion in a man's life. William Fenner defined proper zeal as the greatest possible desire of the soul and therefore, "it must needs be idolatry to place it anywhere else but in the service of God." To think more of the world than of God makes thoughts idolatrous. To sorrow more for "crosses, and losses, and disgraces" than for sins makes grief idolatry, said Fenner.[5]

The puritan tendency to define all sin in terms of idolatry was an outgrowth of the more specific meaning they gave it within the context of the duties toward God derived from the First Table. The puritan movement in England originated early in Elizabeth I's reign as a protest against the refusal of the authorities (Elizabeth and her bishops) to rid the Church of England of the "dregs of popery" which the Puritans thought remained in its liturgy and government. The Puritans insisted that God should never be worshipped except by the methods prescribed in the Scriptures. Any forms of words, vestments, or implements used in worship services were considered idolatrous if they were not of scriptural provenance.[6] Yet care must be taken to avoid the impression that Puritans were simpleminded literalists in their insistence upon scriptural sanction or "warrant." Their hatred of "human" (i.e., devised by men) traditions was no mere liturgical and ecclesiological antiquarianism. Luther, Calvin, Zwingli, and the other great reformers had

5. Fenner, *Affections*, pp. 147–48. Occasionally the sin of adultery was given this comprehensive meaning. John Benbrigge said that sin is "soul-adultery, spiritual adultery, . . . all sin is a spouse-breach" because "God's people are married to him." *Christ*, pp. 42–43. Thomas Case used both terms this way when he wrote (during his imprisonment for complicity in the Love plot), "Art thou in captivity, in prison, in distress, etc. Thank thy idolatry and thy adulteries whereby thou hast forsaken the Lord thy God." *Correction*, pp. 115–16. His 1647 fast sermon, *Spirituall Whoredome Discovered*, is a comprehensive treatment of this theme. Cf. Sibbes, *Cordialls*, p. 218; Preston, *Life*, pt. 1, pp. 88–90; Perkins, 3:36.

6. Sir Herbert Grierson found this rigorousness to be the central characteristic of seventeenth-century Puritanism. "What distinguished them was an immovable conviction that all worship which has not scriptural sanction, especially the use (and here the note of passion comes in) of any rite sanctioned by the Roman Catholic Church (i.e., by Antichrist), was Sin, Idolatry, a thing neither to be practised nor tolerated. This was the spirit which precipitated the Puritan Rebellion." *Cross-Currents in English Literature of the Seventeenth Century*, pp. 11–12. Although this statement needs qualification (see also the first two chapters of Coolidge's book), it does accurately suggest where puritan emphasis lay. Cf. Collinson, pp. 36, 65, 202, 235, 321, 367–71.

all shared this antipathy. The Puritans were striving to be the instruments through whom God would advance the process of purgation and enlightenment which He had initiated in the sixteenth century. Its goal was freedom, a true Christian liberty, from what seemed a vast, thick, suffocating fog of superstition which had enveloped Christendom for many centuries. "In Protestant mythology," writes Keith Thomas, "the Middle Ages became notorious as the time of darkness, when spells and charms had masqueraded as religion and the lead in magical activity had been taken by the clergy themselves." Most Anglicans were satisfied with the largely doctrinal reforms which had been carried out under the Tudors—some (especially such Laudians as Cosin) felt the earlier reforms had gone too far. Indeed, N. R. N. Tyacke has found that "many English Arminians regarded themselves as engaged in a counter-reforming movement dedicated to undoing the Protestant damage of the Reformation."[7]

For Puritans in our period, however, the battle cry sounded by Perkins spoke with the clarity and power of Joshua's trumpets. One of the purposes of his *Warning against the Idolatrie of the Last Times* (1601) was "to inform the ignorant multitude touching the true worship of God. For the remainders of popery stick in the minds of many of them, and they think that to serve God is nothing else but to deal truly with men and to babble a few words morning and evening, or in the church, though there be no understanding." The requirement of what Luther had called "the additions of men" which encouraged or even permitted anyone to continue to think of worship in the old way was an affront to the God who had cast such a generous measure of new light to cut through the blinding medieval fog. Despite what their critics said, the Puritans' objection to ceremonial observances was not really based on a literalism about details. The details of worship could vary from time to time and from place to place so long as God was worshipped without the idolatrous "remainders of popery" and with obedience to the true spirit of scriptural commandments about worship as summarized in the First Table. As J. S. Coolidge has persuasively argued, every-

7. Thomas, *Religion and the Decline of Magic*, p. 68; N. R. N. Tyacke, "Puritanism, Arminianism and Counter-Revolution," in *The Origins of the English Civil War*, ed. Russell, p. 140.

thing done in worship must "edify." Worship must build toward a true conception of God and the life of faith—it cannot sink back toward "subjection to things without life, to idols." Bread and wine are bread and wine, not the body and blood of Christ, and merely to teach this was not enough if the gestures and vestments which were used were connected with those superstitions which "yet stick in the minds of many." The truly converted man would know that he was consuming bread and wine but nothing must be allowed to permit the "ignorant multitude" to remain in its ignorance.[8]

When the work of enlightenment was done, when the old habits of mind and the old erroneous doctrines had been completely eradicated, then and only then could there be no harm in the use of *adiaphora*—"things indifferent." Meanwhile, as Thomas Hill told the members of the Long Parliament in July, 1642, acquiescence in "the pomp of human ceremonies" was a betrayal of the message of the Gospel. "Never say they are indifferent," cried Hill, "if indifferent only, they may the better be spared." Nor would Hill accept the anglican argument that reformed doctrine made the ceremonies acceptable; it was better to "have the stumbling block removed out of the way."[9] The notion that ecclesiastical authorities, even "reformed" bishops under the wing of a Protestant monarch, could command the use of a liturgy which contained such adiaphora was repugnant to the revealed Word. Puritan ministers had long objected to such things (e.g., the requirement that they wear the surplice), but during the long tenure of George Abbot as Archbishop

8. Perkins, 3:670; Coolidge, p. 47. On the way in which Perkins's Ramist thought is antimagical and hostile to the use of images to aid the memory, see Francis Yates, *The Art of Memory* (Chicago: University of Chicago Press, 1966), pp. 266–79. See the first two chapters (on puritan scriptural "literalism" and puritan notions of Christian liberty and edification) in Coolidge's important book.

9. Thomas Hill, *The Trade of Truth Advanced*, pp. 58–59. Hill's sermons are full of explicit and colorfully expressed advice for the completion of the reformation. J. H. Hexter noted Hill's "elaborate indirection" against Lord General Essex in *The Reign of King Pym*, p. 118. Trevor-Roper suggests that he participated in Vane's fight for the Self-Denying Ordinance. "The Fast Sermons of the Long Parliament," in *The Crisis of the Seventeenth Century*, p. 320. Hill had lived for a time with John Cotton in Boston, Lincs., and was a member of the Westminster Assembly. From 1645 to his death in 1653 he was master of Trinity College, Cambridge (after a brief headship of Emmanuel). *DNB*. Note the important distinction between wings of the puritan party which objected to certain Prayer Book ceremonies as "indifferent or inherently evil" in Collinson, p. 463.

of Canterbury they had found it possible to ignore or modify many of the objectionable ceremonial regulations.

Yet even before the "Arminian" controversy waxed hot with Montagu's *Appello Caesarem* (1625) and Cosin's *Devotions* (1627), there was an important respect in which the touchstone of opposition to "idolatry and superstition" was used by Puritans.[10] On the continent of Europe, the reformed churches were feeling the military might of the Counter-Reformation. One of the many territories which were returned to "popery" was the Palatinate, where James I's daughter Elizabeth had reigned with her husband until they were forced into exile in 1620. The continuing progress of Roman Catholic armies made the 1620s a fearful period for Protestants everywhere. Puritans in parliament agitated for an aggressively protestant foreign policy and puritan preachers made concern for the continental Protestants a touchstone of saving faith. In 1625, John Preston said that the reason that "religion suffers an eclipse in any place" is that the people are not sufficiently chagrined and angered by dishonor falling upon "the things that belong to God." For example, if "you find that you can hear of the desolation of the churches and of the increase and growing of popery, and yet . . . you do not grieve for it, it is a sign that you want love to the Lord." Among the examples he chose to illustrate this injunction to "holy anger" over dishonor to God, Preston used that of Moses whose "zeal was kindled in his breast, when he saw the idolatry of the people." He went on to list the "superstition and idolatry of the people" first among the causes for the plague which afflicted the Israelites (Num. 25) and to imply that the same consideration applied to the plague afflicting England in 1625.[11] The famous Northamptonshire preacher, Robert Bolton, was another Puritan who lacerated those who did nothing to help the continental Protestants;

10. On Montagu, the section entitled "Puritans and the 'Idol of Our Godly Brethren,' " in chap. 5, below. One brief account of the puritan reaction to Cosin's book is in John Cosin, *A Collection of Private Devotions*, ed. P. G. Stanwood, pp. xiv–xviii.

11. Preston, *Breast-Plate*, pt. 2, pp. 88–90, 91–92. Preston also here cited Jeremiah's anger (36:24) when "the King had done an abominable action" which dishonored Jehovah. See *WP*, 2:91–92, for Winthrop's reaction to the affliction of the reformed churches. See also J. H. Hexter in *JBS* 8 (1968): 66–67, Zagorin, pp. 106–07, and Marvin Arthur Breslow, *A Mirror of England*.

he called them "profane Esaus, swinish Gadarenes, senseless earthworms." He regarded the matter as "an evident touchstone, to try whether our profession be vital or formal." Thus one of the fruits of an effective conversion had to be a deep sympathy for the victims of the Roman Catholic resurgence in Germany, France, and the Low Countries. Sir Richard Baker, in one of the few personal notes in his massive and popular *Chronicle of the Kings of England*, remarked that he had given £50 to a fund intended to finance a military expedition to recover the Palatinate. Isaac Pennington, a leading puritan alderman in London, was active in a campaign to collect money to succor the Protestants of the Palatinate. But the time was at hand when the demonstration of Christian discipleship by opposing idolatry could be made on matters closer to home.[12]

The rise of William Laud in the estimation of Charles I and the rise with and through him of such "Arminian" prelates as Richard Montagu, Richard Neile, William Pierse, Francis White, and Matthew Wren convinced the Puritans that the headway they had been making, however slight it may have been, was to be reversed. Michael Sparke, writing in 1652, remembered fondly the days of "that learned, pious, painful, preaching Bishop Abbot." Had Laud "been as constant a preacher, and as mild in his carriage and countenanced godly preachers," Sparke thought that things would have been very different. Although the puritan bookseller's estimation of Abbot's qualities may have been nostalgically generous, he was right to say that Laud changed the direction of the Church of England. Sparke called the archbishop "that little high spirited bishop . . . who sought not only the ruin of us [i.e., Prynne, Sparke, and their circle], but also of all such as would not bow to his Baal, for which he spilt the blood of the innocent, for which the just hand of God was upon him seven years after that time."[13]

12. Bolton, *Works*, 3:345–46; Baker, *A Chronicle of the Kings of England*, p. 419. On Pennington's role, see Pearl, pp. 178–79. The clergymen involved were Sibbes, Gouge, John Davenport, and Thomas Taylor. Puritans continued to be concerned about the troubles of the continental Protestants for many years. Cromwell's last letters were addressed to the problem of the persecution of the Piedmontese Protestants. See Abbott, 4:812–15. See also Caryl, *Job* (chaps. 1–3), pp. 308–09.

13. Sparke, *Crumms of Comfort. The Second Part* (1652), sigs. ¶7 (recto and verso) and ¶8 (recto). William Lamont, in his excellent biography, *Marginal Prynne*, does not mention Sparke. On "Arminianism" in England in this period, see my bibliographical note.

Laud's program clashed with puritan convictions in three utterly crucial ways, each of them derived from the puritan conception of the duties owed to God and arising out of the First Table. (1) Laud ordered the use of all the ceremonial observances in the Prayer Book and in the Canons of 1604, many of which had long been omitted by puritan ministers. He added some of his own requirements as well, such as bowing at the name of Jesus and treating the communion table as an altar, railed about and placed in the east end of the chancel. Puritans hated these "innovations" because they smacked of "popish" and therefore merely human additions to divinely ordered services. (2) The archbishop's reissue of the king's *Book of Sports* in 1633 was another serious affront to puritan sensibilities on the subject of how the Sabbath ought to be honored. Puritans saw in this royal and episcopal licensing of Sunday recreations a direct breach of the Fourth Commandment. A puritan minister in London obeyed the order that he read the *Book of Sports* from his pulpit, but he also read the Decalogue. He then said, "Beloved, ye have heard the commandments of God and man, obey which you please."[14] (3) Laud's enforcement of his program led to the suspension, silencing, and ejection of puritan preachers and to the blocking of puritan attempts to install "godly preachers" in as many pulpits and lectureships as possible. His biggest coup was the suppression of the Feoffees for Impropriations in 1633. Oliver Cromwell's plea for the restoration of a lectureship demonstrates the way many puritan laymen reacted to Laud's policies and the high regard in which they held preaching: "It were a piteous thing to see a lecture fall, . . . in those times wherein we see they are suppressed, with too much haste and violence, by the enemies of God his truth."[15]

Laud's requirements appeared to the Puritans as a calculated plot to undermine their attempts to obey the first four Commandments. In the last years of his life as an exemplary member of the spiritual brotherhood of puritan preachers, John Preston said that every man who truly loved the Lord would "find some business

14. Gardiner, *History*, 7:322.
15. Abbott, 1:80. Thomas Hill suggested in his 1642 fast sermon before the Commons that the Feoffees be revived as part of the "Scripture Reformation" that he beseeched the members to press toward. *Trade of Truth Advanced*, p. 47.

to do wherein he may bring glory to God's name and advantage to
his cause." Only true lovers of the Lord would risk all and, if need
be, suffer all for "God his truth" and only they could have any
confidence of the truth of their profession of faith. The archbishop's
activities gave them ample opportunity, especially in the business of
the First Table. As the above sketch suggests, there were three areas
in which the Puritans were particularly anxious to demonstrate their
obedience—the opposition to ceremonial innovations, the defense of
"godly preaching" and lecturing, and the demand for precise
observation of the Sabbath. All are familiar enough as puritan
concerns. The purpose here is to show that these things were used
as touchstones of the validity of a Christian's conversion. Both
godly preaching and the criticism of ceremonies had been present in
Puritanism from its inception. Sabbatarianism had a long history as
well, but apparently did not become a party issue between Anglicans and Puritans until early in the seventeenth century.[16]

The little archbishop had ample intelligence of the opposition
that his policies stirred up among the Puritans. Though he had a
measure of success at censoring the printing of puritan propaganda
during the 1630s, stopping the mouths of the host of puritan
preachers all over England was much more difficult. His agents
suspended and deprived Puritans right and left, only to have them
spring up, hydra-like, more vigorously than before. Thus his dean
of the Court of Arches was informed by a Robert Aylett, an Essex
correspondent (on March 21, 1637), that no sooner had Laud's
vicar-general left the country, "but one sits up to confute that he
had delivered." The confuter was Edward Sparhawke, a suspended
minister who, according to the informant, had "maintained conventicles in Coggeshall, where they refuse both the first and second
payment for ship-money nor will yet be brought by the sheriff to
make a rate." Aylett enclosed notes which had been taken three
weeks earlier on a sermon preached by Sparhawke at a christening.
The suspended but as yet unsilenced Puritan had sought to explain
how it was that "the saints of God may be in calamity and expect

16. Preston, *Breast-Plate*, pt. 2, p. 129. On Sabbatarianism see Collinson in *SCH*
1 (1964):207–21 and C. Hill, *Society and Puritanism*, chap. 5. On preaching and
lecturing, see the works by Knappen, Collinson, C. Hill, Haller, and Seaver (esp.
chap. 2 on preaching and chap. 8 on Laud's campaign against the lecturers).

delivery and yet their hope of salvation may be frustrated." He
noted the ways in which their afflictions had increased, men-
tioning specifically "the heavy impositions and cursed adorations
newly laid upon Christians." He denounced "our altars and such
superstitious adorations and bowing at names and such new
idolatrous mixtures of religion and the treading down of God's
people . . . the profanation of the Lord's day." Unless the in-
former's notes were inaccurate, the "idolatrous mixtures of religion"
which Laud was enforcing were regarded by Sparhawke as both
judgments and causes of judgments at the same time.[17]

It is almost certainly these same "provoking sins" which are the
subject of a doleful and yet defiant lamentation written by Sir
Thomas Wroth to a puritan preacher in London on September 12,
1635. Sir Thomas was a Somerset landowner, a lawyer, a share-
holder in the Virginia and New England ventures and later a
member of the Long Parliament. His letter was addressed to his
sister in Coleman Street, London, but was actually intended for Dr.
John Stoughton, the minister at Saint Mary's, Aldermanbury. In
this clandestine missive, Sir Thomas said,

> I collect by what you wrote that all things go on from worse to
> worse in your parts, and the face of the affairs where I am hath
> as unpleasing an aspect, so that I see no hopes of amendment.
> Nor are the churches abroad . . . like to have any sudden
> rest. Now is the time to show our courage; if now we stand to
> our captain Christ Jesus and forsake not him, we are sure to be
> well paid for our service . . . It will be a great evidence of true

17. State Papers (Domestic) 16/350/fols. 54 and 54I, Public Record Office,
London. See *CSPD (Charles I)*, 10:513–14. The writer, Robert Aylett, enclosed a
list of "studies to be searched" for more seditious material. He also thanked the
dean, Dr. John Lambe, for a letter he had written to Aylett's dying father. Aylett's
letter affords an interesting example of the spiritual tug-of-war between Anglicans
and Puritans, for Aylett said that his father "delights only in prayer, but most in the
prayers of the church, which I the rather mention because Dr. Bastwick had done
his utmost to corrupt him, but now he abhors his errors and follies." Aylett's subject,
Sparhawke, also gave the siege of Rochelle as an example of the way God's people
could be troubled. According to a note in the margin, "Mr. Dod the Elder" had also
criticized the "new mixtures" in a sermon on Nov. 9, 1635. It is not clear whether
Sparhawke cited Dod as an authority, or whether the informant was adding this
in order to incriminate Dod. This Dod was vicar of Coggeshall and not the more
famous puritan patriarch of that name (on whom see Haller, p. 58).

Christian resolution if we suffer *usque ad sanguinis effusionem* [all the way to the effusion of blood] for preservation of faith and a good conscience.[18]

The long muted voice of puritan opposition to Laudianism was heard as soon as the Long Parliament opened. Thomas Case preached before "sundry" members of that body and his sermon perfectly expresses not only the central grievances which Puritans felt but the injured and angry spirit of grievance as well.[19] His text (Ezek. 20: 25) was chosen in order to give him the opportunity to present a puritan history of the Laudian decade. The prophet Ezekiel had explained how God had judged the sinful Israelites with "evil statutes and destroying judgments." The prophet Case explained how God had afflicted Israel (and by obvious implication, England) by allowing her authorities to "make and command these wicked and idolatrous laws and statutes." He then allowed the false prophets of the time to try to "make the people believe that whosoever did refuse conformity and obedience were none but a company of factious and seditious fellows, enemies to the state and government." The result was terrible. Adulterers, idolaters, and drunkards "might go scot-free," while the authorities persecuted righteous men; men "who made conscience of obeying God, rather than man," men whose consciences would not "stretch to the lati-

18. *CSPD (Charles I)*, 8:377–78. For details on Sir Thomas, see Thomas G. Barnes, *Somerset, 1625–1640*, pp. 8, 14–16, 27, 237, 277. Barnes describes the letter quoted above as "mildly seditious" (p. 16*n*). This accounts for Sir Thomas's subterfuge in the address, a subterfuge which clearly failed. On February 25, 1642, he addressed the Commons as the bearer of a Somerset petition. He spoke in strongly puritan terms against the bishops and against pluralism. He also compared a meeting of Parliament to "the Day of Judgment, for in Parliament we are called to account for our actions, both good and evil." *A Speech Spoken by Sir Thomas Wroth* (1642), sig. A2 (recto). Dr. Stoughton "was one of the many clerical clients of the Earl of Warwick, the greatest noble patron of the opposition to Charles I." Trevor-Roper, *The Crisis of the Seventeenth Century*, p. 258. Coleman Street was Isaac Pennington's base and "a center of Puritanism on the Faubourg St. Antoine of London." Pearl, pp. 183–84.

19. Case, *Two Sermons.* These sermons are identified as being among a small but important group of sermons which John F. Wilson has grouped as "Sermons to sundry members." Although not preached by official invitation, they are clearly in the "fast sermon" tradition which was soon to be established firmly. *Pulpit in Parliament*, pp. 8, 43–54, 275–80. I have used the second edition of these two sermons by Case. Although the precise date cannot be fixed, they were preached during the spring of 1641.

tude of an universal blind obedience to human authority (which the
cathedral priests of those times so much cried up.)" Not only did
the authorities fail to execute God's commandments—they dishonored and despised God by defiling "God's ordinances with
ingredients and mixtures of their own inventions." They said
"down with preaching, down with these sermons," and persecuted
the true Isaiahs and Jeremiahs. They accused the true prophets of
being "the troublers of church and commonwealth; men that are
always bawling against idolatry and through the loins of idolatry,
strike at any 'harmless and profitable ceremonies,' whereby the
people may be edified; men that are always preaching hell and the
law and strictness and preciseness, [so] that we do not know how to
behave ourselves among them." The civil authorities of England/
Israel further demonstrated their true, wicked colors by "persecuting the ways and people of God," and by describing the
"Sabbath as a ridiculous or at least as a superfluous ceremony."
Last, but not least, they committed idolatry with the flimsy excuse
that they were bowing down, "not to the shrines themselves, but to
God under those shrines." They said that such things were not an
"essential part of God's worship, but . . . a circumstance of worship that was in the power of authority, the prince and the arch-
priest, to alter and determine as they please." These were among
the "wicked and lying inventions wherewith the court chaplains
of those times did flatter and indurate the king and his courtiers."[20]

Case's sermon is one of many preached during the early 1640s
which represent Puritanism in its most political form. The parliamentary fast sermons preached by such men as Case, Stephen
Marshall, Edmund Calamy, and Cornelius Burges led the royalist

20. Ibid., pp. 7–12. Case also here expressed his attitude toward anglican
sermons. "They" say that "if we must have preaching, let us have it of another
strain. Prophesy not unto us right things, speak unto us smooth things, oiled
sermons, plausible discourses that may not disquiet and perplex tender consciences." Later in the sermon, Case amplified his argument against anglican
worship: "God cannot endure mixtures. . . . Leave us not I beseech you an high
place in the land, leave us not one house for Baal, not an utensil of idolatrous worship, leave us not a rag of the Whore of Babylon, the plague may lie in it, and
break out into a destroying pestilence many years hence, when you are asleep in
the dust," p. 17. Case also frequently referred to dutiful keeping of the Sabbath as
a requisite to assurance of salvation. See, for example, his *Correction*, pp. 102–03,
247–48.

Thomas Knyvett, who was in London in November, 1640, to write to a friend: "And now reformation goes on hot as toast. I pray God the violent turning of the tide do not make an inundation; if thou didst hear what sermons are preached to the Parliament men, thou wouldst bless thyself, and I go to church now to learn the old way to heaven." Clearly, for Knyvett the "old way to heaven" included Laudian ceremonies, for he reported in shocked tones of the way the "Parliament men would not receive the communion at St. Margaret's Church in Westminister before the rails were pulled down and the communion table was removed into the middle of the chancel." The arguments against "idolatry" presented by Case and his colleagues had been accepted by the members. When Case finished his extended comparison of the way that Israelite idolatries had been repeated in England, he again excoriated the failure to honor the Sabbath properly and the itch "to set up altars and crucifixes and all our fathers' Romish trumpery." The only reason that England had not gone the way of Israel was that "there hath somebody been a praying (conventicling as they call it), some Noahs, Jobs and Daniels making intercession." In a manner which managed to combine careful humility with ominous threatening, Case admonished the Parliament against the fatal error of missing its God-given opportunity for a thorough reformation. The godly people of the kingdom had taken the brunt of prelatical persecution, but God would not wait forever. Without repentance and reformation on a broad, national scale, the final judgment could no longer be held off, even by the Noahs, Jobs, and Daniels of England.[21]

In the meanwhile, Case and many others continued to pound away at the familiar themes. The glorification of God without stain of idolatry or superstition, with the proper respect for the Fourth Commandment concerning the Sabbath, and with vigorous preaching of the Word—support for these had been prominent among

21. *The Knyvett Letters, 1620–1644*, Bertram Schofield, ed., p. 30; Case, *Two Sermons*, pp. 14–15. Knyvett's correspondent was John Buxton of Chanonz who had been the Sheriff of Norfolk in 1638 and had been a successful (and therefore hated) collector of ship money (p. 96n). For a discussion of three sermons preached in 1640 and 1641 by Marshall, Calamy, and Burges, see the appendix. All contain the same themes expressed by Case, articulated in very similar terms. See the bibliographical note for a discussion of F. Ernest Stoeffler's suggestion that we should distinguish between "pietistic" and "political" Puritans.

the signs by which the true converts could be identified during the dark days of persecution, and they continued to be touchstones of a lively faith during the civil wars and thereafter. It was just as important as ever that the puritan saints be able to identify each other by outward actions, and these continued to be the badges on their uniforms. On March 30, 1642, Simeon Ash told the fasting members of the Long Parliament that oppression "fastens a black mark of gracelessness upon them who use it." He defined oppression at some length. Patentees and monopolists were oppressors because they injured people's estates unjustly. Rack-renting landlords were oppressors. But Ash insisted that the worst oppression of all was not of estates, civil liberties, or bodies—it was of souls; the worst were those who "poison or starve souls by imposing popish innovations, polluting God's ordinances, inhibiting sermons, etc."[22] Thomas Hill, preaching from the same pulpit a few months later, denounced the "soul-poisoning innovators" who adorned chapels and cathedrals with "vestures, . . . gestures, . . . images"; and he pointedly asked if there were "no worshipping of the sun there, yet do not too many plead for and practise an ungrounded worshipping toward the east?" William Gouge, also preaching at a parliamentary fast in the spring of 1642, compared the task which faced the members to that of Nehémiah after the Hebrew return from Babylon. Nehemiah was among the elect of God, and he had demonstrated his divine calling by the way that he had redressed state grievances, removed church corruptions, and "withal settled the Sabbath's sanctification." Two years later, the aged Gouge helped the City celebrate the anniversary of Queen Elizabeth's succession to the throne with a sermon preached in Saint Paul's. He dedicated the printed version to the Lord Mayor, Thomas Atkins, and praised him for the way he had fulfilled his duties as alderman for the ward in which Gouge resided. There had, said Gouge, been none more careful and industrious in all respects, "and that which sets the crown above all, [none] more pious in preventing all manner of

22. Ash, *The Best Refuge for the Most Oppressed*, pp. 33, 30. Ash had himself been deprived of his Staffordshire benefice for refusing to read the Book of Sports and for other inconformities. *DNB*. He became more explicit on the subject of ecclesiastical oppressions at the end of the sermon, attacking the bishops for having silenced and deprived "many able ministers of the Gospel" because of the "pressing of ceremonies" (pp. 58–61).

profaneness on the Lord's days and procuring people . . . to observe the holy ordinances thereof." And before the dwindling remnant of parliamentary peers in September, 1645, Gouge exulted in the overthrow of those who had tried to adhere to the "innumerable, unwarrantable, and intolerable rites, which on mere human invention are obtruded on the people." He had in mind specifically "matters about divine service: as in fair embroidered copes and other ministers' vestments, in high standing altars, in low cringings and bowings, in turning to the east . . . when they pray."[23]

The voice of puritan outrage against Laudian violations of the First Table was not heard only in Saint Margaret's, Westminster, and the City of London. Thomas Hooker of Old and New England thundered against all "idle persons and such as follow pleasures and cards and dice on the Sabbath. God forbids you, but you will have them, wherefore they be your Gods." Clearly, Hooker's concern was mainly with the attitude which breach of the Fourth Commandment betrayed. God had decreed that Sunday be reserved for worship, and yet carders and dicers would put themselves "above God and his commands." As Sibbes had earlier said, "We should resort to the preaching of the Word while we may." He considered as accursed any study—even biblical study—which occupied a man "when he should be at God's ordinances; and the good that is gotten at home, when we may go to church on the Sabbath, is as the water of cursing because it is gotten in contempt of God's ordinances." John Benbrigge, a native of the Sussex port town of Rye, attempted in 1645 to give his auditory there a set of marks by which they might know if they were among the fortunate souls who "prizeth Christ aright." The soul which has, he said, been taught "the mystery of godliness" by Christ highly prizes Sabbaths and sermons: "Truly Beloved, if any of you prize not the day of the Lord, you

23. T. Hill, *Trade of Truth Advanced*, pp. 50–52; Gouge, *The Saints Support* (1642), pp. 3–4; Gouge, *Mercies Memoriall*, sig. A3 (verso); Gouge, *The Progresse of Divine Providence*, pp. 22–24. Thomas Atkins was a well-known Puritan—see Pearl, pp. 311–13. John Milton denounced "the dark overcasting of superstitious copes and flaminical vestures; wearing on their backs, and, I abhor to think, perhaps in some worse place the unexpressible image of God" (i.e., notes the editor, wearing "the sign of the cross on their backsides"). Don M. Wolfe, ed., *Complete Prose Works of John Milton* (New Haven: Yale University Press, 1953), 1:827.

do not prize the Lord of the day, neither have you any saving grace in you." The saved soul also loves "to hear Christ preached out of his Word; and truly he prizeth Christ preached more than Christ read, because there is usually more in the former . . . of the life, light, and quickening power of Christ." In a sermon preached in 1646, Benbrigge criticized as "formal professors" those who took tradition as a guide in reformation of the church. "Formal professors" were those who claimed to be truly converted but whose actions belied their words. One act which was a mark of "formality" in religion was satisfaction with the anglican liturgy. "Alas beloved, we must not in matters of God's worship and service take up anything upon the practice of our ancestors, except they had therein the prophets and apostles for their guides and examples."[24]

It is significant that Benbrigge restricted the guides and examples which true Christians might lawfully use to those given by prophets and apostles. He did not include the Fathers of the early church. Many puritan divines were as widely read in ancient writers, both sacred and profane, as were Hammond and Farindon. But Benbrigge used a favorite puritan word when he denounced those who were content to live, raise children, and die in the religion of their ancestors. It was, he said, "a practice very unwarrantable." Age was no defense for an unjustified ceremony or observance. No humanly invented authority could make it so by calling it a "thing indifferent." Nothing unsupported by scriptural warrant would do. The opposition between nature and grace, man and God, was too great. To think that the gap was bridgeable by human effort or that grace came easily was a corollary of the popish doctrine of human merit; it was to think that man could build himself up until he could create something acceptable in God's sight. It was to imply that human beings could perfect themselves, and that was a notion created by Antichrist to lure men to everlasting destruction. It was to imply that Christ's sacrifice had been unnecessary because men could live up to God's covenant with Adam, the covenant of works. All Puri-

24. T. Hooker, Lessons, p. 38; Sibbes, Works, 7:171; Benbrigge, Christ, pp. 31–32; Benbrigge, Gods Fury, pp. 93–94. On this point see also Watson: "A fourth sign of sanctification is the spiritual performance of duties, . . . The sanctified soul prays out of love to prayer and 'calls the Sabbath a delight,' " p. 246 and Isa. 58:13. "Such as pollute God's Sabbath, oppose his saints, trampling those jewels in the dust . . . engage the infinite majesty of heaven against them" (p.44).

tans knew that that covenant had been destroyed by Adam's sin and that man's only hope was to recognize his own sinfulness and to pray for the grace to grapple with it. The Bible was the *only* source of models for personal and social behavior. Puritans insisted on the importance of godly preaching so that all men might find out what was warrantable and what was not. Even in an age of increasing literacy, the preaching of the Word had to remain central. Puritan divines published their sermons as sermons, as treatises, and as commentaries and urged that their parishioners read them. Sibbes, however, spoke for them all when he said that "the expressions of a gracious heart by lively voice breed deeper impressions (God attending his own ordinance of preaching with a more special blessing)."[25]

Sibbes's comment on preaching appeared in the dedication of a colleague's sermon to the "fathers and brethren of the Company of Haberdashers." One of them, Sir Nicholas Rainton, had been chairman of the City Feoffees for Impropriations and was to be, according to Dr. Pearl, "the only senior Alderman to show any real sympathies with the parliamentary puritans before 1642." His work as a Feoffee demonstrated his support of godly preaching. There were many other laymen who demonstrated the marks of true conversion as delineated by the divines. Sibbes himself had preached the funeral sermon of Mr. Sherland, the recorder of Northampton. Sherland had collected "choice things out of the sermons he heard about death, many years before he died, to lay up store of provision against that time." Sibbes praised him for being a good keeper of the Sabbath and for always retiring after the sermon to ruminate on it. He had shown "his love to the church" by giving £400 for the purchase of impropriations. Another of the Feoffees was a lawyer, John White. He was one of the most vigorous critics of the bishops, and his speeches before the House of Commons rang with denunciations of their "innovating religion, joining with the Church of Rome, approving as well of the doctrine as ceremonies thereof." He condemned Laud's order that prayers be read at the upper end of the chancel with the priest facing eastward, the treatment of the communion table as an altar, and other regulations. White believed

25. Benbrigge, *Gods Fury*, p. 94; Sibbes, *Works*, 7:561. For Gouge's use of the term "warrantable," see *Gods Three Arrowes*, pp. 39–45.

that such things led back toward the doctrine of transubstantiation and adoration of the elements and other "abominable idolatries." He charged that Laud and his bishops had filled eight tenths of the benefices in England with "idol, idle or scandalous ministers" while suspending or depriving any "godly, learned and painful preachers" who scrupled at a trifling ceremony ("though indifferent in their own account"). In a survey of ministers the bishops had approved, White gave many examples of the sort of First Table offenses the Puritans despised. There was, for example, the minister in Essex who bowed twelve times to the altar upon every entrance into the chancel but rarely preached more than once a month. There was a Surrey Anglican who, according to White, had said that "long sermons, like long swords, cut off both [ears] at once, and that surfeit of the Word is of all most dangerous." For Puritans, there could be no such thing as a "surfeit of the Word." The suggestion that there might be was evidence of ungodliness.[26]

While White and other puritan parliamentarians lambasted the idolatry of popish ceremonies and ungodly preaching in the House of Commons, Lord Saye was reminding his fellow peers of the reasoning which underlay puritan efforts to honor the First Table injunctions of the Lord. Laud had accused him of separatism for his unwillingness to join with the peers in prayer. Saye opened his rejoinder with pointed references to Laud's mean origins and cagily replied that "some set forms of prayer by some men, in some cases, may be lawfully used." What troubled him was that some men had usurped the power to enforce set prayers and "forms of divine service" upon everyone else. The effect, he said, was to throw out "gifts and graces which Christ hath given . . .and introduce a device of men." Lord Saye used the term "lawful" as we have seen Benbrigge use "unwarrantable." That which comes merely from men cannot be lawfully or warrantably used in the worship of God.

26. Pearl, p. 304 (on Rainton); Sibbes, *Cordialls*, pp. 206–08; *Mr. Whites Speech in Parliament on Monday, the 17th of January* (1642), p. 5; *A Speech of John White* (1641), sig. Iiii3 (recto), Iii2 (verso); John White, *The First Century of Scandalous, Malignant Priests* (1643), pp. 6–8. Paul Seaver wrote that "the mark of the lay Puritan was his demand for constant preaching." *Puritan Lectureships*, p. 42. See also pp. 40–54 where he discusses evidence that attendance and support of lectures was "a public action that revealed the inward character of the saint."

Those who forced or acquiesced in the enforcement of what the puritan peer called "ceremonies and things to you indifferent" were guilty of a serious offense against Christ.[27]

Both Lord Saye and John White were among the original subscribers of the Massachusetts Bay Company. The papers of John Winthrop, long the governor of the colony, provide full confirmation of the high esteem in which puritan laymen held the duties derived from the First Table of the Decalogue. From the time of the first stirrings of grace in his soul, Winthrop sought to examine his thoughts and deeds for signs of good or evil. He expressed very well the theme which underlay all his efforts when he wrote: "Oh I see, if we leave, or slightly exercise ourselves in the Word, faith will starve and die and our hearts embrace any dotages of man's brain sooner than God's eternal truth, as I found by dangerous experience." Winthrop found that by hearing, reading, and meditating upon the Bible and then doing his utmost to practice what he learned about divine injunctions, he could keep on his course for salvation. He found that those who were dissuaded from Christian duties by the "opinion of others, their own corrupt reason, common experience, etc. shall never enjoy the comfort of living by faith." The "child of God" had to do all that his profession of faith required regardless of the impediments the world set in his way. What was required was, as Winthrop told himself, a willingness to "set upon any duty, whilst I beheld my warrant in God's book." He vowed that God's commandment would be "sufficient encouragement and warrant to me in any thing."[28] Winthrop recorded these convictions in his spiritual diary in 1616 and 1617. The diary also notes at various points his

27. William Fiennes, Viscount Saye and Sele, *A Speech of the Right Honorable the Lord Viscount Say and Sele*, pp. 2–3, 5, delivered February 22, 1642. Further, he states, "as if because some men had need to make use of crutches, all men should be prohibited the use of their legs and injoined to take up such crutches as have been prepared for those who have no legs."

28. *WP*, 1:208, 215. See 2:158 for Margaret Winthrop's use of the term "warrant." Winthrop received advice to this effect from his friend, John Humfrey, in 1630. Of the many difficulties which the young colony faced, Humfrey wrote, "Let us hear what the Lord saith by them, and so far as they weigh every pin of the tabernacle in the scales of the sanctuary, follow and obey them. [But] where any, yea, though an angel from heaven shall obtrude any thing upon us without warrant from the Word, avoid them, yea, let them be in that anathematiad" (2: 333). For the connections of Saye and White with Massachusetts, see Hexter, *Reign of King Pym*, pp. 77–80.

specific resolutions to apply this doctrine. Upon recovering from a "tedious quartan," he resolved in 1613 to "diligently observe the Lord's Sabbath" by eschewing worldly business and concentrating upon the "religious spendings of such times as are free from public exercises . . . in prayer, meditation and reading." The public exercises were, of course, church services in which the preaching of the Word was central. After hearing one of the local puritan preachers on the subject, Winthrop later proposed a still stricter regimen. The doctrine he had heard was that a "Christian is bound to make use of his Sabbath business all the week after," and that to do so would fend off spiritual discontent. A time should be set apart each weekday for further work upon the preceding Sunday's spiritual business, "for certainly the Sabbath is the market of our souls."[29]

The important role which First Table duties played in puritan thinking appears in the debate among Winthrop and his friends over the warrantableness or lawfulness of leaving Old England to build up a plantation in New England. The validity of the warrant was of the utmost significance because the proposed endeavor was bound to entail a great deal of suffering. The settlers might perish by shipwreck, starvation, sickness, or sword if they were attempting something which was not a part of God's plan. On the other hand, if it was God's intention that they expose themselves to the wilderness, He would care for them. As Winthrop put it, "If this course be warrantable we must trust God's providence for these things, either he will keep these evils from us or will dispose them for our good and enable us to bear them." This did not mean that they could expect to set out in a dory and expect manna from heaven on the North Atlantic. The age of such miracles was past, and they fully intended to take all possible precautions to insure success. Not to use

29. *WP*, 1:168, 198. See pp. 199–200 for an account of one of Winthrop's Sundays which included two trips to church and reading from Mr. Rogers on "the covenant of certain Christians" and from Mr. Perkins on "the estate of a Christian." Other references to the Sabbath (not cited in the index) are on pp. 168, 187, 189 (where Winthrop calls heaven "an holy, everlasting Sabbath") and 208. The Independent lawyer and regicide, John Cooke, affords another example. In the Tower awaiting execution in 1660, he wrote to his wife: "Tell Sister Jones that she keeps but two or three Sabbaths in a week but in prison every day is a Christian Sabbath. . . . I can but smile to think they cannot hinder me from preaching, for I preach every day to myself." *Speeches and Prayers*, p. 50.

"good means" was to "tempt God"—a dangerous error. One clear part of the warrant was provided by God's command that the Gospel be preached to all the world. The building up of particular churches by faithful people would give glory to God in many ways, including the creation of a "bulwark against the kingdom of Antichrist" (then under construction by the Jesuits) and the encouragement of "the faith of God's people" remaining in England. To the objection that the Church of England would need the services and support of its Winthrops in the troubled times that had begun and would continue, the governor-to-be replied that the church of the Jews had been well served by the withdrawal of Mary and Joseph, "that their Messiah might be preserved for them against times of better service." He feared that the Church of England was in danger of the destruction which had fallen upon the German Protestant churches and that the saints of New England might be its saviors eventually. A more general and less apocalyptic warrant was derived from God's order that men should multiply, replenish, and subdue the earth (Gen. 1 : 28).[30]

Perhaps the most prominent factor in the emigration debate, however, dealt not with what could be accomplished in the New World, but with what was happening in the Old. An unknown correspondent had apparently opposed the colonial scheme by arguing that the condition of the godly in England was satisfactory. Only a fragment of Winthrop's reply survives, but that fragment burns with absolute conviction. "If our condition be good," he demanded, why do God's "ambassadors" (the puritan preachers) "so constantly denounce wrath and judgment against us?" His answer is a series of scriptural denunciations of idolatry. "One calf set up in Israel removed the tabernacle out of the host, and for two [i.e., two shrines to calves] God forsook them forever." The presence of some good Israelites (such as the prophets) did not save Jerusalem from the Babylonians. There were "good prophets and seven thousand good Protestants in Ahab's time," but judgement came despite their

30. WP, 2:114–16, 125. For a deft distinction between miracles (which God no longer worked) and "wonders" (which God still worked) much along the lines of Winthrop's argument, see Preston, Breast-Plate, pt. 2, pp. 163–65. On the emigration debate, see E. S. Morgan, The Puritan Dilemma, pp. 40–48, 69–71.

prayers. The rhetorical question which ended this passage referred to England in 1629: "If it be thus with us," asked Winthrop, "where then is the happiness we should rest in?" Idolatry, lukewarmness, superstition, abominations—the peoples of the Old Testament had suffered for these, and all were rampant in England. One correspondent, the Suffolk antiquary Robert Ryece, who had originally opposed the colonial venture, changed his mind after reading Winthrop's defense of it and agreed that the time might be ripe for leaving. He said that England in 1629 was a place "where well doing is not maintained or the godly cherished, but idolatry, popery and whatsoever is evil is countenanced." Even the least of these was, he thought, cause enough to "make haste out of Babylon." Ryece said that Winthrop was right to give up his magistracy because, as things stood, the justice of the peace who was "true and strict for the due execution of his place, especially against popery or against the common sins of the time, is altogether discouraged and discountenanced."[31]

For both clerical and lay Puritans, the sins against the First Table of the Decalogue and the duties of worship which it required formed a consistent, coherent, incessantly reiterated theme. Its elements were logically interlocking. The fountain of all truth was the Bible, and it provided warrants for all that men ought to do and injunctions against all that they ought not to do. God was to be worshipped by the hearing of his Word and the doing of his will as proclaimed in sermons. The hearing of the Word required a trained body of preachers from the universities and adequate compensation for them in their pulpits. The use of idolatrous means to worship God was not only unwarrantable in itself, but it usually took away from attention to the Word. So did the profanation of the Sabbath by sports and other activities not appropriate to the Lord's day. Opposition to or scorn for those who sought to obey the First Table by supporting godly preachers, hindering idolatrous ceremonies,

31. *WP*, 2:121–22, 130, 128. See 1:295–310, for a detailed list of the grievances apparently prepared for presentation to the 1623–24 session of parliament. They include enforcing of the recusancy laws, stopping the silencing of "painful ministers," punishing of pluralists and scandalous ministers and other standard puritan complaints.

and sanctifying the Sabbath was evidence that the opposer or the scorner was unregenerate. Sibbes said that "it comes near to the sin against the Holy Ghost, to hate any man for goodness."[32]

The willingness to face opposition and scorn in pursuance of these godly activities was evidence of regeneration. These signs and marks derived from the Word by the puritan prophets were not always considered absolutely conclusive proofs of a man's spiritual estate, but they always gave a strong presumption of it. Human reason was frail and human will was depraved. The only course which offered any safety or comfort was following these scriptural guidelines and praying for more grace to do better by them. To do well and to countenance other well-doers was to court much worldly affliction, but the rewards were greater than any the world could offer. These concerns were still central for Puritans even after 1660—after the collapse of the attempt to build a godly commonwealth by the saints. Thomas Doolittle, an ejected Nonconformist, found causes of the Great Plague and the Great Fire in "strange fire in the worship of God." Worship that is "not commanded by the Lord must be put away, if God's fiery anger is to be put out." Doolittle made his meaning perfectly clear slightly later as he denounced such provoking First Table breaches as worshipping "the true God in a false manner of our own devising, contrary to his Word, which is the perfect rule of worship," profaning the Sabbath by gaming, selling, drinking in alehouses, and swearing "horrid oaths."[33]

It should not be thought that the heavy emphasis Puritans placed upon performance of the First Table duties and the corollaries thereto was accompanied by a disinclination to obey the commands of the Second Table. Nor should the next section of this chapter be taken as arguing that Anglicans ignored the First Table and preached only obedience to the Second. Both anglican and puritan saints obeyed all ten of God's commandments to the best of their ability. John Benbrigge might have been speaking for them all when he denounced "the civil man and formal professor." Divines, he said, had distinguished between "civility, a Second Table-man, and . . . formality, a First Table-man." He explained that this

---

32. Sibbes, *Cordialls*, p. 202.
33. Doolittle, *Rebukes*, pp. 84, 88, 92–93. See p. 94 for his reprise of the old puritan hymn about the "dumb dogs, that cannot bark." See also Watson, p. 8.

meant that the former "made it his whole religion to be just and true in all his dealings with men, not once thinking of giving God his due," whereas the latter quite reversed these priorities.[34]

The performance of duties toward God and man was essential for both Anglicans and Puritans. The point is rather that, by comparison, the Puritans tended to emphasize the First Table more heavily and to make it a touchstone to the Second. The famous puritan preacher, Thomas Hooker, exhibited this tendency when he denounced mere "civil righteousness" as one of the "false shadows of the state of grace." A man in this state, said Hooker, lives peaceably with his neighbors, indeed, would not "hurt so much as his neighbor's dog, pays every man his own, . . . no drunkard, adulterer or quarreler." He takes pride and pleasure in his just dealings with men "and hopes by this to do as well as the best." But such men deceive themselves because in most of them Hooker found "a manifest gross transgression of the duties of the First Table that do more immediately concern the worship of God." Most are "negligent regarders of the ministry of the Word," and they "break the Sabbath." Like Benbrigge, Hooker warned of the danger of "formal righteousness"—observance of duties toward God without true inward regeneration. Doubtless they agreed with Archbishop Ussher's observation that in Scripture "breaches of the First Table are to be more severely punished, than the breaches of the Second," and that men who believed that "the works of the Second Table, as charity, alms-deeds and the like" were "the most meritorious good works of all" had been duped by "the crafty practices of papists." If a man did not perform his First Table duties in the proper way, his hopes for salvation were likely to rest on sand. E. S. Morgan has written that the Puritans did "not differ so much from their contemporaries in their views about salvation as much as they did in their views about behavior."[35] This is true so long as it

---

34. Benbrigge, *Gods Fury*, p. 53. It is well known that Puritans were avid penalizers of immorality. In New England adultery was a more serious crime than it was in Old England. See E. S. Morgan, *The Puritan Family*, pp. 38–41.

35. T. Hooker, *Lessons*, pp. 211–16; Ussher, *The Principles of Christian Religion*, p. 170; Morgan, *Puritan Family*, p. 2. Despite his high position and his staunch defense of episcopacy, there are good reasons to think of Ussher as strongly inclined to the puritan side. Throughout the sermons appended to the *Principles*, Ussher strongly emphasizes the difficulty of conversion and the justifiability of frightening men

is remembered that their views about desirable forms of behavior were influenced by their beliefs about salvation. As we have seen, strong opposition to even the least manifestation of "human wit" in the worship of God, constant support for "godly preaching" and careful sanctifying of the Sabbath were prominent among the activities English Puritans preached and practiced. The Puritan whose behavior exhibited them could consider them as evidences of saving grace and thus gain assurance about the only matter which really mattered—the state of his soul. Assurance of salvation came by rather different marks to his anglican contemporaries.

ANGLICANS AND THE SECOND TABLE

In terms of emphasis, Anglicans reversed the relationship between the two tables of the Ten Commandments. They made Second Table duties the touchstone to the First. They could do this because they believed that the Church of England was not, as the Puritans thought, an ugly caterpillar struggling toward the exquisite completeness of the butterfly, but rather a liturgically beautiful and spiritually satisfying offspring of the travail of the Reformation in England. For Puritans the rise of the Long Parliament was the beginning of a God-given opportunity to complete the religious reformation which had been threatened by Laudianism. For Anglicans it was the beginning of what could only be a temporary eclipse of the shining light of holiness cast by the established Church of England. It is the purpose of this section to demonstrate first,

---

toward it (pp. 17–18, 33, 52–64, 96) and the inadequacy of human will and "common grace" (pp. 24, 35, 55, 85, 118). The last of the sermons printed in this group was preached before the king at Greenwich on June 25, 1627; it is a vigorous attack on Arminianism in Holland and England. Conrad Russell describes Ussher as "a puritan bishop" and notes that the "official articles of the Irish church, drafted in 1615 under the influence of Ussher, . . . explicitly supported the puritan position" on the subject of predestination. *Crisis of Parliaments*, pp. 343, 212. For his association with such Puritans as Preston, see I. Morgan, *Prince Charles's Puritan Chaplain*, pp. 34–37, 42–43, 130, 202. But Ussher's recent biographer, S. Buick Knox, considers him a thoroughgoing Anglican, consistently Calvinist and consistently Episcopalian. Ussher will always be difficult to classify because, as Knox concludes, he "had firm convictions, but these convictions were not always compatible or easily harmonised with one another." *James Ussher, Archbishop of Armagh*, p. 190. See chaps. 8 and 11 for discussions of his views on church organization and Presbyterianism.

that Anglicans regarded the First Table requirements as entirely fulfilled by honest participation in the prescribed rituals and that puritan attacks upon those rituals were unjustified; second, that the mark of a good Christian was avoidance of theological controversy and concentration upon Second Table duties; and finally, that an acceptable measure of perfection in those duties was attainable by using Christ as an exemplar.

The recurrent note of anglican apologetics was struck by Dr. Sanderson before the king and his courtiers at Berwick. The Scots were in rebellion, Edinburgh had rioted, and deputations were being exchanged between the king and the Covenanters. "Now it is our great comfort, blessed be God for it," said Sanderson, "that the doctrine established in the Church of England . . . is such as is not justly chargeable with any impiety contrarious to any part of that duty we owe either to God or man." With this assertion confidently made, he ejaculated, "Oh that our conversations were as free from exceptions as our religion is!"[36] If, as Clarendon's chaplain, Lionel Gatford, wrote in 1648, "the Church of England in its reformed established religion was not only a defence and a refuge, but the glory and honor of all the reformed churches in Christendom," then the arrangements made by its authorities for the observance of the Christian man's First Table duties toward God were beyond reproach. Anglicans objected to the prelatical pomp of Rome, but also to the bare bleakness of Geneva and Zurich. Farindon put it well when he complained against "these present times, which have thought fit to reform the Reformation itself." Clarendon himself wrote that the entire quarrel in religious matters boiled down to this, that Anglicans "love the habitation of the house of the Lord and the place where his honor dwelleth; that we abhor sacrilege" and the "profaning of the place of his worship." Anglicans, he said, sought simply to "perform these ceremonies, and observe those decent circumstances in our devotion, which either himself [the Lord] enjoined, or his church commanded, for the more reverent setting out and adorning his service." The conjunc-

36. Sanderson, 2:225. Further, "upon this point we dare boldly join issue with our clamorous adversaries on either side, papists, I mean, and disciplinarians." For a description of the tense atmosphere in which this sermon was preached, see Gardiner, *History*, 9:33–55.

tion "or" is crucial. Puritans looked upon the things commanded by the Church and yet not enjoined by the Lord himself as idolatrous breaches of the First Table. The clash was unavoidable— because the ceremonialism which profaned the worship of God by its presence for the Puritans profaned that service by its absence for the Anglicans. For Jeremy Taylor, those who refused "to worship God with lowly reverence of their bodies, according as the church expresses her reverence to God externally" were guilty of sin against the Second Commandment, and those who profaned "churches, holy utensils, holy persons, holy customs, holy sacraments" were breaching the Third. Clarendon could no more believe, as he put it, that the church should "be naked and without any ornaments of state of decency," than his adversaries could believe that many of these "things indifferent" were not sins against the First Table.[37]

From the anglican point of view, those who opposed ceremonies of the established Church of England and who sought to mar its comeliness and decency by changing the form of its observances were merely repeating old errors. They would suffer the fate of previous heretics and slanderers. Early in 1644, John Bramhall compared such men to the Ammonites who had fought the Israelites. The Ammonites had jeered at the Jewish religion, "even as some of late have ludibriously abused those holy garments and books and vessels, which we use in the service of God." Humphrey Sydenham mentioned "Sabbatarianism" as an example of his contention that "all new ruptures in the church are but the grey hairs of an ancient schism, new combed and colored, or the bones of some primitive heresy revived." He explicitly included both old heresies (Donatism, Catharism, and Anabaptism) and new ones (Brownism, Barrowism, and Familism) under the single name, "Puritanism." He reminded his listeners that to suffer for any of these doctrines was not the way to martyrdom and eternal life—but rather the way to hell. Those who would, he said, "pull down ceremonies and build up anarchy . . . under the pretence of an immediate calling" which was in truth nothing but the "heart-burning and proud discontent" of their own spirits, were demonstrating their own reprobation. He

37. Gatford, *Englands Complaint*, p. 14; Farindon, 1:300; *Contemplations*, p. 438; Taylor, 4:488–90; *Contemplations*, p. 490.

fiercely denounced the man who "tortures an innocent piece of glass for the limme [likeness] of a saint in it; . . . pulls down an organ and advances an hour-glass; . . . this malicious disrobing of the temple of the Lord is no better than spiritual theft." Sanderson similarly argued in 1655 that "all errors, sects and heresies" originated in some true doctrine which was somehow twisted or misapplied. Thus "our late sectaries, . . . anticeremonians" had begun with the excellent principle of "the perfection and sufficing" of the Bible, but they had then proceeded to the "unsound corrupt principle [that] nothing might lawfully be done or used in the churches of Christ unless there were either command or example for it in the Scriptures." This, thought Sanderson, had been the "root of bitterness" from which had sprung "all these numerous branches of sects and heresies wherewith this sinful nation is now so much pestered."[38]

Anglicans did not merely defend ceremonies. They were frequently skeptical about the value of what Puritans insisted was the staff of spiritual life, the sermon. Henry Hammond, urging the duty of almsgiving upon the lord-mayor and aldermen of the City in 1640, caustically dismissed those men among whom the notion that " 'we have heard so many sermons' passes for a sufficient pretension to heaven." According to Izaak Walton, Sanderson was so saddened by the results of "irregular and indiscreet preaching [upon] the generality of the nation" that he advocated replacement of extemporaneous preaching and praying by the reading of an annual course of homilies containing the full "body of divinity (or so much of it as was needful to be known by the common people)." Robert Gell, later to be a chaplain to Archbishop Sheldon, said in 1649 that although England was full of preaching and hearing, "yet how few, alas, how few come unto Christ" as had the three oriental kings at Christ's nativity "to whom God gave neither preacher nor Word." The puritan practice of leaving shops and benches to hear weekday sermons and returning to discuss them was criticized by Anthony Farindon. He described such listeners and talkers as

38. Bramhall, p. 93; Sydenham, *Occasions*, p. 266, 31, 28, 258–59, 29–32; Sanderson, 2:6–7. See also Chillingworth, 1:23–24, for a defense of Laud's policy of adorning and beautifying "the places 'where God's honour dwells,' " and making "them as heaven-like as they can with earthly ornaments." Also, Falkland, pp. 177–78.

"monks at large" who called their practice a devotion; but in reality they were afflicted by "the itch and wantonness of the ear, which wasteth their devotion and sometimes their estates." The true Anglican was innocent of such breaches of the First Table as profanation of holy places and sacrilege toward the ceremonies within them. He was also innocent of supporting preachers who preached otherwise.[39]

The anglican defense of Prayer Book ceremonies was in part based upon the overriding duty of obedience to the king and the established ecclesiastical hierarchy. This political obedience will be discussed more fully in the next chapter. There was, however, a theological aspect as well. We have seen how central the ministry of the Word was to the puritan conception of First Table duties. But many Anglicans maintained what J. F. H. New has called "dynamic expectations of grace through the sacraments."[40] These expectations recur frequently in anglican writing and the tone of them is clearly indicated in Jeremy Taylor's *Christian Consolations*. Taylor wrote that "as many spouts should open into one cistern, so all comforts conspire to meet in the sacrament of the Lord's Supper." The liturgy proclaims that the Christian may enjoy "holy security against all fears" because "the Lord hath put himself into my hand and into my mouth and into my spirit."[41] One of the most worrisome problems Anglicans faced during the Interregnum was that of the spiritual damage done by lack of regular access to the sacraments. After the observation of the sacraments according to the Prayer Book rite had finally been outlawed, John Evelyn asked

39. Hammond, p. 255; Walton's "Life" in Sanderson, 1:40–41; Robert Gell, *Stella Nova*, p. 15; Farindon, 1:346. See also Chillingworth, 3:52–53; Cudworth, p. 54. For similar criticisms of Elizabethan Puritans, see Collinson, pp. 373–74.

40. New, *Anglican and Puritan*, p. 76. See pp. 64–76 for his discussion of the puritan view of the sacraments (which stressed "prevenient grace") and the anglican view (which saw in them "a conspicuously effective means of grace"), p. 64. I argue below, however, that we should consider Hales, Whichcote, and others who do not emphasize such an interpretation of the sacraments to be Anglicans.

41. Taylor 1:160. Bishop Heber includes *Christian Consolations* in Taylor's works for reasons cited in his introduction, pp. clvi–clix. The authorship of it has been disputed. For a review of the controversy, see Allison, *The Rise of Moralism*, pp. 215–17. Internal evidence indicates that the tract was written before 1660, though it was first published in 1671. See, for example, p. 101: "Now I live in all disorder of church ordinances, in distraction of schisms, in the filthy stench of old and new heresies."

Taylor (May 18, 1654), "Where shall we now receive the viaticum with safety? How shall we be baptized?"[42] Another layman, the banished Earl of Clarendon, was similarly troubled. During his final banishment he wrote bitterly that, whereas he had enjoyed the services of a chaplain during his first exile, he now had no "exercise of that religion which I have always embraced with my soul, and in which I resolve to die, how destitute soever I may be of the exercise of it at my death." George Morley, who had been Clarendon's chaplain at Antwerp, attacked the puritan notion that the sacraments "ought not to be administered upon any occasion, but in a church and after the preaching of a sermon too." It was not sermons which validated baptism and communion—rather, he insisted, it was "the sacramental words themselves, which make them to be sacraments, [which] are absolutely and essentially necessary to make them efficacious and effectual."[43]

It is important to recognize that even those Anglicans who did not lay much emphasis upon "dynamic expectations of grace through the sacraments" did nevertheless insist upon the primacy of Second-Table duties. Benjamin Whichcote, for example, said that there are "but two things in religion: morals and institutions." The latter "depend upon Scripture" and were "once commanded by God and were acceptable to him" but only "if men were not wanting in moral duties. . . . He will not take sacrifice [i.e., worship] at our hands, if we be not refined in our spirits and reformed in our lives." Therefore Whichcote preferred to "lay stress upon the indispensable necessity of morals," which were "nineteen parts in twenty of religion." John Hales warned that no man should "flatter himself in his outward conformity and correspondence with the church's constitutions" because "neither is ceremony now, neither was sacrifice then esteemed necessary." What remains forever necessary is obedience to "those main fundamental laws . . . against theft, against murder, against dishonoring of parents or the like." Those laws were not written by men, "neither were they the effects of any parliamentary sessions; they were written in our souls from the beginning." Hales's friend, Anthony Farindon,

42. Ibid., pp. cccxxii–cccxxiii.
43. *Contemplations*, p. 374; Morley, *Several Treatises*, pp. x–xxi. See also Hyde, *The Mystery of Christ in Us*, p. 87.

said that to make more of the Word and the sacraments than they
are "is to make them less than they are." Thus, "to attribute virtue
and efficacy to the sacrament, yet to be fitter to receive the devil
than the sop [is] at once to magnify and profane it; to call it the
'bread of life' and make it poison." He pointed out that in Old
Testament times, "when sacrifices were omitted, and the Sabbath
for some reasons was not observed, God complained not." What did
anger God was not the failure to perform those duties which were
not limited to times and places but were required at all times because their performance "requireth no more than our will."
Despite his sadness and anger over the results of the puritan destruction of the established church, Farindon stood in his London pulpit
through years of army rule and repeatedly reminded his large
audiences that at "the day of judgment . . . We shall not be asked
what we thought, but what we did." Clarendon, despite all his
reverence for the established church and its ceremonies, reiterated
the necessity of a good life, a life of obedience and charity to all
men. He warned against the danger of limiting all devotion to the
church's "ivory palaces and to her raiment of needlework, to outward forms and ceremonies, to the gaudry and pomp of divine
worship, without much considering the inward operation and
effect of religion." The true Christian, as described by Chillingworth, could not content himself "with going to church, saying or
hearing of prayers, receiving of sacraments, hearing, repeating, or
preaching of sermons, with zeal for ceremonies, or zeal against them;
or indeed with anything besides constant piety towards God,
loyalty and obedience toward our sovereign, justice and charity
towards all our neighbors."[44]

It is against this background that Dr. Thomas Pierce's dictum
that obedience to the Second Table was the true Christian's touchstone to the First must be understood. If idolatry was the most comprehensive and evocative word in the puritan vocabulary of sin,
disobedience held that place for Anglicans. But the obedience

44. Whichcote, 1:122, and in Cragg, p. 429; Hales, 2:303–04, 308–09 and 3:16;
Farindon, 1:469, 134–35, 533–34; *Contemplations*, p. 489; Chillingworth, 3:31.
See also Taylor, 2:342ff; Cudworth, p. 17; Sanderson, 2:58; "Obedience is a thing
wherein God more delighteth than in sacrifice; and the keeping of the commandment will phase him better than a bullock that hath horns and hoofs."

Anglicans had in mind was obedience to a man, albeit a divinely appointed man. The Second Table deals with relations among men, and it is here that anglican emphasis lay. They were living in an age of vigorous and violent theological and liturgical contention which had, so they thought, arisen because ambitious, sinful private men had sought to arrogate to themselves the right to make decisions which properly belonged to the established authorities. Dr. Edward Hyde, therefore, denounced idolatry as the worst of sins, and said that the very men who thought themselves least guilty of it were most at fault: "When thou followest thine own fancy in serving God thou worshippest Baal, that's now thine idol, nay indeed thy lord and master, and hath gotten dominion over thee. Nor is there any image more dangerously worshipped than thine own imagination."[45] John Wenlock, a royalist lawyer of Suffolk, condemned Roundhead ideas as "fantastical and fanatical opinions of men." When the Suffolk parliamentarians insisted that he obey the Long Parliament's ordinance that all arms be surrendered for militia use, Wenlock refused and deepened his unpopularity with his neighbors by telling them "that they professed themselves to be great haters of idolatry, and yet it appeared they were much infected with superstition, a grand limn thereof; for they had as reverend a conceit of their parliament, as the papists have of the pope, which is, that he cannot possibly err in his function."[46]

Thus Anglicans denounced "opinions of men" just as strongly as Puritans did—but for diametrically opposed reasons. Puritans insisted that the Scriptures had to be obeyed whenever mere men, regardless of their temporal authority, commanded the performance of things which were not warrantable. Laudian ceremonies were the outstanding example. Anglicans, however, found no idolatry in the ceremonies, and thus the puritan condemnation of them was based on mere "opinions of men." This was one of the grounds given by Lord Treasurer Weston in 1633 when he sought dissolution of the

45. Hyde, *Legacy*, pp. 64–65. This was a favorite theme for Hyde. He described a true conversion in part as follows: "It is not a violent but a voluntary motion of the affection that is here required. . . . Not turn seeker after men's new fancies but after God's old mercies."
46. John Wenlock, *The Humble Declaration* (1662), pp. 22–23. This part was written, according to Wenlock, in 1643.

Feoffees for Impropriations. "They must," he said, "have an opinion of sanctity in themselves more than in others. They must devise, determine, judge and then their disciples must follow them." Ralph Cudworth in 1647 criticized those who "spend all their zeal upon a violent obtruding of their own opinions and apprehensions upon others." He feared that many who "pull down idols in churches" and "quarrel with painted glass" were in fact setting up idols and lusts of another kind within their own hearts and "committing continual idolatry with them." John Bramhall echoed the point when he said that "the duties which many men pay to the Deity are nothing but opinions and crotchets; and for these they think it lawful for private men to mingle heaven and earth together, for subjects to invade their sovereign's dominions."[47]

The anglican response to the puritan "opinion of sanctity" was to insist that holy mysteries had to remain holy mysteries. To pry into the deep mysteries of godliness too closely was to court grave danger. The good Christian avoided theological disputation and cleaved to moral improvement. "God hath revealed himself and his good pleasure towards us in his holy Word sufficient to save our souls, if we will believe," Sanderson said, "but not to solve all our doubts, if we will dispute."[48] In the same year that Sanderson preached thus (1639), Sir Henry Wotton died, leaving this epitaph for himself:

> Here lies the first author of this sentence:
> 'The itch of disputation will prove the scab of the church.'
> Inquire his name elsewhere.[49]

47. Weston in I. M. Calder, ed., *Activities of the Puritan Faction of the Church of England*, p. 123; Cudworth, sigs. 3 (verso), 4 (recto); Bramhall, p. 102. Sydenham described the process by which those "rebellions to God or his church" occurred as one in which some men are "pre-occupated by a hasty belief of particular men and their opinions, subscribing wholly to their bare asseveration or negation." *Occasions*, p. 259. See also Hales, 2:57; Whichcote, 1:156–59.

48. Sanderson, 2:216. Gerald R. Cragg has written that this kind of thinking was the characteristic note of "a non-controversial type of Anglicanism which was widely held after the Restoration." *From Puritanism to the Age of Reason*, p. 26. See his discussion of Sanderson, pp. 22–30. I agree with Cragg and wish to emphasize that this attitude was also prevalent long before the Restoration. However, Sanderson and others who held it used it in a polemical way (to be discussed more fully below).

49. Quoted in Logan Pearsall Smith, ed., *The Life and Letters of Sir Henry Wotton*, 1:219.

Wotton was described by Izaak Walton as "a great enemy to wrangling disputes of religion," whether with the enemies of the Church of England on the right or on the left. Although he did not find himself in full agreement with Arminius, he was critical of "men that are but preachers, and shall never know, till they come to heaven, where the questions stick betwixt Arminius and the Church of England (if there be any)." Yet such men would, while on earth, "be tampering with and thereby perplexing the controversy and do therefore justly fall under the reproof of St. Jude, for being 'busybodies' and for 'meddling with things they understand not.'" These were the same foolish preachers assailed by Humphrey Sydenham because they "thrust into the closet of the Almighty; nay, into his very bosom, ransack his secrets there. . . . know at a hair's breadth whom He will save or damn, so manacling his incomprehensibleness to their reason."[50] There is "no warrant in Scripture," said Ralph Cudworth, "to peep into those hidden rolls and volumes of eternity. . . . God's everlasting decree is too dazzling and bright an object" for us to gaze upon. It were much better to remain in what Whichcote called the "learned ignorance" of knowing "no more than God doth say." It were, said Farindon, folly to be "lost in the search of those things which are past finding out," and which, "if they could be known, yet would not advantage us."[51]

Like Arminius and his friends in the Netherlands (and like Erasmus before them), Anglicans were convinced that the things essential to salvation were easily comprehensible and few in number.[52]

50. "Life" by Walton in *Reliquiae Wottonianae* (1672), sig. d3 (recto), d4 (recto); Sydenham, *Occasions*, p. 254. Sydenham elsewhere says that "to be curious (here) is to be quaintly mad and thus to thrust into the bedchamber of the Almighty is a frantic sauciness." *Sermons*, p. 114. Taylor called such "curious inquirers" into divine mysteries breakers of the Third Commandment. 4:489.

51. Cudworth, pp. 8–9; Whichcote, 1:154–55; Farindon, 1:387. See also Chillingworth, 3:47, 69, 89; Pierce, p. 451. Cf. Porter, *Reformation and Reaction in Tudor Cambridge*, pp. 342–43.

52. As Arthur J. Slavin has written, the argument that "reform and heresy could be sharply distinguished in terms of the idea of things indifferent to salvation and things necessary" can be traced back in England to Thomas Cromwell's associate, Thomas Starkey. *Humanism, Reform and Reformation in England*, p. 121. Therefore matters inessential (adiaphora) were subject to regulation by the established authorities. See Starkey's *An Exhortation to the People, instructing them to Unity and Obedience* (1536), sigs. B1–4, C4, R1, S2, U2, Y1–4. W. Gordon Zeeveld argued that Starkey borrowed this adiaphorism from Melanchthon. *Foundations of Tudor Policy*, pp. 141–51. James K. McConica argues that Melanchthon's views on this were in

All that was needed was the effort of will required to make use of them by applying them to conduct. The myriads of puritan sermons, like swarms of bees, merely obscured these fundamentals and made difficult what it should have been the practice of churchmen to make easy. "It was never the intent of the Holy Ghost," said John Hales, "to make it a matter of wit and subtlety to know how to be saved." Even the most ignorant man may "with ease apprehend what is necessary to save him." Lord Falkland was adamant that "in the Scriptures . . . all that is necessary is clear." Further, any man who "strives to square both his actions and opinions" by the clear meaning of the Bible will find that if he happens to "fall into any error (for which his understanding is only at fault and not his will), it shall not hinder his rising to heaven." In another passage, Falkland wrote that "God will either give his grace for assistance to find the truth or his pardon" if it is not found because it accords not "with the goodness of God to damn men for not following his will" when they have sincerely sought it. Whichcote's view was the same: "All things necessary to salvation are clearly taught in the Scriptures," and "he who with an honest intention of finding out the will of God" studies them carefully "will miss of nothing saving." The fundamental truths "are so clear that there is little danger of good men differing about them," and "the light of them is so full, so clear, so satisfactory that no ingenuous, unengaged, teachable mind . . . can be mistaken about them."[53]

This belief that the way to salvation is easy to understand led Anglicans to argue that Puritans had substituted for the superstition of Roman Catholicism a different but equally insidious error, a sort

---

turn those of "the whole Erasmian party." *English Humanists and Reformation Politics* pp. 4, 159–60, 170–71. See also A. G. Dickens, *Thomas Cromwell and the English Reformation*, pp. 80–87.

53. Hales, 3:14; Falkland, p. 95, sig. A3 (recto); Whichcote in Cragg, pp. 41–43. See also Chillingworth, 3:7–9; Cudworth, p. 19; Farindon, 1:116, 164. On this conviction in the writings of Arminius, Uytenbogaert, and Episcopius, see W. K. Jordan, *Development of Religious Toleration in England*, 2:323, 332, 338–40. Cf. Erasmus's "Paraclesis to the New Testament" in J. H. Hexter, ed., *Traditions of the World Western* (Chicago: Rand McNally, 1967), p. 299. Erasmus was quoted liberally by Falkland, pp. 108, 111, 123, 147, 155, 161, 187, 217. There are a number of ways in which the distinctions I am drawing between Anglicans and Puritans are paralleled by John O'Malley, "Erasmus and Luther, Continuity and Discontinuity as Key to their Conflict," *Sixteenth Century Journal* 5 (1974):47–65.

of neo-gnosticism. According to Cudworth, too many had come to think religion "but a little book-craft, a mere paper-skill. . . . The vulgar sort think that they know Christ enough, out of their creeds and catechisms," and if they know those and have "like parrots conned the words of them" they think themselves saved. But in all those things which were most germane to the all important matter of salvation, God's plan required no special knowledge, no adherence to the opinions of private men, no disobedience to the state or to the church. "He is the best Christian," said Cudworth, "whose heart beats with the truest pulse towards heaven; not he whose head spinneth out the finest cobwebs." Hales called it "one very general gross mistaking of our age" that "discourses concerning the notes of a Christian man, by what signs we know a man to be one of the visible company of Christ" indicate that if a man "hath conned his creed by heart" he is saved. The description of Strafford given by his tutor and chaplain could stand as the anglican ideal. Although "bred up in Calvin's opinions," he later became "more moderate" and preferred "piety before contention, laboring to be well grounded in fundamental truths than to trouble himself with disputes." This attitude was an important part of the ideal sketched by Bishop Hall. The Christian

> hath fully informed himself of all the necessary points of religion, and is so firmly grounded in the fundamental and saving truths, that he cannot be carried about with every wind of doctrine. . . . He is ever suspicious of . . . untrodden paths. . . . He dares not be too much wedded to his own conceit, and hath so much humility to think the whole church of Christ upon earth wiser than himself.[54]

Anglicans felt that laymen could safely leave theological disputes to the divines because one of their functions was to combat errors. Sanderson told the royal court in 1639 that "it concerneth every Christian man . . . whatsoever becometh of doubtful controversies, to look well to his life" while leaving the disputes to those "whose

---

54. Cudworth, pp. 3, 14; Hales, 2:71; Hall, 7:173–74. The comment on Strafford is quoted in C. V. Wedgwood, *The King's Peace*, p. 458. See also Hyde, *Legacy*, p. 25; Sydenham, *Occasions*, p. 134.

gifts and callings serve for it." The arena for the ordinary Christian man's duel with the devil was in his relations with other men. He was not to change the established religion by embracing novelties—he was to practice it by behaving in a truly Christian way upon truly Christian principles. It was, said Farindon, "to honesty and sincerity of conversation with men" that one had to look for "the true face of Christianity." The anglican strategy of opposition to the puritan interpretation of Christian duties was, in effect, a detour around the First Table to the Second. It rested upon two stout and endlessly reiterated arguments. The first was that no man could consider himself anything other than damned if he were a rebel and a schismatic. To disobey the prince by rebellion and the Church of England by schism was the deadliest kind of sin and a conclusive sign of reprobation if it went unrepented. The second argument was that no man could have assurance of salvation if he were guilty of the sin of uncharitableness. One form of uncharitableness was the judging of others by calling them superstitious idolaters, oppressors of Christian liberty, and the like. The second part of chapter 4 deals more fully with the anglican conception of obedience, and the second section of chapter 5 treats that of charity. What needs to be stressed here is that both of these duties are performed toward and for men and are therefore derived from the Second Table of the Decalogue. The Anglicans reacted against the theological and practical intricacy of puritan arguments against idolatry and for justification and sanctification by dogmatically asserting the authority of the king and his bishops and by insisting upon a distinctively anglican moral order. It was a moral order resting upon their conceptions of obedience and charity and reinforced by the dispensation of grace through a unified national church. Clarendon exemplified all this perfectly. "Let us not," he wrote, "perplex ourselves with hard words of justification and merit, which signify no more or less than they who use them intend they should." Puritans had been accused of boiling down all religion to the ear, but Anglicans could equally be accused of contracting it to the hand. "Though it is not easy to know all that we may believe," wrote Clarendon, "it is not at all hard to know what we are to do."[55]

55. Sanderson, 2:226; Farindon, 1:221; *Contemplations*, pp. 414, 424. Richard Bancroft (the year before he became Archbishop of Canterbury) spoke at the

Although the most prominent aspects of the anglican moral order are to be treated in subsequent chapters, something more may be said here of the anglican method of preaching and practising moral duties.

Underlying the anglican conception of a moral order characterized by obedience and charity was an assumption about human nature. The assumption was that whatever the distance of Adam's fall and whatever the extent of damage to human moral faculties from it, it was still possible to think in terms of the *Imitatio Christi*, not only as a goal but as a goal capable of a considerable measure of fulfillment. Anglican divines frequently recommended that Christians use Christ as an exemplar for human behavior, and laymen took the doctrine quite seriously.[56] Puritans, on the other hand, spoke a great deal of the importance of "possessing" Christ or having an "interest" or "portion" in him, but they rarely suggested the use of Christ's actions as a model. Professor A. G. Dickens has noted that Tudor Puritans did little in the way of developing a Christology. They did little more in this direction as they developed their covenant theology in the seventeenth century. The puritan relationship with Christ was often intimate, but seldom imitative. Thomas

---

Hampton Court Conference in favor of a praying rather than a preaching ministry and denounced those who place "all religion in the ear." In Barlow's account, excerpted in Robert Ashton, ed., *James I By His Contemporaries*, p. 179.

56. In this Anglicans were following a pre-Reformation tradition. Norman Pettit cites Thomas M. Lindsay's view that the question of how man attains saving grace "divides Medieval reformers, such as Wycliffe, from Reformation thinkers. . . . The Medieval solution, he points out, is by the imitation of Christ, while the Reformation answer is justification by faith." *The Heart Prepared*, pp. 29–30n. Roger Lovatt traces the movement of manuscript copies of Thomas à Kempis's famous devotional work before the appearance of the first printed editions in "*The Imitation of Christ* in Late Medieval England," *Transactions of the Royal Historical Society*, 5th ser., 18 (1968): 97–121. Gordon Rupp noted that in à Kempis there is a "moralism" which "incorporates a good deal of Stoicism in the tradition of Boethius." Further, in Erasmus's *Enchiridion* (influenced by à Kempis), "To a dangerous extent classical morality has replaced the Biblical ethic." "Patterns of Salvation in the First Age of the Reformation," *AR* 57 (1966): 54–55. This sentiment seems to have carried over into the seventeenth century. Gerald R. Cragg, writing of anglican theology after 1660, concluded that "there was no longer any deep concern with the doctrine of grace; men emphasized the beneficial example which Christ had left us, not the atoning work he had wrought on our behalf." *From Puritanism to the Age of Reason*, p. 30. As my following paragraphs suggest, I think that this attitude was characteristic of many Anglicans well before the Restoration. See also Allison, *The Rise of Moralism*, chaps. 3, 4.

Hooker suggested the reason when he said that "two contrary extremes cannot meet together. . . . That Christ and ourselves are two such contrary extremes is easy to see from their contrary originals, contrary effects." Our "selves" are of earth and thus carnal and sensual, whereas Christ is of heaven and thus heavenly.[57] This radical view of human depravity militated against the more optimistic anglican view of human perfectability (or, at least, a less dire depravity). The distinction is again a relative one, but it is nonetheless significant. Anglicans did not preach that moral perfection could be attained in this life. Indeed, they explicitly rejected the possibility of it. But, as we have seen, they did generally regard the human will as more puissant than the Puritans did.

While Puritans such as Hooker hammered on the contrariety of grace and nature, Anglicans such as Farindon said that "Christ came not to destroy the law of nature but to establish and improve it."[58] God's grace was involved in every choice of a good action and every rejection of an evil one, but the human will played a more active part in the choosing process. It is in this sense that Clarendon wrote of God's grace in enabling us "to perform our duties to men with reasonable perfection." It was also what Jeremy Taylor had in mind when he asked John Evelyn for an account of his "progression in religion" by which he meant "that state of excellency" at which "good persons . . . arrive after a state of repentance and caution." Farindon spoke of the angels who, after our regeneration, delight to see us grow in Christ, becoming daily more and more like him. "They would," he said, "have us grow to ripeness and maturity, and be perfect men in Christ Jesus." It was the possibility of this kind of "reasonable perfection" which gave plausibility and force to the

57. A. G. Dickens, *The English Reformation*, p. 321; T. Hooker, *Heautonaparnumenos*, pp. 47–48. Others scholars who have mentioned this point are M. M. Knappen, *Tudor Puritanism*, pp. 376ff. and Roger Sharrock, *John Bunyan*, p. 77: The "figure of Christ in his human nature enters little into puritan piety . . . but a central place is given to Christ's sacrifice on the Cross." For examples of puritan terminology see Doolittle, *Rebukes*, p. 117; Case, *Correction*, pp. 99–100; *WP* 1:240, 253

58. Farindon, 1:221. This view rested in turn upon a more generous conception of nature and natural man. Farindon argues that the Golden Rule is taken from nature, "our first schoolmistress." Nature was not a wholly malignant teacher because the "rule of behavior which our Savior set up is taken out of the treasury of nature."1:217.

Anglicans' frequent injunctions to use Christ's behavior as a model. His actions were touchstones by which the true Christian's life could be assessed.[59]

Benjamin Whichcote, Provost of King's College, Cambridge, pointed to his differences on this subject with the puritan Anthony Tuckney during an exchange of letters (probably in 1650 or 1651). Tuckney, then Master of Emmanuel College, had objected to the content of Whichcote's weekly sermons in the University church, Great Saint Mary's. In Tuckney's view, Whichcote was undermining Christ's atoning role by preaching "a kind of moral divinity . . . only with a tincture of Christ added, nay a Platonic faith united to God." Whichcote answered that although we had to know about Christ's atonement for our sins and profess our belief in it, we must also become "truly God-like or conform to God, through Christ being formed in us." He wrote, "I cannot but marvel to see you balance matters of knowledge against principles of goodness and seem to insist on Christ less as a principle of divine nature in us than as a sacrifice for us." Similarly, Ralph Cudworth in 1648 spoke of the way in which "the life of Christ deeply rooted in his heart . . . is the chemical elixir" upon which the true Christian feeds; "without the life of Christ dwelling in us, whatsoever opinions we entertain of him, Christ is only named by us, he is not known." God became man "not only to cover sin by spreading the purple robe of Christ's death" over it but to free us from sin itself "by the spirit of Christ dwelling in our hearts."[60]

The elevated tone of the anglican Imitatio Christi theme is contained in Archbishop Leighton's plea to good Christians to attain a likeness to Christ himself: "There is a noble guest within us, O, let all our business be to entertain him honorably." The Scottish prelate was a reader of Thomas a Kempis's devotional classic, the favorite devotional work of Anthony Farindon's intimate friend, the "ever memorable John Hales." It is not unlikely that Hales's affection for the book warmed after he bade John Calvin good-night. Bishop Jeremy Taylor, however, produced the most ex-

---

59. *Contemplations*, p. 535; Taylor, 1:xciii; Farindon, 1:55. See also Chillingworth, 3:39; Whichcote, 1:153; Cudworth, p. 46.

60. Tuckney and Whichcote in Cragg, pp. 36, 39, 49; Cudworth, pp. 16, 18, 29–30.

tensive anglican elaboration of the idea. *The Life of Christ: or the Great Exemplar* was first published in 1649 and was extremely popular thereafter. Taylor wrote it for the expressed purpose of drawing Englishmen's attentions away from acrimonious debates about church government and toward the essentials of the Christian faith. In the dedication to Lord Hatton, he wrote that he was "weary and toiled with rowing up and down in the seas of questions" which had agitated Christendom. He admitted uncertainty about many of them but he was "most certain that by living in the religion and fear of God, in obedience to the King, in the charities and duties" proper to Christianity, he would attain "that end which is perfective of human nature, and which will never be attained by disputing."[61] Taylor sought to bypass disputation by making the imitation of Christ the method of truly religious practice. In doing so, he and many other Anglicans developed a theme which was almost as distinctive of Anglicanism as covenant theology was of Puritanism. The Anglicans emphasized the "Word Incarnate" rather than the "Word Preached" and concentrated upon the Second Table virtues of obedience, charity, unity, and peaceableness.

Jeremy Taylor's "Exhortation to the Imitation of the Life of Christ" (part of the preface to the *Life of Christ*) states that it was part of God's plan that Christ's example should provide light for all men to walk by and to be a "guiding star, and pillar of fire to us in our journey." This must have been God's design because, Taylor argued, only "one minute of his intolerable passion" would have been more than sufficient atonement for the sins of "ten thousand worlds." Thus the atonement for human sin, for all its awesome importance, was not all of the Son's mission to men. His life provided a model, an ideal, a standard, and a vision of holiness for all to emulate. The actions of men offered all sorts of good and bad examples, but as Sanderson told Charles I's court at Greenwich in 1637, a man's example shows only that a thing is possible—"it is Christ's example only that can render it warrantable." Anthony Farindon reflected that, as God made us in his own image, "so in Christ, who came to renew it in us, 'he hath showed us a more

61. Robert Leighton, *Works*, pp. xvi, xviii–xix; Taylor, 2:xiii–xiv. Hales's break with Calvinism is documented in Farindon, 1:xlix.

excellent way' " to work out our salvation in "this common shop of change." Through him we learn to obey God's commands because he was "the best teacher and the greatest example of obedience." Thus the following of Christ's example became in itself a means of grace. Taylor explained this phenomenon as comparable to the development of habits. "The very exercise of the action" of imitating the life of Christ produces, he said, "a facility of the action, and in some proportion becomes the cause of itself."[62]

This dynamic conception of the duty of imitating Christ was tenable for Anglicans because they believed that men were equipped to perform it. Taylor interpreted Paul's injunction, "Put ye on the Lord Jesus Christ" to mean that Christ's example is a garment fitted to man's proportions. As a garment fits the part of the body, "so should we put on Christ, and imitate the whole body of his sanctity, conforming to every integral part, and express him in our lives." Not only was it possible for men to imitate Christ—it was easy. In matters of faith as well as in matters of morality, Taylor held that Christ's rule was "fitted to every understanding; it was true, necessary, short, easy, and intelligible," and therefore "it is a very great stupidity and unreasonableness not to live with him in the imitation of so holy and so prompt a piety." The important fact here was that Christ had been a man and knew and understood human infirmities. His compassion was great. "It is no wisdom," said Farindon, "so to honor Christ as to take from [Him] his humanity." According to Taylor, this experience of common humanity underlay the "easiness, compliance and proportion to us" of Christ's example. He lived and worked, not among captains of state or great mystics, but among ordinary, humble folk. Except for the miracles, the examples of piety were "the actions of a very holy, but of an ordinary life."[63]

The assiduous imitation of the Great Exemplar necessarily produced certain fruits in the behavior of the imitator. Thomas Pierce urged his listeners to "put ye on the Lord Jesus Christ and adorn his doctrine by a conformity to his life." This was, said Pierce, nothing less than to "prove that we are in Christ, by that demon-

62. Taylor, 2:lix–lx; Sanderson, 2:207; Farindon, 1:101, 30; Taylor, 2:lxv–lxvi. See also Sanderson, 2:306.
63. Taylor, 2:lxi, lxiv, lxv; Farindon, 1:248; Taylor, 2:lxiii.

strative argument of our becoming new creatures." It was to demonstrate conversion to Christ by exhibiting his virtues. Always prominent in the lists of these were peaceableness, obedience, charity, and other such Second Table duties. In the welter of parties and opinions, John Gauden characterized the virtues which conform us "most to that highest and divinest pattern of Christ's mind and conversation" as those whose effect is to make us "more godly, more holy, pure, just, good, humble, peaceable, charitable, self-denying and conscientious" in all things. It is "the circumstance of our Savior Christ's example," said Hales, which urges upon us the duty of dealing tenderly with our erring brethren. "If you cannot find yourselves arrived as yet to that height of perfection" in the obedience of divine commandments, proclaimed Chillingworth, "take an example above all examples, an example beyond all imaginable exceptions, even our blessed Savior Jesus Christ himself." Sydenham chose to emphasize that "there is no reconciliation with God, except there be first peace with thy brother." Since righteousness and peace were characteristic of God the Father and God the Son, he insisted that we who are "his sons by adoption" must also be his sons "by imitation." As we shall shortly see, when Anglicans used such terms as obedience and peaceableness, they were condemning all who disturbed the civil peace, regardless of claims to religious sanction for their actions. Taylor was careful to remind his readers that Christ had been "as obedient to government as the most humble children of the kingdom." Heaven, said Farindon, had received Christ and would "receive none but those who are like him; . . . not those many antichrists whose whole life is a contradiction to him," however they tried to justify their malice and oppression with his name. It was in the nature of things that such men would persecute the true, charitable Christians who, as Farindon put it, went about "doing all those things which Jesus did and taught"—works of charity for the lame, blind, hungry, widowed, orphaned, and all other suffering human beings.[64]

The obedient, charitable Christians would be slandered and assaulted as Christ had been, but their duties toward their fellow

64. Pierce, p. 25; John Gauden, *The Love of Truth and Peace*, p. 27; Hales, 2:88–89; Chillingworth, 3:178–79; Sydenham, *Occasions*, pp. 182–83; Taylor, 2:lix; Farindon, 1:51, 431. See also Whichcote, 1:128, 165.

men had been clearly demonstrated by the Great Exemplar. In
the affliction which the world would heap upon them, they would,
as Clarendon wrote, "come the nearer to the sufferings of our
Savior himself, which is a great honor and glory to us." Those
Christians who did succeed in the effort to "imitate his meekness
and humility and patience in the bearing of them, so far imitate him
as he hath put into our power to do," could be assured of "such a
reward" that there need be no regrets for worldly troubles. Clarendon's cousin, Dr. Edward Hyde, gave his fellow Anglicans the same
reassurance. The greatest comfort available to the afflicted man was
"the comfort of salvation," and assurance of it came with the imitation of Christ. This was so, he said, because Christ "most sees his
own image in you . . . when he sees himself fully represented,
not only in your doings, but also in your sufferings." The imitation
of Christ, most notably of those precedents which fitted the moral
order which we have begun to describe, was thus a prominent and
important means to attain a firm hope of Christ's favor as He judged
both the quick and the dead. Unlike Puritans, Anglicans found it
possible to think of themselves as achieving a significant measure of
perfection in their "conversation" among men. They could achieve
what He asked, because He had not asked for more than they could
do. They believed that Christ's example was clear enough for all
to see and understand—there was no need, and there could be
danger, in the attempt of the Puritans to make every man a theologian. The anglican view of the potential goodness of the human
will made the imitation of Christ not just a possibility, but a positive duty. It was, as Farindon put it, Christ's duty to be like us.
Therefore, "a great necessity will lie upon us, by our covenant
with him, to be like unto him; and woe unto us, if we be not!"[65]

65. *Contemplations*, p. 544; Hyde, *Legacy*, pp. 105–06; Farindon, 1:45.

4

THE FRUITS OF
CONVERSION:
OBEDIENCE AND PEACE

It is all one to them, what the people do, or how they are instructed, provided they be obedient; and according to their worldly wisdom, they esteem it a great piece of folly, to attempt any
alteration or reformation, as if it were a piece of great wisdom,
and a desirable thing to command a people involved in a brutish
ignorance of things necessary, and especially of their salvation.

Sleidanus to Protector Somerset (May 1548)

You that be of the court, and especially the sworn chaplains, beware of a lesson that a great man taught me at my first coming to
the court; . . . 'Contrary not the King, . . . follow him, go with
him.' Marry, out upon this counsel. . . . The drop of rain maketh
a hole in the stone, not by violence, but by oft falling. Likewise
a prince must be turned not violently, but he must be won by a
little and a little. He must have his duty told him, but it must be
done with humbleness.

Hugh Latimer to Edward VI (1549)

Mr. False-peace, thou art here indicted by the name of False-
peace . . . for that thou didst most wickedly and satanically
bring, hold and keep the town of Mansoul, both in her apostacy
and in her hellish rebellion, in a false, groundless and dangerous
peace and damnable security, to the dishonour of the King, the
transgression of his law and the great damage of the town of
Mansoul. What sayest thou? Art thou guilty of this indictment,
or not?

John Bunyan, *The Holy War* (1682)

His principles are like chaos, a gallimofry of negatives. He talks of
nothing but new light and prophecy, spiritual incomes, indwell-

ings, . . . to the which the zealous twang of his nose adds no
small efficacy. . . . He prays for the king, but with more distinctions and mental reservations than an honest man would
have in taking the Covenant.

Anti-Whig tract (ca. 1679)

Woe to him that claims obedience when it is not due;
woe to him that refuses it when it is!

Thomas Carlyle, *Heroes and Hero-Worship* (1841)

On Christmas Day, 1647, a riot occurred in the City of London. An
account of it was quickly published by an apoplectic gentleman who
identified himself only by his initials, "G. S." The people had,
despite ordinances prohibiting the "superstitious" celebration of
that feast, "set up holly and ivy on top of a pinnacle." The lord
mayor sent a marshal to "pull down these gawds," but the crowd
threatened him, and he barely escaped a beating. The lord mayor
himself then went to the scene with a group of halberdiers, one of
whom struck a member of the crowd abusing him, a Welshman
named Williams. The man soon recovered—but the Devil, that
"father of lies and liars," spread the rumor that Williams was an
apprentice and had been killed on the lord mayor's orders. G. S.
hotly insisted that the man was not an apprentice but a servant,
and that the mayor, far from ordering that the man be struck down,
had reprimanded the soldier who had struck the blow. In any case,
the false rumor soon inflamed the apprentices—the rebellious
students of their day—who quickly posted notification of meetings
for the planning of their revenge. G. S.'s account, obviously rushed
into print in an effort to head off further trouble and to defend the
mayor, depicted the confrontation using elements familiar to
newspaper readers today: an assembly of a large number of "demon-
strators," the intervention characterized by "police brutality," the
accidental creation of a "martyr," and a confused aftermath of
angry charges and countercharges.

G. S.'s explanation of the cause and cure of this trouble is, at first,
less familiar. "That all this is but the fruit of God's anger against us
for our sins, I know," he said, and "this iniquity will be our ruin, if
not timely prevented by humiliation and by reformation." G. S. was,
however, certain that the heart of the matter was that the ap-

prentices should remember their place in the social order and obey all who were above them in it. He indignantly asked, "Is not Jane in her own conceit as good as her lady? Doth not Jack think himself a gentleman?" They should repent of their "horrid wickedness" in spreading lies about his honor, the lord mayor, and humble themselves before God for daring to "speak evil of dignities."[1]

In his treatment of this trivial incident, G. S. raised the most momentous question in English political life in the middle decades of the seventeenth century—that of the meaning of the Christian doctrine of obedience to the higher powers.[2] To him, of course, there was no question involved—the apprentices should cheerfully and unreservedly obey their superiors. He called his little tract *A Word in Season: or A Check to Disobedience*, cited Romans 13:1 and 5 on the title page, and thought nothing more need be said. The doctrine embodied in the thirteenth chapter of Paul's letter to the Romans seems quite unequivocal: "Let every soul be subject to the higher powers. For there is no power but of God: the powers that be are ordained of God." Those who resist the powers that be are resisting God, and they shall therefore "receive to themselves damnation" (verse 2). Subjection to these powers is not to be performed merely from fear of wrath, "but also for conscience sake" (verse 5). Obedience to the higher powers is required of all Christians in the revealed Word of God. It is part and parcel of the duty of Christian obedience of the whole body of divine law for man.[3]

1. "G. S. Gent.," *A Word in Season* (1648). Thomason's date is Jan. 13. Some attitudes never change. A letter to the *Times* (15 Dec. 1967), in answer to the question, "What is the malaise affecting the English people?" said, "It is the lack of respect towards those in authority."

2. This entire subject with its varied ramifications has received a great deal of attention from many historians. The following works are particularly useful: Margaret Atwood Judson, *The Crisis of the Constitution*, esp. chaps. 4, 5, 8; A. S. P. Woodhouse, ed., *Puritanism and Liberty*, introduction and pt. 3; Edmund S. Morgan, ed., *Puritan Political Ideas*, esp. introduction and pts. 1, 2; Richard Schlatter, *Richard Baxter and Puritan Politics*, introduction; J. W. Allen, *English Political Thought, 1603–1660*, vol. 1 (1603–44); William M. Lamont, *Godly Rule*; J. H. Hexter, *The Reign of King Pym*; Michael Walzer, *The Revolution of the Saints*; Richard Tuck, "*Power* and *Authority* in Seventeenth-century England," *HJ* 17 (1974): 43–61. Among the many treatments of this subject in the Tudor period, see Christopher Morris, *Political Thought in England: Tyndale to Hooker*; Whitney R. D. Jones, *The Tudor Commonwealth, 1529–1559*, chap. 4.

3. For a good example of a sermon which presents this argument in a straightforward way, see Farindon, 4:629–40.

It need hardly be said that the apparent clarity of Saint Paul's dicta on this subject is deceptive. No Stuart Englishman maintained that the higher powers had to be obeyed in *everything*. If, for example, the Turks had suddenly conquered England and ordered that all Englishmen worship Allah, no one would have held that Pauline doctrine bound them to do so. All agreed that there were some situations in which obedience could not rightfully be demanded. Dr. Sanderson told the royal court at Whitehall in 1632 that there might come times when we are not bound to please "our earthly masters, or captains, or parents, or princes" by obeying them. "If it be their pleasure we should do something that lawfully we may not: we must disobey, though we displease." He was quick to close the door he had just unlocked by warning against "an evil disobedience" that pretended "an unlawfulness where there is none." Oliver Cromwell wrote to his friend Colonel Hammond that "Authorities and powers are the ordinance of God. This or that species is of human institution, and limited, some with larger, others with stricter bands. . . . [But] I do not therefore think the authorities may do anything, and yet such obedience [be] due." Cromwell went on to assert a right of resistance. Anglicans such as Sanderson and Clarendon limited men to a passive disobedience. All clearly agreed that situations were conceivable in which the true Christian would have to disobey the higher powers. "Indeed, dear Robin," continued Cromwell to Hammond (then serving as Charles I's jailer on the Isle of Wight), "the query is, whether ours be such a case? This ingenuously is the true question."[4]

Anglicans and Puritans had different answers to Cromwell's "true question." These answers will not be found in simple stereotypes. Few Anglicans were slavish toadies to Charles I or his son. Few Puritans were revolutionary ideologues, seeking revolution for its own sake (or, as some now have it, for the fun of it). Seventeenth-century Englishmen were striving to understand and to obey God's will because only by doing so could they achieve any confidence that

---

4. Sanderson, 2:55; Abbott, 1:697 (25 Nov. 1648). Cromwell's letter is reprinted in Robert S. Paul, *The Lord Protector*, pp. 406–10. See also *Contemplations*, pp. 508–09 and Taylor, 4:145: "We must obey all human laws appointed and constituted by lawful authority, . . . all laws, I mean, which are not against the law of God."

their souls were saved. "And who knows not," asked Sir Richard Baker, "that obedience is better and to God more acceptable than any sacrifice?" "There can be no excuse for swerving from the precise rule which God hath prescribed to us," wrote Clarendon in his first exile. A failure of obedience in any "fundamental point of our religion," whether to save either fortune or life "from the fury of cruel and bloody tyrants" was, he believed, an insult to God's "all-seeing providence." All human life was the reaping of a sad harvest of troubles of body and soul, and the only comfort which could be gleaned was that which came through a conscientious effort to obey God's will. As the anglican Anthony Farindon put it, obedience to divine laws and commands is "the true mark and character of a servant of God. . . . obedience is the only spring from whence the waters of comfort flow, an everlasting foundation on which alone joy and peace will settle and rest." The puritan Richard Sibbes defined the ungodly as those who "obey not the Gospel." He maintained that "a little obedience is worth all the discourse and contemplation in the world"; only the power of godliness expressed in a man's life by obedience to God's will could "yield real comfort in the day of trial."[5]

Farindon was a generation younger than Sibbes, and he spoke after witnessing the collapse of the Stuart monarchy and the Church of England under the pressure of the men of the Long Parliament, many of whom had much the same understanding of Christian obedience as Sibbes had. A good many of them had doubtless learned it from Sibbes himself in his sermons in Cambridge and at Gray's Inn (John Pym was one of the executors of Sibbes's will). Yet both Sibbes and Farindon (and indeed Anglicans and Puritans generally) shared the conviction that there could be no comfort in this life or the next for rebels against God's will. Although such rebellion was clearly the most heinous of sins, it was logically separable from rebellion against the will of the prince. Clarendon and Sanderson, no less than Cromwell, said as much. As the preceding chapter demonstrated, Laud's insistence upon what he called

5. Baker, *Meditations and Motives for Prayer Upon the Seven Dayes of the Weeke* (1642), p. 42; *Contemplations*, p. 498; Farindon, 1:196, 195; Sibbes, *Cordialls*, pp. 263, 267. See also Preston, *Life*, pt. 2, pp. 150–52, and T. Hooker, *Lessons*, p. 28: "Try thyself by sincere obedience, canst thou speak the language of universal obedience? If not, you are not true Christians."

"the external decent worship of God"[6] and his prosecution of those who contended it had convinced the Puritans that the ecclesiastical authorities were adamantly opposed to the puritan conception of God's will as revealed in the First Table. They felt forced to choose between obedience to the higher powers and to God himself—a dilemma which should never have occurred, especially as God had shown Englishmen so much light in the "first reformation" in Tudor times. It is the purpose of this chapter to explore puritan and anglican conceptions of the obedience a good Christian owed to the authorities, and to show how they were based upon the values attached to the duties of the Two Tables. These values and the priorities which they established led to the elaboration of a set of interrelated imperatives for Christian conduct.[7] To abide by these imperatives was outwardly to exhibit the fruits of true, inward faith. The imperatives were the marks, signs, or touchstones by which true obedience was tested.

THE PURITAN IMPERATIVES

The City of London in March, 1643, was, to put it mildly, an awkward place and time for a sermon commemorating the inauguration of King Charles I. Puritans were always delighted to celebrate November 5, the anniversary of the Gunpowder Plot. That occasion offered great scope for denouncing the papists and their fellow travelers. Equally welcome was November 17—the anniversary of the accession of "Queen Elizabeth (that glorious glorious Deborah)." Melodious were the changes that could be rung not only upon the deliverance from "the idolatry of the former reign" but the joys of having a godly magistrate.[8] But March 27 carried with it no such pleasant overtones. Joseph Caryl had the

6. From his speech at the censure of Prynne, Bastwick, and Burton in Star Chamber. In S. Prall, *The Puritan Revolution*, p. 84.

7. I am here borrowing and adapting to my purposes J. H. Hexter's notion of a "fabric of imperatives." See his article, "The Loom of Language and the Fabric of Imperatives: The Case of *Il Principe* and *Utopia*," *AHR* 69:(1964) 945–68.

8. Burges, *The First Sermon*, p. 53. Marshall preached, on the same day, *A Sermon* (1641). These sermons are analyzed in the appendix, below. See also Gouge, *Mercies Memoriall* (1645). For examples of "Powder Day" sermons, see Burges, *Another Sermon*; Matthew Newcomen, *The Craft and Cruelty of the Churches Adversaries*; Sibbes, "The Saints Safety in Evill Times," in *Cordialls*.

delicate and difficult task of preaching before the lord mayor (the leading City Puritan, Isaac Pennington), the aldermen, and the "worshipful companies" on the eighteenth anniversary of the beginning of the first Charles's troubled reign. London was in full scale rebellion against the king. On the very day that Caryl spoke to the City leaders, the parliament at Westminster passed an ordinance for the sequestration of the estates of all who supported the king. Earlier in the month, the parliament had ordered the fortification of London, and even the lord mayor, together with his equally puritan wife, busied himself in the work along with thousands of others.[9]

The sermon which Caryl preached that day (and later published with a dedication to Pennington) faithfully reflects the central themes of puritan preaching on the subject of obedience to the higher powers during the middle decades of the seventeenth century. His text was the prayer of David, the kingly psalmist, that Jehovah would grant to his son Solomon "a clear light to understand his will and intent" in matters "relating to government." Caryl maintained that it was as true for the king as for any man that although "the word of God in general" had been given to the church long ago, yet it "may be truly said to be given to every soul, in the day of their conversion." In the unlikely event that the aldermen missed the drift of his discourse here at the outset, Caryl went on to make his meaning unmistakable—magistrates, and most of all the chief magistrate, should be truly converted, godly men. The "special endowments of a king" are an ability to judge according to divine precepts and "a righteousness of God, which some neglecting, take in and trust to a righteousness of their own." Magistrates could not be ignorant of God's revealed will, nor could

9. Pearl, p. 183 (see pp. 176–84) for her sketch of Pennington. A critic said that London's citizenry elected him to the Long Parliament "for his known zeal by his keeping a fasting Sabbath throughout his shrievalty." Zagorin, p. 146. His wife had been converted while reading Preston on prayer. C. Hill, *Puritanism and Revolution*, p. 245. Caryl preached his sermon at Christchurch in Newgate Street—"a large structure where the two houses of parliament, the lord mayor, aldermen, and common council were in the habit of meeting on important occasions." Haller, *Liberty and Reformation in the Puritan Revolution*, p. 226. See Hexter, *King Pym*, pp. 103–16, for an account of the early months of 1643, the beginning of the Roundheads' worst troubles. On the sequestration ordinance, see Gardiner, *War*, 1:98–101.

they "establish their own righteousness," for those who did so had "repealed God's judgments, and enacted their own." In Caryl's text, David had said that when God's people were governed righteously, even "the mountains shall bring peace to the people." Caryl's gloss upon this phrase is a thundering indictment of Charles I's Personal Rule, and an explanation of the cause of the Civil War.

> While error was maintained, which is unrighteousness in opinion; while idolatry was winked at and superstition contended for which are unrighteousness in worship; while profaneness was encouraged, which is unrighteousness in practice; while oppression was countenanced, which is unrighteousness in government. Can any one be to learn why the mountains and the hills brought forth war? . . . While many . . . of God's people and of God's poor . . . were stubbed up and rooted out of most places in the kingdom, not only from great towns and cities, but from the very mountains and hills, so that they could not live quietly anywhere.[10]

Unrighteousness in church and state matters had, the City fathers were told, provoked God's judgment of civil war upon a sinful nation. There was, Caryl continued, "a great cry for peace, desire is upon the wing to overtake and recall our departing if not departed peace." The negotiations for the Treaty of Oxford were in progress as Caryl spoke, and the preacher said that it is "our duty to cry after it." "Only let the point in hand direct us in this pursuit. For what though . . . the King and Parliament at this day treat for peace? Yet all this cannot obtain peace, unless there be a cry after, a treaty about, yea an entreating for righteousness." No good man could forbear tears at "the wounds of this nation, weeping aloud every day; and yet if we should skin over those wounds, before righteousness hath searched them to the bottom, I tremble to think how quickly they will fester."[11]

10. Caryl, *Davids Prayer for Solomon*, pp. 3, 6, 24. Note also Preston's view that all men, including magistrates, had their general and particular callings from God. Thus "every man that doth anything for his own end arrogates that to himself which is the Lord's . . . an high kind of idolatry." *Life*, pt. 1, p. 147. On the puritan doctrine of calling, see E. S. Morgan, *Puritan Political Ideas*, pp. xvii–xiix, 35–55.

11. Caryl, *Davids Prayer*, p. 25.

It was not until the end of his sermon that Caryl referred to the anniversary he sought to commemorate. "I know," he said, that this is usually "a day of anointing the king with praises," but he urged his listeners to pray for the king instead. It was a time not for rejoicing but for lamentation. "Yea I hope it will not be distasteful, I know it is seasonable at this time to say even unto the king and unto the queen, as the prophet Jeremiah directs . . . 'sit down, humble your selves.'" With a curious mixture of caution and boldness, Caryl prophesied, "I will not add that which follows, I have no commission for it, 'for your principalities shall come down, even the crown of your glory.'" The sharp point of this ominous jeremiad was slightly—but only slightly—blunted in its peroration as Caryl urged that all the higher powers, "king . . . princes . . . nobles . . . magistrates . . . prophets," bow down and confess their sins in the hope of divine mercy for bleeding England and Ireland. Then it could be hoped that "holy prayers will at last over-match unholy counsels."[12] One is not surprised to read that when Charles I was offered the assistance of a committee of puritan divines which included Caryl shortly before his execution, he refused to see them.[13]

Caryl's sermon contains what might be called the puritan imperatives on the subject of obedience to the higher earthly powers. No Puritan who hoped for heaven—which is to say no Puritan—could fail to observe these dicta conscientiously. They were the signs and marks of the "new obedience" of a truly converted man. The contrast between these and the anglican imperatives discussed below will be apparent. The Puritans were convinced that (1) the true Christian would fully and cheerfully obey the commands of godly magistrates, but that he would not actively obey ungodly commands issued by other magistrates, most especially those relating to First Table duties. (2) He would, on the contrary, beware of acquiescing in the sinfulness of rulers or any other men because it was just such sins which God judged with afflictions like tumult and war. (3) He would instead contend for the true religion, regardless of the consequences for the civil peace, because only by doing so could he

12. Ibid., pp. 36–38.
13. Daniel Neal, *History of the Puritans*, 2:94. The others were Calamy, Viner, Dell, and Goodwin—Caryl may have been the most moderate of the lot. According to C. V. Wedgwood, the Goodwin was John Goodwin. *The Trial of Charles I*, p. 188.

maintain the only peace that good men would be likely to have in the world, the inward peace of a good conscience.

Obedience Insofar as the Word of God Allows

Implicit in Caryl's sermon, and implicit or explicit in most puritan writing, was the conviction that the truly godly man could perform cheerful, complete obedience only to equally godly magistrates. Puritan preachers preferred to accentuate the positive when the subject of obedience was raised. They spoke fulsomely of the rich benefits of a godly magistracy for the temporal and spiritual estates of all subjects. Caryl hoped for a new day in which "His Majesty judging with righteousness and his people obeying with cheerfulness, the mountains may bring forth peace to all, and all may bring glory to God in advancing the kingdom of our Lord Jesus Christ." The general of the London militia, Philip Skippon, paraphrased from Scriptures an equally glowing vision of a future time when "the Lord will restore good government among us, namely good judges and counsellors as former times . . . so that all good government in the Commonwealth shall be maintained," and when "the Lord will restore his pure worship among us . . . we shall be freed from evil teachers and [He] will provide for us good teachers." Caryl returned to the matter in the course of his sermons on Job. To honor all magistrates was "required in the Fourth Commandment; we must honor our civil father, the father of our country, as well as our natural father, the father of the family." The duty of honoring and obeying good magistrates for conscience's sake was, he continued, clearly exemplified in the story of David. It was of such an excellent magistrate that Samuel, "the divine historian, takes occasion to report the people's satisfaction with all his actions." Caryl was careful to say that this did not mean that "the people swallowed all the king's actions by an implicit faith or cried up . . . his vices for virtues." It did, however, mean that "David was so . . . righteous in all his administrations to the people, that they took high content in him and were pleased with him to the full."[14]

14. Caryl, *Davids Prayer*, p. 36; Skippon, pp. 190–91; Caryl, *Job* (chaps. 27–29), pp. 487, 501. The reference to the Fourth Commandment is a slip—he must have meant the Fifth. William Lamont has rightly emphasized that almost all writers between 1603 and 1660, Anglicans no less than Puritans, were intent upon main-

To obey such a righteous prince or chief magistrate as David or Job was a fundamental duty, and Puritans were agreed that no man could have any assurance of the validity of his conversion unless he performed it. But the inevitable and doubtless intentional effect of all this preaching of the ideal godly prince was to emphasize the width of the gap between the ideal and real in Stuart England. The puritan saint obeyed all "lawful," "warrantable," "godly," "righteous" commands not only of godly magistrates, but of all magistrates. Caryl pointed out that when Paul wrote that every soul is subject to the higher powers, he wrote it to Roman Christians who were under Nero's authority—and Christ's injunction to render unto Caesar his things had been in reference to Tiberius Caesar. Tiberius was no saint and Nero was "a monster of men." Nevertheless, conscientious obedience was due to them and to all in authority at all times and in all places—with one utterly crucial reservation. It was due only insofar as the Word of God allowed. This proviso was stated in various ways by various writers. One typical formulation occurs in the notes taken by one of the members of Sir Thomas Barrington's family in Essex. Sir Thomas represented Essex in the Short and Long Parliaments, and his chaplain, James Harrison, was one of the many puritan lecturers who had been suspended on Bishop Wren's orders. Harrison was discussing the text in which Paul reminded his Hebrew followers of the story of Moses, whose persecuted parents had hidden him from the pharaoh's agents, "and they were not afraid of the king's commandment" (Hebrews 11:23). The suspended lecturer told the assembled Barringtons: "And here we are occasioned to consider how we ought to obey magistrates—which is with subordination of obedience to God, as wherein we cannot obey both in any act which will not consist with our obedience to God."[15]

Puritans agreed that under ideal circumstances domestic, religious, and civil obedience should not conflict, but should blend harmoniously together in perfect service to God's injunctions. But

taining or obtaining obedience to godly magistracy in some form, and that the different forms were derived in part from differing millenarian expectations. See his *Godly Rule*.

15. Caryl, *Job* (chaps. 27–29), p. 488; Harrison on Hebrews 11:23. See also Walzer, pp. 233–34, 262–63, 293.

persons in authority were men, and by no means all of them were
regenerate.[16] Indeed, the great majority of men were not and could
never be regenerate—hence the need for the qualifying proviso.
John Benbrigge, a presbyterian minister of Ashburnham, Sussex,
asked his parishioners in the spring of 1646 to examine themselves
carefully in order to determine whether their sins were responsible
for England's continuing troubles (i.e., the continuing opposition to
the righteous leadership of the Parliament). Benbrigge was certain
that they were the expression of God's continuing anger at incom-
plete and imperfect reformation in family, church, and state. He
began with an extended survey of the domestic duties of husbands,
wives, parents, children, masters, and servants. During the course of
it, he interrogated children as to whether they were more obedient
to their parents "so far as may stand with your obedience to your
heavenly Father?" Benbrigge was preaching in fast-day exercises at
a time when the puritan movement was breaking into pieces. He
was deeply concerned in his sermons to oppose the looming danger
of Independency in the Parliament, in the army, and in the streets.
He stood in the uncomfortable shoes of the rebel who, after the successful conclusion of his revolt, finds the fruits of victory slipping out
of his grasp. All his instincts urged him to struggle against the
disorder and confusion which he saw to his left and to shore up the
authority of the presbyterian majority in the House of Commons.
Yet he could not betray his intellectual heritage by forgetting, even
when addressing himself to children, to include that historic proviso,
"so far as may stand with your obedience to your heavenly Father."
Henry Burton, an Independent who had been one of Laud's famous
victims in 1637, urged the same reservation upon his London
audience in 1641. Natural relationships must not "call me to stand
in opposition to Christ." The Christian must "deny obedience to his
father, so far as" his father hinders his "coming to Christ." "We
must not acknowledge father and mother in bidding us to do that
which Christ forbiddeth." Nor did Burton hesitate to point out the
corollary: "A Christian must deny himself in all civil relations, if
princes or states make laws against the law of Christ, against his

16. For example, Caryl, *Job* (chaps. 4–7), p. 214; "We know that kings are men,
and that's enough to prove they may do wrong."

religion, and his pure ordinances, threatening punishment to those that will not observe them."[17]

The proviso occurs again in an interesting context in the papers of John Winthrop. In the list of grievances "groaning for reformation" which was prepared for the 1624 Parliament, Winthrop included an objection to the "strict oath" which the ecclesiastical authorities required of churchwardens and other parish officials. The oath contained "more than fifty articles . . . and many of them are of little use, as whether is there bowing at the name of Jesus? whether do any go to hear a sermon abroad when none is at home? whether any work on the days called holy days?" The suggested remedy was simple—the oath should henceforth be administered with a short reservation: " 'So far as you are bound by God's law and standeth with a good conscience' or some like mitigation." The wording of the proviso clearly implies that Puritans objected to bowing at the name of Jesus and to restraining people from attending sermons, not because of their uselessness, but because obedience in these matters led Christians out of the narrow path laid out by God for their walking. Although the effect of such a "mitigation" would have been to emasculate an important means of enforcement of the program which Laud was to announce, it was perfectly reasonable from Winthrop's point of view. In this he seems to have been following Calvin almost to the letter. The great Genevan had written that the obedience due the higher powers must be performed—always with "this exception . . .; that it be not incompatible with obedience to Him to whose will . . . kings should be subject, . . . And indeed how preposterous were it, in pleasing men, to incur the offence of Him for whose sake you obey men!"[18]

17. Benbrigge, *Gods Fury*, p. 103; Burton, *A most Godly Sermon* (1641), sigs. A2 (verso), A3 (recto). Cf. Burton quoted in Zagorin, p. 196. Haller (pp. 150–59) provides a vivid account of the "martyrdom" of Bastwick, Burton, and Prynne and points out that Burton's troubles with Laud began with the sentiments which he expressed in a Gunpowder Day sermon. This proviso is in a sense the theological counterpart of the "legal doctrine of the prerogative" in Hexter's treatment of obedience theories (*King Pym*. pp. 180–90).

18. *WP*, 1:306; Calvin as quoted in A. S. P. Woodhouse, ed. *Puritanism and Liberty* p. [61]. In England, use of this proviso goes back at least as far as the reply of the bishops to Henry VIII in 1531—the document is reprinted in G. R. Elton, ed., *The Tudor Constitution*, p. 330. Archbishop Cranmer used it in a sermon against the Prayer Book rebels in 1549. Jasper Ridley, *Thomas Cranmer*, p. 297. Cf. Collinson, p. 266.

William Fenner, a puritan minister in Essex who was well known
as a casuist, sought to give his parishioners and his readers a sure
means of avoiding the offence to God which came from obeying
magistrates too uncritically. Although all obedience was for conscience's sake, he argued that Christians should distinguish between
a primary and a "secondary or relative bond of conscience." The
supreme or primary bond is "God's word," and the relative bond
"is only in relation to God's word, because God's word putteth
authority upon it." In this second category lay the authority of
parents over their children and masters over their servants as well as
magistrates over the people. Fenner took one page to explain "how
far the laws and commandments" of those authorities bind the
Christian conscience—and five pages to explain the circumstances in
which their commandments lost the power of binding conscience.
He maintained that authorities need not be obeyed when they
command acts which are "unlawful in themselves and contrary to
the word of God" (as worship of images) or which, if performed,
would necessarily lead to sin. Further, they cannot "overthrow the
liberty of Christianity" (as, for example, to enforce Jewish dietary
regulations), "for nothing can bind conscience when Christ doth
loose it." Finally, they are not to be "actively" obeyed when "they
command things indifferent to be absolutely necessary, to make
them idolatrous or superstitious." Fenner defined "idolatrous"
things in part as those which "are commanded for the substantial
perfection of religion, as though religion were imperfect without
them." Although he gave no examples at this point, one can hardly
doubt that such things as bowing at the name of Jesus and other
Laudian requirements were the targets of his casuistry. He added
that indifferent things which were not idolatrous were to be
obeyed.[19] As we have seen, however, the puritan conception of
idolatry was based on a comprehensive and distinctive interpreta-

19. Fenner, *Looking-Glasse*, pp. 176, 194–200. Fenner (1600–40) was a client and
at one point a chaplain to the Earl of Warwick. *DNB*. His works were apparently
popular—these two were collected editions in folio, 1651 and 1657. Parts of them
were printed in octavo as *Foure Profitable Treatises Very Useful for Christian Practise*
(1657) "for those that cannot go to the price of the greater volume." It was Fenner's
preaching in 1637 which began the conversion of John Rogers (later a leading Fifth
Monarchy man and troubler of Cromwell). Philip. G. Rogers, *The Fifth Monarchy
Men*, pp. 22–23. Cf. Nathaniel Bernard preaching in 1629 as quoted in Seaver,
Puritan Lectureships, p. 249.

tion of First Table duties. In matters of worship, little was indifferent. In this way, idolatry became central to the puritan technique for distinguishing between the will of God as revealed by his Son, his prophets, and his scribes, and obedience to the will of the Stuarts as revealed by Strafford, Laud, and Clarendon.

It is against this background that puritan injunctions to obedience to human authorities must be read. Puritans agreed that disobedience to "lawful," "warrantable," "godly," "righteous" commands was evidence for the absence of saving grace. But these apparently innocuous adjectives concealed a barb set to hook the ungodly holder of authority when he issued an order which contradicted the Word of God as they understood it. Those adjectives were almost invariably present in their discussions of the obedience due to principalities and powers. They could be read straightforwardly and unsuspiciously as meaning that all the magistrate's commands were indeed all that they should be. Anglicans often used them in just that way. But the terms were ambivalent, and Puritans used them with equal weight upon both their positive and their negative aspects. Active obedience was due only in response to commands which were in no way repugnant to the Word. Commands issued by rulers whose godliness was suspect were to be subjected to careful scrutiny, especially when there was even the faintest hint of idolatry. Fenner cited "that dreadful anathema at the end of God's book," which made it a damnable and unpardonable sin to add to or subtract from the Bible. The enforcement of a "thing indifferent" was just the sort of thing anathematized. He held that just as it is "a sin to add a new law in the material book to bind men, then it must needs be a sin for any creature to put a new law into conscience, which is the spiritual book of God." Henry Burton was equally certain that in "matters of duty, that is toward God, . . . those are true, which are set down in Scripture, and none else; for God will be served of himself, he commandeth not as man prescript."[20]

Warning against the Sins of Ungodly Rulers

The rejection of idolatrous "things indifferent" in worship led

20. Fenner, *Looking-Glasse*, p. 180; Burton, *A most Godly Sermon*, sig. A2 (recto). Fenner's reference is to Rev. 22:18,19.

the Puritans to a curious reversal of anglican thinking on the subject of the public peace. Anglicans—as the second half of this chapter will demonstrate—saw in any breach of the peace a sinful disobedience of Saint Paul's commands. If the civil peace were disturbed when Puritans declined to perform acts which were idolatrous in their eyes, or if there were troubles in the church as they organized means of defending or advancing godly preaching, who was really to blame for the disturbance? Anglicans and Puritans agreed that God would punish disturbers of the peace, and that civil war and all the horrors that accompanied it were indeed part of that just punishment for breaches of God's commandments. But which sins, and which commandments? Sibbes, preaching well before the Civil War, offers evidence that from the puritan point of view blame had to rest on whoever was responsible for the orders which forced godly men into dissimulation and disobedience. It was inconceivable that God would punish his people for their attempts to obey him. "What hurt have we ever had," asked Sibbes, "by the reformation of religion?" None—on the contrary—it had always "been attended with peace and prosperity." Therefore the righteous Christians who, for example, reminded "those that are called to places of dignity" of the great need for setting "up some lights in all the dark corners of this land" (i.e., providing godly preaching wherever it was yet lacking in England) were only doing their duty. They were trying to save England from the troubles which King Manasseh's sins had brought upon his kingdom. Christians were, Sibbes continued, in duty bound "to have a care that there be no breaches made upon the sound doctrine that is left unto us, and hath been sealed up by the blood of so many martyrs." The Reformation had uncovered the shining, saving beacon of true Christian doctrine; its preservation and dissemination into all the dark corners would bring England peace and prosperity. If such works were not continued, England would suffer indeed. "The greatest enemies of a church and state," Sibbes proclaimed, "are those that provoke the highest Majesty of heaven against the light that shineth in their own hearts."[21]

21. Sibbes, *Cordialls*, pp. 156, 178–79, 157. Although I have been unable to date this sermon precisely, it was probably preached in response to the Arminian advances of 1625–26 and thereafter.

Though the troubles of the godly were in most instances fatherly chastisements for their sins, there was no sin in disobeying the unwarrantable commands of earthly authorities or in performing works of obedience to God which the authorities opposed. Fenner cited the "lamentable example" of the men of Ephraim who had obeyed their king's command that they worship calves in Bethel (instead of Jehovah in Jerusalem); they were "utterly destroyed for obeying their king rather than their God. . . . Beloved, God's commandment is sovereign. . . . Whatever commandment is repugnant to God's word, woe to us if we do it." Not for Puritans then was the comfortable Anglican argument that if the higher powers erred in some indifferent matter, God would judge only them. Sibbes had used the example of Meroz, who was cursed for "not helping the Lord against the mighty," to prove that the man who "suffers evil to be done which he might have opposed and hindered, brings the guilt thereof upon his own head." Especially in matters of worship, there was no way to share the fault of sin. Fenner's answer to "the calumnies and slanders of wicked and ungodly men" who called the Puritans "despisers of authority" was simply that obedience to God came first.[22]

The argument that civil peace was disturbed not by the refusers of unrighteous orders but by the issuers of them appeared in a sermon preached by John Owen before the members of the Rump in January 31, 1649—the day after Charles I was beheaded. Two months later Owen accepted Cromwell's invitation to serve as his chaplain in Ireland, thereby taking a major step toward assuming his role as "the Melanchthon of 'orthodox' Independency and Cromwell's chief advisor in ecclesiastical affairs."[23] Owen's main purpose on January 31 was to urge a measure of religious toleration—he made no direct reference to the dreadful event of the day before. His introductory remarks were, however, so apposite that their implications were clearly intended. He set out to vindicate the "equity of God's righteous judgments" in destroying the kingdom of Judah. Jeremiah had said that the Hebrews would be dispersed "into

22. Fenner, *Looking-Glasse*, pp. 203–04; Sibbes, *Cordialls*, p. 157. The example of Meroz was later put to explosive use by Stephen Marshall and other parliamentary fast-day preachers. See Trevor-Roper, *Crisis of the Seventeenth Century*, pp. 307–08.
23. Paul, *The Lord Protector*, pp. 203–04.

all the kingdoms of the earth because of the sins of their king Manasseh" (Jeremiah 15:4). On the face of it, God's justice did need some
defense, for it seemed that the people were punished not for their
sins, but for the sins of their king. Owen began by suggesting that
the "deposing of divine and human things is oftentimes very opposite." In the "spiritual body" the sins of God's people had led to
the punishment of Christ, the "Head" of that body. But in "the
civil politic body the head offends, and the members rue it: Manasseh sins, and Judah must go captive."[24]

Owen offered a three-part apology for divine justice in this case.
First, there was a sense in which the people were responsible for
Manasseh's sins, for "they that set him up may justly be called to
answer for his miscarriage."[25] Second, and more ominous, "the
greatest part of the people" had either for fear of cruelty or hope
of gain by flattery "apostatized from the ways and worship of [the
good king] Hezekiah," and thus followed Manasseh's wicked lead.
"When kings command unrighteous things, and people suit them
with wicked compliance," then God's judgments upon them are
undoubtedly just. Third, and still more ominous, was Owen's statement that God's action was just "because the people, *by virtue of
their retained sovereignty, did not restrain him in his provoking ways.*"
Owen's argument here is extremely interesting in relation to the
obedience due monarchs because he is saying that since the people
did not stop Manasseh from sinning, they made his sins theirs. "And
therefore, those things being written for our example," it must
be vital for the Rump and all Englishmen "to know what were

24. Owen, pp. 127–62. The title is "Righteous Zeal Encouraged by Divine
Protection." Owen's remarks in a funeral sermon he preached for Ireton make
it clear that he saw divine providence in the execution of Charles I. Owen
compared Ireton to Daniel, who had received from God "visions of providential
alterations, disposing and transposing of states, nations, kingdoms and dominions.
What he had in *speculation* was [Ireton's] part to follow in *action.*" Owen, p. 351.
See Tuveson's remarks on another sermon by Owen in 1649, a sermon in which
"the good commonwealth" is equated with "the millennial period." *Millennium and
Utopia*, pp. 89–91. On Owen's interpretation of Revelations, see Walzer, pp. 297–99
and Peter Toon, ed., *Puritans, the Millennium and the Future of Israel*, pp. 36–39.
25. Owen, pp. 135–36. The people had "set him up" in that they had originally
desired the institution of a kingship (see 1 Sam. 8—Samuel thought it a mistake).
They had also elected to follow Omri rather than Tibni, in that the former defeated
the latter (1 Kings 21:22). Neither of these examples necessarily implies that Owen
intended to build his argument upon any democratic premises.

those sins which wrapped up the people of God in irrevocable destruction." Owen reduced these to two categories: (1) "False worship or superstition" (citing a reference to "altars for Baal," 2 Kings 21:3), and (2) "Cruelty" which resulted either from the king's "tyranny in civil affairs . . . or . . . his persecution in subordination to his false worship." Owen's example here was papal persecution, but in the next paragraph he made it clear that his argument applied to all "human-invented worship."[26] "Human-invented" or "humane" worship was, as we have noted, a puritan way of referring to the ceremonies required by Laud.

Owen's sermon was a determined if oblique defense of the successful rebellion that the Long Parliament had completed. Puritans rarely argued for rebellion as such, but they consistently held to two principles: (1) that terrible national judgments such as civil war were caused by disobedience to God, and (2) that the enforcers of "human-invented" worship were sinners of the worst kind. It was the true Christian's duty to disobey them. Though passive disobedience was usually counselled,[27] sufficiently widespread and persistent passive disobedience allowed the relatively small numbers of more militant parliamentarians to prosecute the war against the royalists. Puritans vigorously rejected the anglican charge that they were provoking God by leaving their places in the social and political order; in their view, it was the authorities commanding idolatry who were leaving their places by exceeding the limits of a magistrate's calling. Just such a consideration must have underlain Oliver Cromwell's statement to the House of Commons after the taking of Bristol: "God hath put the sword into the Parliament's hands for the terror of evil-doers and the praise of them that do

26. Ibid., pp. 136–37. Emphasis added.
27. For example, Fenner, *Looking-Glasse*, pp. 199–200: "Nay, though they command that which is utterly unlawful, we must not rise up against them, for if we do, we rise up against God." We must obey and when we cannot obey fully, "yet we must passively obey, suffering and submitting to their penalties." Fenner died in 1640. By the time Owen wrote, the situation was very different. On this subject, see George L. Mosse, "Puritan Political Thought and the 'Cases of Conscience,'" *CH* 23 (1954): 109–17. Mosse notes that William Perkins had no trouble preaching that authorities should not be resisted. William Ames, writing a generation later, did not justify resistance—but it may be significant that he "does not go to the length of Perkins in exalting kingship. . . . [and] the word 'just' is significantly interspersed in his principal passage about the magistrate" (pp. 114–16).

well.''[28] That was the classic description of a godly king's duty from
1 Peter 2:14—but the king's government had persecuted godly
preachers while it spared ungodly papists. One suspects that most
Puritans, lay and clerical, had taken the "evil-counsellors" explanation of Charles's ungodly conduct very seriously indeed. Their
innumerable pious prayers that he would see the light and change
his ways, however unrealistic they now sound, were not empty
rhetoric. Nor were they, as the Anglicans thought, mere camou-
flage for ambition and greed. Diocletian had been succeeded by
Constantine, and there was no reason to think that God could not
work such a change if He chose to do so, even within one man's
reign. It will not do to underestimate the force of the puritan desire
for godly leadership, and to estimate it properly is to understand the
depth of their disappointment when they did not get it. Such prayers
were uttered even on the scaffold in 1660 by men about to undergo
the full horrors of a traitor's death. Colonel Daniel Axtell, who had
commanded the troops providing security in Westminster Hall
during Charles I's trial, prayed before his execution as a regicide
for the conversion of Charles II: "The chief magistrate of this nation, that thou wouldest give him a glorious Christ unto his poor
soul, . . . that he may . . . reign in righteousness; and may be a
terror to evil doers, and a praise to them that do well."[29]

This is not to imply that such prewar puritan luminaries as
Preston, Sibbes, Fenner, and Gouge, or even such fiery parliamentary fast-day preachers as Burges, Ash, Case, and Hill, con-
doned regicide. It is rather to say that the whole weight of the
puritan rhetoric of obedience depended not upon an obedience to
princes which issued in civil peace, but upon the primacy of obedience to God, whatever might become of the civil peace. "Preaching
the saving Word was more important than preserving the public
peace," writes Paul Seaver. The effect was to change the terms

28. Abbott, 1:365–66 (14 September 1645). Cromwell went on to urge the
members not to let any one wrest the sword out of their hands. Any man who did
not cooperate in its use for God's purposes "knows not the Gospel."

29. *Speeches and Prayers*, p. 95. See pp. 19, 31 for prayers for a godly magistracy
by regicides Carew and Cooke. The latter, who was Charles I's prosecutor, intended
to argue at the trial that Charles's unfitness as a ruler was because he was "a stranger to the work of grace and the spirit of God." The speech was never given.
Quoted in Russell, *The Crisis of Parliaments*, p. 365.

connected with obedience. Puritans rarely used the word "obedience" without referring to one of the members of the Trinity as its
object, and they rarely spoke of "rebellion" except as against God
the Father, Son, or Spirit. Anglicans used them primarily in reference to the higher earthly powers. The term "boutefeu," which
Anglicans applied to rebels and schismatics whose wicked actions
set the social universe on fire, was used by the puritan John Benbrigge to describe the profane person whose sins of drunkenness,
swearing, lying, coveting, Sabbath-breaking, and fast-breaking
made him "one fire-brand that helps to burn England. . . . Condemn him then for a boutefeu, of this our present misery." He defined a true Christian man as one whose soul plays upon a single
string, that "Christ must be obeyed, Christ must be pleased, Christ
must be honored." The goodness of any act was, he maintained,
tested by whether a man was moved to it by love of and obedience
to Christ.[30]

Preston gave it as a necessary mark of regeneration that a man set
up Christ as his "chiefest commander" and be ready to "obey him,
and obey him rather than any other." Thus he distinguished true
believers in Christ from "a man that is out of Christ, [who] thinks
that the favor of or the wealth of the king" is of greater value than
that of Christ. The regenerate man, said Preston, disregards "any
command, contrary to that which Christ commands"—his conscience ("Christ's vicegerent") is supreme. To disobey God's plan
for man as revealed in the Word was purely and simply sin; and to
sin, especially against the light, was, said Thomas Goodwin, to
"rebel against God's Spirit . . . to sin against light is called rebellion." Thomas Case spoke against the refusal to learn from God's
teaching hand in chastisements, for "to continue in wonted sins,
against such sensible and real proclamations to desist, is professed
rebellion against God." John Winthrop bewailed his state "when
the flesh hath prevailed in me, all hath been out of order, . . .

30. Seaver, *Puritan Lectureships*, p. 204; Benbrigge, *Gods Fury*, pp. 60–61; Benbrigge, *Christ*, pp. 28–29. Anglican usage of *boutefeu* is discussed at the end of this
chapter. For some interesting examples of what Melvin Lasky calls "the incendiary
image" in the seventeenth-century metaphor of revolution, see his article in
Encounter 34(1970):30–42. See also Zagorin, pp. 9–18 and Walzer, chap. 5 (on
puritan use of metaphors). Lamont comments upon Walzer's arguments in *Godly
Rule*, pp. 24–25 and 138–40.

strangeness towards my God, a guilty heart inclining to rebellion."
But he was delighted when "it pleased God to have mercy upon
me, . . . for my former boldness in sinning and dalliance with the
breach of his Commandments . . . my former rebellions, ingrati-
tude, self-love, sloth, carnality, time-serving, etc. . . ." The way
the puritan value system had of turning the customary usage of
words around and placing them in a new moral context is vividly
illustrated in Thomas Hooker's denunciation of Sabbath-breakers
and similar offenders against the puritan conception of proper
obedience to the first four commandments: "For shall it be a good
plea for a traitor against the state to pretend his righteous dealing
with his fellow-subjects? No more will God accept of such a service,
where there is high treason against his Majesty, though there be
some petty duties performed to men."[31]

Maintaining the Inward Peace of a Good Conscience

The puritan predilection for using rebellion as a synonym for
sinful disobedience of God's Word led to a conception of the meaning of peace which is quite distinct from the anglican conception
considered below. Anglicans believed in the orthodoxy of the king
and his bishops and in the lawfulness of their commands. They
therefore evaluated an individual's obedience largely in terms of its
effects upon the civil peace—hence upon other men. This ran parallel to their insistence upon making obedience of the Second Table a
touchstone to the First. Puritans, on the other hand, evaluated
obedience in terms of its tendency to advance "godliness" or retard
its opposite. According to Thomas Goodwin, there is a "new
obedience" by which a justified man sanctifies his behavior. It is his
duty to "yield a constant obedience to all God's commands, and
avoid the contrary." He is "to hate whatsoever is known or suspected to be a sin; and . . . to love and delight in those contrary
ways of holiness and righteousness God hath chalked out in his
Word, and all this for God's cause." Goodwin offered as an example
of this "new obedience" the proper performance of the duties
derived from the Fourth Commandment. The "Sabbath, . . . if

31. Preston, *Cuppe*, pp. 23–26; T. Goodwin, 3:297; Case, *Correction*, p. 195;
WP, 1:210, 214; T. Hooker, *Lessons*, p. 216. See also Caryl, *Job* (chaps. 22–26),
p. 308; T. Goodwin, 7:554; Preston, *Life*, pt. 2, pp. 81, 97, 100.

sanctified as it ought, in thought, speeches, and actions, is the darling and delight of the Lord." The truly converted Christian would therefore make it his "darling day too." The difficulty was that the actions which Puritans regarded as necessary tended to get them into trouble with the authorities. The Puritan who left his parish to hear a sermon, or who opposed the profanation of the Sabbath by others with their gaming and Morris dancing, or who refused to bow his head at the name of Jesus or kneel to receive communion, might easily find himself called up before the bishop's court and traduced. "And whereas drunkenness and profaneness, contempt of God and goodness, may pass and travel," Goodwin told his Cambridge listeners that "godliness, under the suspicion of being a factious spy, is everywhere stopped, examined (though it have a passport of conformity to show for itself), yea, and is sometimes whipped out of town for a renegade." With imagery steeped in bitterness, he added that godliness had come to be "like Samson, brought up upon stages, which are often the devil's pulpits, though under another visor, to make the Philistines' sport; yea, set up as a mark to be shot at out of God's place, the pulpit, and Puritanism set up as the stalking-horse to stand behind, while they shoot through the loins of it."[32]

In such times, and under the authority of such men, there could be no stable, lasting civil peace. Something was rotten in the state of England, and God's judgments would find it out and destroy it sooner or later. Without thorough reformation at all levels of English society, there would never be a civil peace worth having. As Caryl had said in 1643, all good men should seek peace, but no peace which was not based on righteousness would endure. The wounds caused by the grievous sins of idolatry, profaneness, and abuse of godliness would fester horribly if not fully cauterized instead of merely skinned over. Part of Owen's message to the Rump was similar. He derided the "poor creatures" who cried "Give us peace, give us wealth,—give us as we were, with our own, in quietness . . . yet if peace were, and wealth were, and former things were, and God

---

32. T. Goodwin, 7:562, 555, 556, 547. These quotations are from a pair of sermons which Goodwin preached in 1628 as Preston's successor in the lectureship of Trinity Church, Cambridge (2:359). Early in the first sermon he referred to the necessity for searching out "national sins," not daring to "leave any of Rachel's idols hid in the straw" (7:545). Equally specific denunciations of "Arminianism" follow in the sermon. See also Fenner, *Looking-Glasse*, pp. 134–35, on this theme.

were not, what would it avail you?" To desire a godless peace, peace for its own sake, was an indication that one lacked saving grace. Cromwell said as much in a letter to his dear friend, Colonel Hammond: "Peace is only good when we receive it out of our Father's hand, it's dangerous to snatch it, most dangerous to go against the will of God to attain it."[33] One of the Lord General's chaplains, Nicholas Lockyer, explicitly rejected the notion that peace with fellowmen could be treated as an indication of true faith. "Peace," he said in 1644, "may be in a sinner's mouth, and wrath in God's," and a soul given over to the devil might be as quiet as anyone could ask. A good, true peace came of true faith and true obedience to all God's commandments against sin. John Preston said that "to have a peace not well bottomed, is the greatest judgment in the world." He defined such an "unsound peace" as that of a man "secure and at rest," his mind not "occupied about sin, or about matters of salvation; I say, it is a sign that such an one God hates."[34]

For Puritans, an individual's role in maintaining the public peace could be a touchstone to try his estate with God only under a truly godly magistrate. Each new demonstration of the ungodliness of the higher powers—and there was no shortage of these demonstrations in the late 1620s and 1630s—merely confirmed the Puritans in their deep distrust of any who seemed to be returning to the superstitious and idolatrous ways of benighted ancestors. Not long before his death, Preston was asked what the saints should do to demonstrate their true love for God, considering that "it is time now for men to be working more than ordinary." His answer was, "My brethren, 'Contend for the faith once delivered to the saints,' mark it, the work must be to contend for it, you must be men of contention." Thomas Hooker's counsel was the same; "Contend for the faith.

33. Caryl, *Davids Prayer*, p. 25; Owen, p. 135; Paul, *The Lord Protector*, p. 403. Paul here reprints the letter (Nov. 6, 1648) along with information on the sources which justify attribution to Cromwell. Cromwell continued, "War is good when led to by our Father, most evil when it comes from the lusts that are in our members."
34. Lockyer, *Baulme for Bleeding England and Ireland*, pp. 188–89; Preston, *Breast-Plate*, pt. 2, pp. 105–06. See also Sibbes, *Works*, 7:350; Watson, pp. 262–63; Calamy, quoted in Russell, *Crisis of Parliaments*, p. 204; Benbrigge, *Christ*, p. 38, said that to fast and pray "for no other end but out of a desire of peace" was to put the cart before the horse, to ask for an end to deserved judgments before the receipt of saving grace.

Contention implies opposition, . . . when love is in most opposition, it is most violent in resolution."[35]

On innumerable occasions, puritan ministers explained the disturbances which rocked church and commonwealth as the results, not of disobedience to the prince but of opposition to those who contended for the truth as revealed in Scriptures. All trouble arose from sin and all sin was idolatrous preference for and indulgence in activities forbidden by the Word. Godly ministers, whose calling it was to preach the Word, necessarily ran into opposition when they demanded that men uproot all their false gods, i.e., their public and private sins. Joseph Caryl said that "ministers are often persecuted and reproached," and the better they preached, the more so; "to preach the Gospel fully as it should be preached, is to provoke thousands and bring the world about our ears." Thomas Hooker said that wicked men always opposed godly preaching because the "god of heaven by the Word would pluck away these dunghill-gods; hence comes an uproar in the town and family." Drunkards railed at ministers because "they would have their God Bacchus still, and therefore they are up in arms to maintain it." Robert Bolton gave a similar explanation for the way the wicked men "combine furiously to be rid of" good preachers and good magistrates. Using the Manichean imagery which figures so strongly in the Gospel of John, Bolton said that there is "an implacable and everlasting enmity between the children of light and the children of darkness" which drives the latter to hate God's children and to become "notorious instruments and means" for afflicting and vexing them. This reasoning is prominent in lectures on John's Gospel given by James Harrison to the Barrington family at Hatfield Broad Oak. "The world," he said, "hates the ministry . . . of the Gospel which gives them all to see their evil courses," and further, "the world hates you. The grace which is in the children of God is the cause of the world's hatred." Cain hated Abel for his good works, thus demonstrating that there is "a root of bitterness which is in all mankind which opposes all goodness and holiness."[36]

35. Preston, *Breast-Plate*, pt. 3, p. 211; Hooker, *Lessons*, p. 78. See also Sibbes, *Cordialls*, p. 178. See Christopher Hill's essay on Preston's political sermons for a brilliant depiction of the context in which this and similar sermons were preached (in *Puritanism and Revolution*).

36. Caryl, *Job* (chaps. 32–34), p. 381; Hooker, *Lessons*, p. 42; Bolton, *Cordiall for*

In this analysis, then, the gift of saving grace would be displayed by a complete, sincere, active obedience to the divine will, and such an obedience would in all likelihood lead the Christian into tumults as he struggled against sin in himself and others. If some of the higher powers issued unwarrantable commands, the tumults would be the more disruptive of the public peace. If this happened, and if there were no lawful means of evading the controversy, then the earthly authorities were in the wrong, and the chips would have to fall where they would. Such tumult was a signal to Anglicans that someone was not in due Christian obedience. To Puritans it could be a sign that the magistrate or the bishop was demanding disobedience to God. When Laud and his colleagues began systematically to oppose the puritan attempt to complete the reformation of the Church of England, and especially when they began to muffle puritan preaching and lecturing, then the Puritans could continue to obey the higher powers fully only at the risk of their assurance of eternal life. Leading puritan preachers often told their congregations that they must expect to have to face reproach and persecution. Sibbes, in explaining why the rebellious plot of Absalom and Achitophel against David failed, said that sinners always hate goodness because they envy it. Worldly men always plotted against godly men because the latter are not at home in this world, and their very presence in it is a standing rebuke to those who are. Thus a story which in an anglican sermon usually led to a homily on obedience to prince and prelate became, for Sibbes, evidence that godly men and their works are always marks set up to be shot at by wicked men. He turned a homily on obedience to a man into a homily on obedience to the Son of Man. He was convinced that God cared for only two things in this world, "his truth, and his church begotten by his truth." He urged his listeners to "get a strong resolution against all oppositions, for (know this) scandal will come, difficulties will arise."[37]

Harrison warned the Barringtons in the same way, stating it as a doctrine that every "Christian man in his course must look to

---

a Fainting Christian, pp. 11–12; Harrison on John 14:18, 15:19–20. For examples of this imagery, see John 1:4–10, 8:12, 12:35–36, 46; Sibbes, *Cordialls*, p. 142 and *Works*, 7:350.

37. Sibbes, *Cordialls*, pp. 142–43, 149, 186. On the anglican approach to Absalom, see Sanderson, 1:266–67, 2:344.

meet with scandal." He defined "external scandal . . . as when anything is done whereby (it being repugnant to God's Law . . .) a Christian is hindered in his Christian course." Owen had sought to bolster the zeal of the Rumpers in similar terms, reminding them that "great works for God will cause great troubles among men." Jesus Christ, the "holy, harmless Reconciler," had told his followers to expect "the sword to attend his undertakings for and way of making peace" (Matt. 10:34). If Christ had said as much, Owen continued, then the "right honorable" members of Parliament would surely not lack "experience of that opposition which is raised against the visible instruments thereof." As the "visible instruments" of godliness, they could expect to suffer as Moses did from Korah's conspiracy. That godly man had led the Hebrew nation away from sin, but there would always be Korahs entering "into a conspiracy and revolt, consulting to cast off his government, . . . and with a violent hand to return to their former condition."[38] In Owen's sermon, another favorite story in the anglican liturgy of obedience is thus read against the background of a puritan set of values. The Parliament which had, like Moses, led Englishmen out of the Egyptian darkness of sin and idolatry, would not be thanked for it by the Korahs of England who had enjoyed the fleshpots of Egypt and preferred to worship at the altars of Baal. Korah's sin lay not in opposing magistracy as such, but in opposing a godly magistracy which aimed to restrain sin and establish righteousness.

Owen sought to strengthen the Rumpers in the task they faced by assuring them that "God will so secure the instruments of his glory against a backsliding people, in holding up the ways of his truth and righteousness, that all attempts against them shall be vain, and the most timorous spirit may be secure, provided . . ." Provided? Just as Benbrigge repeated to the children, Winthrop to the 1624 Parliament, Harrison to the Barringtons, so Owen to the Rump some twenty four hours after the decapitation of Charles I declared that God will protect even "the most timorous spirit . . . provided he go not out of the Lord's way." Moses was delivered from Korah's

---

38. Harrison on John 16:1; Owen, p. 129, 151. See also Preston, *Cuppe*, pp. 26–27; Caryl, *Job* (chaps. 4–7), p. 379; "Though usually they who [are] in a nearest league and covenant with God, are most warred with and opposed by the world."

plot, but "falling into one deviation, in one thing, from close following the Lord, was taken off from enjoying the fruit of all his labor."[39] The sword—and the axe—was in the hands of Parliament, a worldly authority no less enjoined to righteous use of its power than the late king had been. Owen had great hopes that the members would persevere in the right way and honorably fulfill the duties of their high calling. The whole burden of his sermon was to urge these duties upon them and to bolster their confidence against the opposition they would meet. But if they failed to measure up to the high standards of godliness, the cautionary proviso remained, floating like a mine just beneath the waves of encouraging rhetoric.

Despite all the scandals, oppositions, contentions, afflictions, tumults, wars, and rumors of wars which would accompany the profession and practise of sincere commitment to the saving truth of the Gospel, Puritans insisted that the true Christian would have peace. He would have it whether he were called to serve in Parliament or to suffer in prison. Puritans distinguished carefully, however, between outward and inward peace. The former was useless without the latter; indeed, as we have just seen, outward peace could not even be expected. The only peace worth having was that which followed upon a full conviction of the heinousness of sin, a hearty repentance for it, and a turning to the ways of righteousness revealed by the preachers of the Word. Although John Preston made peace one of the signs of a justifying faith, he took care to explain that he meant the kind of peace which came after war upon sin. He explicitly rejected the "blind peace" of a man who had not seen and fought down the danger of sin but simply had never seen the danger. Such men "were never acquainted with the doctrine of justification, and of sanctification" and their peace rested upon a false foundation. Preston went further and argued that even a true Christian's inner peace as well as his outer peace would be disturbed: "If it be true peace, if Satan be cast out, he will not let thee alone, thou shalt be sure to have thy peace troubled, he will make many rebellions against thee by the flesh and the world." Preston offered David as proof. During the rebellion of Absalom and Achitophel, David was able to lie down and sleep even while his enemies sought his destruction because his heart was at peace and his faith in the Lord was

39. Owen, pp. 150–51.

secure. Like Preston, William Fenner rejected the peace of those who "have peace of conscience because they know not what belongeth to trouble of conscience." Peace could come only after conversion, and for Puritans conversion did not come easy. "If our quiet and peace of conscience be good," continued Fenner, "it is accompanied with such a life as is agreeable to the will of God; it avoideth sin, as the thing that disturbeth the peace."[40]

THE ANGLICAN IMPERATIVES

"My Lord, I have lived to see religion painted upon banners, and thrust out of churches," wrote a saddened Jeremy Taylor in 1653 as he dedicated his *Holy Living* to his patron and protector, the Earl of Carbery. Times and men were terrible, and they were made worse because "the ministers of religion are so scattered, that they cannot unite to stop the inundation." Neither from pulpits nor from tribunals could they, in Cromwellian England, "chastise the iniquity of the error, and the ambition of evil guides, and the infidelity of the willingly seduced multitudes." Taylor believed deeply that the Church of England would surmount the troubles in God's good time, that He would turn "our persecutions into joys, and crowns, and scepters." But what of the interim? What, asked Taylor, of "those few good people, who have no other plot in their religion but to serve God and save their souls"? Many such lived where they had no access to an orthodox minister who could "assist their endeavors in the acquist of virtues, and relieve their dangers, when they are tempted to sin and death." Taylor sought to help them in the only way open to him. He composed "a collection of holy precepts" which they could use in the absence of the "personal and attending guides" who would be available under normal circumstances. In the dedication, he listed a group of signs by which any man could "give sentence concerning the state of his own soul."

40. Preston, *Breast-Plate*, pt. 2, pp. 101–03; Fenner, *Looking-Glasse*, pp. 100, 102. See also Sibbes, *Works*, 7:350, 353. For a comparable treatment of Absalom's rebellion, see Sibbes, *Cordialls*, pp. 139–40. For another treatment of David in affliction, see Case, *Correction*, pp. 59–60, 65: " 'Put not your trust in princes nor in the son of man;' and gives the reason of it, there is no help or salvation in the best of men . . . Peace, constant and everlasting peace is the portion of him that liveth by faith, so far as he liveth by faith."

Taylor regarded these as sufficiently comprehensive so that "the man that hath these twelve signs of grace and predestination, does as certainly belong to God, and is his son, as surely as he is his creature."[41]

The substance of Jeremy Taylor's twelvefold description of a truly saved Christian would have been acceptable to most Puritans. The Christian believes the fundamental doctrines of Christianity and seeks to widen his knowledge of them. He is baptized and "worships God diligently, frequently, and constantly." He lives humbly, contentedly, chastely and mercifully; he "despises the world, . . . is just in his dealing, and diligent in his calling." He is dutiful out of love to God and is prepared "to suffer affliction for the cause of God." Puritans certainly would not have quarreled with the requirement that the Christian be "obedient to government."[42] But they were, as we have seen, quick to insert the proviso that Christians should be obedient only insofar as the Word of God allows. It is the purpose of this section to examine the anglican conception of obedience to the higher powers on earth. We will do so in terms of three imperatives, each of which was a prerequisite to peace of conscience: (1) the Anglican owed obedience to the crown and mitre, and support for (2) maintaining ecclesiastical unity, and (3) preserving the public peace and the natural order. Taylor and his colleagues held that obedience resulted in peace in the state and unity in the church, and they defined peace and unity in such a way as to indict the Puritans for disrupting them. Anglicans were incessantly urged to ask themselves whether their actions contributed to and supported the maintenance of civil peace and religious unity. Any man who could answer that question affirmatively and also lived an upright, moral life, could account himself a good Christian and take comfort against whatever tribulations he faced. He could look upon his troubles as the chastisements of a loving Father and not as the punishments of an angry Judge. For Anglicans, inner peace and outer turmoil were integrally related. If there were public tumults, a man

41. Taylor, 4:ii–v.
42. Ibid., pp. iv–v; "These are the marks of the Lord Jesus and the characters of a Christian: this is a good religion." There is one requirement—that of "a frequent sacrament"—which Puritans would have disliked, not because they disliked the sacrament itself, but because they abhorred the "popish" trappings with which the Anglicans performed it. Taylor had at one time been one of Laud's protégés.

could retain his inner peace only if he were in no way responsible for them, and if he did whatever he could to restore peace and unity.

Obedience to the Higher Powers

The cornerstone of anglican thought—and the basis for the insistence that civil peace and ecclesiastical unity were the fruits of true Christian obedience—was the belief that the Church of England, as constituted under the leadership of Charles I, was a true church. It was acceptable in the sight of God and was therefore a safe and satisfactory guardian and guide for the souls of Englishmen. Taylor held that a Christian was in duty bound to obey "prince and prelate, provided that his duty to God be secured by a precedent search." In other words, he should first inquire as to "whether the civil constitution agree with our duty to God; but we are bound to inquire no further."[43] Once it was established that the head of state was a Christian prince and that his ecclesiastical arrangements fulfilled the essential requirements of a true church, capable of extending the requisite aids to salvation to its members, then there could be no justification for disobedience to government. Charles I was such a prince and the Church of England was such a church—of those central affirmations there was no doubt for Anglicans.

Reservations on the duty of obedience to the prince were pro forma for the Anglicans. They were made to maintain logical consistency in an imperfect and changing world. They were a remembrance of times past (e.g., the Marian persecution) and a hostage to future, unlooked for and unlikely rule by a popish or even pagan tyrant. In the real, contemporary world, the rightful king was a good Anglican, a godly prince in the glorious tradition of David, Josiah, Constantine, Elizabeth I, and James I. Charles II, not long after his father's death, heard Henry Byam proclaim that "we had no Amon, no idolater, but a defender of the faith, and for that cause martyred by his own subjects." Dr. Edward Hyde, writing in 1657, said that the ordinances of the Church of England were God's ordinances, and that to deny the same was anti-Christian, indeed, the work of the Beast. The best way to prevent terror of the Day of Judgment was to use the church's help in the leading of a godly, righteous and sober life. Yet some men, according to Hyde, refused

43. Ibid., pp. 152–53. See also Sanderson, 2:290.

to accept such "sound divinity, if it be taught them by the church (thereby showing themselves . . . no less unthankful to God's mercy, which gave them a church to teach them the true way of godliness, than undutiful to God's authority, that they will not be taught)." John Bramhall, preaching in Dublin in celebration of the restoration of Charles II, expressed the characteristic pride of Anglicans in their religion. It was, he said, "a good religion":

> A religion, not reformed tumultuously, according to the brain-sick fancies of a half-witted multitude, dancing after the pipe of some seducing charmer, but soberly, according to the rule of God's Word, as it hath been evermore and everywhere interpreted by the Catholic Church, and according to the purest pattern of the primitive times. . . . A religion, which is neither garish with superfluous ceremonies, nor yet sluttish and void of all order, decency, and majesty in the service of God. A religion which is as careful to retain old articles of faith, as it is averse from new articles. . . . The terror of Rome—they fear our moderation more than the violent opposition of others. The watch tower of the Evangelical Churches—I have seen many churches of all sorts of communions, but never any, that could diminish that venerable estimation which I had for my mother the Church of England. From her breasts I received my first nourishment, in her arms I desire to end my days.[44]

As Bramhall looked back over two decades of strife, he was convinced that the "true Israelites" in England were those who had suffered in the struggle to maintain "their spiritual Head," Christ; their "political head," Charles I and then his son; and "their ecclesiastical head, or lawful superiors in the church." It was their glory in this life—one which would be rewarded in the next—that they had "never bowed their knees to Baal Berith, the God of the Covenant, but continued loyal subjects and orthodox Christians."

44. Byam, p. 8; Hyde, *Legacy*, p. 187; Bramhall, p. 123, See also Taylor, 6: cccxxxii, cccxlii; Hales, 2:29–30. "S.P. of Cambridge" (possibly Simon Patrick) similarly praised "that virtuous mediocrity which our Church observes between the meretricious gaudiness of the Church of Rome and the squalid sluttery of fanatic conventicles." *A Brief Account of the New Sect of Latitudinarians*, p. 7. On Bramhall's political theory, see J. W. Daly, "John Bramhall and the Theoretical Problems of Royalist Moderation," *JBS* 11 (1971):26–44.

This kind of confidence in the Church of England was the firm foundation upon which the anglican conception of obedience rested. Anglicans were the beneficiaries of a partnership with the Stuart monarchy and the inheritors of the tradition of the "judicious Hooker." Their particular idea of the "true" church was established. Any attack upon it or its head, the king, could only be regarded as a sinful attack upon a system sanctioned by God and thereby an attack upon the truth as well as the peace. Clarendon equated rebellion with atheism because in his eyes the sinfulness of rebellion was so absolute that none could commit it and believe in the existence of God at the same time. He "who lifts up his hand against his lawful sovereign, and . . . bathes his hands in the blood of those who are loyal to him" is a grievous oppressor whom God will condemn "to the pains of hell-fire." The great earl's sometime chaplain, Lionel Gatford, told his former neighbors of Suffolk in 1648 that it was "the continuing in our sins, and the not acknowledging of our rebellions against God and his vicegerent, but the justifying of them" which heightened God's anger and caused the continuation of "his heavy judgments upon us." Robert Sanderson, preaching at Hampton Court on July 26, 1640, recalled the familiar story of Saul and David in making the same point. Upon several occasions, David had the opportunity to destroy Saul, and he did not lack plausible reasons to do it. David, however, clearly understood "the thing itself, to offer violence to the Lord's anointed, to be utterly unlawful, and that was it that stayed his hand." Preaching after the Civil War was under way, Chillingworth found it incredible that those who had "made no scruple of fighting with his sacred majesty and shooting muskets and ordnance at him" could be ignorant of "the example of David, recorded for their instruction, 'whose heart smote him, when he had cut off the hem of Saul's garment.' "[45]

One important consequence of the thoroughgoing anglican acceptance of the existing civil-ecclesiastical arrangements was a categorical rejection of civil disobedience in any form. Even passive disobedience was unwarrantable if the commands of the civil author-

45. Bramhall, p. 136; *Contemplations*, p. 401; Gatford, *Englands Complaint*, p. 1; Sanderson, 2:271–72; Chillingworth, 3:11–12. See also Ferne, quoted in Haller, p. 369. Apropos of the sin of rebellion, Taylor wrote, "Nay, the good angels of an inferior order durst not revile a devil of a higher order." 4:151.

ities required no betrayal of the Christian man's duty to God. Since Anglicans found nothing repugnant to God's commands in the Church of England, disobedience of or rebellion against the Stuarts could not be justified by any religious scruples. Taylor made this point succinctly in the preface to a sermon preached in Dublin two weeks after Bramhall's sermon quoted above. Taylor said, "Men pretend conscience against obedience, expressly against Saint Paul's doctrine, . . . but to disobey for conscience *in a thing indifferent*, is never to be found in the books of our religion." In his *Enchiridion Ethicum* (1667), the Cambridge Platonist, Henry More, considered it axiomatic that " 'tis good to obey the magistrate in things indifferent, even when there is no penalty to disobey." Elsewhere he wrote that "no interpretation of divine writ that justifies sedition, rebellion or tyranny, can be any inspiration from God." Sanderson had, back in 1633, scathingly dismissed the men who claimed to obey as Saint Paul had required, but glossed the text, "by putting in a conditional limitation, . . . as thus, the magistrate shall have his tribute, the minister his tithe," but only "if he carry himself worthily, and as he ought to do in his place." And who, Sanderson asked, "must judge of his carriage, and whether he deserve such an honor, yea or no?" It was a basic principle of justice that no man should be the judge of his own cause. But, Sanderson argued, quite aside from the irrationality of such a distinction, no distinction could be allowed. "Where God commandeth he looketh to be answered with obedience, and dost thou think to come off with subtiltics and distinctions? The precept here in the text is plain and peremptory . . . and will not endure to be eluded with any forced gloss." A favorite application of this doctrine for Anglicans was that God did not hold a subject responsible for examining the lawfulness of his superior's orders. If a man were satisfied that there was no apparent sinfulness in a command, Sanderson said he should obey it "without any more ado. . . . Let them that command us look to that, for it is they that answer for it, not we." Taylor reminded his readers of the "great peace and immunity from sin" which lay in "resigning our wills up to the command of others." It was not for the subordinate to judge of the superior's performance; another would do that.[46]

46. Taylor, 6:cccxxii (emphasis added); More in Cragg, pp. 269, 145; Sanderson, 2:80, 290; Taylor, 4:149.

The duty of a due obedience to government, unqualified by "subtilties and distinctions," did not rest solely upon the strictures of Saint Paul. It was derived from the most authoritative of all laws, the Ten Commandments. More specifically, it was derived from the Fifth Commandment in the Second Table: "Honor thy father and thy mother." Anglicans were fully agreed that the duty of obedience to the powers that be was implied in this law. The king was the father of the nation, and the church was often referred to as the holy mother of its members. Hammond, in his widely used *Practical Catechism*, simply assumed that "honor of father and mother, obedience to superiors, magistrates, etc." were part and parcel of the Fifth Commandment's meaning. Sanderson said in 1640 that "to disobey lawful authority in lawful things is a sin against the Fifth Commandment." Taylor asserted the same in his famous tract, *Holy Dying*, saying that "to obey kings and all that are in authority" was a duty of the Fifth Commandment.[47]

In addition to the authoritative dicta of Moses and Paul, there were the famous examples of rebellion and conspiracy against the higher powers in the Old Testament in 2 Samuel 15 and 16 (Absalom and Achitophel) and Numbers 16 (Korah). There are innumerable references to these stories in anglican writing. An anglican preacher at Paul's Cross in 1609 criticized the puritan lecturers as "oily mouthed Absaloms" who would "bring the people out of love with their true father . . . their David." While struggling with Absalom's rebellion, David and his servants had been railed at and cursed by one Shimei (2 Sam. 16:5-7). Archbishop Laud, hounded on his way to the Tower in 1641 by the "clamor and revilings" of the mob took pride that his "patience was not moved. I looked upon a higher cause than the tongues of Shimei and his children." George Morley, arguing in 1641 against

47. Hammond, *Catechism*, p. 183; Sanderson, 2:288; Taylor, 4:490. See also Hammond, *A Paraphrase, and Annotations Upon . . . The New Testament* (7th ed., 1702), p. 810. Schlatter, in his lucid introduction to excerpts from Baxter's political writings, quotes Baxter's statement that the "power of kings [does not] arise naturally from paternal power." In a footnote, Schlatter says that this apparently refers to Filmer's theories. But as this and the preceding quotations suggest, the analogy of paternity was common—Baxter need not have known of Filmer to find it. *Richard Baxter and Puritan Politics*, p. 25. For some interesting comments on Calvin's thought, see Walzer, pp. 32-33. See also C. Hill, *Society and Puritanism in Pre-Revolutionary England*, pp. 460-61.

the replacement of episcopacy with Scottish Presbyterianism, urged his readers "to remember that there may be as much ambition in Korah, as in Aaron, and as much pride in refusing to be governed, as in desiring to govern." Charles I (or his ghostwriter) grimly amused himself in his "Meditations upon Death" with the thought that "the more insolent and obstinate" of his enemies might, like Korah, be swallowed up in a pit suddenly opened by God for their destruction. Taylor said that there was "no sin in the world" which God had judged with "so great severity and high detestation" as disobedience. The proof was the punishment of Korah and his henchmen. "For the crime of idolatry God sent the sword amongst his people; but it was never heard, that the earth opened up and swallowed up any but rebels against their prince." The Korah and Absalom stories were appointed for reading in a special fast-day service added by royal proclamation to the anglican liturgy in 1643. The service was to be performed on the second Friday in every month "for the averting of God's indulgence now upon us; for the ceasing of this present rebellion."[48]

Anglicans also insisted that the religious duty of obedience meant a good deal more than merely not rebelling violently against the higher powers. It should be, said Farindon, not just the "casting down of the eye" or "the bend of the knee" but the "yielding up and surrendry of the whole man," hand, tongue, and thought. There were many sins of disobedience short of outright rebellion, and there were many duties of obedience which went beyond a grudging submission. As sinners against the Fifth Commandment, Taylor listed those who "curse the king in their heart, or speak evil of the ruler of their people" and who "refuse to pay tributes and impositions imposed legally." He spoke scornfully of "consciences so tender, that a ceremony is greatly offensive, but rebellion is not; a surplice drives them away, . . . but their consciences can suffer them to despise government, and speak evil of dignities, and curse

48. Paul's Cross sermon quoted in Seaver, *Puritan Lectureships*. p. 201; Laud quoted in Trevor-Roper, *Archbishop Laud*, p. 406; Charles I, *Eikon*, pp. 177–78; Taylor, 4:150; *A Forme of Prayer* (Oxford, 1643). The epistle appointed for this service was Romans 13; the sermon was the Elizabethan homily against disobedience and rebellion. For other references to Absalom or Korah, see *Eikon*, pp. 120, 130, 133; Sanderson, 1:266–67, 2:343–44; Chillingworth, 3:13; Whichcote, 1:186.

all that are not of their opinion, and disturb the peace of king-doms." Henry Byam urged his listeners to "fly from those . . . double-headed, doublehearted serpents. Those 'despisers of govern-ment,' and such as 'speak evil of dignities,' . . . That curse the king, not in their thoughts alone, but in words and works, too."[49]

Anglicans were not so naive as to assume that all human laws and authorities were perfectly wise and just. Nevertheless they would have agreed with Taylor that the good Christian "must not be too busy in examining the prudence and unreasonableness of human laws." Although he need not "believe them all to be the wisest," no inquiry into their lawfulness or wisdom, whatever its findings, could be used to justify the disparagement of "the person of the lawgiver, or to countenance any man's disobedience, much less our own." Because obedience had to be performed for con-science's sake, the wisdom of any particular human law was irre-levant. Taylor said that "although the matter before the making of the law was indifferent, yet now the obedience is not indifferent." Bishop Hall characterized the true Christian as the man who "dares not curse the king, no not in his thoughts, nor revile the ruler of his people, though justly faulty; much less dare he slander the footsteps of God's anointed." In this analysis, the man who privately criticized the wisdom of the ruler in any but the most circumspect terms was guilty of a sinful breach of the Fifth Commandment, even if he outwardly obeyed the law. The anglican casuist, Sanderson, held that it was lawful for private men to petition "modestly" about things which might "seem to them inexpedient," so long as the thing was under discussion by the councils of the higher powers. Once the appropriate public authorities had made and promulgated their decision, Sanderson held it utterly indefensible for "private men to put in their vie, and with unseasonable diligence to call in question the decency or expediency of the things so established, yea, with intolerable pride to refuse obedience thereunto." Further, this right of modest petition applied only to "indifferent things," i.e., matters not pertaining to the fundamental doctrines of re-ligion.[50]

49. Farindon, 3:635–36; Taylor, 4:490, 6:cccxxv; Byam, p. 51. It will be re-membered that the courts had upheld impositions and ship money. On the duty of paying taxes, see also Hammond, *Catechism*, p. 183; Hall, 6:173.
50. Taylor, 4:146–48; Hall, 6:173; Sanderson, 2:287.

It was on this same kind of reasoning as to the sinfulness of any but the mildest kind of political or religious dissent that such anglican laymen as Clarendon, Wotton, and Wenlock based their condemnation of the Puritans. Clarendon condemned the slandering, lying tongue because it "dissolves kingdoms and governments by raising jealousies, slanders and calumnies against princes and magistrates, thereby lessening the awe and reverence due to them." Such tongues "are the seedplots of sedition and rebellion." John Wenlock was in his home county of Suffolk in 1642 when he found many of his neighbors using their tongues in just such an "irreligious and undutiful discourse tending to the slighting and undervaluing of your Majesty's proclamation and the applauding of the Parliament's designs" on the militia. Wenlock's neighbors accused him of calling the ministers who engaged in such discourse "pulpit-knaves." He replied that he deeply reverenced "all honest divines, but such as nowadays come up to preach sedition and to abuse the King and his liege people, I know another place more fit for them than a pulpit." The seditious incitement to disobedience by such "pulpit-knaves" was also vigorously impeached by Sir Henry Wotton. He called the Covenanters' oath in Scotland "a sacred cover of the deepest impiety. . . . Never was there such a stamping and blending of rebellion and religion together."[51]

In the full anglican signification then, the duty of obedience to government was a good deal more than a civic duty. It was integrally related to eternal salvation and its religious importance was greater than its civic importance. It required more than a mere avoidance of acts of outright rebellion or defiance—it required willing and cheerful performance of the king's orders and outlawed even murmuring against them. The man who was not fully and truly obedient to the will of Caesar in the things that were Caesar's could have no assurance of salvation—indeed, he could expect damnation, regardless of his pretensions to religious justification for his conduct. In 1649 Robert Gell (later a chaplain to Sheldon) stated it as an axiom that "if rebellion or sedition be born in us, . . .

51. *Contemplations* p. 504; Wenlock, *The Humble Declaration*, pp. 22, 28; Logan Pearsall Smith, ed., *The Life and Letters of Sir Henry Wotton*, 1:407. Almost equally guilty in Clarendon's view was "the busy information whispering tongue, which spoils truths in the repeating them and tells them to those to whom they ought not to be known." *Contemplations*, p. 504. See also Farindon, 4:635–36.

Christ's innocency is not born in us" (i.e., we are not truly converted to Christianity). Hammond was quick to point out that Christ himself had been careful to live "in subjection to the known laws" of his time and place. As a "private man," he had left "the woman taken in adultery and all other offenders to the ordinary legal course." Hammond's conclusion was that Christ's example in these matters was a strong denial of "those doctrines of ambitious men which have made Christian religion a ground or excuse of moving and disquieting of states and shaking, if not dissolving, of kingdoms." Byam was another of the many Anglicans who maintained that to "honor the king" and obey him was "a duty taught by Christ both by precept and example, . . . though these days breed men of another temper who can distinguish between the person and his authority."[52] Anglicans thus made the imitation of Christ's example of obedience to the higher powers an essential mark or touchstone of saving faith. The king, however, was more than the highest civil authority—he was the supreme head of the Church of England as well. Anglicans placed heavy emphasis on the duty of political obedience and on the value of the public peace which was its result, but they emphasized even more heavily the duty of maintaining unity in the Church.

Maintaining the Unity of the Church

Peace in the state and unity in the church were inseparable in England and indeed in Western Europe generally until the doctrine of religious toleration gained widespread support. So long as the institutions of church and state were not separated, trouble in the one led to trouble in the other. "Know, dissension is the very gate of ruin and the breach at which destruction enters. Civil wars are as dangerous in matters of religion as state, and prove the earthquakes both of church and commonwealth." So warned Humphrey Sydenham prophetically on July 9, 1626, from the pulpit of Saint Mary's, the university church in Oxford. The dissension against which he thundered was the turmoil which the Puritans had raised against the doctrines in Montagu's *Appello Caesarem* (published early in 1625). The puritan attack on Montagu did not impress Sydenham: "Against the sins of the time they clack loud and often," but they

52. Gell, *Stella Nova*, p. 12; Hammond, *Catechism*, pp. 183–84; Byam, p. 50.

are like "mills driven by a hasty torrent which grind much but not clean." The heat of their zeal was, he said, like that of molten glass, in that its form was given to it by the fancy of those who blew it. The form it usually took was that of a venomous serpent, for their "every word is a sting against the church, her discipline, truth of government." Although the Puritans claimed that their sermons and speeches were based upon the testimony of Christ's twelve apostles, Sydenham supplied an easy formula by which this claim could be tested. The original apostles spoke not from "a cloister, a barn, a wood, a conventicle," but from "the temple," that is, from the church. Further, they spoke with "one office, one spirit, one mind, one faith; not here a Separatist, there a Brownist, yonder a Familist, near him an Anabaptist." Those apostles had one faith which was apparent in their lives, and that "was not religion with them which was divided, nor that unity of opinion, which they would not burn for."[53] The true Christians were those who shared the same faith, who were united in the truth and would not, even under the pain of a martyr's death, abjure that truth and unity.

Just as civil obedience was, for the Anglicans, more than absence of rebellion, so was religious unity much more than the absence of schism. It was a good in itself, the sine qua non not only for civil peace but also for salvation itself. Sydenham, in dedicating a group of his sermons to Laud in 1637, accurately identified "the main anvil most of my sermons hammer on . . . [as] . . . a general harmony, as well in doctrine as in discipline." It was also the main anvil upon which Laud himself pounded. When the 1628 Parliament opened at Westminster, Laud told the assembled members that any man who sought to be worthy of his calling as a Christian had to "endeavor to keep the unity of the Spirit in the bond of peace" (Ephesians 4:3). Unity was such a good "that none but the worst willingly break it," and those who did so were so ashamed of their crime that they disguised it by trying to "appear holier than the rest, that they may be thought to have a just cause to break it." Later Laud explicitly identified the means that his enemies had used to break the peace. In the early Church, "God appointed the foolishness of preaching" as a means "to save those that believe." However, "if the distempers

53. Sydenham, *Sermons*, pp. 34–37. He was then a Fellow of Wadham College. For evidence that he meant Puritans as well as sectarians, see footnote 57 below.

of the pulpit should grow in any national church so high, so seditious, so heretical and blasphemous, so schismatical and outrageous,
as many of them have been of late in this distracted church of ours,"
then other means were needed. Sermons which taught "nothing but
disobedience to princes and all authority, under a false pretence of
obedience to God" could not be tolerated. Laud's vision was of an
England and a Church of England, peacefully united in one faith,
and continually expressing that faith in an orderly and dignified
set of ceremonies as well as in the upright lives of its communicants.[54]

The cry for unity and against contention came not only from
Laudians but from those we have characterized as moderate Episcopalians. John Hales, for example, criticized those who "stand so
much upon state and ceremony in the church" and believe that "the
service of God doth necessarily require this noise and tumult of
outward state and vanity." He spoke eloquently of the need to deal
gently "with our weak brethren." "If we can by our behavior remedy their imbecilities, we make them the better; if not, by endur-
ing them we shall make ourselves the better." Despite these un-
Laudian tactics, Hales's Anglicanism is apparent in his persistent
emphasis upon man's ability to know and to act upon the few and
simple essentials of faith. Furthermore, he held that true Christians
(unlike Puritans and sectarians) are aware that although ceremonies
are not essential, "if we live in places where true religious persons
do resort and assemble for the service of God, it were a sin to neglect
it." Again unlike Puritans, true believers do not seek "to establish
an unity of opinion in the minds of all," especially about God's
"undiscernible . . . manner of proceeding in predestination."
Such a unity is unattainable, and it is for Hales more important "to
provide that multiplicity of conceits trouble not the church's peace."
The English withdrew from Rome because "she added unto Scripture her glosses as canonical," and to "set up our own glosses . . .
were nothing else but to pull down Baal and set up an ephod; to
run round and meet the church of Rome again at the same point in

54. Sydenham, *Occasions*, sig. A4 (recto); Laud, *Sermons*, pp. 173, 177; Laud,
History of the Troubles and Tryal, quoted in Seaver, *Puritan Lectureships*, p. 244. For a
description of a masque performed for Charles I's court at Oxford and based on
Laud's ideas about the sin of rebellion, see Trevor-Roper, *Archbishop Laud*, pp.
291–92.

which at first we left her." Benjamin Whichcote, as we have seen, did not emphasize ceremonies either but he did insist that "the reformed church" does not "hold any principles of disturbance but maintains principles of peace." He quoted from the homily against "contention and strife, and particularly that which is occasioned by principles of religion." The reformed church's "principle of peace and charity" is that all "who do agree in the main points of religion" are members of the church, "notwithstanding any different apprehensions in other matters." Any man who professes to be of the "reformed religion" but does not affirm this "is so far popish in the Protestant profession." A Church of England led by men like Hales and Whichcote would have been more tolerant of differences of opinion but no less opposed to organized attempts to preach or establish those differing opinions. It would not have waved the red flag of ceremonies before the puritan bull—but its theological Arminianism would have been much more blatant. What methods it would have used to defend itself must remain a matter for conjecture.[55]

The anglican vision of a unified, peaceable church appears again and again in Sanderson's court sermons. In 1633 he described the Church of England as a "house and family" in which all the baptized were "fellow-citizens with the saints, and of the household of God." As with an earthly household, "jarring, and snarling, and fighting" were ugly and painful to see, but it was "a goodly sight, when they dwelt together in love and unity." At Theobalds in July, 1638, he preached on Paul's injunction to the Christians at Rome, "Be like-minded one towards another" (15:5). Exactly three years later at Whitehall, he took the next verse, "That ye may with one mind and one mouth glorify God." He defined like-mindedness in Cranmer's familiar terms, praying God's gift of "unity, peace and concord; but especially that all they that do confess his holy name may also agree in the truth of his holy word, at leastwise in the main and most substantial truths." Such doctrinal unity, if accompanied (as it should be) by unity in inward affections and outward behavior was both "profitable (like the dew upon the mountains, that maketh

55. Hales, 2:299, 54–55, 310, 94–95, 36; Whichcote, 1:175, 181–82. For the "ephod" as an image, see Judges 17:5. For more on the "peace" theme, see Falkland, pp. 126, 265; Hales, 3:12–16.

the grass spring) and comfortable (as the smell of a precious ointment). And what can the heart of man desire more?" It was basic Christian theology that man was created to glorify God, and Sanderson held that "God is much glorified by unity, peace, and concord."[56]

The corollary to the beauty of unity was a horror of its opposite or anything which tended toward its opposite. Bishop Hall's son, later a prelate himself, spoke dejectedly in 1655 of the way that the church, "Christ's coat hath been miserably rent, in the whole cloth, as well as in the fringe." Some of its members had apostatized in the direction of Rome, while others were "crumbling away into conventicles, . . . and so making God's Israel to become a speckled bird of several colors, of all varieties of religions." Sanderson said that it was "odious to God, . . . grievous to every godly man, . . . the deep scandal of the reformed religion, and eternal infamy both of our church and state," that in 1641 in pamphlets and pulpits, Englishmen were almost at each others' throats over different forms of church government. Sydenham said in 1633 that this is "our misery, . . . so many opinions almost as pastors and factions as congregations." He sadly reflected that "religion begins to look asquint, and hath one eye cast for Geneva, another for Rheims, another for Amsterdam." The spectacle of such unchristian wranglings was as terrible to Clarendon as to the churchmen. He wrote that "when the Church is disunited and broken into schisms, and churchmen entertain that horrible sacrilege in their hearts, of hope to thrive and prosper by the ruin of the Church," then it is no wonder that God's judgments roll down as a mighty torrent upon a guilty, sinful nation.[57]

56. Sanderson, 2:87, 197, 194, 196. See also Sydenham, *Occasions*, p. 303; "Unity, unity, unity the Church groans for."

57. George Hall, *Gods Appearing for the Tribe of Levi*, pp. 25–26; Sanderson, 2: 308–09; Sydenham, *Occasions*, p. 301; *Contemplations*, p. 428. Sydenham clearly meant to include Puritans in his condemnation. "There was a time when faction was neither so strong nor so bold, when the chief patriarchs and founders of it had for their cities of refuge only woods and barns, and [for] their disciples but the suburbs and the offal of the people. But now forsooth . . . great men are become both their proselytes and protectors. . . . They earth themselves in corporations and peculiars where they are shot-free of the power of a consistory; an *injungendo mandamus* cannot reach them, or if it do, a common purse defends them both from bruise and battery so that the mouth of the canon cannot reach them" (p. 302). Sydenham's reference to Rheims is probably to the college of English Roman

Despite the beauty of unity and the ugliness of schism, there were schismatics, and it was in the nature of their activity that they claimed to be acting out of the best of religious motives in an attempt to practice what the Bible preached. Many of the Puritans were as anxious as the Anglicans for unity, though upon rather different terms. Each of the "factions" clamoring for dominance in the 1640s had a different platform of church government which it believed the Word of God required. Anglican apologists could and did criticize each of their opponents individually and collectively. Historians have rightly given much attention to the major controversies, but it is worth noting here that the Anglicans had one stick which could be used handily against all of their critics. It was agreed by all controversialists that the good Christian was obligated to follow the counsel of Saint John whenever he was confronted with the claim that this or that doctrine was of divine origin. He was to "believe not every spirit, but try the spirits, whether they are of God" (1 John 4:1).

There had been false prophets, deceitfully claiming divine inspiration in order to proclaim their own covetous and misguided nostrums, from the earliest times up to the present. Anglicans such as Sanderson, Hammond, Sydenham, and Stampe provided the method by which any doctrine could be "tried." They recommended the test used for the discovery of false prophecy by Christ himself: "You shall know them by their fruits" (Matt. 7:16). In other words, the Christian was to determine the practical effects of the practising of any doctrine. If the practise, as Sanderson put it in 1639, "tendeth to make men unjust in their dealings, uncharitable in their censures, undutiful to their superiors, or any other way superstitious, licentious or profane," then it could in no way be "heavenly doctrine." There was, he admitted, such a thing as "liberty of judgment" in indifferent matters—that is, matters not pertaining to the "most necessary truths" of salvation; but it was a liberty which dissenters could enjoy only "so long as they keep themselves quiet, without raising quarrels, or disturbing the peace of the church thereabouts."[58] Anyone who disturbed the peace of the church was guilty

Catholics which moved from Douai to Rheims in 1578 (*ODCC*, s.v. "Douai-Reims Bible"). Cf. Collinson, p. 235.

58. Sanderson, 2:225, 218. He added, however, that they that "have traveled farthest in these matters, with a desire to satisfy their own curiosity, have either

of abusing this liberty and was propagating false doctrine as well. Hammond's *Practical Catechism*, true to its title, provided a similar test beside the marginal heading, "Marks of False Teachers." Hammond told his readers that "the surest way to discern [the false teacher] will be to observe the effects and actions discernible in him or which are the fruits of his doctrine." In the detailed listing of effects which unmask Satan's agents, Hammond included any which "tend to injustice or uncharitableness toward men, or (under that head) to disobedience, sedition, rebellion, faction, speaking evil of dignities."[59]

Anglicans thus suggested the use of a kind of litmus paper test for claims of prophecy. If the paper turned to the blue of obedience, unity, and peace, then the prophet should be honored. If it turned to the red of sedition, schism, and rebellion, the prophet should be stoned (or at least turned over to the higher powers). Instructions for the use of the test were often accompanied with a warning that the falsest of prophets might appear to be a godly man loudly proclaiming the purity of his motives. Sydenham said that no matter how complete his knowledge of the Scriptures, no matter how apparently orthodox his doctrine; "yet because in some things thou hast made a breach of this harmony in the Church, then thou art a rebel both to it and thy Christ." Sanderson said in 1639 that "shows of sanctity and purity, pretensions of religion and reformation, is the wool that the wolf wrappeth about him when he meaneth to do most

dashed upon pernicious errors, or . . . by God's mercy . . . have been thereby brought to a deeper sense of their own ignorance" and a higher apprehension of the way in which God's counsels are past finding out. Examples: the controversies surrounding original sin, angelology, free will, and predestination. Anglicans took pride in this carefully regulated liberty of judgment in doctrinal matters because they felt that it distinguished what Henry Ferne called their "due submission" from Rome's "absolute submission" and "blind obedience." Replying in 1653 to a Catholic critic, he said that "it is to be desired rather than expected, that Christians should be all of one mind, and a due liberty of dissenting in points, wherein (*salva pietate et charitate*) good men may differ, makes for preserving of peace and unity." This was, he maintained, much better than the peremptory pronouncing of anathemas on all sides—a tactic which both the Romanists and Puritans used. *Certain Considerations*, sigs. A5 (verso) and A6 (recto). See also Whichcote, 1:156–59; Jasper Mayne, *A Sermon Concerning Unity and Agreement* (Oxford, 1646), pp. 10, 56–57.

59. Hammond, *Catechism*, pp. 318–39. See also Henry More, *Enthusiasmus Triumphatus*, p. 39, and in Cragg, pp. 142, 145.

mischief with least suspicion." Then Sanderson was issuing a caution, but by 1647 he was struggling to explain how the false teachers had been so successful. Part of his explanation was that they had proceeded as had David's unworthy son, "the grand rebel Absalom, by discrediting his father's government, pretending to a great zeal of justice and making shows and promises of great matters to be done by way of reformation" if he were in power. William Stampe, writing in 1650 from his Dutch exile to his former parishioners in Stepney, also said that evil fruits were the "characteristic mark, whereby we may receive satisfaction" in discerning the wiles and stratagems of "the great red Dragon, the old Serpent, the Devil . . . the Beast and the false prophet, [which] are all of a piece." Although "damnable doctrines may have a saint-like holiness attending upon them," the honest Christian could discover the hypocrisy in any preacher who was "persuading and inclining a people unto any apparent corruption in religion or good manners; or . . . promoting of sedition and rebellion to the prejudice of the peace and safety of any church or kingdom."[60]

There was only one conclusion that could be drawn about the place of origin and destination for all who failed the test of obedience, peace, and unity. From the Devil they came and to him they would return. All their pretenses of piety made their damnation that much more certain. Henry Byam said in Sydenham's funeral sermon in 1650 that it was too easy to meet the kind of man who "together with his dog" would come to church and "talk and tumble out as much divinity as may win him the name and reputation of a zealous gentleman." Such a man, Byam continued, was like the Jew who could cite a scripture to justify the murder of Christ —they were like the man who could "find a law to manacle those hands which reach to him the blessed sacrament."[61] Knowledge of Scriptures, "godly" behavior, prayers, and fastings were of no avail

60. Sydenham, *Waters of Marah*, pp. 28–29; Sanderson, 2:224, 344; Stampe, *Spiritual Infatuation*, pp. 96–100. See also Sydenham, *Occasions*, pp. 267–68. Sanderson alluded to the way that the Pharisees had used their "long-winded prayers" to obtain a good place in "the opinions of some and the estates of others" (2:343).

61. Byam, p. 220. Byam's younger brother was rector at Dulverton, where Sydenham was born and where he died. Byam was himself rector of Luckham in the same archdeaconry of Taunton, Somerset. Like Sydenham he was ejected for his royalism. *DNB, WR*, Bosher.

to any who disturbed the peace of the Church. Sydenham leaned on the authority of Saint Augustine to assert that all the "gifts and rewards of beatitude, which God hath treasured up for his children and elect, . . . are appropriate only to the sons of peace." The man who disseminated doctrine which resulted in disobedience and disunity was, willy-nilly, demonstrating that he was no true son of God. No true doctrine could have seditious, schismatic fruits in Stuart England. As Dr. Edward Hyde put it, "the spirit of verity is always the spirit of unity, speaking indeed by several mouths but still one truth." A clear conscience, the only foundation of assurance of salvation, was something "which they cannot have who are guilty of faction." In a sermon preached before the assembled clergy of Bishop Pierse's diocese of Bath and Wells in 1636, Sydenham condemned the occupants of "our western pulpits" who were preaching such "seditious doctrines" as Catharism, Donatism, Anabaptism, and Sabbatarianism (all of which could be collected under the name "Puritanism"). Although the seditious preachers claimed that these and other heresies were "the doctrine of the Reformed Church," Sydenham maintained. on the contrary, that "their main ring-leaders and seedsman have been such, as universities have vomited either as their burdens or their trifles, and authority justly condemned to silence or suspension." He was convinced that they were moved, not by a spirit of reform, but by a spirit of greed.[62]

Sydenham was not crying wolf where there were no wolves. The number and vigor of puritan preachers in Somerset had been increasing since Elizabeth's reign. There were a number of incidents —such as the widespread resistance to the reading of the *Book of Sports*, the stubborn struggle of the Beckington churchwardens against the diocesan's order to move their communion table to the east end of the church and rail it in, the dogged opposition to Pierse's silencing of lecturers and preachers—which indicate that the embattled tone of Sydenham's sermons was not empty rhetoric but a response to a strong puritan movement in the county.[63] During

62. Sydenham, *Waters of Marah*, pp. 42–43; Hyde, *Legacy*, pp. 22, 191; Sydenham, *Occasions*, pp. 266–67.

63. For details see the sketch of Pierse in the *DNB*; S. H. Cassan, *Lives of the Bishops of Bath and Wells*, pt. 2, pp. 63–68; *V.C.H. Somerset* (1911), 2:42–46. Thomas G. Barnes's excellent study, *Somerset, 1625–1640*, has little to say on the influence of

the 1640s, the worst fears of Sydenham and other Anglicans around
England came to fruition. Laud himself was executed in 1645. How
the bishop of Bath and Wells, William Pierse, escaped a similar fate
(or at least the extended incarceration suffered by that other
prominent persecutor of Puritans, Matthew Wren) remains a
mystery—he was, in any case, among the group of bishops imprisoned at the end of 1641. Sydenham and Byam were among the
hundreds of anglican ministers deprived of their preferments for
their support of the royalist cause. The unified structure of doctrine
and discipline which they had sought to forge and maintain was
shattered.

Preserving the Public Peace and the Natural Order

Anglicans continued, in the changed circumstances created by the
victory of the rebels, to preach that the truth of any man's profession
of Christianity could be judged by its tendency toward harmony,
peace, and unity via obedience. Richard Harwood, in a sermon
preached before Charles I at Oxford in February, 1643, condemned
all those heretical opinions of the time which claimed to be true
religion, yet were belied by "their bloody effects, the murders,
treasons, and rebellions they do produce." Over two years later
(and only a short time after the disastrous battle of Naseby), he
sought to encourage dispirited royalists at the university church.
He told them that, although the Church was then almost buried in
its own debris, God would "repair it into its former beauty and
luster." He counselled withdrawal from the tumults raised by
enemies into a private world of Christian living, patience, and
prayer until such time as God chose to restore the Church of
England. This was the course followed by John Evelyn as he
related it in a letter to Jeremy Taylor (possibly when Taylor was in
prison in May, 1665). Evelyn said that "Julianus Redivivus" (i.e.,
the reincarnation of the persecuting Roman Emperor in the form of
Oliver Cromwell) could do whatever he liked, but he could not
"hinder our private intercourses and devotions where the breast is
the chapel and our heart is the altar. Obedience founded on the
understanding will be the only cure and retreat."[64]

Puritanism in the county—but see his article on Somerset churchales in the *Transactions of the Royal Historical Society* 9 (5th ser., 1959):103–22.
    64. Harwood, *King David's Sanctuary*, p. 22; Harwood, *Loyall Subject's Retiring*

Anthony Farindon used much the same terms in his discussion of the suppression of the celebration of Christmas by the puritan higher powers. He regarded its celebration as fully justifiable by Scripture, councils, and Fathers. Nevertheless, "I do not stand up against power . . . [but remember] Him whose memory we so much desire to celebrate, who was the best teacher and greatest example of obedience." He urged Anglicans instead to understand that "where the church is shut up, every man's chamber, every man's breast, may be a temple, and every day a holy day."[65] Farindon was among the small but important group of anglican divines who managed to continue their public ministries by one means or another after the initial round of ejections early in the 1640s. He was ejected from the Berkshire vicarage of Bray; but despite his counsel of passive obedience to Cromwell, he was by no means a model for that pusillanimous vicar of later rhyme. He was a keen judge of men. When Cromwell's future son-in-law and right-hand man, Henry Ireton, was a student at Oxford in 1626, Farindon disciplined him for "some insubordination" and predicted that he "would prove either the best or the worst instrument that ever this kingdom bred." Ireton got his revenge after the second battle of Newbury when he plundered Farindon's vicarage. Farindon also lost the divinity lectureship at the royal chapel of Saint George at Windsor, a preferment originally secured through Laud's interest. But in 1647, through the influence of Sir John Robinson (a kinsman of Laud), he was chosen minister of Saint Mary Magdalene in Milk Street, London. The church became popular with Anglicans and was known as "the scholars' church" because many divines (including Hammond and Sanderson) went there.[66] As one of the few Anglicans preaching in the politically sensitive and volatile center of London, Farindon's position was extremely vulnerable. He nevertheless succeeded in

---

Roome, p. 11; John Evelyn, *Diary and Correspondence*, ed. W. Bray, pp. 566–67. Also in Taylor, 1:cccxxii–cccxxiii. The dating of the letter is discussed on pp. cccxxiv–cccxxvi.

65. Farindon, 1:30.

66. *DNB, WR*, p. 68; "Life" by the Rev. Thomas Jackson in Farindon, vol. 1. He was also sequestered for an undetermined period at the end of 1651 or the beginning of 1652. Robinson took office as Lord Mayor in 1662 and was son-in-law to Sir George Whitmore, an important City merchant and royalist (Pearl, pp. 306–07). Farindon preached at Whitmore's funeral in 1654. For more on Anglicans in England during this period, see Bosher, chap. 1.

examining many subjects thoroughly, not least of which was exploring the meaning of the doctrine of Christian obedience as most Anglicans understood it. Indeed, we can treat his formulation as a model of anglican thought on this subject.

Although we have been considering the anglican notion of obedience in the realm of religious and secular politics, no survey of this matter could be complete without reference to the natural and cosmic realm upon which the more immediate social and political realms depended, and to which they corresponded. Farindon and his colleagues saw each true Christian striving for a perfection which was none the less to be striven for because it could not be completed in this life. The Christian's attempt to perfect himself is, said Farindon, an attempt to partake as fully as he can of the attributes of God's nature. He can come to see God only by doing his utmost to be like him.[67] God's center is himself and there is only order and peace, not turbulence and change; so we should "in this be like unto God himself,—have our centre in ourselves, or rather make peace our centre." God's kingdom is similarly orderly and peaceable; in it everything is "in its order. There is something first and something next to be observed, and every thing to be ranked in its proper place." In the kingdom of nature things are ordered and ranked; heavy bodies do not ascend, nor do light ones descend; "and so it is in both church and commonwealth. . . . We cannot be quiet and rest but in our own place and function."[68] Whenever a man is out of his place, his movement can only be disorderly. He can only cause trouble when he steps into the sphere of a superior, a sphere where he has no business. The tumult which ensues in human affairs is analogous to that which follows upon the arrival of a

67. Farindon, 1:184–86. On Hooker's statement of this, see McAdoo, *The Spirit of Anglicanism*, p. 7. A good short introduction to this important subject, the correspondences between the cosmic and social universes, is in Christopher Morris, *Political Thought in England: Tyndale to Hooker*, chap. 4. On the "imitation of God" theme, see Whichcote, 1:32–33, 149–50; Cudworth, pp. 33–34, 46, 51.
68. Farindon, 1:336, 127, 338. Sydenham said that Christians must be peaceable because servants should imitate their masters and "the Lord is not the God of tumult but of peace." *Waters of Marah*, p. 6. He also said "no bishops, no king; and if neither bishop nor king, how a God? God professeth an order in his universal government, and without those, there would be some manifest breach and flaw in the carriage of inferior things. . . . And certainly episcopal honor hath gone down the wind since this dream of parity first started in the church." *Occasions*, p. 299.

meteor upon the earth or "a stone in the firmament." In church and state as in those other spheres, Farindon held that the result is that "the whole course of nature will be set on fire, . . . the foot shall stand where the hand doth; the ear shall speak, the tongue hear, and the foot see."[69] It is on the basis of this analogy that Jeremy Taylor compared rebellion to witchcraft, "that sin, which of all sin seems the most unnatural and damned impiety."[70]

In addition to the analogies from God's attributes and the hierarchical order of his kingdom, Farindon argued that the obedience was required because Christians should imitate Christ. The Anglican told his beleaguered parishioners that Christians are obliged to raise themselves nearer their Savior "by a holy and diligent imitation of his obedience." It is a willing obedience to God's laws and commands which is "the true mark and character of a servant of God." If the spirit of Christ truly dwells in us, then it "worketh in us 'the obedience of faith' "; that is, an obedience which is "universal and equal" (obeys all the divine injunctions and not just some of them), "even and constant" (obeys continuously and not only now and then), and "sincere and real" (obeys out of a desire to do so and a love of God—not hypocritically and fearfully). Most Puritans would have fully agreed with these adjectives (though they would not have been so ready to speak of the imitation of Christ's example). If, however, they had been present, they would have certainly known whom the preacher was criticizing in his sermons on Thess. 4:11 ("study to be quiet, and to do your own business"). In these sermons Farindon clearly and carefully explained how this kind of obedience was related to peace in church and state. "The great mistake and fault of those who profess Christianity," he said at the outset, is that they have emphasized only one doctrine—say, repentance, or zeal, or piety, or faith—at the expense of complete and full holiness. They are not at peace with

69. Farindon, 1:338. Further, "all shall be prophets and teachers. I might say, all shall be kings, and I might add, all will be atheists." See also Bishop Hall's eloquent and extended analogy between "faction" in church and state and earthquakes ("strange and unnatural things") in nature; the sermon was preached before the king in 1641. Hall, 10:500–19.

70. Taylor, 4:150. The text for this is 1 Sam. 15:23: "Rebellion is the sin of witchcraft." It was the text for Stampe's *Spiritual Infatuation*. M. A. Judson cites another example of its use in one of Isaac Bargrave's sermons. *Crisis of the Constitution*, pp. 183–84.

others, though at peace with themselves; they are "very religious,
and very turbulent, have the 'tongues of angels,' but no hand at all
'to do their own business, and to work' in their calling." Farindon
held that such "partial holiness" was worse than useless. According
to him, Paul had taught the necessity not only of such "domestic
and immanent virtues" as faith and hope, which are useful only to
their possessor, but also "emanent, public and homiletical" virtues
which are useful to others. These included patience, meekness,
generosity and "love of quietness and peace"[71]—all arising from
Second Table duties.

Such a full and complete holiness is the "queen in the midst of
the circle and crown of all the graces, and claimeth an interest in
them all," and it is no accident that the component virtue upon
which Farindon chose to enlarge was the last named, the love of
quietness and peace. To be quiet is, he thought, to be peaceful at all
times and in all places; it is to so compose ourselves that we retain a
calm and even temper, never attacking others because they say
things we would not hear, do things we would not have done,
"though their thoughts be not as our thoughts, nor their ways,
though they be contrary to us." More particularly, the quietness
which is essential to full holiness requires that "we do not start out
of the orb wherein we are fixed, and then set it on fire, because we
think it moveth disorderly."[72] It is clear from the examples Farindon
cited that he was defining the notion of calling and of place very
carefully indeed. The man who performed an act which was "in
itself lawful and most expedient to be done" was guilty of a sin if
the act were "another man's duty." Uzziah, a layman, was struck
with leprosy when he went to the sanctuary to burn incense—only
the priests were called to burn incense (2 Chron. 27:16–21). Absalom was hanged because "he would up into the tribunal which
was none of his place." Just as pointedly, Farindon noted that there

71. Farindon, 1:30, 196, 489–90, 305–10. He states also, nothing is more repugnant to true religion than "a mixed and compounded Christian, made up of a
bended knee and a stiff neck, of an attentive ear and a hollow heart, of a pale
countenance and a rebellious spirit, . . . and real disbedience" (pp. 571–72). See
also Whichcote, 1:183–84.
72. Farindon, 1:312. Hales also spoke against those who go about " 'making the
right somewhat righter,' . . . out of desire to amend what is already well." His
quotation is from Saint Gregory of Nazianzus.

had been Christians who had, "out of a wanton and irregular zeal," destroyed heathen images and been slain by the heathen for their trouble. Nevertheless, the church had rightly censured them as "disturbers of the peace." Good and pious intentions were no excuse for going beyond one's calling. The "enemy of the truth" had never lacked for agents who had "unseasonably disturbed the public peace and their own, whose business it was (and sure it could be none of their own) to teach pastors to govern and divines how to preach; every day to make a new coat for the church, to hammer and shape out a new form and discipline, as if nothing could be done well because they stood not by and had a hand in the doing it; and so maketh the church not so fair, but certainly as changeable as the moon."[73] A more direct slap at Puritans of all shades would not be easy to find. Sanderson preached similarly before the King in 1647; "A regular minister sitteth quietly at home, followeth his study, . . . keepeth himself within his own station and meddleth no further." Unfortunately there were others—"schismatical spirits . . . [who] will not be contained within their own circle, but . . . [are always] offering, yea, thrusting themselves into every pulpit before they be sent for, running from town to town, from house to house, that they may scatter the seeds of sedition and superstition at every table and in every corner."[74]

Farindon did not hesitate to link the inner peace of the human conscience with the outer peace of society. Faith was the rock upon which the church was founded, but, as he said, "faith imparteth practise," the practice of virtues requisite in members of both the church and the commonwealth. Despite the vulnerability of his position in Cromwellian London, Farindon left no doubt that in his view no man who "at pleasure breaketh those ties which nature and religion have linked him in a body politic, and that (many times) under pretence of religion, [could] boast or comfort himself in his relation to Christ." In other words, a man who troubles the state in any way, though ostensibly for conscience's sake, cannot

73. Farindon, 1:336–37. Sydenham told the assize judges at Taunton in 1634 that it was not his "practise to . . . school (as some do) a magistrate and catechize a judge." *Occasions*, pp. 76–77. Puritans might try to tell a judge how to do his job— but for him the word "judge" meant "a king one way and a God another, and what is that but a God and a God?"
74. Sanderson, 2:348.

have inner peace. He cannot have any confidence that he will be saved from the fires of hell. "He that is not a good member of the commonwealth is not a true member of the church." For Farindon, as for all Anglicans, the test which had to be applied to instructions which were said to be from God was to determine whether they aimed to advance Christ's kingdom by promoting men "in the ways of innocency and perfect obedience." Any doctrine had to be tested by its fruits, and if these were such as "tread down peace and charity" then they were not of God and could not help men toward that plenitude of holiness which Christianity requires.[75]

At the heart of Farindon's view of the Christian life was the conviction that true religion is "not to hear, and talk, and fill the world with noise and confusion, 'not to exercise ourselves in things too high for us'; but to fight against our lusts and trouble none but ourselves." Our duty, when the world is "out of order," is not to break it into smaller pieces by trying to settle it, but to "establish this order, this peace, this heaven within our selves." Inward peace and quietness is "the work of the gospel, the sum of all, the end of all that it teacheth,—to work this quietness in us, that we may raise it up in others, . . . that there may be no deceit, no envy, . . . no violence, . . . no complaining in our streets." Further, there is "no truer method" for gaining this quietness than "to abide in our calling, . . . in our proper place and sphere, . . . in that state and condition in which the hand of providence hath placed us." There were Anglicans, such as Clarendon and Hammond, who were taking a more active part in restoring the political and social order which had been so rudely shaken, and by this time they had a good many allies from among the earlier shakers. Without, however, going quite as far as Farindon did in applying this pacific doctrine to the situation in the 1650s, they fully agreed with him that disturbers of the peace of the church and the kingdom had disobeyed the will of God. Anglicans were united in believing that any man who thought that obedience to the divine will required that he leave his particular station in the Great Chain of Being by challeng-

75. Farindon, 1:351, 121–22. Hammond (p. 16) said before the king at Carisbrooke in 1647 that men who had not achieved peace with others lack "sure sanctity, . . . in despite of all glorious appearance to the contrary, [such men] have received the name, the grace of Christ in vain."

ing the policy of his superiors was obeying not God but Satan. Although he might honestly believe that the salvation of his soul in the next life (and thus his assurance and comfort in this) might depend upon action injurious to the peace, he was nevertheless badly mistaken in the only matter which ultimately mattered. "Christianity bindeth us to our own business; and, till we break loose, till some one or other step out of his place from it, there is peace; we are safe in our lesser vessels, and the ship of the commonwealth rideth on with that smoothness and evenness which it hath from the consistency of its parts in their own place."[76]

The doctrine of obedience and peace preached by Sydenham, Laud, Hammond, and Farindon was still very much in use after 1660. Although not one of them survived to taste the fruits of the restoration of the Stuart monarchy, their successors in the Church of England kept the doctrine handy both as a prescription for political behavior and as a weapon to brandish over their defeated opponents. Anglican clergymen reveled in the orgy of loyalty which ensued, and it was quite unthinkable that the God who had so gloriously delivered England by restoring the monarchy would ever allow the king or his successors to turn toward Rome or Geneva or any city besides Canterbury. Dr. Thomas Pierce, a chaplain-in-ordinary to Charles II (soon to be the president of Magdalen College, Oxford), told the House of Lords on the first anniversary of the Restoration that they must not forget that they were deeply indebted to God for delivering them from "the land of Egypt, . . . the house of bondage," that is, the government of the militant saints. But it was equally important that they remember God as represented in his vicegerent, Charles II, and do all that could possibly be done to enable him to "be indeed what he is styled, *Defensor Fidei*." Insofar as the peers did support and obey the king, according to Dr. Pierce, by so much the greater would be their glory, both here and hereafter. He went on to put in a special plea for the restoration of the bishops to their full antebellum authority, a step which he thought was essential to the maintenance of royal authority. Christians should, he thought, fully appreciate that they, unlike the heathens, "had the glory to be subjected by a most

76. Farindon, 1:329, 317, 332, 335. See also Hales, 3:50–51.

honorable obedience."⁷⁷ A little over three years later, preaching in the university church in Oxford, he gave further details of the meaning of the obedience which was expected of Christians. He was speaking to many who would soon occupy pulpits all over the country, and he made it very clear that there was one thing that they must never do. They must never preach with "fiery, cloven tongues, unless they are cleft and set on fire by the spirit of unity and truth." Nowhere, he said, could one ever see "so sad and so deplorable a spectacle" as when a minister transformed himself into "the absolute guise of a son of Belial" and despised "his own soul . . . and the house of God by an applauded defamation of his superiors."⁷⁸

The concept of Christian obedience as understood and preached by Anglicans in the middle decades of the seventeenth century cannot be separated from concepts of harmony in church and state, uniformity in doctrine and practice, and acceptance of orders and ranks in the social as well as the natural universe. Defamers of superiors were one category of those disturbers of the public peace which were, in Hammond's phrase, "the only *boutefeux*, . . . the disquieters of the honor and peace of Christendom." King Charles also used this word, and it means "an incendiary," a kindler of "feuds and discontents." "He is the *boutefeu*," said Sanderson of the proud, impatient man "that beginneth the fray." Men who were boutefeux were, whatever they said and however they appeared, not yet converted to true Christianity. The doctrine of obedience interpreted in this way made the effect of a man's actions on the peace of the community and the unity of the church a guide to the truth of his profession of faith. It urged all men to evaluate the results of their actions in terms of the public peace. Peace, Farindon had said, should be "the only judge to set an end to all contro-

77. Pierce, pp. 71, 68 (19 May 1661). Pierce described Phocas, the Roman Emperor who allegedly sold the title of supremacy among bishops (thus beginning the papal usurpation of supreme authority in the church), as "the greatest villain in the world, excepting Cromwell and Pontius Pilate" (p. 336).

78. Ibid., pp. 332, 335. Further, "as if on the tip of a man's tongue stood all religion. For let his alms be never so great, his fastings never so many, his prayers never so long, . . . yet if he bridleth not his tongue from injurious calumnies and falsehoods, he is a man either of none, or a vain religion."

versies."[79] Only the man who made peace his judge could consider
himself a true Christian, and only true Christians could face the
ills to which flesh and spirit were heir with equanimity and hope.

79. Hammond, p. 13; *Eikon*, p. 16; Sanderson, 2:194; Farindon, 1:312. For
Bramhall's use of the term, see the *OED* entry. Anthony Wood used it to describe
Thomas Case. *DNB*, s.v. "Thomas Case." Cf. Montagu, *Appello Caesarem*, p. 79.
That its implication was pejorative for royalists is further indicated by S. Pordage's
modifier in his poem, *The Loyal Incendiary, or the Generous Boutefeu*, "A Poem Occasioned by the Report of the Owners Bravely Setting Fire to the Rye House, as
the King came from Newmarket" (1684).

5

THE FRUITS OF CONVERSION:
FELLOWSHIP AND CHARITY

TIMOTHY: Christ commanded us to give to everyone who asks. If I did that, I'd have to beg myself within a month.
EUSEBIUS: I believe Christ meant those who ask for necessities . . . it's robbery to bestow on those who will use it ill what ought to have relieved the instant distress of our neighbors. Hence those who adorn monasteries or churches at excessive cost, when meanwhile so many of Christ's living temples are in danger of starvation, shiver in their nakedness, and are tortured by want of necessities, seem to me almost guilty of a capital crime.

Erasmus, Colloquies (1522)

The worthy poor do not realize that their function is to exercise our generosity. . . . I slip a small coin into their hand . . . they must love me, and that love will beautify their lives. I know that they lack necessities, and I take pleasure in being their superfluity. Besides, whatever their poverty, they will never suffer as much as my grandfather did: when he was little, . . . in winter, he had to break the ice in the water jug in order to wash. Happily, things have since been put to rights. My grandfather believes in Progress; so do I: Progress, that long, steep path which leads to me.

Jean-Paul Sartre, The Words (1964)

We are all worms. But I do believe that I am a glow-worm.
Winston Churchill to Lady Bonham-Carter (1907)

"We know that we have passed from death unto life, because we love the brethren." This text (1 John 3:14) is one of many in the Scriptures which say that no man who does not love his fellow Christians and express that love in acts of charity has been truly converted to the religion he professes. Anglicans and Puritans in

Stuart England were fully agreed that "loving the brethren" was an essential mark or touchstone of salvation. Henry Hammond's message for the king and his shrunken retinue at Carisbrook Castle in 1647 was that there was only one way that disciples of Christ could be distinguished from other men. It was only by the charity they displayed to one another; " 'behold how they love,' how they embrace." This was, he said, because Christ had come into the world in order to introduce faith and "brotherly charity into his church, this being the most strict, and most frequently reiterated command of Christ." Richard Sibbes, speaking at Gray's Inn for the last time just before his death in the summer of 1635, told his listeners that "love to the brethren" is a grace and that "every grace is but faith exercised." Therefore, if they sought proof that their faith was truly and deeply rooted, their love to fellow Christians provided that proof: "For the root and branches be together, though the root is not always discerned. And therefore when we discover any true faith in the fruit of it, let us support and comfort ourselves with it."[1]

Anglicans and Puritans also concurred on the truth of the corollary—that hatred of the brethren, whether expressed in thought, word, or deed, was a sign of reprobation. As Hammond put it, "there is no possible separating the hatred of the brethren from enmity to Christ." Thomas Hooker accounted it "a great character of the devil, he is an 'accuser of the brethren' " (Rev. 12:10). At first glance then, the anglican and puritan conceptions of the virtue of Christian charity are similar. In its broadest sense, charity consists of loving one's fellow men and of doing good to them at all times and upon all occasions. It requires ministering to their needs and wants when they are in any way afflicted. Relatively little was said about loving heathens because there were no outright heathens upon whom charity could be showered in seventeenth-century England. The fundamental duty of loving one's fellow Christians was, however, a prerequisite to assurance of salvation. But as Charles and Katherine George have rightly noted, "brethren" was a "weighted word" in early Stuart England.[2] It

1. Hammond, pp. 17–18; Sibbes, *Works*, 7:353–54.
2. Hammond, p. 19; T. Hooker, *Lessons*, p. 85; C. and K. George, *English*

is the purpose of this chapter to see just how it was weighted by considering puritan and anglican conceptions of the duty of loving the brethren.

PURITANS AND THE "IDOL OF OUR GODLY BRETHREN"

The sentiments expressed in the *Appello Caesarem* so angered many of the members of the House of Commons in 1625 that they ordered its author, Richard Montagu, into the custody of the sergeant-at-arms. King Charles I quickly moved to protect the cleric by making him royal chaplain (he later became a bishop). Montagu's puritan critics doubtless found cause for offence throughout the book, but few statements would have incensed them more than his charge that their aim was to build up the power of that great "moat-in-the-eye unto popular irregularity and puritanical parity, the idol of our godly brethren." There was nothing that Puritans loathed more than idolatry, and Montagu here suggested that they had made an idol of their "godly brotherhood." Equally sarcastic objections to the puritan notion of brotherhood were made by other Anglicans. Humphrey Sydenham tartly dismissed those preachers who complained of persecution and impoverishment after they had been ejected from their benefices for refusing to wear surplices. Then, "a brethren-contribution more fats them than all the fortunes they were masters of before." By January 1640, the tables were turned, and the Puritans were about to oust all the clergymen who did not measure up to their standards for a godly preaching ministry. Sir Thomas Knyvett, an Anglican, wrote to his wife that there would be "such a purgation of black-coats . . . if the Parliament entertains all the complaints of the brethren, I know not where they will find new ones to put in." Jasper Mayne, who often preached before the royal court in Oxford during the Civil War, complained in 1646 of the puritan preachers then about the country who claimed the art to heal and reconcile men; their followers called each other "brethren" and boasted of their charity. "But," said Mayne,

---

Protestant Mind, p. 401. My argument is that "brethren" was considerably more weighted than they think.

"they call only such as are of their own confederacy brethren."
Christ had used the word as a mark of unity and peace, but they
degraded it by using it as "the sign and mark to know a faction
by."[3]

These charges were not without foundation. Lay and clerical
writers from one side of the puritan spectrum to the other in Stuart
England did indeed place great emphasis upon the importance of
belonging to a group composed of "godly brethren." They used a
wide variety of terms to refer to such a group or to a coalition of
such groups. Cromwell, as we shall see, referred repeatedly to
"the people of God," "honest godly men," "the saints," "the godly
party." In this section we will first determine how the Puritans
identified each other as "godly brethren." What were the most
important signs and marks used by Puritans to designate others as
either "well-affected" or ill-affected, "malignant" opposers of
God's truth or benign members of a godly fellowship. Secondly,
we will discover what kinds of charitable services were owed to
these brethren as distinguished from other mortals, and what were
the benefits of performing such acts of charity. Here, as in the
preceding chapter on obedience, there is a sizable area of overlap
between anglican and puritan conceptions of the duty of charity—
but there are also emphases which clearly differ, and differ in ways
that carried important political implications.

Love to Brother Saints

Oliver Cromwell, when he convened the Parliament of the Saints

3. Montagu, *Appello Caesarem*, p. 3; Sydenham, *Waters of Marah*, p. 32; *The
Knyvett Letters (1620–1644)*, p. 98; Mayne, *A Sermon Concerning Unity and Agreement*
p. 25. Peter Heylyn described the Feoffees for Impropriations as "a secret combination of the brotherhood." Quoted in C. Hill, *Economic Problems of the Church*, p.
255. Cf. Collinson, pp. 212, 234, 294, 324–28, 339, 343–45. On the reaction to
Montagu and to "Arminianism" in the 1620s, see Gardiner, *History*, 5:351–64,
399–402; Trevor-Roper, *Archbishop Laud*, pp. 73–77; C. Hill, *Puritanism and Revolution*, pp. 243–49; Hillel Schwartz, "Arminianism and the English Parliament,
1614–1629," *JBS* 12 (1973):43–58; N. R. N. Tyacke, "Puritanism, Arminianism
and Counter-Revolution," in C. Russell, ed., *The Origins of the English Civil War*,
pp. 119–44. Irvonwy Morgan has noted that Montagu, when writing to his friend
John Cosin, "often used the words 'The Brethren,' instead of 'Puritans.' " *Prince
Charles's Puritan Chaplain*, p. 41n. See also p. 71. for examples of the use of "Brother"
by lay Puritans.

on the hot fourth of July, 1653, occupied himself at some length with a justification of his peremptory dismissal of the Rump. One of his reasons had been the Rumpers' plan to hold new elections without excluding those "Presbyterians" who had been ready to betray the parliamentary cause to Charles I and later to his son. The lord general and his fellow officers felt very strongly that none who had "deserted this cause and interest upon the king's account" should have any power in a new parliament. In recounting all this to Praise-God Barebones and his colleagues, Cromwell added that "it is one thing to live friendly and *brotherly*, to bear with a[nd] love a person of another judgment in religion; [and] another thing to have any so far set into the saddle . . . as . . . to have all the rest of their *brethren* at mercy."[4]

Emphasis has been added to "brother" and "brethren" because the use of these terms in this speech and elsewhere in Cromwell's writings serves as a good starting point for analysis of the duty of charity or "love to the brethren" as the Puritans understood it. Despite the perfidy of Love's plot, of Scottish presbyterian military support for the Stuarts, and of presbyterian plots against the army, Cromwell continued to think of the Puritans who wanted a presbyterian system of church government as godly brethren and saints. Three years earlier, he had described to his son-in-law Ireton the reluctance of his army to fight against the Scots at Dunbar. "We made great professions of love, knowing we were to deal with many who were godly . . . we begged to be believed that we loved them as our own souls." Despite their deluded opposition to the cause they had earlier supported, there were "many who were godly" among the Scots. Cromwell again demonstrated his awareness that they too deserved the love owed to fellow saints in his first speech as lord protector. A few minutes after uttering the statement quoted above, he urged his listeners to remember their duty of being "faithful to the saints." He had not, he said, intended to criticize

4. Abbott, 3:59. The additions in brackets are mine and follow Carlyle's improvement of the coherence of this passage. In a letter to his son Henry, who was in command in Ireland, Cromwell expressed the same attitude toward the Anabaptists: "I know they are weak because they are so peremptory in judging others. I quarrel not with them but in their seeking to supplant others." Abbott, 4:146 (April 21, 1656). On the use of "brother" in Pym's circle, see Zagorin, p. 102n.

too harshly "those of the presbyterian judgment. I think if you have not an interest of love for them you will hardly answer this [duty] of faithfulness to the saints."[5]

In Cromwell's usage then, the "brethren" are synonymous with the Saints, the Honest Party, the People of God, the Children of God and a host of similar terms. John Preston was another of the many influential Puritans for whom the saints and the brethren were simply identical. The Word, he said, gave it "as a peculiar sign by which we may judge of our love to the Lord [i.e., of the truth of our conversions], it must not be passed by, and that is our love to the saints." For proof he cited 1 John 4:20: "Wilt thou say thou 'lovest God whom thou hast not seen, and yet lovest not thy brother whom thou hast seen?' "[6] A saint was a brother and a brother was a saint—but this was automatically to limit brotherhood to a circle whose radius was much shorter than that of the baptized membership of the Church of England. As the second part of this chapter will demonstrate, Anglicans insisted that no man on earth was entitled to circumscribe his "love to the brethren" to his own notion of a brotherhood within the established church.

Puritans, however, customarily lowered the mantle of brotherhood only upon "men who know the Lord,"[7] regenerate men who had experienced something more than the common grace with which all too many were satisfied. Preston put this distinction in theological terms when he described baptism as "a single covenant" in which God promises that "if you will believe and repent, and walk in my ways, you shall be saved." This is to say merely that baptism seals the covenant of works; but no man since the fall of the first Adam is capable of performing this side of the covenant. The saints are those who are parties to "a double covenant" in which God says, "I will give you an heart, and you shall repent, and believe, and be saved."[8] The Puritans thought of the fellowship of

5. Abbott, 2:326; 3:62.
6. Preston, *Breast-Plate*, pt. 3, p. 100. See also Sibbes, *Cordialls*, p. 162. The phrases are sprinkled throughout Cromwell's letters and speeches. Hence Sir Charles Firth could write that Cromwell's highest priority was his "duty to a section of the English people." *Oliver Cromwell*, pp. 482–83.
7. The phrase is Cromwell's, here used to describe the kind of men who had been chosen for the Parliament of the Saints. Abbott, 3:60.
8. Preston, *Life*, pt. 2, pp. 86–87. On covenant theology, see Leonard J. Trin-

the "godly brethren" on earth as an admittedly imperfect but nevertheless essential approximation of men whom God had elected to participate in the "double covenant" which went beyond baptism. The brethren were members of the invisible church which their fellowship in this life represented. The distinction between the visible church—a body composed of all who were baptized and professed belief in the fundamental doctrines of Christianity—and the invisible church, the fortunate body of elect saints predestined to eternal life—was a seventeenth-century commonplace and indeed was long a central theme of Christian history. Puritans did not claim to know with absolute certainty who was regenerate and who was not, but they were quite ready to make guesses on the basis of criteria derived from their reading of the Scriptures.

The common element running through these criteria for identifying the saints is the one suggested by Preston when he asked, "What is grace, what is that you call Christianity else, but to do that which another man cannot do?" If you would "show your grace, show your regeneration," then do it "by exposing your selves to that danger, to those losses for any good cause, . . . by keeping the Sabbath better than others do, by being more exact in looking to your ways." The saints, because they have received grace which makes them new, regenerate creatures, are able to rise above ordinary professing Christians in obeying God's commandments. They are, as John Winthrop insisted, not like "our common Protestants . . . who in the depths of their devise, will be wiser than Christ and his apostles" by trying to love both the world and him. Common Protestants, men who by common restraining grace and fear of punishment live moral lives and profess belief, are not saints. "The very naming" of the title of saint, said Thomas Goodwin, "dasheth morality and formal profession out of countenance, as light doth a glowworm, as importing a more divine workmanship created, and some singular thing, . . . even holiness in truth." True saving grace does not, according to Preston, merely "make a

terud, "The Origins of Puritanism," *CH* 20 (1951): 37–57; Perry Miller, *The New England Mind*, chap. 12. For a study of the way that Independents made this concept a basis of church organization between 1640 and 1660, see G. F. Nuttall, *Visible Saints*, pp. 70–100. Particularly useful among recent studies bearing upon this subject is Coolidge, especially pp. 26–54.

little light alteration on the superficies of the heart, but alters the very frame of it." It brings with it not only the power to resolve for good works, but "the power and strength to perform them." It does not, Preston continued, "put upon us a washy color of profession," but instead "dyeth us in grain with grace and holiness. . . . This, my beloved, differs from common graces, from the common form of godliness which is in the world, as much as life differs from the picture, or the substance from the shadow." There were those who maintained that none could tell the true believers from the wicked, but Thomas Goodwin dismissed that notion firmly. "Now surely," he said, "there are many rules in the Word whereby it is meet to judge who are saints." Those who professed "to know God" but whose works were "so abominable" as to demonstrate their reprobation could not be saints. "It is not," he insisted, "a profession of faith joined with morality, and no grand scandal, but a profession of such a strictness that will rise to holiness, that you are to judge men saints by."[9]

Goodwin, who was among the most influential of the Independents, wanted churches composed only of saints, but this did not mean that he did not regard as brethren the Puritans who did not agree with his ecclesiastical polity. He welcomed the eminent Presbyterian John Howe into the congregational church he organized as president of Magdalen College, Oxford, during the 1650s. In the university church in 1651 he preached a sermon which explained how "the saints shall, and must be one, and reconciled in the end," even though there would be "enmities . . . amongst the people of God themselves" in this life.[10] There were many Puritans who did not find it necessary to separate from the "common Protestants" or even the obviously reprobate. Goodwin's mentor, Richard Sibbes, flatly rejected the notion that the godly brethren must have a church purged of the wicked. He told his audience at Gray's Inn that the unregenerate members of the Church of England were not really members at all, and that God

9. Preston, *Breast-Plate*, pt. 3, pp. 204–05; *WP*, 1:123; T. Goodwin, 1:11; Preston, *Cuppe*, pp. 29–30; T. Goodwin, 1:12–13. See also Preston, *Life*, pt. 1, p. 62.
10. T. Goodwin, 2:xxxv, 361–62. God has indeed foreordained that there would be enmities "in the hearts and lives of those he intends to save" (p. 368).

would extrude them on Judgment Day: "There is a mixture in the Church (as in a house) of good and bad vessels, but the godly are especially God's house. As for hypocrites and fake professors, they are no more in the house than the excrements are in the body. They are in the body but not of the body, and therefore as Ishmael they must be cast out at length."[11] Quite regardless of whether the unregenerate were to be received into church membership or not, Puritans were certain that they could identify most of their godly brethren. There would be errors—of failure to perceive the presence either of hypocrisy in some or of grace in others. But the crucial distinctions could nonetheless be made in most cases. Cromwell charged those who had been chosen for membership in the Parliament of the Saints with the duty of "bearing good fruits to the nation, to men as men, to the people of God, to all in their several stations." He reminded them that Moses and Paul had had spirits "not for believers only but for the whole people."[12] The true Christian had duties to both believers and unbelievers, regenerate and unregenerate—but he had a special relationship with those who were "especially God's house."

In principle then, the godly brethren could be identified because they were different from other men. The essence of this difference was that they transcended common forms of godliness to what Goodwin called "a strictness that will rise to holiness." Further, "those who are children of His begetting through the Spirit" (another of Cromwell's phrases) were not limited to one kind of ecclesiastical polity. "I say, when I say the people of God," Cromwell told the saintly Members of Parliament, "the large comprehension of them under the several forms of godliness in this nation." The Rumpers had failed "as plain a trial of their spirits" as anyone could ask when they had not maintained the Commission for the Propagation of the Gospel in Wales, "it being known to many of us that God did kindle a seed there, indeed hardly to be paralleled since the primitive

11. Sibbes, *Cordialls*, p. 215. Richard Bancroft had condemned this puritan attitude forty years before from the anglican viewpoint. As Collinson quotes Bancroft: "Although the puritan ministers preached 'in our material churches,' the parish in which they preached was not the church 'properly in their sense, but as many thereof only as are joined unto them' as a godly company" (p. 381).

12. Abbott, 3:61–62.

times." For once, Cromwell was not mixing his metaphors, because as Carlyle noted, "kindle" used in this way comes from a German verb meaning "to give birth to" or "to create."[13] God had begun the process of conversion of many Welshmen from the unregenerate to the regenerate state, from wickedness or at best merely common goodness to true godliness of carriage and conversation. The saving transformation from "civility" and "morality," both of which had been achieved by pagans and heathens, to that higher pitch of belief and behavior which only saints could reach was an inward change. The change itself could not be seen by the outward, bodily eye, but the fruits of the holy seed of grace could be discerned as believers grew into "trees of righteousness" (Isa. 61:3). There were, therefore, certain outward and visible signs by which truly godly men demonstrated their inward and spiritual grace.

The most important of these outward signs—and indeed the one from which all the others were in one way or another derived—was that godly men put obedience to the comand of God and delight in the things of God above everything else. They were different from other men in that they had a different scale of values. The duties enjoined by the first four of the Ten Commandments provided the crucial test. In general, said Preston, "every man that doth any thing for his own end, arrogates that to himself which is the Lord's; which is a high kind of idolatry." If he made his goal wealth or fame, he was an idolater, and in particular, if "he seeks not the Lord in that which is done to his worship," then it was certain that he was not truly seeking the Lord in his "outward works." If he were not "faithful in the greater, and that which God doth immediately command in his worship, he will never be faithful in those things that are further off, that are of less consequence." And for Puritans, the most important public ordinance which God "doth immediately command in his worship" was, as the text Preston cited here indicated, that of giving "ourselves continually to . . . the ministry of the Word" (Acts 6:4). Therefore it was a mark of reprobation if "your hearts and sanctifying the Sabbath will not agree."[14]

13. Ibid., 4:148, 3:57. The footnote explaining "kindle" is omitted from the S. C. Lomas edition of Carlyle's collection but appears in others (e.g., the one published by Chapman and Hall, 1871, 3:211). On the Commission, see Austin Woolrych in R. H. Parry, ed., *The English Civil War and After*, p. 66.

14. Preston, *Life*, pt. 1, pp. 147, 150; *Breast-Plate*, pt. 3, p. 132.

The godly brethren hated to fail in their Sabbath duties of worship because they valued the pleasure which was derived from performing them. This matter will be dealt with more fully below, but it must be mentioned here because a proper attention to these duties is part of the definition of puritan sainthood. Joseph Caryl said that they "who are godly indeed, delight in God," and further, that if "we delight not in God only, we delight not in God at all." The godly brethren are those who delight in anything "which carrieth the appearance, or bears the image and impression of God upon it. Thus they delight in the word of God, in the works of God, . . . in the ways and ordinances of God, in the servants and people of God." Caryl said that a true Christian's joy in God "belongs to the First Commandment"—it is "natural worship, (not natural, as natural is opposed to spiritual, but as natural is opposed to formal or instituted worship)." David was an excellent example of this aspect of saintliness; "he loved those that feared the Lord," said Preston, and he hated those that loved "vain inventions." The latter were precisely the "unnatural," "formal," and "popish" liturgical practices "instituted" by men rather than warranted by divine command. Thomas Goodwin spoke with nostalgic longing for the "infant times of our first Reformation" and of the splendid example of "pure religion and undefiled" which had been set by Tudor Puritans. Those "blessed men" had both professed and practiced the "duties of godliness. . . . Spiritual preaching was then prized; men might go far to hear sermons and repeat them to their families and be reverenced. Men might have pleaded for the Sabbath and sanctified it in the utmost strictness, spent it wholly in heavenly exercises (as our homilies' words are), and not have been accused of Judaism." They could have done all these things and more to obey and rejoice in First Table duties then, but in 1628 "a generation is come on that know not these Josephs; and now their brethren that worship God after the same way that they did are cried down."[15]

Men who took pains to sanctify the Sabbath by hearing the read-

15. Caryl, *Job* (chaps. 27–29), pp. 104–07; Preston, *Breast-Plate*, pt. 3, p. 120; T. Goodwin, 7:546. The reference to Joseph is a double entendre—it was the pharaoh who "knew not Joseph" (Exodus 1:8) who enslaved the Hebrews. For a richly detailed portrait of the object of much of Goodwin's nostalgia, see Collinson, pp. 333–82.

ing and the preaching of the Word, fortifying themselves in the knowledge of it (while eschewing forms of worship the origins of which were human rather than divine) would naturally seek out each other's company. Robert Bolton listed three things required of one who is "rightly cured" of the disease of sin: he casts himself upon Christ as his Savior, and then takes Christ as his king, and

> he presently associates himself to the brotherhood. . . . He now begins to delight in them whom he heartily hated before, I mean the people of God, professors of the truth and power of religion; and that, as the most excellent of the earth, the only true noble worthies of the world, worthy forever [of] the flower, fervency and dearness of his most melting affections and intimate love. And he labors might and main to ingratiate himself into their blessed communion by all engagements and obligations of a comfortable, fruitful and constant fellowship in the Gospel.

They would do all this because, as the chaplain to one of the leading gentle families in Essex said, the world would try to seduce the children of God away by temptations, or to drive them away by tribulations. It was therefore all the more important to "esteem highly of them that are Christian, and labor to be their fellow members."[16]

Desire for and delight in such fellowship is a duty, but it comes naturally to the truly converted sinner. The values of the godly brethren become the values of the convert. Such men have the image of Christ and of God in them because they have by God's grace been granted new natures and are different from other men. John Winthrop explained it so to his little godly fellowship on the way to New England in the *Arbella*. All men are like Adam after his breach with God: "Every man is born with this principle in him, to love and seek himself only and thus a man continueth till Christ comes and takes possession of the soul, and infuseth another principle, love to God and our brother." After this regeneration, Winthrop continued, "the Lord loves the creature, so far as it hath any of his image in it, He loves his elect because they are like himself."

16. Bolton, *Works* (1641), 1:343–44; Harrison on Heb. 4:25 ("Choosing rather to suffer affliction with the people of God . . .").

The regenerate in turn through a highly selective narcissism admires, esteems, and loves others because among "the members of Christ, each discerns by the work of the spirit his own image and resemblance in another, and therefore cannot but love him as he loves himself." The saints love each other and enjoy each other's fellowship and company because, as Winthrop's examples of Adam and Eve, David and Jonathan, Ruth and Naomi indicated, the living soul "is of a sociable nature" and will cleave to saintliness wherever it is found. He values things according to how much they are like God. "A man that is in Christ," said Preston, "sets so much by himself, and by every man as he is in God's book," just as worldly wealth is rated in "the King's books." The true Christian then "settest so much by [himself] and by every man else, as he is in God's favor; as he hath the eminency of grace and holiness above others."[17]

It seems safe to conclude that the Puritans believed that it takes a saint to know one—indeed, that only a saint could identify grace in others and in himself. He would seek godly company because it is his natural tendency to do so, and he would relish the good opinion of godly men. Preston said that, all good professions notwithstanding, it was an "infallible sign" that the man who would "desire to be in any company rather than in theirs" was not a true lover of God. Further if, "when you are among them, you are as if you were out of your element, you move as if you were out of your own center," then the truth of any professions of love to the brethren was in doubt. "It is impossible but that those that are moved by the same spirit should be best pleased when they are in one and the same society." John Benbrigge spoke in similar terms to his Sussex hearers. When men have been "made partakers of the divine nature," that is, "when they are born of God, sin becomes quite out of their element; and therefore it is as troublesome to be in the company of wicked men, as it is to a fish to be in the air, amongst the birds."[18]

17. *WP*, 2:292–93; Preston, *Cuppe*, pp. 8–9. Similarly William Gouge: The saints have "that stamp or impression of God's image which the Holy Ghost hath set in them and whereby they are sealed unto the day of redemption." *The Saints Support*, pp. 32–33.

18. Preston, *Breast-Plate*, pt. 3, pp. 102–03; Benbrigge, *Gods Fury*, pp. 39–40. R. P. Stearns and D. H. Brawner have written that "in short, saints recognize one another by virtue of that which Richard Baxter called 'connaturality of spirit,' or, less mystically, by a combination of common sense and intuition." "New Eng-

Thomas Doolittle, writing after the Restoration, used another familiar image to explain why the saints flocked together. "Christ's sheep," he said, "are sociable creatures, . . . love to be with sheep, but not with wolves." They therefore choose "to converse with those that fear God, and love their company for their grace's sake, and for God's sake, whose image is enstamped upon them." That they used their sense of ease or discomfort in the company of the saints as an indication of their spiritual condition is apparent from Winthrop's diary. He wrote that the "society of the saints" had seemed contemptible to him when he had been backsliding toward worldliness. But when he succeeded in fighting down his desire for a good reputation in the world and overmastering his misguided avoidance of having "an ill name with the most where I lived," he felt better. "I will say with Paul, I pass not for man's judgment. . . . Walk with God, and never fear but thou shalt be honored of the godly." That he desired to be honored by them is clear in a letter he wrote in 1630 to his close friend, Sir William Spring, one of the representatives for Suffolk in several parliaments. The "love or esteem" he had from Spring "and some others,whose constance and godliness hath made me sometimes proud of their respect" caused him to thank God for putting "this honor upon me, (a poor worm, and raised but yesterday out of the dust)."[19]

There is therefore a certain truth in the anglican charges that the Puritans made an idol of their "godly brethren," and that they made their conception of brotherhood "a sign and mark to know a faction by." They did place a high value on membership in an earthly communion of saints, meaning a brotherhood of regenerate Christians who transcended ordinary goodness. They could be identified by the devoted way in which they sought to perform a cluster of First Table duties—duties which were linked together by powerful desires to hear the Word preached, to aid in its further dissemination, and to reject categorically an unwarrantable adiaphorism in matters of worship. They addressed each other as

land Church 'Relations' and Continuity in Early Congregational History," *Proceedings of the American Antiquarian Society* 75 (n.s., 1965), p. 25. My argument is that this "common sense and intuition" rested heavily upon the puritan conception of First Table duties.

19. Doolittle, *Rebukes*, p. 534; *WP*, 1:197, 209–10, 2:203–04. See also 1:215, 2:205–06.

"brethren," and careful attention to the context in which this term was employed usually shows that it was not used in such a way as to include the unregenerate (except insofar as there were—and there always were—souls among the unregenerate which were destined for regeneration). They were believers, not in a catholic human brotherhood, but in a brotherhood of grace. As we will shortly see, this did not mean that true Christians owed no charity to unregenerate men, whether carnally wicked or possessed of a merely "civil" or "moral" righteousness. The form which love to the godly brethren ordinarily took, and the benefits which redounded to the brethren involved, will be surveyed after two frequently employed applications of this definition of the godly brotherhood have been considered.

The first use is irenical, for it is in the light of this definition of godliness that puritan appeals for love, peace, and unity must be considered. In the preceding chapter we noted the polemical use that Anglicans made of Paul's injunction to the Christians at Ephesus (3:14) to preserve "the unity of the spirit in the bond of peace." Well before the disastrous fragmentation of the puritan movement in the 1640s and 1650s, we find Sibbes preaching for unity among the people of God (probably during the late 1620s or early 1630s). "Oh let us esteem the treasure of the Gospel," he said, seeing "how it is slighted by most of the world, how they shake the blessed truths of God." The Gospel was the "glory of England," and it was incumbent upon the godly to work to maintain it. "We should every one in his place labor to stop dissensions in this kind, and knit our hearts together in unity and concord."[20]

Sibbes, a patriarch of the puritan brotherhood, was hoping to maintain a solid front against Arminianism and popery on one side and separatism and worse on the other. But by 1646 one senses a note of desperation as Independents and Presbyterians struggled to continue thinking of one another as brethren. Moderate Independents resented the hysterical attempts of some Presbyterians to tar them with the brush of antinomianism, while the Presbyterians resented the army's forestalling of the installation of their policy and

20. Sibbes, *Cordialls*, p. 224. For a discussion of the irenic program urged by Jeremiah Burroughs, see Winthrop S. Hudson, "Denominationalism as a Basis for Ecumenism: a Seventeenth-century Conception," *CH* 24 (1955):32–50.

blamed the "dissenting brethren" of the Westminster Assembly for
encouraging the army in its actions. "It is a sad thing to me," said
Henry Wilkinson, one of the members of the committee of divines
sent to evangelize Oxford after its fall, "to think that they which
look on one another as saints, should behave themselves each to
other as the Jews had wont toward heathens."[21] Saints who were of
different persuasions about the ecclesiastical polity required by the
Word were, as a group of presbyterian ministers in London put it in
September 1645, "perplexed and amazed" at the way "the present
reformation" had not gone to the completion God obviously intended. These Presbyterians petitioned the Parliament to establish
their system, so that "all the brethren (though now of different
opinions) may sweetly join together in the worship of their God,
. . . and all gracious spirits at home, together with all our godly
friends abroad, may heartily cry Grace, Grace." Independents were,
as Cromwell's rejection of presbyterian church government quoted
above indicates, equally perplexed that the men who had stood with
them against idolatry and for godly preaching would seek to impose
a spiritual tyranny scarcely distinguishable from the prelacy they
had jointly opposed. Amidst all their bitter quarrels, one finds
many references to a sense of kinship. Christopher Love, on the
scaffold in 1651 for plotting to bring in royalism and Presbyterianism, declared that "the union for which I plead is a church-union;
to wit, love among the godly; . . . that those that fear God might
walk hand in hand in the fellowship of the Gospel."[22] An anonym-
ous broadside of 1647 has an engraving which depicts "a godly dissenting brother" clasping hands with "a godly brother of the presbyterian way" and saying, "Let there be no strife between thee and
me for we are brethren."[23]

21. Wilkinson, quoted in Haller, *Liberty and Reformation in the Puritan Revolution*,
p. 224 (from a sermon preached July 21, 1646). Haller's book provides a good
introduction to the conflict between "religious Independency" and "religious Presbyterianism." For a brief statement on the complicated meaning of the terms in political matters, see Austin Woolrych in E. W. Ives, ed., *The English Revolution,
1600–1660*, p. 24. For full details, see Underdown, *Pride's Purge*.
22. *The Humble Petition* (1645), broadside, B. M. Press-mark 669. f. 10 (37); *The
Whole Tryall of Mr. Christopher Love*, p. 124. The presbyterian divines Ash, Calamy,
and Manton attended him there.
23. *A Pious and Seasonable Perswasive To the Sonnes of Zion Soveraignely usefull for
Composing their Unbrotherly Devisions*, entered by Thomason on March 11, 1647.

This puritan irenicism, comprehending all who had similar conceptions of First Table duties, appears frequently in Cromwell's thinking. We have already noted the expressions of it in his speech opening the Parliament of the Saints. He concluded his account of the storming of Bristol in September, 1645, by saying that "the people of God" in the army, in London, and all over England had been God's instruments in the victory. "Presbyterians, Independents all had here [in the army] the same spirit of faith and prayer; . . . know no names of difference: pity it is it should be otherwise anywhere." His reason was that "all that believe, have the real unity, which is most glorious; because inward, and spiritual, in the body and to the head [Christ]." Three years later he wrote to his Scottish allies that one of God's purposes "in permitting the enemies of God and goodness in both kingdoms to rise to that height and exercise such tyranny over his people was to show the necessity of unity amongst those [godly people] in both nations."[24] One of the lord protector's subordinates later showed this spirit shortly before his execution as a regicide. Colonel Daniel Axtell was asked whether he had any message for "the good people in the country" of Gloucestershire. "Bid them keep close to Christ, and let them not touch with surplice or common-prayer-book," he replied, "and bid them (what ever they do) love the image of Christ where ever they see it in Presbyterian, Independent, Baptised or other." On his way to the gibbet, he spoke to "an eminent godly minister of the presbyterian way," saying, "it is much upon my heart, that one great cause why the Lord thus contends with his people, is for want of love towards them that were not of their minds."[25]

The second application of this definition of the godly brotherhood was polemical rather than irenical. It was aimed at those who considered themselves truly Christian, and yet criticized puritan

24. Abbott, 1:377, 653. For his inclusion of Anabaptists, see 1:278, 4:271. From Ireland in 1649, he wrote of his hope that "these unspeakable mercies" (i.e., his numerous victories there) "may teach dissenting brethren on all sides to agree, at least, in praising God. And if the Father of the family be so kind, why should there be such jarrings and heart-burnings amongst the children?" 2:173.

25. *Speeches and Prayers*, pp. 84–85. He was an Independent (see p. 87). On his last evening his friends heard him "bewailing the great divisions amongst God's people," p. 86. Similarly: "Mr. Cooke said, 'Blessed be God, brother Peters, we are going to heaven where the saints are all of one mind, which my soul hath long desired to see' " (p. 24)

188 THE GODLY MAN IN STUART ENGLAND

godliness as hypocritical. "Many call themselves Christians," said Thomas Watson, "but blot out the word saints. . . . To deride sanctification argues a high degree of atheism." Robert Bolton said that the scorning of saints "is a certain mark thou art a limb of Satan." Even though there were some hypocrites among those who professed to be the children of God, he insisted that there was no excuse for opposing God's truth and the professors of it: "be careful therefore you speak not, nor oppose any more the members of Christ for he is their head." Thomas Hooker had a similar warning for scoffers: "You love Christ you say, but you hate his members because they are hypocrites; tush, that is a fancy; can a man say, I love your head well, and yet would chop off your arms?" John Preston said, after completing his lengthy presentation of the duty of love to saints: "You will object, I do love the saints, but who are they? I love not hypocrites." He called this "a notable excuse," but an unacceptable one. "I will not wish thee to love hypocrites, only take heed thou suffer not the imps and instruments of the Devil to paint out the true saints unto thee in the colors of hypocrites." This had been done to the saints and "holy men in all ages," and those who did it were "the devil's factors, though they think not so." They invented "slanders and false reports" to hurl upon "holy men, especially . . . the ministers of the Gospel, and so upon all the ways of God."[26]

"All the ways of God" for the Puritans meant a cluster of First Table duties the performance of which increasingly led to trouble with the higher powers in the 1620s and 1630s. With arguments such as these, puritan preachers encouraged the godly to persevere against derision and persecution, and at the same time warned the deriders and persecutors that they were living in glass houses on sandy foundations. When and if they were converted they would, like the apostle Paul, see how wrong they had been to persecute even what Preston called "shows of holiness." He reminded them that "it is the common condition of men whose hearts are not upright, that they

26. Watson, p. 247; Bolton, *A Cordiall for a fainting Christian*, pp. 10–11; T. Hooker, *Lessons*, p. 20; Preston, *Breast-Plate*, pt. 3, pp. 102–03. Note the warning in *Breast-Plate*, pt. 3, pp. 120–21, to beware of regarding as hypocrites those who "fear the Lord and hate vain inventions. . . . I say, do not deceive yourselves in this, for as they rejected Christ under the person of a counterfeit and of a wine-bibber, so thou mayest persecute Christ under the person of a hypocrite."

are not able to judge aright of the ways of God." There was no possibility that "a man that hath not grace himself" can "judge aright of grace in others." Thomas Case's view was similar. "The men of the world are incompetent judges of the state and condition of God's children," he wrote. "God's day is coming when things and persons shall be valued by another census or rate."[27] It is precisely the exclusiveness of the puritan "godly brotherhood" and the smugness of the judgments derived from its values which so enraged the anglican critics quoted at the beginning of this section. Having surveyed the puritan approach to determining who were the persons with whom fellowship should be sought, we may move on to a consideration of the charitable services which should be performed and the benefits to be derived from performing them.

Charity to the Poor in Spirit

Charity in any form is a good work, and all English Protestants regarded works of charity as evidences of true and lively faith in the doers of them. Puritans, however, relative to Anglicans, emphasized the importance of what might be called "spiritual charity"—works aimed at benefiting the souls of their recipients. The earliest extant letter written by Oliver Cromwell (January 11, 1636) gives an excellent illustration of the reasoning behind this emphasis. It was addressed to several wealthy London citizens who had endowed a puritan lectureship in Cromwell's "country" of Huntingdonshire. "Mr. Storie, Amongst the catalogue of those good works which your fellow-citizens and our countrymen have done, this will not be reckoned for the least, that they have provided for the feeding of souls. Building of hospitals provided for men's bodies; to build material temples is judged a work of piety. But they that procure spiritual food, they that build up spiritual temples, they are the men truly charitable, truly pious."[28] The highest and best kind of charity, as Cromwell clearly stated, was the performance of works which tended to the saving of souls. This puritan emphasis upon spiritual charity may be considered under two aspects. First, there is the

---

27. Preston, *Breast-Plate*, pt. 3, pp. 103–04; Case, *Correction*, pp. 199–200.

28. Abbott, 1:80. On Sept. 8, 1641, the House of Commons passed a motion legalizing the setting up of lectureships in parishes. The mover was Oliver Cromwell. P. Seaver, *Puritan Lectureships*, p. 268.

giving of money, land, lodging or other material aid to godly persons, either to preserve them from want or from the rage of persecutors, or to allow them to work for the spiritual improvement of others. Second there is the expression of "love to the brethren" which occurs within a church fellowship of the regenerate, the earthly communion of saints.

When charity in the former sense was being discussed, Puritans emphasized the great virtue of giving material aid to poor saints. The many biblical texts which urged charity to the poor, needy, and oppressed were usually taken by Puritans to command aid to regenerate or at least apparently regenerate persons. Joseph Caryl explained the reason in his sermon on Psalm 72:1–3. The apposite part of the text is David's prayer that Solomon "shall judge thy people with righteousness, and thy poor with judgment." Magistrates at all levels were in duty bound to care for the poor because "God cares most for his poor, and men ought." But "the poor" to Caryl often meant the "poor in spirit"—that is, those individuals of whom it could be said that "God is their portion for ever, and his righteousness ought to be their portion here." There is, he said, "one thing very emphatical in the text, which may be as a nail to fasten home" the duty of righteous treatment of the saints by all who are "in the place of God; it is said, they are God's people, and God's poor; 'Thy people, and thy poor.'" All the "people of Israel" were, he conceded, comprehended within David's prayer. It applied to the entire Hebrew nation—but "at this time, there is no whole nation hath such a privilege." The privilege had devolved upon God's "special covenant people, his peculiar ones in every nation, . . . and though all others are God's people, as men, and the princes' charge too, yet for the sake of these chiefly, governors are set up, and princes sit upon the throne." Others were, Caryl thought, God's people "as men"— but the touchstone of the righteousness of a government was its treatment of "God's people and God's poor." Caryl meant by these the Puritans who had been persecuted by Laud in the 1630s.[29]

As Caryl used the terms, poverty in the conventional sense is not in itself relevant to the duty of charity. The richest man in the world

29. Caryl, *Davids Prayer*, pp. 18–19. For analysis of the political content of this sermon see the section entitled "The Puritan Imperatives" in chap. 4, above.

might be "poor in spirit" if he had been truly humbled for sin, seen the depth of his iniquity, and experienced the liberating, saving regeneration which followed upon real humiliation. John Benbrigge gave it as an essential mark of a true convert that he "prizeth the poorest man or woman who is rich in Christ." Benbrigge cited James 2:5, "Hearken my beloved brethren, hath not God chosen the poor of this world, rich in faith?" The Sussex preacher's aim here was to denounce those who despised saints because they preferred "rich worldlings before poor Christians" and to insist that "Christ this jewel" was no less to be sought and loved in another because "wrapped up in a leathern jacket, or a threadbare coat." But neither was he to be despised in a costly habit because apparel did not proclaim the spiritual rank. Cromwell repeatedly used the word "poor" in reference to the saints, rather than to the destitute. "I find this only good," he wrote to Fairfax in 1646, "to love the Lord and his poor despised people, to do for them, and to be ready to suffer with them." Again to Fairfax: "Surely it is not the poor godly people of this kingdom should still be made the object of wrath and anger." He addressed Lord Wharton, "My dear lord, I, poor I, love you!" and said in another letter to him, "the best of us are, God knows, poor weak saints, yet saints, if not sheep, yet lambs, and must be fed." Stephen Marshall, in the first of his many fast-day sermons before members of the Long Parliament, said that it was the godly man's duty to do good unto the poor. The poor, he explained, were those that Christ said would, unlike Christ himself, always be present. "So I say, you have not Christ with you in his person. But you always have his cause, his truth, his ordinances, his day, his ministers, his children, the tears of the afflicted." All of these (with the possible exception of the last) concern only the regenerate or potentially regenerate. These are the puritan poor, poor in spirit and therefore rich or destined to be rich in grace.[30]

This puritan tendency to identify the poor with God's cause and God's people in the world was a strong one, but we cannot leave this subject without a measure of qualification. That charity was thought of as being primarily a spiritual duty with spiritual recipients and purposes (defined, as always, along First Table lines) did not mean

30. Benbrigge, *Christ*, p. 33; Abbott, 1:429, 619, 646, 2:328; Stephen Marshall, *A Sermon Preached* (1641), p. 42.

that the unregenerate could be scorned. First, there were among them some who would ultimately be saved. The provision of godly preaching all over England was a vital service not only to comfort and guide the already converted, but to bring in those who were predestined to enter into the earthly communion of saints. Preaching had been the immediate cause of many a conversion, and no Puritan could consider God's cause in the world properly provided for until preaching of the right kind was everywhere available. Only by this means could the Reformation which God had begun in Tudor times move toward its completion.

Second, there was the undeniable fact that the hungry, needy, sick, widowed, fatherless, helpless, and oppressed residents of England deserved all the help which Christians could give them. Sturdy beggars should be made to provide for themselves, but the helpless needed help. Puritans were forever distinguishing between godly and ungodly acts and persons, and it was the frequency with which they did this that required them to remind themselves occasionally that the unregenerate also had to be treated decently and charitably. Preston, for example, in his extensive discussion of the duty of love to the saints, halted to meet an objection. "But will you say, would you have us to love none but the saints?" No, he replied, "it is true, we ought to love all others with a love of pity, we should show abundance of this love to all mankind." Then he went on to expound upon the higher love due to the saints. Thomas Doolittle told the members of his plague-ridden London conventicle in 1666 that they must "have a fellow-feeling of the miseries that others are urged with . . . and this regardless of their spiritual condition." Sir Richard Baker reminded his readers of David's tears of supplication and compassion for those who hated or opposed him; he prayed "that God will either convert or confound them; . . . for such is the tenderness of a godly eye, that it hath tears to shed even for enemies." William Gouge told the saints that even though the sins of those who wronged them often pulled down judgments "upon their own pates, our endeavor must be to help them, to heal them."[31]

31. Preston, *Breast-Plate*, pt. 3, p. 102; Doolittle, *Antidote*, p. 134; Baker, p. 122; Gouge, *Gods Three Arrowes*, p. 48. According to Clarke, Gouge was himself "very charitable, especially to the godly poor. . . . He maintained some poor scholars in

To say therefore that the Puritans preached a doctrine of "spiritual charity" is not to maintain that they urged the withholding of material aid to their fellowmen, regenerate or not. They did make a great virtue of financial support for such directly spiritual ends as the support of preaching and preachers and such indirectly spiritual ends as education. Equally prominent in their economy of exhortation was material help to their fellow saints in time of need. The duty of charity in its more conventional sense was mentioned infrequently—and then often in an offhanded way—not because it was unimportant but because it was too obvious to require much elaboration. It was a Second Table duty; even heathens and pagans had realized the justice and necessity of it. The duty of living in peace with one's neighbors and behaving toward them in a loving, charitable way had, said Thomas Goodwin, "taken the deepest impression upon the most vulgar apprehensions of all that profess Christianity." Puritans aimed above this "common godliness." Their critics charged that in doing so they lost not only common goodness but religion as well. For Goodwin, however, "to be in charity with their neighbor, &c., hath remained in all ages of the church, upon the spirits of the most ignorant and superstitious, when those higher ends and intendments of it were forgotten." Thus John Winthrop, detained on business in London ten days before Christmas, wrote telling his wife to "let provision be made; and all our poor feasted, though I be from home, so I shall be the less missed; such as are of the middle sort let alone till I come home." Arrangements for Christmas charity were ordinary matters, dealt with in a brief matter-of-fact way.[32] In seeking to recover and practice the true spiritual worship that God had commanded in the First Table and to associate with others of like minds and hearts, Puritans did not want to lose sight of Second Table duties among men. Such duties as feasting the poor were to be performed; absence of them was sign of damnation. But as they could also be performed by unregenerate men, safer, and surer

the university." *A Mirrour or Looking-Glasse*, 2:68. Clarke collected other examples—see pp. 54–71. For more puritan exhortations to this broader charity, see Gouge, *Saints Support*, pp. 21, 24–25; Caryl, *Job* (chaps. 18–21), pp. 60, 501, and *Job* (chaps. 27–29), pp. 516–19, 542–43; Perkins, 2:143–44.

32. T. Goodwin, 2:385; *WP*, 1:293. That they were indeed very charitable has been demonstrated by W. K. Jordan. See his *Philanthropy in England, 1480–1660*. See my bibliographical note for further discussion.

evidences of election were sought by Puritans. They were found in the activities pertaining to the "higher ends and intendments" which God had revealed first in the Word and then in the history of the true church throughout the long ages of "popish" darkness and superstition—and finally in the glorious light of the still unfinished reformation.

Much more prominent in puritan thinking than any of the forms of material "love to the brethren" was the brotherly love which they gave and received within an earthly communion of saints. This is the second (and to them the more important) of the aspects of "spiritual charity" which we will consider. It was more important for the same reason that the soul is more important than the body. Food for a brother's stomach would soon be consumed. Even if such charity took the more advanced and enlightened form of providing means for a poor man to lift himself out of poverty, his body would eventually die.[33] This did not mean that bodily needs were to be neglected—God held each man responsible for the proper stewardship of all the earthly things committed to his care, including his own body and his worldly estate, however grand or humble. But the first and highest charitable responsibility of the puritan saint in this life lay in service to the spiritual estates of his fellow saints. If he were truly regenerate he would recognize this and exemplify his recognition of it in acts of spiritual "love to the brethren."

The saint would above all things be active in the kind of godly fellowship which the puritan commissioners who were sent to Oxford in 1645 sought to establish there. Their aim was "to unite the godly citizens and scholars" in "a spirit of communion . . . a visible way of heavenly partnership." These saints would observe each other "with a godly and friendly jealousy, provoke one another to piety, and upon every good opportunity according to their several abilities instruct, admonish, reprove, exhort, encourage, comfort, support, relieve, serve one another in love and prudence, as their several necessities should require." This rather formidable list of activities

33. Christopher Hill has rightly argued that this kind of charity was rapidly replacing indiscriminate almsgiving in the sixteenth and seventeenth centuries. But Hill conveys the impression that this kind of thinking was limited to (or at least more typical of) the Puritans. *Society and Puritanism*, pp. 259–97. My doubts are expressed in the bibliographical note.

has one central thread; it is the duty of each member of an earthly communion of saints to do all that he can to help his fellow saints stay on the narrow path which leads to heaven. A saint who saw a brother straying into the broad way which led to hell failed in his duty if he issued no warning. Equally essential was the encouragement to all those who were on the right path to stay on it, to persevere in the way, and not to be drawn off by worldly temptations or pushed off by worldly persecutions. These were the advantages that Sibbes had in mind when he spoke of the "Christian society with the saints of God, to whom you might make known your griefs, and by whom you might receive comfort from the Lord and encouragement in your Christian course." It was, he thought, dangerous not to partake of "the benefit of their holy conference, their godly instructions, their divine consolations, brotherly admonitions and charitable reprehensions." God was pleased by the presence of such fellowship and angered "when there is not that sweet communion of saints among them [true Christians] to strengthen and encourage one another in the ways of holiness. . . . When there is not a beauty in their profession to allure and draw on others to a love and liking of the best things." Bolton described the "blessed body and brotherhood" of all the truly converted as "an humble mutual intercourse and communication of holy conference, heavenly counsel, spiritual encouragements, consideration one of another, confirmation in grace."[34]

John Winthrop's diary offers specific examples of the kind of brotherly aids to sanctification which Bolton, Sibbes, and other puritan divines praised so highly. Even the saintliest of saints would from time to time slip from his course, for none contended that perfect sanctification could be achieved by the justified sinner in his life. His sins, whether great or little, would drive away his sense of assurance. He would need instructions, admonition, and comfort, perhaps all at the same time. Progress toward his goal was not smoothly linear; it was not the movement of a steamship steadily ploughing the waves to its port, but of a sailing ship, veering and tacking, struggling against winds and currents, spars broken, sails torn and pumps manned continuously. All of the loving service to

34. *An Account*, pp. 6, 12; Sibbes, *Letter*, pp. 1, 4, and *Cordialls*, p. 222; Bolton *Works*, 3:344.

fellow saints, and the benefits reaped by performing them as well as by receiving them, were necessary because the saints could not remain perfectly on course. Winthrop wrote: "Having occasion of conference with a Christian friend or two, God so blessed it unto us, as we were all much quickened and refreshed by it. The matter of our conference was not doubtful questions to exercise our wits, etc., but a familiar examination of our own experiences." In other words, "Christian conference" for Winthrop and his brethren was not theological disputation, but a mutual recounting of experiences of God's grace in their lives. Sibbes spoke of it as one of the "sanctified means" (along with prayer and reading and hearing the Word) the use of which was often fruitful because "by conference God works strangely many times." In this sense, "conference" had something approaching a sacramental character for Puritans. Winthrop often found that when he left the company of his godly brethren, he was more "disquieted" and "unsettled" than before he had joined them. "God sends it as a punishment upon me," he thought, "for not making the good use of such company as I ought; or . . . their godliness doth stir up and check some secret evil within me that disquiets my mind."[35]

It would often be the case that the example of the saints was in itself a powerful force. The backsliding brother would know that something in his conduct was amiss because, like Winthrop, he felt uneasy in godly company, The standards which they set became normative. Oliver Cromwell, upon learning that his son Richard had overspent his allowance and gone into debt, wrote angrily that although he did not begrudge the young man "laudable recreations," he would not support him "if he should make pleasure the business of his life." Richard would have from his father "not only a sufficiency but more"—but he would have it only so long as his behavior was answerable to "the will of God" and to what was "comely before his saints." Cromwell, in making comeliness before the saints a guide to conduct, was doing what many puritan divines suggested. Where Anglicans tended to recommend Christ as a moral

35. *WP*, 1:202; Sibbes, *Works*, p. 170; *WP*, 1:207. Also, Doolittle, *Rebukes*, p. 574; "Christian conference; by this believers build up one another in . . . faith." See the remark on conference by William Kiffin quoted in Zagorin, p. 183 and M. M. Knappen, ed. *Two Elizabethan Puritan Diaries*, pp. 4, 8.

exemplar, Puritans such as Joseph Caryl spoke of imitating the saints. "It is profitable for us to look to the example of the saints, either those departed or those alive, and by them to examine both what we do and how we suffer." Caryl felt that "God hath given us, not only his Word for a rule, but he hath given us examples as a rule to walk by." Preston told his audience to "consider but that holiness that is expressed in the book of God, and that is expressed also in the lives of the saints who carry his image stamped on them" is the way to heaven. If there were "a kind of contrariety between your ways and theirs," then they were right and you were wrong.[36]

If the force of example did not prove sufficient to reclaim an erring brother, then it became the duty of his saintly colleagues to reprimand him. "Being admonished by a Christian friend that some good men were offended to hear of some gaming which was used in my house by my servants," John Winthrop decided "not to use any cardings" himself and to suppress gambling by others so far as he could.[37] He did not look upon this intervention into his household as nosiness. He knew that, as Thomas Hooker later said, "the strongest bones need sinews, . . . So in the church, the strongest members in the same need advice." To those who objected that offering such counsel was "to play the bishop in another man's diocese and to row in another man's boat," Hooker replied that "every saint hath to do with one another, we are our brothers' keepers, except we be Cains and will have Cain's wages." True Christians understood that "the richest man must use the market; so none can live without the market of the society of saints; and there is need of help to the best." Another objection might be that the counsellor was unfit in some way or was a young upstart. Hooker answered this with a tart question: "Wilt thou refuse physic, because it comes in an earthen pot, and not in a silver cup?" The justified saint, in his sincere quest for sanctification, would be able to distinguish godly from

36. Abbott, 2:425; Caryl, *Job* (chaps. 4–7), pp. 174–75; Preston, *Breast-Plate*, pt. 3, p. 132. Cf. Perkins, 3:39.

37. *WP*, 1:66. This is an example of an old and important aspect of the puritan movement which many historians have noted. See, for example, the description of "local self-government by the godly" in Walzer, pp. 219–24; also Collinson, especially, pp. 346–55. L. J. Trinterud, ed., *Elizabethan Puritanism*, reprints Fulke's *Brief and Plain Declaration* (1584), of which pp. 247–49 and 278–82 are especially useful on the subject of "discipline."

ungodly criticism because he could, as we have noted, perceive God's image in others. He would shun worldly criticism (and worldly praise too), but he would accept censure from kindred spirits with alacrity. "Let a friend strike me, and it shall be a balm to my head. . . . The striking of a friend is out of love, and intends amendment," wrote Sir Richard Baker. Robert Coachman, a lay Independent, felt that "it is no small privilege for [the godly] to live in such a society, as where the eyes of their brethren are so lovingly set upon them, that they will not suffer them to go on in sin."[38]

38. T. Hooker, *Lessons*, pp. 3–5; Baker, p. 345; Coachman, *The Cry of a Stone*, p. 21. Coachman's tract, published in 1642, is interesting in several ways, and it is therefore the more regrettable that the only extant information about the author himself is in the tract. I have found only two secondary references to him. The first is in Reinhold Niebuhr's *Nature and Destiny of Man* (2:169n.). Niebuhr mistakenly gave the title as "The Glory of a Stone" and refers to Coachman as "a sectarian Leveller of the Cromwellian period." Niebuhr almost certainly took his reference from T. C. Pease, *The Leveller Movement*. Pease gave precisely the quote Niebuhr used, plus a few more sentences, in a short appendix entitled "Alleged Independent Exclusiveness," pp. 84–85. Since the tract is rare (all four copies that Wing lists are in England), it seems safe to conclude that Niebuhr borrowed from Pease without remembering that Pease did not identify Coachman as a Leveller. He may have been a Leveller later on, but there is no solid evidence for it in this little treatise. The title is taken from Luke 19:40 ("I tell you that, if these should hold their peace, the stones would immediately cry out"). A tract with the same title was published in 1653 by Anna (or Hannah) Trapnel, a woman who claimed to have had (as her subtitle says) "Visions of God. Relating To the Governors, Army, Churches, Ministry, Universities." Professor Abbott called her a Fifth Monarchist (*Bibliography of Oliver Cromwell*, #718), and her *Cry of a Stone* is one of several works which bear him out. It is full of mystical, garbled doggerel far removed in style and content from Coachman, though both writers spoke warmly and frequently of the pleasures of godly fellowship.

Coachman was a layman (sig. A7 [recto]) whose aim it was to describe in a straightforward way the benefits of membership in a "gathered church." His experience "of ten years in a society of as excellent Christians, and under the purest orders and most profitable means that (I think) in this frail life can be obtained" (sig. A5 [verso]) impressed him so deeply that he felt a responsibility to publicize it that others might also share the experience. He was not, however, a rabid sectarian clamoring against the bishops and all that they represented. As Pease wrote, "Coachman had the fairness unusual among Puritans to protest against attributing such conditions entirely to the sloth and negligence of the bishops, or to the corrupting influence of the ceremonies." It is the essential tolerance, moderation, and sanity of Coachman's views that make him interesting, for in 1642 there was a dearth of these qualities. He is careful, when criticizing the Church of England, to distinguish between "the personal graces, knowledge, and learning" of the Christians who are in it, and "the confused manner of gathering churches by house rows of all sorts" (sig. A7 [verso]). In denouncing "the Churches of the Separa-

Besides counselling and admonishing his fellow saints, each member of the earthly communion of saints was bound to try to bring in others to join it. He proselytized knowing full well that God had already written the names of all the saints into the Book of Life. But to be a part of the means to another's conversion was spiritual charity at its sublime best. Thomas Goodwin said that the desire "to make disciples, and bring men thoroughly to Christ" was one of the "most sure and certain signs of regeneration, . . . the distinguishing character of a son of God." God's greatest mercy was the gift of salvation to the elect. Therefore, Goodwin asked, "you that have received mercy from God, wherein is your mercy to be shown most to others? In endeavoring to pull them out of hell, and save them from the wrath to come." Sibbes made the same point by referring to the example of Saint Paul: "When we find ourselves . . . delivered from the lion's mouth, we cannot but show that pity to others, which we felt from God ourselves. Paul thirsts as eagerly after the conversion of others now as ever he did for their blood before." John Benbrigge told the congregation of a parish adjoining his own in Sussex that "every soul that prizeth Christ is still motioning of him to others" and laboring to "kindle in their friends a love of Christ" that he might not go to heaven alone. The duty of proselytizing was not lost on puritan laymen. John Winthrop found that one of the effects of the early stirrings of grace in his soul

tion," he distinguishes between the principle of separating from the profane world (a good principle) and that of condemning all who do not agree with the separatists in every detail (a bad one). It was sad but true that some "of the strict separation, seeing if a man agree with them in all points, save one only (though it be but about hearing a sermon in an old temple) they will account him as bad as the worst" (sig. A4 [recto]).

Coachman argues instead for a voluntary congregationalism in which each congregation of godly men and women is free to operate according to the light it has received from God. Churches, like men, have their periods of infancy, in which they do only those things which they understand at the outset. They will proceed to higher things as God gives them the knowledge and means for progress in the faith (p. 2). Coachman foresaw in 1642 the enmities which were developing among different groups of godly brethren. He looked upon these enmities as yet another example of "the strength of man's corruption, and the marvelous operation of God's grace" (p. 37). He was lonely in his calm equanimity. In his lay mind we may witness the maturation of his thoughts on the necessity of toleration—a toleration based on a sense of the gradual clarification of the meaning of earthly Christian fellowship in practice—and we may suspect that a very similar process had also begun in the mind of Oliver Cromwell.

was that he had "a great striving in my heart to draw others to
God." Sir Richard Baker defended the study of divinity by laymen
and insisted that they were bound to communicate such divine
knowledge as they could obtain to others. If they did not, they
ignored Christ's parable of the talents. "Shall a godly man meditate
in the law of God, day and night," he asked, "and shall God's
blessing such meditation bring forth nothing that may be worth
the writing?" "O happy conversion," he later wrote, "that is not
barren, and ends in itself . . . but, as a fruitful mother, continues
a race of conversions, and shall therefore make the converter shine in
heaven."[39]

In addition to the duty of proselytizing, there was for saints the
spiritual charity of prayer. All the saints spent much time in prayers
both of supplication and of thanksgiving, and they believed that God
listened with special—if not exclusive—attention to their prayers.
John Preston told his listeners that "all the prayers of the saints
made upon earth, are assuredly heard in heaven." Moreover, he
insisted, "Take the prayer of a saint and the prayer of a wicked
man . . . you shall find some times the prayer of a godly man more
cold and less fervent," and that of the other man better phrased,
perhaps; "yet because this comes from such a person, the Lord
regards it not." Obviously, this was not to say that the Lord would
always answer in precisely the way or at exactly the time the saint
desired, but he could at least be assured of a hearing. Cromwell said
that the Lord expects praises only from "such as the Lord forms for
himself." Only their prayers could bring results; this seems to be the
assumption which underlay the many requests for the prayers of the
godly in the papers of John Winthrop. The *Humble Request* of the
leaders of the Massachusetts-bound Puritans began with a statement
of the encouragement they had received "by the procurement of the
prayers and blessings of the Lord's faithful servants: . . . those
whom God hath placed nearest his throne of mercy." The offering
up of the prayers for the people of God in New England was just as
much a duty as was praying for the members of the reformed
churches in Germany and elsewhere on the continent of Europe.

39. T. Goodwin, 6:517; Sibbes, *Cordialls*, p. 202; Benbrigge, *Christ*, p. 34; *WP*,
1:156; Baker, *Apology for a Lay-Mens Writing in Divinity*, sigs. C2 (recto)–C3 (verso);
Baker, pp. 211–12.

Caryl gave this doctrine a political twist when he said that whatever a prince loses, "he may comfort himself so long as he doth not lose the prayers of the godly." He can lose nothing that cannot be recovered by prayers "sent up to heaven by those that are the favorites of heaven, and have through grace the ear of God."[40]

The spiritual charity of praying for the godly illustrates the reinforcing mechanism of puritan fellowship. Each duty performed within the earthly communion of saints was an obligation fulfilled by the doer of it and an act of brotherly love to the receiver of it. It helped the doer assure himself of his election because he knew that it was in the character of a saint to be, as Sibbes put it, forever asking if there are "any of Christ's posterity here, any of his children in this world, that I may do good unto them." He knew that, as Robert Bolton said, those who did not pray for the people of God thereby "infallibly" demonstrated that they were "no loving members of Christ's mystical body; have no part in the fellowship of the saints, no spark of spiritual life, no acquaintance at all with the ways of God." For the saint who was on the receiving end of the these charitable works, the benefits were equally valuable. There might, for example, be temporal deliverances. God's three arrows, said William Gouge, were plague, famine, and war—but the "supreme Lord of all hath such respect to his faithful ones, as he will rather spare many wicked ones for a few righteous ones." Thomas Mocket thought it a good omen for England that there were so many godly persons working to bring others to the gospel in 1642. God did not destroy nations when the "Lots, Jobs, Samuels, Daniels remain in it and stand in the gap." Sibbes said that the mere presence of a few saints would ward off judgments. "Beloved, it is not for the good of God's children that they live. As soon as they are in a state of grace,

40. Preston, *Cuppe*, pp. 59–60; Abbott, 3:65; *WP*, 2:231–32; Caryl, *Job* (chaps. 27–29), p. 507. For other examples, see Bolton, *Cordiall for a fainting Christian*, p. 3, and *WP*, 1:169, 235, 264; 2:140, 219. Cromwell told Ireton, "I often remember you at the throne of grace" and begged the same of his godly son-in-law. Abbott, 2:327. Thomas Doolittle urged those of his nonconformist flock who were afflicted by the plague to take comfort in the knowledge that Christ and the godly were praying for them: "How do the people of God prize the prayers of the saints on earth! And bespeak their prayers for them in their sickness and say to them that have an interest in God, 'oh pray for me, oh do not forget me when you are on your knees at the throne of grace!' And without doubt it is a singular privilege to have a share in the prayers of the people of God." *Antidote*, p. 135.

they have a title to heaven, but it is for others. When once we are in Christ, we live for others, not for ourselves."[41]

Even the saints who did not escape afflicting judgments in the general scourges which assaulted communities and nations had the great comfort of belonging to godly fellowships in which their brethren would help them maintain and build up their spiritual estates. "Associate with sanctified persons," Thomas Watson said. "They may, by their counsel, prayers, and holy example, be a means to make you holy. As the communion of saints is in our creed, so it should be our company." Puritans believed that God dispensed sanctifying grace through their fellowship with their godly brethren. Sibbes told a Christian who had withdrawn from the fellowship that he could not expect as much profit by his prayers as he had before. The reason was that "as the soul in the natural body conveys life and strength to every member as they are compacted and joined together and not as dissevered, so Christ conveys spiritual life and vigor to Christians, not as they are disjoined from, but as they are united to the mystical body, the church." In other words, the grace of God is ordinarily given to men in their communal and corporate identity as the chosen people of God. The value of such divine ordinances as prayer, baptism, preaching, and communion depended in part upon their communal quality. Professor New has noted that Puritans such as Thomas Cartwright objected to private baptism because the "sacraments were essentially congregational activities." He also showed that one reason for their objection to Laud's requirement that the communion table be placed in the east end of the church was that it made communion "a spectacle, and the opportunity for congregational fellowship had been completely discarded." This certainly was the view of it taken by Thomas Goodwin in 1651. He spoke of "a controversy of late years fomented by some, through popish compliances, that the Lord's Supper might be styled a sacrifice, the table an altar." Goodwin insisted that the Lord's Supper was not a sacrifice but a feast celebrated for two purposes: first, to ratify the covenant of grace which existed between each saint and God, and second, to be "a communion, the

41. Sibbes, *Cordialls*, pp. 180–81; Bolton, *Instructions for a right comforting Afflicted Consciences*, p. 346; Gouge, *Gods Three Arrows*, p. 27; Mocket, p. 61; Sibbes, *Cordialls*, p. 302. See also Doolittle, *Rebukes*, p. 198; *WP*, 1:157; Watson, p. 316.

highest outward pledge, ratification, and testimony of love and amity among his members themselves, . . . a love-feast, in that they eat and drink together at one and the same table."[42]

The emphasis upon the importance of communality is also present in the writings of lay Puritans. Near the end of his sermon on Christian charity preached to the *Arbella* group, Winthrop said that "we must delight in each other, . . . rejoice together, mourn together, labor and suffer together, always having before our eyes our commission and community in the work, our community as members of the same body." Only then could there be a firm hope that "the Lord will be our God and delight to dwell among us." The circumstances in which he spoke were extraordinary. He and his party were setting out on a voyage across the north Atlantic to build "a city upon a hill" in New England. But his godly puritan brethren in Old England were in the same spiritual boat, terribly alone in their voyages across a sea of sin and death. They could look only to each other for comfort, support, and encouragement in their courses, hoping that God would, as he had often promised, bless their fellowship with grace. Robert Coachman listed the "privileges of the saints" as "their free access to God, their fellowship in their Sabbaths, sacrifices, prayers, blessings, seals and 'new songs' of praise." In all these things they meet "with Christ their Savior, and so gather new comfort and refreshing daily, amidst the many crosses and troubles of this transitory world." In the Lord's Supper, for example, the fellowship is spiritual, "and they that feast at it must be united to Christ by one spirit." For Coachman, communality was the essence of the sacrament, "the nearest fellowship that the saints can have in the world, and most resembleth heaven; and it is not only a sure pledge of their fellowship with Christ, but also a demonstration of their unity together." Sir Richard Baker, in explaining why the ungodly cannot stand in "the congregation of the righteous" on the Day of Judgment, said, "It is a company that

42. Watson, p. 249; Sibbes, *Letter*, p. 4; New, *Anglican and Puritan*, pp. 66, 43; T. Goodwin, 2:382. J. S. Coolidge, whose book is vital to understanding this subject, stresses that "the preaching of the Word is the original sacrament of Puritanism, without which the Lord's Supper itself is a dead ritual" (p. 142). For an account of the puritan manner of celebrating the Eucharist, see Collinson, pp. 362–63. On ordination and fellowship, see Nuttall, *Visible Saints*, p. 94.

makes communion, and that none can do but saints, for sinners seek
every one their own, and all are for themselves."[43]

It is this advising, counselling, admonishing, proselytizing, ex-
horting, praying communion of individuals with "higher ends and
intendments" than the mere performance of Second Table duties
among men which lies at the center of puritan practical theology.
In Anglicanism, the doctrine of the community of saints implied, as
New has written, "a distant mystical link with the saints above, but
in Puritanism it involved fellowship with the sanctified both past
and present."[44] Membership in a local communion of saints, and
awareness of membership in an international one, provided indispensable help for the troubled souls who had truly understood the
message of the Gospel and were truly "poor in spirit." They struggled against sin because they knew how vast was the distance of
man's fall from grace, how depraved was his condition, how broken
his faculties. A just God could justly condemn all men to eternal
death, but He had with inscrutable yet infinite mercy elected some
to eternal life. God's people and God's poor would be afflicted and
persecuted in this life, and the only creatures to whom they could
look were those in whom God had stamped his image by regeneration. Their fellowship together was a kind of bank into which the
saints who were thriving in either their worldly or their spiritual
estates deposited the currency of Christian comfort for the use of
those in straits, aware that they might need them in their turn when
bad times came. The borrowers, gratefully receiving charity in
their moments of weakness, could take heart as they beheld the
godliness of their deliverers. The depositors were aware that their
dutiful payments gave evidence of the truth of their own privileged
position as the elect of the earth. This is a nice irony indeed. The
Protestant Reformation had begun with Martin Luther's impassioned protest against the Roman Catholic doctrine of supereroga-
tory works of saints which the pope could dispense from the heavenly
treasury.[45] Yet here English Puritans found comfort in the charity

43. *WP*, 2:294–95; Coachman, *Cry of a Stone*, pp. 13–14, 11; Baker, p. 80.
44. New, "Oliver Cromwell and the Paradoxes of Puritanism," *JBS* 4 (1965):
54.
45. Note the sarcastic reference to "the doctrine of the exchequer of superabun-
dant merits, of which the Pope is Lord Treasurer" by Falkland, p. 163.

that they gave and received (though they would have abhorred the suggestion that they regarded their good works as in any sense meriting God's mercy to them).

The importance of membership in the godly brotherhood was so great for Puritans that when they spoke of being without it, they meant little less than being without religion. Thomas Goodwin raised the terrible specter of Cain, who was "cast out of his father's family and from the ordinances of God there enjoyed and made a vagabond upon the face of the whole earth, which of all curses is the greatest." That is, Cain was one who found himself cast "out of the hearts of God's people, out of their company, out of their prayers, yea and out of their society by excommunication."[46] To be deprived of godly fellowship was a terrible loss, though one which made the loser appreciate it the more. Thomas Case, meditating in prison upon David's psalms, wrote that the "remembrance of the company of the saints, the beauty of the ordinances, and the presence of God, fetcheth tears from his eyes. . . . Oh how amiable are the assemblies of the saints and the ordinances of the Sabbath, when we are deprived of them."

Case used the word "beauty" to describe his feelings about the earthly communion of saints. We are not accustomed to thinking of the Puritans as being much concerned about beauty, but to them the fellowship of the saints was beautiful because it gave them a sight of heaven. They could endure the trials that were set before them in this life because they expected to have their flawed earthly communion with each other translated to heaven where it would be perfect. As Sibbes put it, "our imperfect measure of mortification [deadness to sin] in this life, hinders us from a full content in one another's communion," and we should be eager to go where "we shall fully enjoy one another, without the least falseness or distrust." Bolton said that "if once this divine flame of brotherly love be kindled by the Holy Ghost in the hearts of true-hearted

---

46. T. Goodwin, *The Tryall of a Christians Growth*, pp. 73–75. He further maintained that withdrawal from the fellowship was "a step to the sin against the Holy Ghost . . . when men forsake the assemblies and company of the people of God, public and private, and love not to quicken and stir up one another or begin to shy of those they once accompanied, they are in a nigh degree" to the sin of apostasy— willful sin after receiving knowledge of the truth (Heb. 10:26). Sibbes called such a withdrawal "a grand enormity." *Letter*, p. 3.

Christians, . . . it is never put out . . . but burns in their breasts
. . . with mutual warmth of dearest sweetness here upon earth,
and shall blaze eternally with seraphical heat in the highest heavens
hereafter." Sir Richard Baker, in attempting to depict the "congregation of the righteous in that new Jerusalem," suggested that it
could be thought of as a place where all citizens were "as loving
mutually together as David and Jonathan . . . where there is
holiness immaculate, peace inviolate, joy ineffable, pleasure in-
expressible."[47]

The spiritual charity which was expressed within the context of an
earthly communion of saints was beautiful and sweet because it was
a means of growth in assurance of salvation. It helped the true
believer to keep his feet on the narrow path and his eye on the
transcendent, eternal God, the Creator and Sustainer of all things
and source of all grace, beauty, and joy. Professor Morgan has
written that "the Puritan loved his God with all the sensual abandon
he denied himself in dealing with the world." It might be added
that he found in godly fellowship a sensual pleasure which he denied
himself otherwise. It was dangerous to indulge excessively in
worldly pleasures, however lawful and warrantable in themselves.
But one could not have too much godly company. "It cannot be
expressed either with pen or tongue, what a wonderful pleasure and
sweetness there is in a Christian fellowship," wrote Robert Coachman. "This brotherly fellowship of the church hath been so longed
after, and loved of God's servants," he continued, "that they have
compared it to the most pleasant dew and sweet ointment, the one
ravishing the eye, the other delighting the smell." John Winthrop
wrote that he had "a very sweet meditation of the presence and
power of the Holy Ghost in the faithful, . . . how he unites the
faithful in deed and in affection." Unsatisfied with his attempt to
describe the sweetness of it, he said, "I am not able to express the
understanding which God gave me in this heavenly matter, neither
the joy that I had in the apprehension thereof." There was, he
thought, "no joy on earth like the communion of saints . . . let all
thy delight be in the saints that are in the earth."[48]

47. Case, *Correction*, pp. 14–15; Sibbes, *Cordialls*, p. 161; Bolton, *Instructions for a right comforting Afflicted Consciences*, pp. 344–45; Baker, p. 83.
48. E. S. Morgan, *The Puritan Dilemma*, p. 12; Coachman, *Cry of a Stone*, p. 19; *WP*, 1:196, 213, 192.

If we dismiss as empty rhetoric these and other expressions of the sense of deep pleasure with which Puritans thought of their godly brotherhoods, then we cannot understand Puritanism at all. If paleontologists can offer realistic conceptions from a few bones of what dinosaurs looked like when they roamed the earth, then we too can attempt to conceive of the fervor of the puritan quest for assurance of salvation—and therefore of the beautiful aspect which helps to that assurance must have offered, however remote from modern conceptions of beauty theirs might seem. The admonitions of the godly could be painful, as Winthrop discovered when his servants offended them by gambling. But he could no more resent their censures than the victim of kidney disease can regret the hours he must spend attached to the machine which removes deadly toxins from his blood. To a drowning man, the appearance of the ungainliest tugboat must be as beautiful as a clipper ship under full sail. If we catalogue all our fears—poverty, heart attack, drug addiction, nuclear holocaust—we shall not exceed the puritan fear of sin and everlasting death. Relief from any of our fears in the short term is manna from heaven, and in the long term a kind of heaven itself.

The comforting reassurance that all will be well brings loving glances to the bringer of the comfort, so long as the assurance is firmly based and is not, like that of Job's friends, empty and platitudinous. This is not the less so if the comforter requires some discipline as a condition. "So every man that is in Christ," said Preston, "he hath the comforts of the spirit, the meditation of the privileges that he hath in Christ, the hope of God's favor, these are the things that his soul feeds on in secret." Further, "the very works that he doth in serving the Lord from day to day,"—works which, as we have seen, included love to his brother members in Christ—are "as sweet and acceptable to his soul, as meat and drink . . . to the hunger and thirst of his body." Bolton, Preston, Sibbes, Gouge, and many others were preaching about the duties, joys, and comforts of the spiritual charity of the communion of puritan saints in this world long before groups of illiterate sectaries and their "mechanick preachers" managed to "turn the world upside down" and bring the ideal into temporary disrepute by what seemed a militant and destructive antinomianism. The godly brethren, from a deep concern for their own and others' salvation, helped to breed in each other the kind of confidence which gave peers of the realm, members of the House of Commons, country squires, lawyers, merchants, apprentices, and soldiers the courage to refuse to obey the orders of the king of England because he had commanded things which the Word of the king of Heaven and Earth did not allow. Though persecution and civil war came, the saints persevered, with exhortations like this one from Sibbes ringing in their ears. "Our glory tends to [Christ's] glory; shall we not glorify him all we can here by setting forth his truth, by countenancing his children and servants. . . . Let men be as unthankful as they will, we look not to them but to the honor of God."[49]

ANGLICANS AND THE "CONSTELLATION OF GOSPEL GRACES"

Oxford, the last major stronghold of royalism, surrendered to parliamentary forces on June 24, 1646. The puritan commissioners sent to reform the city, like the carpetbaggers who "reconstructed" the southern states after the American Civil War, ran into a good deal of resistance. One of the stumbling blocks mentioned in their report was that "some of the university" had been taught the erroneous doctrine "that a constellation of gospel graces and sincere obedience to the whole Gospel" were conditions the fulfillment of which would "qualify believers for justification." The Puritans regarded this as tantamount to the popish doctrine of merit which all good Protestants abhorred. In order to combat this insidious, soul-murdering doctrine, the puritan preachers did what came naturally. They set up a "catechism-lecture" to purge the Oxonians of these and other dangerous ideas by again explaining the "doctrines of justification and regeneration." Another indication that Puritans thought Anglicans were preaching justifying works occurs in a piece of doggerel describing a Laudian "new churchman" (perhaps Richard Montagu).

> His divinity is trussed up with five points,
> He dops, ducks, bows, as if made all of joints.
> But when his Roman nose stands full east,

49. Preston, *Cuppe*, pp. 17–18; Sibbes, *Cordialls*, p. 180.

He fears neither God nor beast. . . .
He hopes to be saved by prevision
Of good works, but will do none.
He will be no Protestant, but a Christian,
And comes out Catholic the next edition.

Although Anglicans vigorously denied that they believed that man could by good works earn his salvation, their puritan critics may be pardoned for thinking that they did. Anglicans did emphasize good works so heavily that they seemed to leave out saving grace and thus make sanctification precede justification.[50] We have seen that their interpretation of the duty of obedience rested upon a belief that the human will could choose to obey. This section will demonstrate that Anglicans did place extraordinary emphasis upon the need for a "constellation of gospel graces" which can all properly be described as aspects of charity, and further, that they interpreted the duty of "love to the brethren" in a way which can be clearly distinguished from the puritan conception of it.

The demonstration that Anglicans tended to bring together all the virtues of a Christian man under the heading of charity may begin with Hammond. He extolled the attribute before the lord mayor and the aldermen of the City of London in the spring of 1640. Charity was, he explained, a duty for the Hebrews, and Christ had come, not to abrogate it, but to improve it. He described Christians as men "whose very style is 'brethren' [Col. 1:2], whose livery 'charity' [Col. 3:14], and character that 'they love one another'" (John 13:35). Further, the Greek words for communion or fellowship of saints could be translated as "'the communicativeness,' or 'liberality of administering to the saints,' and is therefore by us rendered 'liberality'" (1 Cor. 16:3). To help our hungry fellow Christians is, he said, "a way of binding up both the tables of the law into one volume, of ministering both to God and man, by this one mixed act of charity and piety, of mercy and of sacrifice." To relieve the "extreme want and necessity of our brethren" was to build "trophies and monuments of virtue to us, of charity, liberality, and magnifi-

50. *An Account*, p. 4; *Diary of John Rous*, M. A. E. Green, ed., p. 79. G. B. Tatham suggested that the puritan commission in Oxford deserves more attention because it affords "an excellent opportunity for the study of these widely differing types which were all included under the name of Puritan." *The Puritans in Power*, p. 152.

cence, of mercy, and bowels of compassion, that most beautiful composition of graces, that most heroical renowned habit of the soul."[51]

Hammond was by no means the only Anglican who spoke so highly and so comprehensively of charity. When the king and his attendants were in the Parliament's custody at Newport on the Isle of Wight in October, 1648, they heard Dr. Sanderson tell them once again of the situation among the Galatians when Paul wrote to them. False preachers had come among them and had "so extremely soured their charity" that they were feuding with one another. The apostle was disappointed, said Sanderson, that the Galatians had suffered "so sore and sudden a decay in the two most essential parts of Christian religion, faith and charity." No less exalted a view of charity was held by Jeremy Taylor. He wrote that, although there are many questions about divinity that remain disputed, there is one way in which "God hath described our way plain, certain and determined: . . . he put it past all question, that we are bound to be charitable." Taylor equated charity with righteousness and justice and declared in a sermon that the "faith of a Christian hath no signification at all but obedience and charity." Clarendon defined charity as "the translating [of] moral virtues into Christian language" and thus an essential ingredient of true religion. Humphrey Sydenham described charity as "the very salt of religion, the seasoner of all our spiritual and moral actions; without which, even our devotions are unsavory, our orisons distasteful."[52]

It is not therefore amiss to say that Anglicans constructed their conception of charity from such materials as liberality, compassion, love, mercy, and brotherliness. The tradition of biblical preaching led to the use of many different terms to describe virtues which were nearly or entirely identical. Sydenham made mercy "the badge and cognizance of a Christian" in one sermon and in another he equated it with love, "but such a love as is inward and from the very bowels." Merciful men were, he continued, those who were "touched even at the marrow and entrails for the miseries of another, they could

51. Hammond, pp. 245, 248, 242.
52. Sanderson, 2:374; Taylor, 2:x, xlix, and 5:192; *Contemplations*, p. 413; Sydenham, *Waters of Marah*, p. 22.

pour out their very bowels for him." As with the "bowels of compassion" in Hammond's sermon, the intention was comprehensive.
Thus, in still another sermon, Sydenham urged his hearers to
eschew "(that soul disease of the times and us), uncharitableness"
and to obtain instead the converted man's virtues, "sincerity, faith,
repentence, sobriety, brotherly kindness, love, and (what without it
disparages the tongue both of men and angels), charity."[53] This
omnicompetent duty of love to the brethren was prominent in
anglican and, as we have seen, puritan writing.

The anglican conception of charity, however, contained two
elements which clearly distinguish it from the puritan conception.
The first was that anglican charity was explicitly extended to all
members of the Church of England, regardless of faction or party.
Puritans were guilty of the sin of uncharitableness because they
insisted on trying to purge the Church of "things indifferent,"
thereby disturbing its peace and confusing the weaker members.
This distinction corresponds to the one made in chapter 4 where
we saw that Puritans were ready to disturb the peace of the established church in order to reform it according to their program (or
at least to prevent what they regarded as the retrogressive "innovations" of Laud) while Anglicans condemned any such disturbance
as unwarrantable disobedience. The second element was that (again
relatively) Anglicans emphasized concern for the material comfort
of their afflicted brethren while Puritans emphasized comfort for
their distressed souls. This distinction meshes logically with that
made in chapter 4 as to the Two Tables. These elements will now
be considered in turn.

Love to All the Brethren

Nowadays charity is, sad to say, a bland virtue. It is difficult to
imagine how it could ever have been a battle cry or a rallying point.
Yet there are American politicians who made the apparently innocuous phrase "law and order" seem to many a euphemism for
repression. It used to be assumed that no politician would ever come
out against motherhood—but now that the politics of ecology is
upon us, even motherhood is no longer sacrosanct. In the seven-

53. Sydenham, *Waters of Marah*, p. 9; *Occasions*, p. 158; *Sermons*, p. 86.

teenth century, the anglican definition of the virtue of charity and the sin of uncharitableness became for many Puritans a euphemism for Laud's persecution of them. The way that this came about gives insight into another area of anglican–puritan opposition. Anglicans made charity (as they defined it) a mark of true faith and thus a prerequisite to the comfort which came with assurance of salvation.

The anglican argument began with the dogma that the church, by definition, was made up of all baptized Englishmen. The Church was the body of Christ and must be, as Bishop Hall put it in 1652, "one entire body: all the limbs must be held together by the ligaments of Christian love." This body was the visible church, and no one claimed that all the individuals within it were also members of the more select body of true saints predestined to salvation, the invisible church. No living man could take it upon himself to circumscribe his charity to the smaller body within the visible church for two reasons. First, he was under explicit command not to do so: "Judge not, that ye be not judged" (Matt. 7:1). Second, that task belonged to Christ alone, and Dr. Edward Hyde warned against usurping it: "Christ is the only over-seer and bishop of our souls. . . . Do not presume to go a visitation in thy Savior's diocese." Or, as Sanderson explained it, "The fan is not in our hand, to winnow the chaff from the wheat, the Lord only knoweth who are his, by those secret characters of grace and perseverance, which no eye of man is able to discern in another, (nor perhaps in himself infallibly)." Therefore the duty of loving the brotherhood had to be discharged toward all who were living "in the communion of the visible church, being baptized into Christ and professing the name of Christ." These "plain and legible characters of baptism and outward profession" were, continued Sanderson, all that one could go by and therefore the terms "brethren" and "Christians" were interchangeable. Jeremy Taylor listed as one of the consolations arising from the sacrament of baptism the thought that "I am no longer a stranger and a foreigner, but a fellow-citizen with the saints, and of the household of God." The gate to felicity was baptism itself, and no baptized Christian could exclude another from the "household of God." In a sermon preached at Whitehall in 1665, Thomas Pierce told his listeners to "make it your boast that ye are members of a Christian Reformed Church" and the children not of Hagar but "of Jerusalem which is above, and therefore the children of the promise."[54]

This inclusive definition of the term "brotherhood" was the basis of numberless polemical uses of the term "charity." The Church of England did not claim perfection, but it did claim to provide for its members all that any institution could provide of the essential elements of religion and therefore of salvation. To separate from it or to agitate for change within it were failures of the charity which brethren owed each other. Anglicans felt that a certain latitude of opinion was acceptable within the church so long as the essentials were unimpaired. Benjamin Whichcote's "principle of peace and charity" was that all who "agree in the main points of religion, may look upon themselves as members of the same church, notwithstanding any different apprehensions in other matters." Bishop Hall called for diversity of opinion without "alienation of affection. That charity, which can cover a multitude of sins, may much more cover many small dissensions of judgment." The proper, charitable course in these matters for the good Christian was to "be silent where he must dissent." Any who did not remain silent in his dissent and who pressed his views openly and actively was guilty of a deficiency of charity. The most obvious targets for this particular line of attack were the various types of separatists. Beginning with the Brownists, separatists had said that the Church of England was insufficiently reformed of popish errors and lacking in some vital way the full character of a true church. Although few of them went so far as to assert that all those who remained in the mother church were destined to perdition, their actions and their rhetoric implied that they feared as much. The orthodox anglican reply might on occasion be magnanimous, but it was nevertheless firm. The church, wrote Hall, is composed of all who consent to "the main principles of religion . . . and if [Christians] admit not of each other as such, the fault is in the uncharitableness of the refusers no less than in the

54. Hall, 7:154; Hyde, *Legacy*, p. 62; Sanderson, 2:83; Taylor, 1:156; Pierce, p. 143. Sanderson's sermon (on 1 Pet. 2:17, "Honor all men, love the brotherhood") was preached before Charles I and his court in 1633. For more on this theme, see Sanderson, 2:203, 339, 390; Hales, 2:14–15, 60–64, 3:305–06. Chillingworth wrote that Charles I had brilliantly defended the Church of England "from all the foul aspersions both of domestic and foreign enemies, of which they can have no ground but their own want of judgment or want of charity" (1:iv).

error of the refused." The "vain and loose stragglers" who insisted on severing themselves were to be assured "that the union of Christ's Church shall consist entire without them; this great ocean will be one collection of waters when those drops are lost in the dust."[55]

Brownists, Barrowists, Familists, Anabaptists—these sectarians were obviously guilty of the sin of uncharitableness. Anglicans also levelled the same charge at dissenters who did not withdraw from the national church. Anthony Farindon struck the characteristic note of anglican polemic when he said "faction cannot be religion, since it cutteth off the fairest part and member she hath—charity." Dr. Sanderson, the king's favorite casuist, had another word for faction—"partiality." He defined it as the restraining of "the brotherhood to some one party or society in the church, such as we think good of, and exclude the rest, as if they had no part nor fellowship in this brotherhood," nor any claim to "that special affection" we owe to the brethren. Such a partiality had been, in Sanderson's view, the "very bane of the church's unity and peace" since the days of the apostles. Like the Donatists and other schismatics and like the Roman Catholics, "our brethren of the Separation" had excluded from heaven all who were not subject to their authority and discipline. In the case of the separatists, this had the ludicrous effect of "unchurching all the world except themselves" and limiting Christ's entire flock to "a private parlor or two in Amsterdam." Unfortunately, he continued, "some in our own church, who have not yet directly denied us to be their brethren, had . . . some of the leaven of this partiality hidden in their breasts." They had such uncharitable opinions of their brethren and inflated opinions of themselves that they used "the terms of brotherhood, of profession, of Christianity, the communion of saints, the godly party, and the like, as titles of distinction, to difference some few in the church (a disaffected party to the established government and ceremonies) from the rest." Sanderson prefaced his conclusion upon this with the requisite note of charitable caution; "I may not, I cannot judge any man's heart." But his conclusion was that any man who annexed

55. Whichcote, 1:181; Hall, 7:154, 175, 156. For more examples of this insistence on the necessity of charity toward all who did not differ on essentials see McAdoo, *Spirit of Anglicanism*, pp. 68ff. Note the praise of "the best unity which is that of charity" by Falkland, p. 139.

the title of "brethren" to "some part only of the Christian church" was failing in his duty of loving the entire brotherhood. Since Sanderson had already described that duty as an essential fruit of true faith, his meaning was clear. The "godly party" was guilty of the kind of "rotten or corrupt partiality" which good Christians avoided.[56]

Humphrey Sydenham's style was quite different from Sanderson's. Sanderson approached his condemnation of the uncharitableness of the "godly party" with cool logic and presented it to his hearers with an air of elegant distaste—as if it were his unpleasant duty to warn them of an ugly danger and then to leave the distressing subject as quickly as possible. Sydenham, on the other hand, led with his right and aimed for a knockout in every round. Despite the virulence of his rhetoric, the argument of this Somerset firebrand was essentially the same as that of the courtly casuist. The tone is set in the subtitle of his *Waters of Marah and Meribah* (1630): "Advice, Refutation, Censure, Against the Pseudo-zelots of our Age." Sydenham recognized that there were occasions when a "Boanerges, . . . a son of thunder," was needed to crack stony, sinful hearts, but he preferred "a Barnabas," a son of consolation. At some length, he eulogized the tender, compassionate method of seeking conversions. In dealing with their fellowmen, Christians should imitate Saint Paul's example and address all men as brethren. Such consideration was owed "not to some only but to all (so says the text), to all, of all sorts, not the particulars of his own cut and garb but even to those without." The Christian should, Sydenham continued, treat all men—unbelievers, neighbors, enemies, and even evil enemies—as brothers to whom sincere charity is due. " 'Tis plain then, where charity is, there is an habitation for the Lord; and where 'tis not, there is a thoroughfare for the Devil. . . . Tell me not of . . . zeal without thy charity; what is devotion when 'tis turbulent, . . . or preaching, when 'tis schismatical?"[57]

From this point on in the sermon, Sydenham became a veritable Boanerges to the Puritans, denouncing their "oral vehemence [which] hath more tongue than heart." What good, he demanded,

56. Farindon, 1:439; Sanderson, 2:89–91. Similarly Hammond, p. 199, on the "pleasures of singularity and being head of a faction."
57. Sydenham, title page and pp. 17, 6, 21–27.

was their "purity, when 'tis factious?" Rather than subscribe to
ceremonies, they underwent suspension or imprisonment. Sydenham
regarded this as proof of their schismatic intentions, for "what
judgment would expose our body unto prison? our calling to the
stain of separation and revolt for a thing merely of indifferency and
ceremony?" His conclusion, like Sanderson, decried those who went
"squadroned into a faction, . . . not only in the state but the
church too" and thus threatened that "unanimity [which] is the
soul of brotherhood." At the end, Sydenham made an attempt to
practice the charity he had preached. He had addressed his factious
enemies as "our brainsick and discontented neoterics at the present." But his peroration was directed to "the peace-less brother"
as a word of advice. The advice might have been taken from Laud's
sermons, but was in fact translated from Tertullian—himself no
mean son of thunder among the early church fathers: "Since we
have one God, our father, one Christ, our brother, one church, our
mother, one spirit, our comforter, let us have all one mind, one
heart, one peace, our director."[58]

The Anglicans felt that the essential thing to remember was that
religion could never be made the excuse for causing schism within
the unanimity of the brotherhood—the national church. The duty
of charity demanded a fervent zeal for the good of the brethren,
but it was an unsound zeal and a mistaken charity if it upset the
peace of the church. Jeremy Taylor, preaching in his Welsh haven
of exile, urged care "that this zeal of thy neighbor's amendment be

58. Ibid., pp. 40–41, 35, 43. Sydenham regarded "the people" as the prime
movers of "the hubbub and outcries in our church. . . . They have gotten
lately [i.e., 1630] into most corporations of the kingdom certain lapwing divines
and featherless professors of their own cut; prescribe them principles which they
may not transgress, and not only their posture, habit and conversation, but the
very method, tone and language cued them. Miserable age, when divinity shall be
thus slaved to a stipend and a trencher! And the apostles of Jesus Christ, for a
morsel of bread or some mechanick or lean-cheeked contribution, shall disparage
the power and sacredness of their keys! But fie on this factious holiness, this Jezebel
in religion." Without the arcane and rather splendid pejoratives, this is a good
description of the puritan practice of building corporate lectureships. However,
Sydenham underestimates the amount of help "the people" got from highly placed
persons. For descriptions of Puritans (not Separatists) as "factious" by such Anglicans as Laud, Chestlin, and Heylyn, see Seaver, *Puritan Lectureships*, pp. 86, 237,
260, 288.

only expressed in ways of charity. . . . 'He that strikes the prince
for justice,' as Solomon's expression is, 'is a companion of mur-
derers.' " The man who "out of zeal of religion, shall go to convert
nations to his opinion" by drawing his sword and dictating "new
summaries of religion" brings forth not salvation but religion which
"serves an interest, not holiness." The essence of the church was,
according to Farindon, compassion, mercy, and charity to the
Christians who constitute it. The difficulty was that each man
preferred to define the church "after his own image . . . so far
as to leave in him a persuasion that he is a true part of it" and to
shut out all others. Thus the schismatic is confident of his salvation
"though he have no charity." In the early church, the Novatians
were, Farindon said, "the 'Puritans' of those times." They so
lacked compassion as to refuse to accept back into the church
repentant apostates after Diocletian's persecution. It was this kind
of proud uncharitableness which caused divisions within the church
and caused Farindon to cry, "Talk not of a visible, infallible, or a
Reformed church: God send us a compassionate church!" The kind
of zeal which "consumeth not ourselves, but others about us," and
is indignant "against sin in all but ourselves," was, he said, a false
zeal, just as "that hand which is so ready to take a brother by the
throat, was never guided by the Author of our religion, who is our
Father."[59]

If reproofs delivered privately and publicly failed to convince
the factiously partial and misguidedly zealous brethren of their
unchristian lack of charity, the devout Anglican had three alternative courses of action. First, he should yield to the pleas of his weaker
brethren for changes in indifferent matters insofar as he lawfully
could. Second, if the dissenters demanded changes which could not
lawfully be granted, true charity might require that their bodies be
punished so that their souls might benefit. Third, if their temporary
triumph made it impossible to chastise them, the good Christian

59. Taylor, 5:210; Farindon, 1:249, 540, 250, 440–41. See also Hales, 2:60–64
and Chillingworth, 3:89: "The time is come when men think they can give no
greater nor more approved testimony of their religion and zeal of God's truth, than
by hating and abhorring, by reviling and traducing their brethren, if they differ
from them in any, though the most ordinary innocent opinions."

might be left with only one recourse—beseeching the Almighty with prayers urging that he force them to a recognition of their uncharity with judicial afflictions.

The first alternative was thoroughly considered by Sanderson in two sermons preached in July, 1640 (one at Whitehall and the other at Hampton Court). The problem, as he saw it, was that the Puritans and their ilk considered a great many things unwarrantable which were merely indifferent. Their mistakes arose from two interconnected sources, ignorance and partiality. Nothing, he said, should be considered unlawful unless its unlawfulness were "sufficiently demonstrated, either from express and undeniable testimony of Scripture, or from the clear light of natural reason" (or at least from proper deductions from them). One of the many dangers of concluding things unlawful upon weak grounds was that "it produceth much uncharitableness" because it was almost impossible not to "think somewhat hardly of these men that take the liberty to do such things as we judge unlawful." If "all walking in the fields, . . . or even moderate recreations on the Lord's day, . . . be grievous profanations of the Sabbath," then men who indulged in them had to be regarded as "grievous profaners of God's Sabbath." Sanderson held it even more dangerous that this rash and ill-considered wielding of the brush of unlawfulness led to a loss of respect for and obedience to the "Christian governors." The higher powers were simply exercising "that power God hath left them in indifferent things, by commanding such . . . things to be done, as namely, wearing of a surplice, kneeling at the communion, and the like." The source of this kind of "ignorance and ill governed zeal" was the "corrupt fountain of partiality [which] maketh a man to look at himself and his own party with favor" and at everyone else with scorn or envy. It was on this rationale that Clarendon criticized all who condemned a man "for not believing all indifferent and circumstantial things which they believe." The effect of exalting trivialities was, he said, that they "make such a fence about their religion, of laws and oaths and obligations" as to drive men away from religion instead of drawing them into it.[60]

60. Sanderson, 2:256–58, 263–64; *Contemplations*, p. 538. See also Hammond, *Catechism*, sig. A2 (recto). For an explanation of how this charge of ignorance was consonant with the variety of learning displayed by puritan writers, see Sanderson, 2:262. He also stated that gaming, dancing, and stage plays were not "utterly unlawful" (2:261).

Despite the corrupt parentage and unlovely offspring of puritan partiality, Sanderson told the royal entourage that Christians "are bound to forbear the exercise of our lawful liberty in indifferent things for our brother's sake." Discretion and charity would have to be exercised in specific decisions as to just how much to yield in each situation in order "to advance the common good by preserving peace, and love, and unity in the church." Sanderson concluded his pair of sermons on this subject with what he called "a caution of some importance." All that he had said about "yielding to the weaknesses of our brethren for the avoiding of their offence" should, he warned, be applied only to things within our power, "no superior authority, either divine or human, having limited us therein." Wherever our choice between expedient and inexpedient things has been circumscribed by legitimate authority, nothing can be yielded. If there were any Puritans in the chapel at Hampton Court on the 26th of July, 1640, they could have found little useful charity in these precepts. All that Sanderson would grant was that, when "things are in agitation, private men may, if anything seem to them inexpedient, modestly tender their thoughts, together with the reasons thereof, to the consideration of those that are in authority." Once a decision had been made and publicly proclaimed, "then for private men . . . with unseasonable diligence" to question or to refuse obedience was utterly indefensible.[61]

As Sanderson knew full well, the degree of charity he described was not enough. Many Puritans had long since demanded much more latitude than the king and his bishops would grant. The anglican insistence on ceremonies, among other things, had led them to question, once again, the warrantableness of episcopacy itself. The anglican response had been to take the second alternative —to move from the charity of consent to the charity of chastisement. They insisted that the underlying purpose was the same. Sanderson made the distinction neatly when he said that the aim of charity is not men's pleasure but their good, "and therefore as it seeketh to please them, if that be for their good, so it careth not to displease them, if that be for their good." Sydenham concurred, with the observation that a "religious chastisement sometimes more profits, then a partial connivance or remission." In all punishments the aim

61. Sanderson, 2:282, 287–88. Similarly Whichcote, 1:159: "This argument of private judgment is modest and humble and grows only in God's garden."

had to be the reformation of the guilty party because in this there was "great charity, that we wish the preservation of the sinner, when we desire the destruction of his sin." When the Civil War began, the Anglicans began to be on the receiving end of this kind of charity. One of the king's chaplains, Richard Harwood, came to see charity as a reason against seeking vainglorious martyrdom. In the sermon he preached in the university church at Oxford shortly after the battle of Naseby, he agreed that the royalist owed "so much charity to his very persecutor, as not to give him an occasion to shed innocent blood."[62] By the summer of 1645, however, the anglican exercise of charity had been largely reduced to the last of the three alternatives, prayer for drastic divine intervention. Royalist arms lay in the dust but the royalist chant rose more loudly now that only prayer was left. Clarendon, idle in exile on the island of Jersey, began his contemplations on the Psalms. The prayers that he attached to each contemplation frequently contained pleas such as this: "Convert and instruct our enemies, that they may be conscious to themselves of their impiety against thee, of their disloyalty against their sovereign, of their uncharitableness and cruelty against their brethren."[63] Clarendon repeatedly prayed for either their conversion or confusion and eventually he got the latter. To read his thoughts is to see the graph of a barometer of anglican hopes from 1647 to the Restoration. When the Scots joined with the young Charles II in 1650, Clarendon exulted and thanked God for "disposing the hearts and affections of one of his kingdoms to return to their allegiance and obedience." He further reflected that the whole brotherhood of the church should feel its load of suffering lightened because "all good and true Christians are one body, and when the least or meanest member of it feels any notable

62. Sanderson, 2:286; Sydenham, *Waters of Marah*, pp. 19, 26; Harwood, *The Loyal Subject's Retiring Roome*, p. 16. Dr. Thomas Pierce, writing soon after Charles II's restoration, insisted that no concessions be made to the Nonconformists because "in the method of healing wounds, . . . there is as charitable cause, both of the probe and the abstersive, as there can possibly be of the oil and the balsam" (sig. A3 [verso]).

63. *Contemplations*, p. 394. Clarendon's chaplain (while in Jersey), Lionel Gatford, later urged the men of his home county of Suffolk not to draw back from repentance of their wicked rebellion out of fear that the king would not be merciful: "Do not ye measure his charity by your own uncharitableness." *Englands Complaint*, p. 8.

ease, any recovery from the pain that possessed it, the whole body must be refreshed."[64]

Clarendon's prayers express the full conception of the first aspect of the anglican definition of charity. True Christians owed the duty of charity to all who were baptized into the Church of England and who professed belief in the articles pertaining to salvation. All such men were "brethren" and should be treated with an appropriate form of charity, even if they belied their profession by causing dissension within the church and commonwealth. The sin of uncharity was, however, a serious matter, because it muddied the waters of the fountain of grace, the national church. Thus the apparently bland virtue of charity became a means of differentiating Anglicans and Puritans.

Charity to the Poor and Hungry

According to the King James translation of Saint Matthew's gospel, Christ blessed those who are "poor in spirit" and who "hunger and thirst after righteousness" in his Sermon on the Mount (Matt. 5:3, 6). In Saint Luke's version, however, He said, "Blessed be ye poor. . . . Blessed are ye that hunger now" (Luke 6:20, 21). This contrast in the first century A.D. between the hunger of the soul and the hunger of the body was present in puritan and anglican conceptions of how good Christians ought to go about loving the brethren in the seventeenth century. As the first part of this chapter demonstrated, Puritans heavily emphasized works of charity that were directed toward the spiritual well-being of their brothers in Christ.

For Anglicans, however, the duty of charity was usually a ministry to those who were poor in estate and hungry for food. Jeremy Taylor felt that although "it is good to give to a church, . . . it is better to give to the poor." Both required help, "yet in cases of dispute mercy carries the cause against religion and the temple." Dr. Hammond called the charity of almsgiving "the queen of heaven." Although, he said, no human merit could be pleaded as a

64. *Contemplations*, pp. 447–48. He did not forget to pray that the Scots' repentance would be true and complete and that they would not be so obstinate as to try to get the king to agree to "anything which in conscience, honor or justice he cannot consent to."

title to salvation, yet almsgiving "is a duty most acceptable in the sight of God, . . . almsgiving is mentioned when assurance is left out, charity crowned when confidence is rejected." The anglican biographer, William Lloyd, praised Bishop Walter Curle of Winchester because he had been "a charitable reliever in all places, of God's poor, his living temples." Gilbert Sheldon, who was shortly to succeed the aged Juxon as archbishop of Canterbury, told his hearers in the royal chapel on June 28, 1660, that they should show their gratitude to God for the "happy return of His Majesty" by relieving the wants of "those especially that have suffered in the late disturbances, the sick, the maimed, the lame, the desolate widows and children of such as fell in the service." That such works of charity would be highly pleasing to God was a certainty. Clarendon wrote that God had not "acknowledged himself so much obliged in our exercise of any Christian virtue as in our charity and giving alms to the poor, and indeed the practice of any other duty is not so evident to be for God's sake as this of relieving the poor."[65]

This is not to say that Anglicans never urged works of "spiritual" charity, just as it is false to say that Puritans never urged "material" charity. The argument is that, by comparison with Puritans, almsgiving and other works of material charity were much more prominent in their thinking and were much more frequently and warmly commended. When Anglicans spoke of spiritual charity in the puritan sense, they were often scornful. Whichcote castigated men whose "finding fault with others, . . . backbiting, . . . busy meddling in other men's affairs, lives and judgments, . . . [and controlling] others' liberty" was reckoned by them to be "reproof of sin, . . . endeavor for reformation, . . . advancement of religion, . . . [and] a care for their souls." Chillingworth was, as we shall see, a great advocate of almsgiving. But he also thought that Christians should contribute to the repair of church buildings—a view he expressed in a vigorous antipuritan way. In a pair of sermons probably preached during the Civil War, he told his listeners that "since God himself is grown so poor and needy (especially in this kingdom), that he hath not means enough to repair his own

65. Taylor, 5:197; Hammond, p. 257; Lloyd, quoted in Cassan, *Lives of the Bishops of Bath and Wells*, pt. 2, p. 56; Sheldon, p. 47; *Contemplations*, p. 477.

houses, nor scarce to make them habitable," they would "do well to rescue God's churches from being habitations of beasts and stables for cattle." Indeed, he suspected that "God has suffered the ancient, superstitious, histrionical adorning of his temples to be converted into the late slovenly profaneness (commonly called 'worshipping in spirit' but intended to be worship without cost), that you may find a happy occasion to restore those sacred places . . . to that majesty and reverence as may become houses wherein God delights that his name should dwell."[66]

Anglicans repeatedly emphasized that works of "material charity" were more truly pious than any amount of more formal piety. Many chose to enlarge upon James 1:27, "Pure religion and undefiled before God and the Father is this, to visit the fatherless and widows in their affliction and to keep himself unspotted before the world." Sydenham, for example, said that he who fulfilled the first part of James's instruction by relieving the afflicted would have little difficulty remaining unspotted. In 1633 he told a group of clergymen in Somerset that there was no proportion "between three sermons a week and but one alms. . . . Let us as well fill the poor man's belly as his ears." Thomas Pierce said that although there might be "a seemingness of religion" in many things, "I am sure its purity consists in these two, the relief of the needy in their afflictions and the keeping of one's self unspotted from the world." Sanderson was equally critical of those who were confident of their salvation because they frequented "the house of God and the holy assemblies." "No man," he said, "hath either more contentment or more religion than he hath charity," referring in this instance to the "dispensation of the temporals God hath bestowed upon him for the comfortable relief of the poor distressed members of Jesus Christ." "I must confess," said Hales with studied sarcasm, "that I have not yet made that proficiency in the schools of our age" as to understand "why the Second Table and the acts of it are not as properly the parts of religion and Christianity" as the First. "If I mistake," he continued, "then it is Saint James that hath abused me for he

66. Whichcote, 1:183–84; Chillingworth, 3:201, 171. See also Hales, 3:57. For straightforward exhortations to spiritual charity, see Taylor, 5:209, and Hyde, *Legacy*, pp. 119–24.

describing religion by its proper acts" says that it is visiting the
fatherless and the widows in their time of need.[67]

Anglicans derived this duty of charity to the poor and oppressed
from the laws both of nature and of grace. Hammond told the City
fathers that "mercifulness, or charity, or giving alms," is not a part
of the ceremonial law of the Jews but rather a part of "the eternal
law of reason and nature," and thus "is all one with humanity, a
precept of the nature, the God, the soul we carry about with us."
Taylor said that "the law of charity is a law of nature" because it
was the result of simple justice among men; "justice to our neighbor,
is loving him as ourselves." Our natural reason, he continued,
tells us that we should do "as we would be done to" and justice and
charity are the result. Sanderson also noted, in an assize sermon in
Kent in 1630, that all men were in duty bound to use their "best
strength to deliver the oppressed." This was, he said, so evident a
precept that even the heathen philosophers had called it "a beam
of the light of nature." Anglicans did not, however, stop with the
dictates of natural reason in this matter. Sanderson went on to say
that, in addition to the rationality of this kind of charity, there were
numerous explicit commands to perform it in both the Old and the
New Testaments, all of which were summed up by the "second
great commandment" of Saint James (2:8), the command to
"love thy neighbor as thyself." The innumerable commands in
Scripture which required succoring the poor and oppressed were
necessary because of original sin. Before his fall from grace, Adam
had behaved according to the law of nature. The entry of sin into
the world had corrupted both his reason and his will. All of the
revelations of God's will by Christ, the disciples, and the prophets
were aimed at restoring this pristine humanity. Under the laws of
nature and the laws of Moses, charity had been a duty of the highest
importance. When Christ came, as Jeremy Taylor put it, He "added
many new precepts over and above what were in the law of Moses,
but not more than was in the law of nature." Christ came, he continued, to make "a more perfect restitution of the law of nature, than
Moses did, and so it became the second Adam to consummate that,

67. Sydenham, *Occasions*, pp. 314–15; T. Pierce, *Philallēlia*, sig. A2 (verso);
Sanderson 2:155; Hales, 2:71–72. See also Hammond, p. 257, Chillingworth, 3:
199.

which began to be less perfect, from the prevarication of the first Adam."[68]

The existence of poverty, hunger, and all sorts of material need among the afflicted members of Christ was itself a result, not of God's plan but of man's sin. Adam, by choosing earthly pleasures despite explicit divine prohibition, had introduced the sins which brought about what Hammond called "the extreme inequality that is now so illustriously visible in the world." The sinful covetousness which drove some men to grind the faces of the poor in order to increase their wealth was no part of God's plan. Faced with man's sinful rebellion, God responded by commanding men to minister to the needs of the victims of evil men. Hammond summed up the "pedigree and genealogy of alms-giving" this way: "covetousness and oppression and rapine brought in emptiness and beggary and want; then God's providence and goodness, finding it in the world, resolves to continue it there to employ the treasures and exercise the charity of others." In a similar vein, Chillingworth pointed out that God could quite easily have so ordered the world that every man would have enough to sustain himself. But then there would have been no need for "two heavenly and divine virtues . . . the poor man's patience and the rich man's charity. The poor man therefore wants that you may have occasion to exercise your liberality."[69]

When money and property were considered in this light, there could be nothing absolute about them. Although the positive law talked of ownership of and "propriety" in material things, the moral law dictated a different attitude. George Hall, son of the famous Bishop Joseph Hall and himself bishop of Chester after the Restoration, told a gathering of the sons of ministers in 1655 that "while so many are in extreme indigency, your purses are not your own, you are but stewards and almoners, not proprietors. And next unto drinking up the tears of widows and orphans is not drying them up when it is in your power to do it." Humphrey Sydenham said that helps given to the poor were not "so properly a lending or benevo-

68. Hammond, pp. 251–52; Taylor, 2:xlix; Sanderson, 2:397–98; Taylor, 2:1. For more on Sanderson's conception of social justice, see McAdoo, *Spirit of Anglicanism*, pp. 42–49. See also Farindon, 1:217.

69. Hammond, pp. 241–43; Chillingworth, 3:171. See also Sanderson, 2:401.

lence as a due. The gleanings of the corn field and the shakings of the vintage were a legacy long since bequeathed the poor man by the Law when the Gospel was yet in her nonage and minority." Speaking on Shrove Tuesday at Eton, John Hales said: "So much as thou needest is thine, the rest thou art but entrusted with for others' good." To hold back food in a barn, clothing in a wardrobe, or money in a treasury is to hold back "the bread of the hungry . . . the garment of the naked . . . the shoe of the bare foot . . . the poor's money." Rich men literally owed alms to the poor: "the hungry man begs at thy gate, . . . thou art in debt to him for his dinner."[70]

Some Anglicans went even farther than this in urging the obligation of charity. Hammond insisted that the withholding of alms was tantamount to murder. Though a man's goods were his own "by right of propriety," yet they belonged to others "by right of charity; the rich man's barn is the poor man's granary." Citing Ecclesiastes 24:21 ("The poor man's bread is his life"), Hammond charged that he who deprived the poor man of his bread deprived him of his life as well. The unmerciful man, he concluded, "is a murderer." The judgment of the casuist, Dr. Sanderson, was the same. He said that "to take away a man's substance, whereby he should maintain his life, is . . . all one as to take away the very life itself. Therefore, as Abel's blood crieth, so the laborer's wages crieth." In this sense, failure to relieve the poor and oppressed was a breach of the Second Table commandment against murder. They did not, by all this, mean to press the old-fashioned style of indiscriminate almsgiving. Sanderson said that to an idle beggar, "it is alms to whip him."[71] But almsgiving in the full sense of material aid to the helpless poor was for Anglicans an essential mark of salvation.

Anglicans alternated, carrot-and-stick fashion, between eulogizing the benefits which accrued from giving alms and decrying the murderous consequences of not giving them. Persons in high places

70. G. Hall, *Gods Appearing*, p. 29; Sydenham, *Occasions*, p. 109; Hales, 2:165, 160. See also Hales, 2:179–81, 3:52–54.

71. Hammond, p. 244; Sanderson, 2:405; Sanderson, quoted in C. Hill, *Society and Puritanism*, p. 285. See also Taylor, 3:66; *Contemplations*, p. 477; Hammond, *Catechism*, p. 130; Chillingworth, 3:199; Hales, 2:161: "Take heed, every vanity, every superfluity, every penny that thou hast misspent to the prejudice of him that wants, when the time comes, shall cry out unto thee."

were especially bound to works of charity because of the opportunities afforded them by their offices and estates. Sanderson described wealth and power as affording "a rich opportunity for every great and good man, especially for every conscionable magistrate, to set in for God's cause and in God's stead." He could "by the greatness of his power . . . stop the course of violence and oppression, and . . . rescue out of the hands of the mighty those that are marked out to destruction or undoing." Sydenham, speaking to the magistrates in Somerset in 1633, said, "O consider this, all you whom God hath advanced either in title or blood above others; . . . you are exalted to protect the innocent, not to oppress them; to relieve the poor man, not to grind him." Those who were in a position to dispense justice and mercy had, for their own good, best do so. God will, he continued, be "a sanctuary for you" who are merciful and a scourge to all who are not. "Remember the greater you are in place, the nearer you are unto God"—a position rich in potential for either felicity or disaster. Jeremy Taylor explained that although great persons were free of many of the temptations and troubles that beset smaller men, yet they had to cast up their accounts upon the basis of all the "powers and possibilities" their positions afforded them. "They are," he said, "to reckon and consider what oppressions they have relieved, what causes and what fatherless they have defended, how the work of God and of religion, of justice and charity, hath thrived in their hands."[72]

Whether addressed to men of wealth and power or not, Anglican appeals for charity toward the poor and hungry and for aid to defenseless widows and orphans were based on a conviction that divine providence operated a kind of pre-Keynesian "multiplier effect" whenever works of charity were done. Charitable men would benefit, both in this life and the next, and the benefit would far exceed the dimensions of the acts of charity themselves. The underlying doctrine was, as George Hall put it, that charitable men would increase their temporal estates "by this most beneficial way of holy usury. Indeed, when accounts shall be cast up, it will be found that the poor are benefactors unto the rich." In the same way, Clarendon was convinced that even men who were not well off would profit by

72. Sanderson, 2:406; Sydenham, *Occasions*, p. 150; Taylor, 5:183. See also Sanderson, 2:155.

almsgiving. "He who can himself live a week without alms can very well give alms half that week." Clarendon believed that "God doth exceedingly bless such compassion and will never suffer the heart that is really and truly charitable to want fuel to maintain that fire, not to have wherewithal to be charitable." This was so in part because just as God punishes men by the "same vices which they have practised to the prejudice and damage of others, . . . so He rewards those who according to their weak ability have served him, the same way they have served him best." Hammond stated as an axiom that "alms-giving or mercifulness was never the wasting or lessening of any man's estate to himself or his posterity, but rather the increasing of it." He challenged the London merchants who were hearing him in Old Saint Paul's to produce even one example of "a prudent alms-giver" who had regularly devoted "some considerable part of his revenue" to the poor and who could say that he had ever missed it. Hammond compared alms-giving to bloodletting, saying that "as phlebotomy hath saved many men's lives, letting out some ounces of blood been the securing of the whole mass," so did charity have "a secret blessing influence upon temporal estates."[73]

At the very least, the careful performance of works of charity for the poor would protect temporal estates by warding off the plagues, famines, or other public judgments that were provoked by widespread uncharitableness. "So long," said Sanderson, "as we think no pleasures too much for ourselves, no pressures too heavy for our brethren, . . . we can expect no other but that the rod of God should abide upon us, either in dearths or in pestilences." Hammond called tithes to the poor "the hedges to our riches" and cited the Hebrew experience of famines and plagues as judgments upon the oppressions of the poor.[74] In the event, however, that the multiplier

73. G. Hall, *Gods Appearing*, p. 29; *Contemplations*, p. 479; Hammond, p. 262. Sydenham used the same image: "Let's abate somewhat our superfluities to supply their necessities; bleed this pleurisy of ours and cordial their consumption." *Occasions*, p. 180.

74. Sanderson, 2:414–15; Hammond, pp. 264–65. The sermon by Sanderson quoted here was delivered before the Lincoln Assizes in 1630, a time when Laud was making vigorous efforts to get the poor laws enforced. See Gardiner, *History*, 7:164; Wedgwood, *Thomas Wentworth*, pp. 94–97; Trevor-Roper, *Archbishop Laud*, pp. 381–84.

effect of charity failed to reward the merciful man in this life, there was no shred of doubt in the anglican mind that he would be rewarded in the next. "The Lord," said Sanderson, "who hath given every man a charge concerning his brother, and committed the distresses of the poor to our care and trust, will take district knowledge how we deal with them, and impartially recompense us hereafter." Farindon was equally confident that our mercy would be rewarded because "God hath set up his assurance-office to pay us back in our own coin, or, if not, in that which cannot be valued, being of an inestimable price." According to Hales, "nothing clears our account with God" short of emptying it to succor the needy. "Secular thrift is seen in saving, but divine thrift is best seen in spending."[75]

Aside from these spiritual and temporal benefits that adhered to works of charity, Anglicans often spoke of three additional motives to almsgiving. The first was that the giver realized the exquisite pleasure of the highest possible degree of participation in the being of God and Christ. To save a worthy human being from starvation by timely aid was for Clarendon "one of the pleasantest things a virtuous and noble mind and the nearest an act of creation human nature is capable of." Jeremy Taylor said that "Christ made himself the greatest and daily example of alms or charity." To love one's neighbor as one's self "concurs rarely with the first reasonable appetite of man, of being like God." Although charity is a commandment, its purpose, said Taylor, was "to make the charitable man happy. . . . And certain it is, there is no greater felicity in the world, than in the content that results from the emanations of charity." Hammond's description of the joys of almsgiving was even more fulsome: "This so delightful a duty, so perfect voluptuousness to any ingenuous man, . . . mercifulness, the pleasurablest burden in the world; there is no such kind of inward delight, and sensuality, as it were." Like Clarendon, Hammond attributed this to the "godlike quality" and "creative power" of saving poor men from starvation or ruin. Farindon too emphasized that the delight of giving is much greater for the giver than receiving is for the recipi-

75. Sanderson, 2:413; Farindon, 1:241; Hales, 2:166. For more examples of this kind of imagery, see C. Hill, *Society and Puritanism*, pp. 290–92. See also Sydenham, *The Rich Mans Warning Peece*, pp. 6–7.

ent. "The poor man rejoiceth as a hungry man that is fed . . . but the merciful man triumphs and jubilees within him. In a word, to love mercy is to be in heaven." In another sermon, Farindon pointed out that Christ had given us an excellent example of ministering to the needs of the poor and downcast. Thus for us "to serve our brethren is to exalt and advance and raise us up to be like him." Farindon admitted that some services might seem debasing (such as the washing of feet or the visiting of prisoners), but they are "our honor, our crown, our conformity to him who was the servant of God and our servant," and it is by compassion that "we come nearest to Christ himself." In almsgiving and other forms of help for the helpless, Anglicans experienced a creative joy which they described in rapturous terms comparable to those used by the Puritans to describe the fellowship of puritan saints.[76]

A second motive to almsgiving for Anglicans was the gratitude and the prayers of the beneficiaries. As we have seen, the Puritans believed that God listened with special attention to the prayers of the "godly brethren" because they were his particular children. Anglicans, however, frequently implied that He listened with special attention to the prayers of his "living temples" and "ambassadors," the poor. Clarendon said that God "readily hears every grateful prayer that is poured out on our behalf, by those who have been refreshed and preserved by our Christian bounty." Sanderson maintained that the man who relieves the poor will reap a rich harvest of "the hearty prayers and blessings of the poor," whereas the man who is able to help them but does not, receives instead their curses. There must, he concluded, be "comfort in the deserved blessings of the poor" or else Job, in the time of his affliction, would not have said, "The blessing of him that was ready to perish came upon me, and I caused the widow's heart to sing for joy" (Job 29:13). Jeremy Taylor spoke caustically of those whose whole religion was a mere avoidance of evil, completely lacking in positive

76. *Contemplations*, p. 478; Taylor, 4:241, 2:xlix–1; Hammond, p. 43; Farindon, 1:256, 111, 248. Similarly Hammond, p. 242 and Farindon, 3:110: "Christ is our pattern, our motive, the true principle of charity." Clarendon also said that helping a virtuous, though destitute, person is "the most lively and pregnant instance of heaven that the sense and understanding of man is capable of, since it so feelingly exceeds all others that can be imagined." *Contemplations*, p. 426. On the rapture of puritan fellowship, see above, pp. 202–07.

acts of charity. Their situation was indeed sad because "they have no catalogue of good things registered in heaven, no treasuries in the repositories of the poor, neither have the poor often prayed concerning them, 'Lord, remember thy servants for this thing at the day of judgment.' "[77]

A third motive to almsgiving was that it could be both a means to conversion and an evidence or sign that true conversion had occurred. It was a means to conversion in the sense that almsgiving could help to prepare the soul for saving grace. Hammond described it as one of the good works which would "naturally incline the subject for the receiving of grace when it comes." As an example, he mentioned the centurion, Cornelius, who was commended for his alms-deeds in Acts 10:2 and converted soon after (ver. 44). Dr. Edward Hyde also cited the example of Cornelius as proof that "if there be not a redeeming, yet there is a breaking off sins by alms-deeds, and iniquities by showing mercy to the poor."[78]

More frequently, however, the Anglicans spoke of almsgiving and other tangible expressions of concern for the material needs of the "poor distressed members of Jesus Christ" as yielding assurance of the validity of conversion. This, as we have seen, was a vital matter because of the danger that inward feelings about it could be misleading. Outward actions thus had both positive and negative significance—positive in that the performance of a particular duty gave strong though not conclusive evidence of the soul's regeneration, and negative in that nonperformance of the duty gave even stronger evidence that the soul was not yet regenerate. To profess faith in the saving doctrines of Christianity was necessary but not sufficient, and Anglicans insisted, as Jeremy Taylor put it, "that charity or a good life is part of that faith that saves us." Further, "nothing but charity and alms is that, whereby Christ shall declare the justice and mercy of the eternal sentence." Almsgiving is "the peculiar character of God's elect, and a sign of predestination." Puritans held that an important fruit of a true faith was "love to the

---

77. *Contemplations*, p. 479; Sanderson, 2:412–13; Taylor, 5:182. Chillingworth, 3:64, spoke against the man who "sees Christ himself, every day almost, hungry, and does not feed him; naked, and does not clothe him; in prison, and does not visit him." All such men, "inasmuch as they do not offices of charity to his beloved little ones," deny Christ. Cf. pp. 79–80, 115.

78. Hammond, pp. 458–59; Hyde, *Legacy*, p. 194.

brethren" within the context of a fellowship of "godly brethren."
Anglicans emphasized instead the importance of the "constellation
of gospel graces" which can be summed up as charity—"love to the
brethren," with "brethren" broadly defined. Faith, said Farindon,
"is naturally productive of good works . . . Charity is the proper
effect of faith, and upon faith and charity, we build our hope."
The law of God, he thought, gave evidence to support human law
on the subject of private ownership of worldly goods, "but it is
evidence against us, if we use them not to that end for which God
made them ours." Christ's law required that men dispense their
wealth by feeding the hungry, visiting the sick, and clothing the
naked, and it was upon such giving that hope of salvation rested;
"alienation is our best assurance, and continueth it to us for ever."
God's own charity in the form of the sacrifice of his only son was
apparent to all Christians. "If there be in thee any true fear of God,"
said Sanderson, "thou wilt obey his command; and if any true hope
in God, follow his example."[79]

In the quest for assurance of salvation and thus of comfort in
affliction, Anglicans made "love to the brethren" the highest of
duties. In the full signification which they gave it, charity was
required for all who were in need. There was no justification for
restricting it to any group within the whole body of baptized,
professing subjects of the Stuart monarchs. On the contrary, any
such restriction was a dangerous error and an evidence of the
reprobation of the restricter. As we have seen, the political implications of this comprehensive aspect of the definition of charity were
and are obvious. As Thomas Pierce put it, "Our love must imitate
the manner and degree of Christ's love" and we must not "love as
they do, whose love consisteth only in this, that they agree in the
hatred of some third party." Pierce's statement sums up the political
implications of the anglican definition of the objects of charity. The
political implications of the material form of that charity are less
obvious, but they could be seen by those who were looking for them.
Anglicans often accused Puritans of being latter-day Pharisees,
preaching and practicing a religion rich in theological phrases and
legalistic morals but devoid of the good works of a loving, liberal,
forgiving Christian spirit. Bishop Curle is said to have defined a

79. Taylor, 5:180, 4:241–42; Farindon, 1:428, 235–36, 239; Sanderson, 2:401.

Puritan as "such an one who loves God with all his soul, but hates his neighbor with all his heart." Sydenham thought in much the same way. God, he said, gave us two hands and one tongue and thereby "would have us distribute as well as talk . . . where the mouth is always open and the bowels shut, we have just cause to suspect that man's religion for imperfect, seeing God is a God of compassion as well as jealousy." In a sermon preached on Christmas Day, 1635 (and in the midst of an extended plea for charity to the poor), Sydenham gave his doctrine an explicitly political application. He condemned "those flinty professors which turn Gospel into law, Christianity into barbarism" by refusing to help the afflicted. These were the same men who were so unconcerned about the fate of the whole nation that they refused to pay ship money. They refused

> a rate to be levied for the royal navy to the honor of their prince, the terror of other nations and the future preservation of their own. They are up presently with their passive obedience. Goods forsooth they have, but in this case money they have none (though all the while they tumble in bonds and mortgages). And why? Tis against the law. Thus, they make the mere letter of the law their oracle.

In other words, charity to the prince required the payment of a tax not required by law. As he neared the conclusion of this rousing Christmas oration, Sydenham gave a brief, bitter catalogue of the sins of his enemies. They made "their religion, faith without works; their allegiance, murmuring; their church, mutiny; their charity, implacableness; their compassion, Bridewell; their alms, a whipping post."[80]

In order to consider himself a good Christian with a well-grounded hope of eternal life, Anglicans required that a man be the opposite of Sydenham's caustic caricature of a puritan saint. He had to eschew attachment to any group of private men within the comprehensive church which considered itself holier than the rest. It is "most sure," said Farindon, that if we entail election "on

80. Pierce, *Philallēlia* (1658), sig. D1 (recto); Curle, quoted in *Diary of John Manningham* (Camden Society Publications, no. 99. Edited by J. Bruce. London: J. B. Nichols, 1868), p. 156; Sydenham, *Occasions*, pp. 315, 180–81.

a faction," then we are without charity and "our 'election is not sure' " (2 Pet. 1:7–10). The anglican saint also had to express his faith in works of charity directed to the material needs of his unfortunate brethren, the poor and oppressed in body and estate. "Shall I tell you in one word," said Dr. Hammond, "that though heaven be given us freely, yet alms-giving is the consideration mentioned in the conveyance, that men are acknowledged the blessed of God and are called to heaven upon the performance of this duty." Next to the duty of obedience to God's anointed, no duty was so fruitful of the comfort of assurance as this. Clarendon concluded that there was "no pillow so soft to rest on as the conscience of having been kind and merciful to the fatherless and the needy."[81]

81. Hammond, p. 257; *Contemplations*, p. 479.

6

THE TRUE ISRAELITE

The English are a mysterious people and require all your attention. The sea which you passed to visit them is an emblem of their
temper and a direction how you ought to steer. . . . The curiosities
of a place are sooner known than either the religion or the politics
of its inhabitants. Time is required to become acquainted with the
factions of the country and much more time to find out a remedy
when the distemper is discovered.

> Cardinal Barberini to the papal emissary in
> England, Gregorio Panzani, March 1635

I knew a witty physician who found the creed in the biliary duct
and used to affirm that if there was a disease in the liver, the man
became a Calvinist, and if that organ was sound, he became a
Unitarian.

> Ralph Waldo Emerson, "Experience," *Essays* (1844)

Middleton, of course, he'd always relied on, but he'd never quite
made the grade. Perfectly right, of course, to follow the thing
through, but there'd been a sort of over-finicking, high-strung,
personal conscience about it that didn't do at all. More like a
Dissenter than a gentleman. But, of course, he probably came
from Quaker stock or something like that. These rich trades-people.
Well, they'd have to see. But you couldn't rely on any of them to
have the right instinct.

> Sir Edgar Iffley in Angus Wilson, *Anglo-Saxon Attitudes* (1956)

Joseph Caryl spent the better part of the three middle decades of the
seventeenth century steadily commenting his way through the Book
of Job. He chose it because he felt that the sad story of saintly Job's
many and terrible afflictions bore "the image of these times and
presents us with a resemblance of the past, present and (much
hoped for) future condition of this nation." In the preface to the

first volume of his lectures (signed in November, 1643), Caryl said that he sought to offer his readers "cordials for the reviving of their spirits and medicine for the care of their distempers. The whole book of Job is a sacred shop, stored with plenty and variety of both." He added that the "main and principal subject" of his book was Psalm 34:29, "Many are the afflictions of the righteous: but the Lord delivereth him out of them all."[1] If a man were righteous, he could gain admission to the "sacred shop" of God's comforts for his peculiar people, the true Israelites. God's promises to the Hebrews of the Old Testament were by virtue of Christ's death and passion translated to their successors, the true, elect Christians of all ages and nations.

As we have seen, however, there were certain signs which gave strong indications that a man's inward estate was unregenerate, whereas there were certain virtues which indicated that regeneration had taken place. "If we are God's people, true Israelites indeed," said the royalist chaplain Richard Harwood, "we should wear the habit, speak the language, and live according to the laws and constitutions of his kingdom." True Christianity, based on a real inward principle of faith in Jesus Christ, would be discernible in certain patterns of behavior. The whole life of the believer would bear the imprint of the divine grace which justified him. In the three preceding chapters, we have examined anglican and puritan conceptions of different parts of these patterns, and it is time to put the parts together. Caryl noted that "painters or picture-drawers, . . . when they are drawing the picture of a man, or of any other thing, frequently turn their eyes upon the prototype, upon that which they are to draw by."[2] The catalogue of the most sinful of sins and virtuous of virtues, taken together, provided for Anglicans and Puritans two portraits of the true Christian, ideal types or "prototypes" with which they could compare themselves.

As these portraits are painted, it must be remembered that both anglican and puritan painters were working from the same palette of sins and virtues. They began with the same tubes filled with the same pigments. Anglicans tended to squeeze dry the tubes labelled

1. Caryl, *Job* (chaps. 1–3), sigs. A2 (recto), A4 (recto and verso).
2. Harwood, *Loyall Subject's Retiring Roome*, p. 8; Caryl, *Job* (chaps. 4–6), p. 174.

"obedience to crown and mitre," "material charity," and other "Second Table duties." Puritans, on the other hand, used up tubes of "obedience to God first," "spiritual charity," and "First Table duties." Anglicans put the hearing of sermons and the careful observation of the Sabbath in their icons but they did so with fine detail brushes rather than with palette knives. Puritans certainly made obedience to the higher earthly powers a part of their portrait, but only against the strongly colored background of a higher duty to God. All English Protestants worked from the same skeletal structure of fundamental doctrine, and they used many of the same models of saintly behavior drawn from the Bible and the history of the church. Skeletons are hard to tell apart, but people are not. Anglicans and Puritans produced portraits which share a great deal and are yet distinct. They were distinct enough so that they could tell each other apart in the seventeenth century, and it should not be beyond the reach of the historian's art to find some of the more important distinguishing marks which they used and to rediscover something of their sense of perspective.

The usefulness of these paradigmatic portraits is in no way vitiated by the fact that seventeenth-century writers did not attach the labels "Anglican" and "Puritan" to them. These writers were not describing one of two models of life patterns which gave evidence of inward regeneration because all agreed that there could be only one such model, only one truly Christian pattern. Throughout his extensive meditations on the psalms of David, Clarendon referred to the actions of the "pious and godly man," the "true Christian," "the pious and faithful man," who not only knows his duty but does it in the face of all the opposition the treacherous world puts in his way. In the writings of such Puritans as John Winthrop and Oliver Cromwell, terms such as these are used for the same purpose of differentiating between truly godly Christians and those who profess Christianity but belie their professions with their sins of omission and commission. Nor is the usefulness of the models lessened by the fact that the differences between them are not always doctrinal. As Dr. Collinson has written, there were "ideological differences which arose between English Puritanism and what we are almost forced, in spite of the anachronism, to call Angli-

canism. These were differences of degree, of theological temperature
so to speak, rather than of fundamental principle."³

The historian's task in discovering these often subtle and elusive
distinctions—distinctions which were plain enough to Clarendon,
Cromwell, Winthrop, and their contemporaries—is made more
difficult by several factors. They used the same words to convey
somewhat different concepts, as we have seen with regard to "poor"
and "brethren." Or they customarily used the same words in quite
different contexts, as "obedience" and "rebellion," and in such a
way as to indicate quite different courses of action. They also used
the same scriptural texts and stories as sources for quite different
morals. For example, Puritans usually spoke of David as the writer
of songs of praise and thanksgiving written in the adversity caused
by the persecutions of ungodly men. He was a splendid example of
a righteous man, worshipping God in spirit and in truth, struggling
against the enemies of the true Israelites, surviving malignant plots
and attacks upon the true religion which he both professed and
lived because he was a legitimate, elect son of God. Anglicans, however, rarely missed the opportunity of emphasizing that he was
King David, "a saint-royal," who overcame rebellions led by ambitious, greedy upstarts because he as one of the "higher powers"
was of divine institution and received divine support. The Puritan
David hated idolatry and rebellion against God's Word; the Anglican David hated uncharitableness and rebellion against God's
vicegerents.⁴

Both Anglicans and Puritans thought of themselves as heirs of the
orthodox Protestant tradition in England. It is easy to see why the
Anglicans, closely associated as they were with their "godly rulers,"
the Stuarts, believed in their own orthodoxy. Yet most Puritans had
no doubt that they were the orthodox Protestants and that Laud
and his followers were the schismatic "innovators." The puritan
incumbent of a Suffolk parish wrote in 1635 that many pieces of
doggerel had been published "on both sides, some against the ortho-

---

3. Collinson, pp. 26–27. See chap. 1, above, for my argument about the importance of "directionality" in these matters. For examples of Clarendon's use of the
terms describing Christians, see *Contemplations*, pp. 387, 389, 413, 455.

4. For more examples of the "Anglican David," see Byron S. Stewart, "The
Cult of the Royal Martyr," *CH* 38 (1969):175–200.

dox, other against these 'new churchmen.' " Professor Barnes has
written that in Somerset in the 1630s "what we call Puritanism was
the established faith practised in the established Church." Collinson notes that such populous areas as York, Lincoln, and Norwich had had sixty or seventy years of "radically Protestant
bishops." He concludes that "for much of the time and in many
localities it must have seemed that puritan aspirations would be
satisfied without schism and without conspicuous conflict. Not until
the rise of Archbishop Laud and his episcopal colleagues in the reign
of Charles I were these tendencies radically reversed."[5] It is this
conviction of orthodoxy which explains the beleaguered, defensive,
and yet defiant tone of puritan rhetoric in the late 1620s and 1630s.
Sibbes, for example, charged his audience at Paul's Cross to "have a
care that there be no breaches made upon the sound doctrine that
is left unto us and hath been sealed up by the blood of so many
martyrs." It was in this conservative and embattled frame of mind
that Sir Nathaniel Bernardiston went to take his seat in the Short
Parliament. "Help, I beseech you, Sir," he wrote to John Winthrop,
"with all the might and force you can make, this great work; which,
if it succeed not well, is like to prove exceeding perilous and dangerous to this church and kingdom."[6]

Anglicans and Puritans denounced with equal vigor what they
called worshipping according to "opinions of men." To Puritans

5. *Diary of John Rous*, M. A. E. Green, ed., p. 79; Barnes, *Somerset, 1625–40*, pp.
14–5; Collinson, pp. 59–60. See also Claire Cross, *The Royal Supremacy in the Elizabe-
than Church*, pp. 95–114; Roger B. Manning, *Religion and Society in Elizabethan
Sussex*; R. C. Richardson, *Puritanism in North-west England*; Kenneth W. Shipps,
"Lay Patronage of East Anglian Puritan Clerics in Pre-revolutionary England,"
Ph.D. dissertation (Yale University, 1971); Zagorin, pp. 168–69, 189. N. R. N.
Tyacke argues strongly that it was not so much "the rise of Puritanism" which
made religion an "issue in the Civil War crisis" as it was "the rise to power of
Arminianism in the 1620s." This was because "in terms of English Protestant
history the charge in 1640 that King Charles and Archbishop Laud were religious
innovators is irrefutable." "Puritanism, Arminianism and Counter-Revolution" in
C. Russell, ed., *The Origins of the English Civil War*, pp. 119, 143. This chapter was
essentially complete before Dr. Tyacke's essay appeared and I was pleased to see
that my sketch agreed with his conclusions.
6. Sibbes, *Cordialls*, p. 178; *WP*, 4:218. See also Sibbes, *Cordialls*, pp. 156, 224;
Preston, *Breast-Plate*, pt. 3, p. 211; T. Goodwin, 7:547, 555–56, 562. W. Lamont
points out that "the most damaging charge that Prynne can make against bishops
is that they were deviating from the principle of the Elizabethan Church." *Godly
Rule*, p. 35 (cf. pp. 44–45, 71–72).

this meant Laudian ceremonies; to Anglicans it meant the exalta-
tion of preaching and lecturing over the performance of "things
indifferent" which the ecclesiastical authorities were entirely within
their rights in requiring. Further, although Puritans have usually
been thought of as extraordinarily zealous in the pursuit of their
goals, we cannot consider the call for zeal a distinguishing mark of
Puritanism. Jeremy Taylor was one of many Anglicans who felt that
"God hates an indifferent spirit . . . a lukewarm religion" and
demands fervency and zeal in a Christian's behavior. Nor did Anglicans shy away from using the rhetoric of sainthood, even though
Puritans are often thought of as having monopolized it. Henry
Byam compared the plight of Charles II and his supporters in exile
to that of "Abraham driven from place to place, at one time ready to
starve; another time his wife in jeopardy to lose her honor; . . .
and yet his bosom now a receptacle for the saints of God." Archbishop Bramhall, speaking of all who had suffered for the Stuart
cause, said, "I know that the saints themselves are involved in
national judgments as well as others."[7]

Another doctrine upon which Anglicans and Puritans agreed was
that although there were many outward signs which indicated inward regeneration, there were no absolutely infallible ones. Bishop
Sanderson said that there were "marks of sincerity for the trial of
our graces," but that there were no "certain rules or infallible
characters whereby to try the sincerity of those marks, so as to remove all doubtings and possibility of erring." This was true because,
as Thomas Hooker put it, "whatsoever a child of God will do by
virtue of sincerity in his heart, that same will an hypocrite do out of
the pride and vanity of his heart." No man could be certain of the
condition of another man's soul because it was possible for hypocrites to counterfeit the coin of true grace. "The web of hypocrisy,"
Hooker continued, "is most cunningly spun, scarcely to be discerned by him that hath the spirit of discerning more than ordinary."[8] Absolute certainty as to the state of another man's soul
was utterly unobtainable in this life. It was, however, equally certain
that all Christians were bound to admire and emulate goodness

7. Taylor, 5:192–93; Byam, p. 54; Bramhall, p. 129. See also Sydenham,
Occasions, pp. 56, 89; Bramhall, pp. 120–21.
8. Sanderson, 2:391; T. Hooker, *Lessons*, p. 230.

when they found it in others and to associate themselves with good men and women. That none of the touchstones was perfectly trustworthy was never an excuse not to use them.

Despite the important and numerous aspects of the idealized portraits of true Christian sainthood which Anglicans and Puritans held in common, there were enough differences to make identification not only possible but necessary and inescapable. All wanted to display in their lives not merely the form of godliness but the power of it as well. The divine Spirit which granted that power was, like the wind, invisible to the eye of mortal men, but the effects of its presence (or its absence) were observable. Oliver Cromwell, borrowing a line from Job (19:28), was proud that the Triers admitted to the ministry only those who had "the root of the matter" in them. Clarendon studied the Psalms in order to find the means to "discern the great difference and inequality even in this world, between honest and upright men who have God and his commandments always before their eyes, and the proud and the wicked who neglect or contemn both." Both would have agreed with John Bunyan when he wrote that "God knoweth their hearts without their outsides and we know their hearts by their outsides." The question for the historian is this: what were the most important outward marks and signs of true Christian behavior for Anglicans and Puritans? On what, for example, did John Winthrop base his opinion that Sir Robert Naunton, though a courtier, would make Suffolk a good shire knight in the 1625–26 Parliament? Winthrop told his wife that Naunton was, in addition to other virtues, "known to be sound on religion." Winthrop's friend, Sir Robert Crane, agreed that Naunton had an "affection to religion." Although it is possible that these eminent puritan gentlemen had actually catechized the prospective member of Parliament, it is more likely that most such judgments were based more on intuition than interrogation. It was well known that Naunton had been a vigorous enforcer of the penal laws—so vigorous in fact that the Spanish ambassador had lodged complaints about him. Although this alone would have been enough to commend him to Crane and Winthrop, the puritan ideal type—like the anglican one—was composed of a complex matrix of interlocking attitudes, values, and virtues.[9]

9. Abbott, 4:496; *Contemplations,* p. 382; Bunyan, *Christian Behavior* (1663), p.

The key to differentiation between the two paradigms lies in the interpretation of and the weights of emphasis upon the duties of the Two Tables. Stephen Marshall, in a parliamentary fast sermon preached in 1640, implored the assembled members of Parliament to be "purgers and preservers of our religion . . . pluck up every plant that God hath not planted." And why? "The Lord interprets them to love him that purely worship him. . . . God will trust them for all his Commandments, whom he finds faithful in his worship." The analogy Marshall offered left no doubt that he believed that God would more readily forgive breaches of the Second Table than breaches of the First. The Lord was, he said, like the "man who finds his wife faithful in the marriage bed" and thereby judges "that she loves him, . . . whatever other infirmities she may have." Puritanism had begun with the goal of purifying the worship of the Church of England of all its "idolatrous," "popish" remnants. Puritans had feuded bitterly with three sovereigns and their archbishops (excepting only Grindal and Abbot) because they could not accept the anglican doctrine of what Collinson has called "the *adiaphora* of God's service, . . . the corner-stone of Anglicanism."[10] They believed that their program would sooner or later succeed because it was God's will. Most could at least tolerate the Elizabethan and Jacobean barriers against their progress. The Elizabethan

---

113; *WP*, 1:325–26; *DNB*, s.v. "Robert Naunton." The three letters in the *Winthrop Papers* (1:324–26) which bear on the Naunton nomination offer fascinating insights into the ways and means of selecting members of parliament in such counties as Suffolk. Winthrop said in a letter to his wife that he had intended to find time to write to their local puritan minister about the proposed nomination. Not having found time, he instructed his wife to show the letter to "Mr. Sandes," their preacher at nearby Boxford and a member of the Dedham classis. This is a clear indication that such puritan gentlemen as Winthrop thought of their ministers as political counsellers. Sir Robert Crane told Winthrop that he had suggested Naunton's name to the town councilmen of Bury St. Edmunds—but they had rebuffed the suggestion. Though they were aware of the advantages which might accrue, especially to their vital cloth trade, by having a privy councillor as their representative, they feared that Naunton "was tied in so particular an obligation to his Majesty as if there was occasion to speak for the country he would be silent." Despite his soundness on religion and his affection to the good of the county and the nation—factors which both Winthrop and Crane mentioned—the burghers "would give no voice to any courtier especially at this time of all others." This time was January 1626.

10. S. Marshall, *A Sermon*, pp. 40–42; Collinson, pp. 27–28. Collinson considers this adiaphorism the cornerstone "if by Anglicanism we mean the claim made on behalf of a national Church to develop its own forms of church order."

Settlement had been doctrinally orthodox in their sense or at least could be so interpreted. James had upheld their views on the theology of grace at Dort. During both reigns they had been able to make considerable progress at the parish and regional levels in various parts of the country. If the tide were not running swiftly in their direction, they could at least feel some confidence that it was not running against them.

Under Charles I, however, a number of factors converged to frustrate their hopes. One effect of the Arminian controversy surrounding Montagu and others like him in the late 1620s was the engendering of doubts about royal "orthodoxy." Other straws in the wind—the pro-Spanish foreign policy, the presumed influence of the Roman Catholic queen, the rumors of court conversions, the lax execution of the recusancy laws—were combined with the most important development on the religious front, the rise of Laud and his party. "Idolatrous" regulations which had long gone unenforced were revived and new ones added. Thomas Watson's feeling about Laudian ceremonial innovations was typical; such things were the "strange fire" for the offering of which Nadab and Abihu had been incinerated. "If God was so exact and curious about the place of worship, how exact will he be about the matter of his worship! Surely here everything must be according to the pattern prescribed in his Word."[11] An equally grave breach of the First Table occurred when Laud sought to restrain puritan ministers from the activity which godly worship most assuredly required—the preaching of the Word. He restricted the supply of puritan preachers by his suspension and deprivation of them—actions which Watson denounced, saying that God's "glory is much promoted by the preaching of the

11. Watson, p. 8 (cf. pp. 47–49). Preston spoke forcefully in a similar spirit when he said that the "disposition of all those whose hearts are perfect with their God" is as follows: "They dare not pare away the least lap from the garment of religion, nor add the least fly to this box of precious ointment. For in this curious clockwork of religion, every pin and wheel that is amiss distempers all. And as we are wont to lay aside cracked vessels and distempered watches, so doth God distempered and mixed religions." *Sermons Preached Before his Majestie*, p. 17. The timing of this sermon and the context of these remarks suggest to me that he was thinking of Arminian theology rather than of ceremonial innovations—but the two were closely linked in puritan minds. Preston's modern biographer suggests that this sermon was aimed against John Cosin's *Book of Hours* (1627). I. Morgan, *Prince Charles's Puritan Chaplain*, p. 187.

Word, which is his engine whereby he converts souls. Now, such as would hinder the preaching of the Word fight against God's glory." Further, Laud forced the reading of the *Book of Sports*—an affront to all who would properly sanctify the Sabbath by hearing and reading the Word—and he tried to enforce the regulations against the leaving of one's parish to hear sermons. For Puritans, there could never be enough godly preaching. Winthrop said that after his conversion, "I had an unsatiable thirst after the word of God and could not miss a good sermon, though many miles off, especially of such as did search deep into the conscience."[12]

There were many puritan gentlemen in the English countryside who, like Winthrop, were appalled by what seemed to them a national change of direction after 1625. They and their forebears had faithfully and untiringly worked for the completion of what seemed to them to be the logical implications of the Protestant Reformation. Suddenly the doctrinal rudder and the liturgical sails on the ship of the state church were, it appeared, altered for a change of course which could only lead back to Rome. As the Civil War approached, those Anglicans who did not share their ideology and the values that it engendered were unable to interpret puritan opposition to royal policy as anything other than ambitious and schismatic. Secure in their confidence about the warrantableness of adiaphorist distinctions between essential and inessential matters, and traditional in their interpretation of the duty of obedience to the sovereign, the Anglicans emphasized instead the Second Table duties between man and other men and made performance of them "the most prominent mark" of the ideal Christian saint. Thomas Pierce told an assembly of Wiltshire gentlemen in London in 1658 that "the true importance of Christianity doth not consist (as some would have it) in . . . posting up and down from sermon to sermon." On the contrary, and despite "whatever some mockers are wont to say, . . . the Second Table is the touchstone of our obedience to the First. Our chiefest duty towards God is our duty towards our neighbor."[13]

12. Watson, p. 19; *WP*, 1:156. For more on the advance of anglican ritualism and the reasons for puritan hatred of it, see New, *Anglican and Puritan*, pp. 71–76. Note especially his discussion of the importance of the ceremonial innovations in Laud's new Book of Fasts (1636).

13. Pierce, *Philallēlia*, pp. 23–24. His identical statement in another sermon was

These differences in the weight of anglican and puritan emphases
upon the parts of the Decalogue reflected a basic difference in
religious and moral values. They were differences which might even
have coexisted in the church of England had not the archiepiscopacy
of William Laud intervened. When the troubles came, all were
agreed that they were the result of God's wrath against disturbers
of the peace. But which sins—and which peace? The evidence
which was presented in chapter 4 suggests that for Anglicans the great
disturber was disobedience to men—meaning the higher earthly
powers, Charles I and his civil and ecclesiastical subordinates. For
Puritans, the troubler was disobedience to God—meaning primarily
the First Table duties as Puritans understood them. For Anglicans
outward civil peace and religious unity were sacred. Pierce said
that "the note of distinction, whereby to know a sincere and a solid
Christian, is such a divine kind of love as tends to unity and
peace." The quality which Sydenham most admired in his patron
and friend, Sir Hugh Portman, was that he had wished "the
walls of our Jerusalem [the Church of England] built up stronger
in unity and peace, and a more temperate and discreet silence
amongst the wayward hotspurs of our spiritual mother." Portman
had been "truly Christian," "a saint," and "an uncorrupted patron,
no firebrand in his country nor meteor in his church," in part
because he had censured "vocal purity and tongue devotion and
furious zeal."[14]

"Firebrands" and "meteors" were for Anglicans damnable
boutefeux. Any who broke the peace were damnable boutefeux
regardless of any justification they might speciously claim. Loss of
peace and loss of unity were to Puritans regrettable but hardly
unexpected casualties of the struggle to complete the Reformation
begun so long before. They put "truth" and inner peace first, outward
peace second. Anglicans did not so much reverse these priorities as

---

quoted in the introduction to chap. 3, above. Prof. David Ogg summarized Charles
II's "Directions concerning preachers" (1662): "They were to emphasize
the moral duties of the individual, as churchman and citizen, and not to perplex
him with the intricacies of speculative theology." *England in the Reign of Charles
II*, p. 98. The "Directions" may be found in Edward Cardwell, ed. *Documentary
Annals of the Reformed Church of England*, 2:306–10.

14. Pierce, *Philallēlia*, sig. A 3 (verso); Sydenham, *The Royall-Passing-Bell*,
pp. 36–37.

deny that they were divisible into different priorities at all. Public tumults were for Anglicans a sign that a few ambitious and avaricious men were "starting" out of their places in the divinely ordained social and political order. Contention was for Puritans the inescapable result of the working out of God's purposes in history. Note that Puritans held this view without rejecting the traditional notion of a hierarchical society, but they applied their distinctive conception of the magistrate's calling to all of the higher powers.[15] The magistrates who used their authority to require things which the Word of God did not allow could not command full obedience.

The great force and dynamic of the puritan movement lay stored up in that short but crucial reservation. Behind it lay the entire matrix of things which Puritans fervently believed that the Word did not allow. There could be no compromise with "popery," no profanation of the Sabbath, and no idolatrous, soul-destroying ceremonialism. There could be no hindering of preaching against those things, nor any obstruction of the piety and moral order which went with them. At least one Puritan recognized that ordinary men might have difficulty understanding what the Puritans were concerned about. "Godliness makes men zealous in such things as others can see no reason why they should," wrote Jeremiah Burroughs. "They think . . . that the ground of their zeal is vanity and turbulency of spirit." The Puritans' overmastering preoccupation with the establishment of their piety and with using it as a touchstone to true morality obscured a fact that is now evident—that the moral order they sought was in many ways the same one that the Anglicans wanted. But Puritans were deeply convinced that the anglican methods for achieving a fully Christian society were tragically wrongheaded and that they led away from fulfillment of God's plan instead of toward it. Not long before his death, Cromwell touched upon the reason when he reflected upon the pre-Civil War years, a time when there had been men who sought "to innovate in matters of religion . . . and so to innovate as to eat out the core and power and heart and life of all religion by bringing on us a company of poisonous popish ceremonies." Puritans had had no choice but to oppose those efforts by seeking to reform English life according to

15. See MacCaffrey, *The Shaping of the Elizabethan Regime*, p. 15; Collinson, p. 27.

their reading of God's plan for human life. They struggled to hold on to the doctrinal core which was the "heart and life of all religion" and to provide for its lively and effective dissemination because only in so doing could they find evidences of their election to eternal life. Inner peace was the only defense against the troubles and temptations which Satan would direct against them. Outward peace was a great blessing when God granted it, but when it was taken away its return could not be an end in itself. They were ready to suffer and to struggle for their objectives because their inner peace rested upon doing God's business. The following excerpt from Thomas Hooker's dialogue between the heart and the will perfectly exemplifies this puritan conviction.

> Is not the sanctification of the Sabbath day better than the profanation of it? Say *Heart*, is not preciseness in a Christian course better than with the harlot to wipe the mouth and say all is well? And all truth, though the least that God reveals, is it not better than all the world? If it be, *Will*, do thou close with it and say within yourselves, here are reasons clear, let heaven and earth meet together, though all the dust on the earth and sands on the shore and spires of grass in the field were devils, I will have that which the Word reveals, though I die for it.[16]

Charity, like obedience, was for Anglicans and Puritans a virtue of transcendent importance. As chapter 5 showed, the possession of it was, with each specific act, a source of rapturous joy on earth, a preparation for the receiving of grace, and an assurance of election to eternal life. The prayers of the brethren who were helped by it were given special attention by God, and hatred or indifference toward the brethren was a clear sign of reprobation. But who were the "brethren," and what were the most important forms which love to them should take? The puritan conception of charity was centered upon the provision and maintenance of godly preachers and help to men who wanted to hear what those preachers had to say several times each week. The charity for which the times called out was spiritual in nature. Thomas Goodwin's exhortation in 1628 is typical: "Do as much as thou canst to others, and use all the abilities and opportunities God hath put into thy hand to the utmost advan-

16. Burroughs, *Irenicum*, p. 249; Abbott, 4:705; Hooker, *Lessons*, p. 11.

tage to do good to men's souls." This is not to say that Puritans opposed charity in the older, more conventional sense of material aid to the needy, but it is to assert that such charity had a lower priority among the marks of sanctification. Thus Christians would perform it as a matter of course; elaborate and frequent exhortations were unnecessary. The ranking of priorities in the use of monetary gifts is clearly indicated by Goodwin: "Do good, also with thy estate, to the bodies of men, especially the saints, and for the propagation of the gospel and the good of the church."[17]

Anglicans vigorously objected to the notion that charity should be directed "especially to the saints" precisely because they saw in such charity an encouragement to sedition and an uncharitable judgment upon fellow baptized Christians. Hammond said that we owe alms "to all whom Christ hath made our neighbors and brethren, and I know not that any are excluded from this title." He noted that Saint Paul had urged the Galatians to "do good unto all men, especially unto them who are of the household of faith," but considered this clause to be no restraint, "all Christians being such." Although Laud and his colleagues did campaign for benefactions for the repair and beautification of churches and cathedrals, the main emphasis in anglican sermons was on charity to the poor, hungry, and oppressed. Farindon expressed this conception perfectly when he said that "to visit the fatherless and widows in affliction" was far more difficult than "to say a hundred paternosters . . . or to hear a sermon every day." A much fairer religion was, he thought, to be found in the man who thought "the bellies of the poor the best granaries for his corn and the surest treasuries for his money," and who could so manage the good things which God had given him as to "return them back by the hands of his ambassadors, the poor, who beseech us in his name."[18]

If it is established that differing interpretations of and emphasis upon the duties of the Two Tables of the Decalogue provide a reasonably trustworthy guide to anglican and puritan conceptions of these two all-important and all-encompassing Christian virtues, obedience and charity, then we must ask how these conceptions

17. T. Goodwin, 7:572.
18. Hammond, pp. 247–50; Farindon, 1:430–31. The text for this sermon of Farindon's was James 1:27.

arose. My own approach throughout has been to seek the methods by which men we know to have criticized, reproached, opposed, and finally fought each other distinguished friend from foe. I have been cautious about placing individuals in this or that "tradition" or in this or that theological "school." The more promising way to assess the role which religion and religious language played in the integration of groups of individuals in our period seemed to be to listen for the strings upon which individuals harped and the chords which they repeatedly struck. What has emerged is not merely two sets of unrelated crotchets but two logical and harmonious visions of the true Christian's behavior. The logic and the consistency within each pattern arises from two underlying sources, one anthropological and theological, the other historical and circumstantial. J. F. H. New has pointed to the first when he wrote that Anglicans felt "though Adam's fall had emasculated his spiritual capacity, not every faculty to good had been crushed out of him. Man was sorely wounded with sin, but not so critically as the Puritans claim."[19] This distinction is related to J. S. Coolidge's comparison of anglican and puritan understandings of the doctrine of Christian liberty. For Anglicans, Christian liberty meant license from God in matters indifferent, but the Puritan saw this liberty "less as a permission than as a command. . . . Far from consigning authority in 'extern things' entirely to the magistrate, Christian liberty engages the subject to civil disobedience on occasion in order to 'use things indifferent to edification and not to destruction.' "[20]

19. New, *Anglican and Puritan*, pp. 6–7. Collinson's review of New's book raises questions about the role of historical circumstance in the development of anglican-puritan opposition. *EHR* 80 (1965):592–93. With New, I find among Anglicans a greater optimism about human moral capacity but I think that New forces this optimism to carry too much of the burden of explanation. He also seriously underestimates the importance of quarrels about predestination in the seventeenth century (as Coolidge has noted, p. 127n). There is a subtle and interesting distinction between the approaches of these two scholars. New bases his case for anglican-puritan opposition on differing views of the moral power of natural man and natural reason, one side being more optimistic than the other. These views are held to underlie the whole range of differences on specific issues. Coolidge argues that the Puritans experienced a fresh and theologically creative insight into the meaning of Pauline theology, insight which they developed into a powerful criticism of Elizabethan conformity. Coolidge explains why Anglicans and Puritans had such difficulty understanding each other, and I find his analysis highly persuasive.

20. Coolidge, pp. 26–27. The quotation within the quotation is from Robert

250 THE GODLY MAN IN STUART ENGLAND

Coolidge is writing here of Elizabethan Puritanism, but his argument holds for Stuart Puritanism as well. Puritans cleaved so tenaciously to the need to establish "godly preaching" and opposed so vehemently the Laudian "innovations" because the former edified and the latter did not. Preaching was the ordinary means by which God dispensed the special grace by which alone men could overcome the moral depravity of their reprobate condition. The regenerate saw through the ceremonies and could not be harmed by them but their use cruelly confused and misled those not yet converted. For Puritans, use of such things was a denial of charity to weaker Christians, a sin which Saint Paul had condemned in the Corinthians when he asked, "And through thy knowledge shall the weak brother perish, for whom Christ died?"[21]

Both Anglicans and Puritans deeply desired a moral reformation in England, an end to the public and private sins which provoked God's chastening and judging afflictions. But they were increasingly divided over the means for bringing such a reformation to pass. Indeed, what was regarded as an essential means by one side was, for one reason or another, anathema to the other. Laud saw in the Feoffees for Impropriations a subtle, dangerous plot to undermine the authority of crown and mitre by weakening their influence over what was said from the pulpits of the land. For Sibbes and his friends, the employment of private funds for the better propagation of the Gospel by preaching was a means to strengthen the kingdom by increasing the number of conversions and thereby the number of men capable of truly Christian behavior. No rightly advised godly prince would oppose it. Anglican homiletical emphasis tended to fall on the ease of conversion, a tactic which seemed to many Puritans a cruel, evil conceit. Puritan emphasis on the enormous difficulty of conversion appeared to Anglicans to frighten people away from religion instead of persuading them to embrace it. Another means to moral improvement for Anglicans, optimistic as they were in their assessment of human moral capacity, was

---

Crowley, *A briefe discourse against the outwarde apparell and Ministry garments of the popish church* (1566), sig. Bii (verso)–Biii.

21. 1 Cor. 8:11, as quoted in Coolidge, p. 40. Coolidge's chap. 2 (pp. 23–54) presents his argument about the vital role played by the notion of "edification" in puritan thought.

exhortation to the imitation of Christ, the "Great Exemplar." Thus
Hammond spoke of the Incarnation as "God the Son pitching his
tent in our nature," thereby "giving us in our flesh such sublime,
visible, elevated copies of charity toward all mankind" as to require us to copy them in our own conduct.[22] This approach seems
to have been for many Puritans a presumptuous affront to God's
glory. They spoke incessantly of the necessity of saints suffering as
Christ did and of having to face bravely and patiently the whips
and scorns brandished by sinful haters of godliness. Puritan saints
had to bear Christ's heavy yoke of persecution and pain, but the use
of Christ as a moral example is rare in puritan writings.

The contrast between anglican and puritan views of man and the
resulting implications for the best means to moral reformation may
be clearly seen in the writings of Clarendon and Winthrop. Writing
sometime in 1649 or early 1650, Clarendon mused on the distinction
between what he called a "mere moral man" and a true Christian.
In terms of outward appearance there was little distinction to make.
"A mere moral man may be very just in doing right to all men, and
very bountiful in relieving all who want, and very magnanimous in
pardoning all who do him injury; but he can never be charitable,
which is practising moral virtues upon Christian principles." Only
the true Christian can be truly charitable because "charity . . . is
but the translating moral virtues into Christian language." This is
to imply that "mere moral men" were, on their natural reason,
perfectly capable of moral behavior and choice. A good and just
society could be composed of such men. Therefore, Clarendon
concluded, "we need not be ashamed of being reproached for living
like good moral men if we do so upon Christian grounds, for love of
heaven and fear of hell we have Christianity enough." Clarendon
was not disturbed at being described as such a "mere, moral man"
because he felt, as his fellow exile John Bramhall later put it, that
"nothing is more hidden than true grace. We know it not in another,
hardly in ourselves." John Hales, Clarendon's friend from the
happy days at Great Tew before the Civil War, said that a man who
knows little or no theology and yet is "of upright life and conversation, such a one we usually name a moral man." Yet "true profes-

22. Hammond, *Catechism*, pp. 190–91.

sion, without honest conversation . . . saves not . . . but a good
life" by itself lessens punishment; therefore, "a moral man, so called,
is a Christian by the surer side." Better to be a "moral man" lacking
knowledge than a knowledgeable man lacking morality. These
Anglicans believed that the moral reformation which England so
desperately needed in the middle of the seventeenth century would
come when divine providence intervened in such a way as to demonstrate these truths to the private men whose sinful covetousness
and carnal pride had so possessed them that they had dared to shake
the political and social order which God had ordained. They had
acted under the iniquitous pretence of obedience to his Word, and
the extent to which their sense of values was perverted was deftly
suggested by Jeremy Taylor when he wrote that "to kneel at the
communion, is not so like idolatry, as rebellion is to witchcraft."
Meanwhile it was the duty of good men everywhere to use the
reason God had given them to order their own lives so as to deserve
the blessings which would come when He decided to give the
boutefeux the comeuppance which was undoubtedly awaiting
them.[23]

John Winthrop, unlike Clarendon, would have been deeply
insulted by any suggestion that he was living like a "mere, moral
man." He "found that a man may master and keep under many
corrupt lusts by the mere force of reason and moral considerations
(as the heathen did) but they will return again to their former
strength. There is no way to mortify them but by faith in Christ and
his death. . . . so a Christian being in him by faith is made really
partaker of his conquest." Without saving grace no man could
achieve anything more than a temporary victory over the lusts of
his corrupt flesh, and this is to say that no meaningful moral reformation was possible without the regeneration wrought not by
"common grace" but by saving grace. This distinction lies behind

23. *Contemplations*, p. 413; Hales, 2:69; Bramhall, p. 120; Taylor, 6:cccxxv. Cf.
Wormald, p. 268. Hales went on to note that "to visit the fatherless and the widow"
is "in an especial refined dialect of the new Christian language . . . nothing but
morality and civility, *that* in the language of the Holy Ghost imports true religion"
(2:71). His biographer thinks that this sermon was preached in the late 1630s. J.
H. Elson, *John Hales of Eton*, p. 26. Whichcote, in the same spirit, concluded, "far
better is nature alone, take it as it is, than that religion which is insincere and false.
. . . man, by his nature and constitution, is a gentle creature, fitted for converse
and delighting in it" (1:168).

Winthrop's many references to the "power" of religion. As a young man of eighteen living under the puritan ministry of Ezekiel Culverwell in Essex, he wrote that there "I first found the ministry of the Word to come to my heart with power (for in all before I found only light)."[24]

Light was knowledge of good and evil which any man might have, but the Puritans believed that the power to act on that knowledge came with something much more than common grace. It is here that historical circumstance came to play a powerful role in reinforcing these differing tendencies in anglican and puritan thought. Puritans looked upon the anglican saint as depicted by Clarendon and others as the "civil," "moral" man whose conduct fell short of that plenitude of holiness which saving grace made necessary. The ideal of Christian saintliness which Clarendon and his fellow Anglicans admired was a godliness conceived in terms of steady devotion to the duties enjoined by the Decalogue. The ceremonies of the Church of England provided all the necessary actions which the First Table obliged. All baptized members of the Church of England who participated in those ritual observances and did so with due preparation and sincerity were assumed to be converted to Christianity unless they demonstrated their continuance in a reprobate condition by schism, rebellion, murder, adultery, uncharitableness, covetousness or other breaches of the Second Table. Anglicans did not hold that all who approximated this ideal were necessarily predestined to salvation, but they were adamant that any man who deviated from it was almost certainly damned if he remained unrepentant. Clarendon was not bothered when Puritans reproached him with being a "mere moral man" because his notion of the true church was established, and adherence to a different vision of First Table duties was not a mark of the validity of his faith.

Puritans, by virtue of the historical circumstance that they were the critics and would-be reformers of the established system of

24. *WP*, 1:155 (cf. p. 193). Culverwell had been "suspended for nonconformity in 1583" and was deprived later (possibly in 1609). He was brother-in-law to Laurence Chaderton and uncle to William Gouge (pp. 88–89n). Roger Sharrock notes that in *Pilgrim's Progress* (pt. II), "Ignorance" is damned at the end not because he is morally corrupt but because "he persists in the greatest intellectual error imaginable to a Calvinist; he relies on his own righteousness." *John Bunyan*, p. 93.

performing First Table obligations, had to hate "idolatry" more in order to demonstrate that they transcended "mere morality." As we have seen, Puritans identified others as fellow saints primarily by noticing whether or not they opposed anything which smacked of "human inventions" in worship. Obviously, anyone who went about wantonly breaking Second Table commandments while proclaiming devotion to godly preaching and hatred of Laudian ceremonialism was a hypocrite. The point is that Puritans believed that none who had not experienced the "power" of religion by inward regeneration could really and consistently struggle against the lusts which held all men in thralldom. No Puritan contended that he and his fellow saints were or could in this life be perfect in their obedience to the moral law, but they did believe that only they could even approximate the pattern of behavior which God demanded of the elect (except for the rare hypocrites who succeeded in counterfeiting grace, at least to outward appearances). Each step taken by Archbishop Laud in his attempts to uphold what he thought of as the "external decent worship of God" in the Church of England was to the Puritans a step away from the only feasible program for bringing about a true moral and spiritual reformation. Each step with Laud was a step back into the darkness of the old religion, obscuring and clouding the doctrine of justification by faith alone by encouraging men to think that they could merit salvation by choosing good actions over evil ones. That all this was unfair to Laud is now clear, but it is equally clear that he made the fatal error of badly underestimating the honesty and depth of puritan fears.

There were other essentially circumstantial factors working against Laud. Puritanism was a "movement" but it was not monolithic; that it lacked a centralized organization was part of the secret of its strength because the authorities could never kill it by striking off its head. The Puritans had successfully withstood highly placed displeasure before by various means. They had blended into their environments in country and town by making ambivalent submissions and turning up in other dioceses to carry on while their places were filled by newer faces. They had preached without benefices as lecturers and chaplains. They had availed themselves expertly of the thousand-and-one hiding places in the thickets of common and canon law. In Laud, the king had found a man fully as tenacious as they. Efficient and industrious, he forced their hand and found it incomprehensibly strong.

Laud also had the misfortune to begin his change of course, slight as it appears in retrospect, in the midst of the most successful military phase of the Counter-Reformation. Protestant and nationalist in his outlook, he failed to perceive the ominous character of his program when it was considered from the international puritan point of view. Had he in fact been what they thought—a crypto-Catholic—he would not have made the mistakes he did. Puritans were extremely conscious of their membership in an international brotherhood of saints. They had long thought of the churches of Geneva, the Rhineland, and other centers of advanced Protestantism on the Continent as the models of the reformation they sought for England. Wherever they were, they were aware, as Cromwell's kinsman William Hooke put it, that "the same thread of grace is spun through the hearts of all the godly under heaven." The doleful course of the Thirty Years' War, in which the godly brethren abroad suffered one disaster after another, was interpreted by Puritans as a series of warnings that God was on the verge of resting a heavy hand of judgment upon England. Winthrop, in 1625, feared the coming of "some heavy scourge and judgment. . . . The Lord hath admonished, threatened, corrected and astonished us, yet we grow worse and worse. . . . He hath smitten all the other churches before our eyes and hath made them to drink of the bitter cup of tribulation." Yet there had been no progress toward the national and public reformation for which the Puritans had struggled for so long. Instead Laud would soon attempt to gain a stranglehold on the preaching and lecturing which they regarded, quite rightly, as their most important weapon in the struggle. Against this international background, the threat which Laud represented was heightened. It led Thomas Goodwin in 1628 to remind his listeners that "there are hours of darkness to the church of God. . . . Popery may have a reviving, as heathenism did after Constantine's reformation, in Julian's time, . . . and then it will prove a time of suffering rather than doing."[25]

25. Hooke, *New Englands Tears, For Old Englands Feares*, p. 17; *WP*, 2:91; T. Goodwin, 7:573. Hooke's sermon, preached in New England, was so popular that

It has become something of a truism that revolutions occur during times of "rising expectations." Such events often seem to be triggered at the moment of slip between cup and lip. From the beginning of their history, Puritans had lived in what may be called a state of almost apocalyptical expectation of the time when they would have the experience of tasting the delicious nectar of truly "godly rule."[26] So long as they could expend their vast energies and strong enthusiasms in constructing their distinctive piety and moral order by supporting godly preaching and all that went with it in town and countryside, the revolutionary potential of the movement remained latent. The king's foreign policy was a bitter disappointment but it could be tolerated. But when Laud began to suspend their preachers for refusing to commit "idolatry," he struck at the heart of Puritanism. It is true that Anglicans also desired godly rule and moral reformation, but they did so within a framework of essentially melioristic assumptions about the means of achieving their goals. Anglicans did not expect that the world would ever be greatly different from the world they knew. Their characteristic tone is fatalistic, stoical, worldly-wise, even occasionally blasé. There is in their writings a persistent notion that human history is cyclical, and that the cycle will continue to go around and around until the world ends. "No sublunary thing is stable," said Bramhall in 1661. "The whole world is a restless whirligig, . . . a tottering quagmire, whereupon it is impossible to lay a sure foundation." After eloquently expounding this theme, he

it went through three editions in 1641 in London. For examples of the way Puritans in the 1640s continued to hark back to the troubles of the Reformed Churches (with the additions of Ireland and Scotland), see Case, *Correction*, p. 230; Caryl, *Job* (chaps. 1–3), pp. 308–09. On the fear of "popery" in the period, see Brian Manning, "The Outbreak of the English Civil War," in R. H. Parry, ed., *The English Civil War and After, 1642–1658*, pp. 3–8; Robin Clifton, "Fear of Popery," in C. Russell, ed., *Origins of the English Civil War*, pp. 144–67; C. Hill, *Antichrist in Seventeenth-Century England*; Caroline Hibbard, "Charles I and the Popish Plot," Ph. D. dissertation (Yale, 1975).

26. W. Lamont, *Godly Rule*, provides many insights into the meanings and magic of this phrase. Not the least of its virtues is that it conveys a reminder that varieties of millenarianism existed across the entire political spectrum. On Brightman, Mede and other key figures in the development of what I consider moderate millenarianism, see Peter Toon, ed., *Puritans, the Millennium and the Future of Israel*, chaps. 2 and 3; Tuveson, *Millennium and Utopia*, chaps. 2 and 3; Capp, *The Fifth Monarchy Men*, chap. 2.

concluded that since God had ordained "such a necessary vicissitude of all things, let us not think vainly to translate this valley of tears into a paradise of perpetual bliss." Sanderson had asked in a similarly pessimistic vein in 1631, "Hath it not been always seen, and still is, and ever will be, (more or less) to the world's end, that extorting usurers, oppressing landlords, unconscionable traders, corrupt magistrates, and griping officers, have gotten together the greatest wealth and most abounded in riches?"[27] Neither of these anglican divines would have argued from this premise that good men should not struggle against the evil in the world, but their struggle could not be carried on with unrealistic expectations of what could be achieved even under the best of rulers.

By comparison, even the most moderate Puritans were visionaries with glowing hopes of the way God would be glorified by moral reformation when true godly rule was instituted. As good Calvinists, they certainly were not thinking of a miraculous transformation of all men, but rather of the beneficent results of properly godly leadership at all levels of society. As more and more of the men and women who were destined to be the happy recipients of the gift of regenerating, saving grace were in fact reached by the preaching through which the Holy Spirit ordinarily worked, there would be more and more who would become better in every sense. It was, said Preston, "a sign of a new creature that he doth judge aright of spiritual things." New creatures would also "judge aright" of outward things and avoid sin, "for if the general frame of the heart be good, there will be a general reformation of the life." These saints, though by no means perfect, would be renewed so that they could work successfully against sin in themselves and in others. They would have new natures and it would, said John Benbrigge, deeply grieve them "to see men be drunk, profane the Sabbath and holy fast days; to see men sleep in the midst of the public assembly; to behold the pride of men and women in their antic gestures and strange apparel." Evil men would lie in wait to attack these saints

27. Bramhall, pp. 126–27; Sanderson, 2:32 (cf. p. 423). See also Zagorin, pp. 13–14 and Joan Webber's description of the "temporal" character of Bunyan's writing versus the "timelessness" of John Donne's. *The Eloquent "I"*, pp. 23–24, 28. Although Bunyan was a sectarian, his thinking is in this respect similar to that of the moderate Puritans about whom I am writing.

whose very carriage was a reproof to them. Benbrigge thought that this was precisely what "the Cavaliers, malignants, papists, atheists and carnal Protestants now amongst us" were doing to "the Parliament and its friends" in the 1640s. "Is it not," he demanded "because there is an antipathy in their natures against godliness and the power of it which that honorable court would set up and settle in this land? The Parliament would have a reformation in church and state, . . . but this to them is as salt to live eels."28 This fervent hope that England could be a better place, that moral reformation was possible, that there was a way out of the tawdriness and turpitude of things was, paradoxically, characteristic of Puritanism. It is the fervency of the hope that helps us to comprehend the suddenness with which the shimmering dream of moral and social reformation faded into despair and disillusionment in the very midst of military and political triumph. The Puritans had long been united in their conviction that obedience to the First Table was the touchstone of the godly man's obedience to God. Strong in opposition, their union was to prove fragile in power.

28. Preston, *Life*, pt. 2, p. 19; *Breast-Plate*, pt. 3, p. 193; Benbrigge, *Gods Fury*, pp. 39, 40–41.

APPENDIX

FAST-DAY PREACHERS
AND FIRST TABLE DUTIES

The long series of fast sermons preached before members of the Long Parliament by leading puritan ministers throughout the 1640s reveal Puritanism in its most political form. In the section entitled "Puritans and the First Table" in chapter 3 above, one of Thomas Case's sermons was quoted at some length to demonstrate puritan hatred of idolatry and devotion to First Table duties. We will here consider three other fast sermons by well-known Puritans—Cornelius Burges, Stephen Marshall, Edmund Calamy—for further evidence of the same attitudes.

Cornelius Burges, preaching on November 17, 1640, told the parliamentarians to condemn and utterly root out "popish masses" and everything connected with them: "Purge out and cast away (as a menstruous cloth) all idols and idolatry in particular. All our lusts are loathsome to His stomach, but nothing is so abominable to his soul as idolatry." If they would not be neutrals but would be "thorough for God and follow him fully, down with all idols and idolatry through the kingdom." They could "talk of a covenant and think to do great matters; but that great God who is so jealous of his glory in that, above all other things, will abhor all covenants with you." There was at last the "opportunity and power" to "cleanse the land of these spiritual whoredoms." If the chance were not taken, the idolatries would "draw down a curse . . . and scatter like poison over all parts and corners of the kingdom." At the same time that idolatry was being uprooted, Burges insisted that they should:

Above all, take better order for the more frequent and better performance and due countenancing of that now vilified (but highly necessary) ordinance of preaching, which, albeit be

God's own arm and power unto salvation, is yet brought into so
deep contempt (and by none more than by those who should
labor most to hold up the honor of it) [i.e., the bishops] that it is
made a matter of scorn and become the odious character of a
Puritan to be an assiduous preacher.

Burges went on to denounce all the various limitations on preaching and the hearing of it which had been initiated and enforced by
Laud, Wren, Pierce, Montagu, Cosin, and company, and to attack
them as "blind guides and idol shepherds [who] care not to erect
preaching where there is none, so do they all they can to cheat and
defraud those of it who do or would enjoy it." They had destroyed
preaching entirely in some places, and in others they had struck
"out the teeth of it, that if men will needs preach, yet it shall be . . .
a frigid, toothless, sapless discourse, never piercing deeper than the
ear." "Wonder not at my length and heat in this point," he said, for
the setting up of "a preaching ministry is one of the best advantages to secure a state," and it should "be put in the head of the
catalogue of your weightiest consultations at this time."[1]

Burges had preached his sermon at the morning service. Stephen
Marshall stepped into the same pulpit in the afternoon. Marshall,
like Case and Burges, reminded his listeners of a time when there
had been among the ancient Hebrews a "horrible apostasy from the
purity of God's worship. Religion was very much corrupted and the
forces of the kingdom were exceedingly weakened." If England
were to escape the avenging sword of divine judgment which had
already overtaken her neighbors, she could do it only one way.
"Read over all the book of God, and you shall never find that a
people are said to come home to God, but when they put away all
their abominations, threw away all their lusts and idols." To be
"a holy people" was in large measure a matter of being "true
worshippers" of God, "maintaining the purity of his ordinances
from idolatry and superstition." Marshall again insisted on the
primacy of First Table duties when he pointed out that each king
of Judah's goodness had been determined mainly by

how he stood affected in point of religion. 'Such a man was upright with God'; the meaning is, all his days 'he maintained

1. Burges, *The First Sermon*, pp. 67–73, 75, 77.

God's worship.' And let me tell you some of their moralities were no better than they should be. Asa in the text was a choleric passionate man and covetous in his old age, and many other weaknesses were found in him, yet because he went thorough-stitch in the reformation of religion, Asa's heart was said to be 'upright with God all his days.' With this God useth to cover all their infirmities as with a veil.[2]

Marshall next turned his attention from Israel to England to ask, "Do we walk according to the rules of Christianity, the sum whereof for the practical part is laid down in the Ten Commandments?" The answer was negative, and it consisted once again largely of a recital of First Table offenses. Though the "generality of people" wore "the Lord's livery (being christened)," yet for the most part they "hated holiness" and cried down any who would not be drunk or swear "with the odious name of Puritan." Further, England had terribly abused "God in point of his worship, which is the defiling of the marriage bed betwixt God and his people." Marshall was horrified that "there hath not been in all the Christian world such high affronts offered to the Lord's day, as of late hath been in England." Many "poor congregations" had been deprived of preaching, "the bread of life," and there had been havoc wreaked "among many faithful and painful ministers, for such trifles as will not endure trial in the day of the Lord's appearing." In addition, not only had there been men who had rejoiced "to see the idolatry and superstition of Rome practised by others, but have dared to set 'their thresholds by God's threshold,' and to dress out all God's worship according to their own fancies." Some thought this unimportant and excused it by making fine distinctions. Not Marshall: "I may say truly of those men (that notwithstanding all their distinctions) little difference is to be found betwixt their practice and the superstitions and idolatries of the church of Rome." The solution for all this Marshall had, though he apologized for the apparent unfitness of prescribing to "such a college of physicians a way of cure." It was the same "catholic remedy . . . even the same which was pressed in the forenoon . . . the promoting, establishing and maintaining

2. Marshall, *A Sermon Preached*, pp. 2, 24, 26–27; succeeding references to pp. 30–34, 48.

a faithful, learned, painful, preaching ministry, [so] that every
candlestick may have a candle."

As a last example of the fast-sermon genre, we may consider a
sermon preached on December 22, 1641, by Edmund Calamy (not
long after the beginning of "the cruel Irish massacre"). He wished
"that our heads were fountains of tears for the idolatry (that land-
devouring sin of idolatry), for the superstition, the apostasy, the
contempt of the Gospel and of the ministers and ministry of it that
reigns amongst us!" He charged his listeners, as "the representative
body of this nation," with bringing about a "general reformation"
by example and by legislation. "Many pollutions have crept into
our doctrine, much defilement into our worship, many illegal
innovations have been obtended upon us." It was essential to "bury
all superstitious ceremonies in the grave of oblivion and perfect a
reformation according to the Word of God." "Pure and undefiled
religion is the ark to preserve kingdoms. But sin betrayeth religion
into the hands of superstition and idolatry." It was sin that had
delayed reformation, and therefore the best way to perfect "this
great work of reformation" was to send "a faithful and painful
ministry throughout the kingdom." The areas "which are rudest
and most ignorant, most irregular, and where the least preaching
hath been, are the greatest enemies of reformation."[3]

3. Calamy, *Englands Looking-Glasse*, pp. 16, 23–24, 28–29.

BIBLIOGRAPHICAL NOTE

In this note I intend to mention recent works which have been most useful in the preparation of this study and then to discuss briefly two controversial matters—Puritans and politics, and Puritans and the poor.

Any study of Puritans in the Stuart century must begin with the Tudor origins of Puritanism. The beginning student would do well to read chapters 12 and 13 of A. G. Dickens, *The English Reformation* (1964), before tackling M. M. Knappen, *Tudor Puritanism* (1939), H. C. Porter, *Reformation and Reaction in Tudor Cambridge* (1958), and Patrick Collinson, *The Elizabethan Puritan Movement* (1967). Knappen's book still provides a lucid introduction to the history and attitudes of the Puritans, and Porter's beautifully written work illuminates the significant theological issues. It is apparent from my frequent references to it that Collinson's book has been extraordinarily helpful. Though mainly concerned with the organization of the puritan movement, it is nevertheless very nearly a history not just of the movement but of Elizabethan society and church as well. It is full of information about the ideas, methods, and attitudes of the varieties of Puritans and their opponents, and will surely remain the definitive treatment of its subject. John S. Coolidge's work *The Pauline Renaissance in England* (1970), a tightly written book, is important in defining Anglicanism and Puritanism and must be read alongside the books by New and Charles and Katherine George (discussed in chapter 1 above). David Little, *Religion, Order, and Law* (1969), has a section entitled "Theology and the Conflict of Order," which is suggestive and in some respects parallel to Coolidge's argument. H. C. Porter, ed., *Puritanism in Tudor England* (1971), provides a handy collection of documents; a larger collection is presented in Leonard Trinterud, ed., *Elizabethan Puritanism* (1971). A valuable recent survey with an excellent bibliography is Patrick McGrath, *Papists and Puritans under Elizabeth I* (1967).

At the end of his book, McGrath rightly reminds us that although there "was continuity between Elizabethan Puritanism, Jacobean Puritanism and Caroline Puritanism, . . . there were, too, highly important differences, and one must beware of the temptation to see Elizabethan Puritanism as leading inevitably to a Puritan Revolution" (p. 396). Puritanism had what Collinson has called a "political potency" (p. 27), but it took specific historical circumstances to bring about the expression of that potency in the form of rebellion and civil war. I have been particularly concerned with those circumstances and the responses which they evoked from the Puritans. Perry Miller, *The New England Mind in the Seventeenth Century* (1939), and William Haller, *The Rise of Puritanism* (1938), continue to provide indispensable information and interpretations for students of Jacobean and Caroline Puritanism. Their other books are also helpful as are the first three chapters of Norman Pettit, *The Heart Prepared* (1966). We should, however, keep always in mind a caution issued by Perry Miller and Thomas Johnson:

> On everything except matters upon which the Puritans wanted further reformation, there was essential agreement [with Anglicans] . . . Puritanism was a movement toward certain ends within the culture and state of England in the late sixteenth and early seventeenth centuries; it centered about a number of concrete problems and advocated a particular program. Outside of that, it was part and parcel of the times, and its culture was simply the culture of England at that moment. It is necessary to belabor the point, because most accounts of Puritanism, emphasizing the controversial tenets, attribute everything the Puritans said or did to the fact that they were Puritans; their attitudes toward all sorts of things are pounced upon and exhibited as peculiarities of their sect, when as a matter of fact they were normal attitudes for the time.[1]

Charles and Katherine George's book is a timely reminder of this principle. I have stated above my reasons for maintaining that we cannot accept all of the conclusions which the Georges wish to

1. *The Puritans*, 1:6–7. Miller's views on some important points are controverted by Coolidge.

draw. Rather a lot of work remains to be done on Stuart Puritanism, a subject which, despite its massive bibliography, has not yet found its Collinson. Recently a linguist, a literary scholar, and an art historian have given us books which approach Puritanism from different angles: M. van Beek, *An Inquiry into Puritan Vocabulary* (1969), analyzes puritan word usage; Owen C. Watkins, *The Puritan Experience* (1972), analyzes their spiritual autobiographies; John Phillips, *The Reformation of Images* (1973), analyzes their iconoclasm. Kenneth Shipps advances our knowledge of puritan patronage in Norfolk, Suffolk, and Essex from 1600 to 1640 in his Ph.D dissertation (Yale, 1971), and R. C. Richardson, *Puritanism in North-west England* (1972), deals with the diocese of Chester to 1642. Paul Seaver, *The Puritan Lectureships* (1970), presents a thorough, careful study of that important "First Table" institution. His first two chapters, "The Importance of Preaching" and "Preaching and Politics," provide good introductions to their important topics. These subjects and many other relevant ones receive attention in Christopher Hill, *Society and Puritanism in Pre-Revolutionary England* (1964), a mine of fascinating information based on the author's very wide reading. This, and Hill's other books, are absolutely essential yet must be used with a little care (see below for some reasons). Michael Walzer, *The Revolution of the Saints* (1965), is another important book describing the relationship between politics and religion. His chapter, "The Attack upon the Traditional Political World" is especially interesting. Throughout, he opposes Hill's approach by treating Puritanism not as "the social religion of the 'industrious sort' (merchants and artisans)" but as the "political religion of the intellectuals (ministers) and gentlemen" (p. 328). Briefer, but subtle and suggestive, is William Lamont's *Godly Rule* (1969). Lamont is acutely aware of the importance of what appear in retrospect to be the little differences between the feuding parties, and he lucidly discusses their differences over means to the mutually acceptable ends. Some of the concerns may also be seen as reflecting differences of emphasis. Lamont's book was the forerunner of a number of books dealing with seventeenth-century eschatological thinking, a subject of great importance. For example, see Peter Toon, ed., *Puritans, the Millennium*

and the Future of Israel (1970); Christopher Hill, *Antichrist in Seventeenth–Century England* (1971) and *The World Turned Upside Down*
(1972); Bernard S. Capp, *The Fifth Monarchy Men* (1972).

Lamont at one point complains that we lack studies of the London "root and branch" ministers as individuals. We do need individual accounts of them, and we need as well more up-to-date
biographies not just of the London Puritans on the eve of the Civil
War but of individual Puritans, lay and clerical, over the entire
period. It is curious that Puritanism has been more thoroughly
studied than Puritans. The value of the biographical studies we
do have merely underlines the need for more—such as Edmund S.
Morgan, *The Puritan Dilemma* (1958), and *Roger Williams* (1967);
Geoffrey Nuttall, *Richard Baxter* (1965); William Lamont, *Marginal
Prynne* (1963); J. H. Hexter, *The Reign of King Pym* (1941); Raymond Phineas Stearns, *The Strenuous Puritan: Hugh Peter* (1954);
Irvonwy Morgan, *Prince Charles's Puritan Chaplain* (on John Preston)
(1957). Many Puritans who deserve study were fast-day preachers,
and John F. Wilson, *Pulpit in Parliament* (1969), analyzes the large
body of fast-day sermons. These sermons have been reprinted by
the Cornmarket Press, and it may be hoped that their wider avail-
ability will bring to them more attention. Wilson underscores
the importance of eschatological expectations in these sermons, a
subject further developed by Tai Liu, *Discord in Zion* (1973).

The only recent survey of the history of the Church of England
in our period is Florence Higham, *Catholic and Reformed* (1962). It
serves as an introduction but is too brief to be much more than
that. A great deal can be learned about the established church from
the books mentioned above by Collinson, Knappen, Porter, and
McGrath on the Elizabethan period. For the Stuart period, the
most important recent book is Christopher Hill's *Economic Problems
of the Church from Archbishop Whitgift to the Long Parliament* (1956).
Hill notes that there is a thirty year gap between the period covered
in Roland G. Usher, *The Reconstruction of the English Church* (2 vols.,
New York: D. Appleton and Co., 1910) and William A. Shaw,
*A History of the English Church During the Civil Wars and under the
Commonwealth, 1640–1660* (New York: Longmans, Green, 1900).
Fortunately, Dr. Collinson is at work on a history of the English
church which will bridge this gap and bring the older books up

to date. William Haller's *The Rise of Puritanism,* though it concen-
trates on the Puritans, is helpful in providing details about the
English church for the interim period. Also, his *Liberty and Reformation in the Puritan Revolution* (1955) may be used very profitably for
the period from 1638–49. N. R. N. Tyacke's essay, "Puritans,
Arminians and Counter-Revolution," in Conrad Russell, ed.,
The Origins of the English Civil War (1973), outlines the important
new interpretation that we can expect from his forthcoming book,
The Rise of Arminianism. Tyacke's argument is also briefly sketched
in Conrad Russell, *The Crisis of Parliaments* (1971), pp. 210–18.

The problem of the gap between the histories of Usher and Shaw
(and the age of those books) can be partly overcome by using some
of the available biographies of Anglicans. Anglicans, it seems, have
been more studied than Anglicanism. Among recent studies we
have: Robert R. Orr, *Reason and Authority* (on Chillingworth's
thought) (1967); Paul A. Welsby, *George Abbot, the Unwanted Archbishop* (1962) and *Lancelot Andrewes* (1958); R. Buick Knox, *James
Ussher, Archbishop of Armagh* (1967). R. W. Ketton-Cremer, *Norfolk
in the Civil War* (1970) has a good account of Matthew Wren, one
of the most hated Laudian bishops (pp. 62–88) as well as information on his successors, Montagu and Hall (pp. 124–33). Henry
Hammond is the central figure in John William Packer, *The Transformation of Anglicanism, 1643–1660* (1969). Hugh R. Trevor-Roper,
Archbishop Laud (1940), remains essential, though one should read
his preface to the paperback edition (1965) for his thoughts as to
how he would write it a bit differently now.

In the preparation of the present work, concentrating as it does
upon the middle decades of the seventeenth century, I have found
that the most helpful secondary works on Anglicanism included
two by Bishop H. R. McAdoo. *The Spirit of Anglicanism* (1965)
stresses that Anglicanism from Hooker through the Latitudinarians
is unified more by its method than by a system of dogma. His
second chapter contrasting Calvinism with this method was especially interesting (though, as Perry Miller has shown, Calvinism
was capable of rather more "latitude" than its critics were aware).
In another book, *The Structure of Caroline Moral Theology* (1949),
McAdoo discusses "practical," casuistical divinity in the Carolines.
Rosalie L. Colie, *Light and Enlightenment* (1957), provides a brief

but well executed study on the relationships between the Dutch
Arminians and the Cambridge Platonists. A sensitive exposition
of the position of one such Cambridge Platonist (Whichcote) is
presented in the introduction by Robert A. Greene and Hugh
MacCullum to their edition of Nathanael Culverwell, *An Elegant
and Learned Discourse of the Light of Nature* (1970), pp. xxxv–xlviii.
Charles F. Allison, *The Rise of Moralism* (1966) is narrowly theological—but he convincingly argues that anglican soteriology
made an unfortunate turn in the direction of moralism and deism
with the theology of Jeremy Taylor. According to Allison, Taylor
held that "a sinner must root out his sin, and the habit of it, and
obtain some measure of the opposite virtue before he can expect
pardon" (pp. 65–6). Allison's survey of anglican soteriology can be
compared and contrasted with puritan soteriology. Canon Charles
Stranks, in the first three chapters of his *Anglican Devotion* (1961),
has a good introduction to the tone and mood of early Stuart
Anglicanism. On the attitudes and activities of the Anglicans during
the Interregnum, Paul H. Hardacre, *The Royalists During the Puritan
Revolution* (1956) is helpful. Robert S. Bosher's *The Making of the
Restoration Settlement* (1951) is an excellent account of the "Laudians"
who kept the Church of England alive and carefully prepared for
its triumph in tandem with the monarchy.

   A persistent problem in the historiography of English religion in
the early modern period has been the relationship between Puritans
and politics. In his recent analysis of puritan spiritual autobiographies, Owen C. Watkins defines Puritanism as "that aspect of
sixteenth– and seventeenth–century religious life in Britain which
was centered on pastoral and personal issues rather than political or
ecclesiastical ones." This is true of most Puritans, but it does not
define Puritanism. The same could easily be said of most Anglicans.
It also ignores the fact that events in the reign of Charles I had an
alarming tendency to force both Puritans and Anglicans to see these
"pastoral and personal issues" in a "political and ecclesiastical"
context. F. Ernest Stoeffler argues that there were two types of
Puritans; there were those whose main concern was the "practice of
piety," and there were others who "were primarily interested in
ridding the Establishment of 'popish' remnants." Stoeffler's discussion of the English Puritans is valuable in that it underscores (as

have Collinson and others) the importance of the *praxis pietatis* which is the "universal emphasis of Pietists."[2] But his division of Puritans into two distinct types is unsatisfactory. As examples of the first or pietistic type, Stoeffler offers Preston, Sibbes, Bolton, Burroughs, and Thomas Goodwin. Preston was as "political" a Puritan as one could find in the 1620s (for example, see the biography by Irvonwy Morgan and the essay on Preston in Christopher Hill's *Puritanism and Revolution*). Sibbes was one of the clerical Feoffees for Impropriations, an organization which, as we have seen, drew Laud's fire in the early 1630s. Burroughs and Goodwin were prominent among the Independents who fought a rearguard action against the imposition of a presbyterian system of church government in the debates of the Westminster Assembly. These men were deeply concerned with the *praxis pietatis*, but they also had deep convictions about the need to establish a framework within which it could be effectively pursued.

Thomas Case affords a good demonstration of the unwieldiness of Stoeffler's types. In the preface and in chapter 3 above, we noticed that he was a hater of Laudianism and a supporter of the parliamentary cause. He had been cashiered in Norfolk by Bishop Wren, but he made his way to Chester and was popular there before the Civil War. Early in the 1640s, he came to London where he held various lectureships and the benefice of Saint Mary Magdalene, Milk Street (until 1648). He was a strongly presbyterian member of the Westminster Assembly and spent six months in the Tower for alleged complicity in Christopher Love's plot to overthrow Cromwell's government in favor of Presbyterianism. He was later satirized in Samuel Butler's *Hudibras*: "Whence had they all their gifted phrases/ But from our Calamies and Cases?" Here, it would seem, is a political rather than a pietistic Puritan. Yet while in prison he wrote his *Correction, Instruction* (1652), a thoroughly pietistic tract. As Stoeffler sees it, "the pietistic Puritans . . . had little enthusiasm for politics. Their sphere of interest was the life of their parishioners which they attempted to shape through preaching, writing of edificatory material, and pastoral work." However, the quotations from *Correction, Instruction* cited above have indicated its

2. Watkins, *The Puritan Experience,* p. 3; Stoeffler, *The Rise of Evangelical Pietism,* p. 9 and chap. 3.

pietistic rather than its political spirit, and the emphasis is under-
scored by its subtitle, "A Treatise of Afflictions: First conceived by
way of private Meditations: Afterward digested into certain Sermons preach'd at Aldermanbury. And now published for the Help
and Comfort of humble suffering Christians." It might be suggested
rather that almost all Puritans were pietists according to Stoeffler's
description—but that inside many of them was a political Puritan
ready to speak out given an occasion when his pietistic convictions
required it. They were playing upon a critical stage of English
history, and they would have to have been made of ivory to have
remained in intellectual or parochial ivory towers at such a time.
That few regarded themselves primarily as political revolutionaries
does not mean that most never thought of achieving their goals in
the political arena when the opportunity arose to do so—or when
persecution of "godliness" made it a duty. As Paul Seaver has
written, "not more than a handful of puritan preachers were self-
conscious revolutionaries: on the contrary, most preachers were the
more effective for clothing their political ideas in the familiar garb
of traditional religious rhetoric."[3]

From Puritans and politics we may turn to Puritans and the poor.
My comparison of anglican and puritan interpretations of the duty
of Christian charity indicates that Anglicans emphasized "material
charity" much more heavily than Puritans did. On the face of it,
this claim runs counter to one of the central themes of Professor
Jordan's important book, *Philanthropy in England, 1480–1660* (1959).
As he sees it, the post-Reformation era was a "period of incredible
generosity" for private charity, and that "most of those donors were
deeply pious men; in fact, a large proportion of the most effectively
munificent among them were Puritans." He notes that thirty-two
of the fifty-one sermons he examined on charity for the early Stuart
period were "by clergy of undoubted puritan persuasion and that
another six of these ministers would seem from the biographical
data or from internal evidence to have been Puritan as well." He
does not argue from this that the literature was expressing "a
factional point of view, but rather that the great strength of the

3. *DNB*, s.v. Thomas Case; Stoeffler, p. 9; Seaver, *Puritan Lectureships*, p. 69. E.
L. Tuveson warns against too great a distinction between "political" and "moral"
applications of eschatological doctrine. *Millennium and Utopia*, chap. 2, n. 102.

charitable impulse, at least in its social aspect, was to be found in the puritan party." We should, however, remember that there were many Anglicans who made impassioned pleas for charity. Bishop Sanderson's thoroughgoing and persistent preaching on themes of social justice has been noted. What must also be remembered is the heavy emphasis the Puritans placed upon "spiritual charity" in the form of endowing lectureships and other "educational" institutions. In this matter, Jordan's statistics (which show a major shift away from giving alms indiscriminately and for religious purposes toward giving for educational purposes) support my findings. The reader should, however, note that Jordan's statistical methods have been attacked with considerable persuasiveness by D. C. Coleman and Alan Everitt.[4]

Another problem which requires comment is his definition of Puritanism. Professor Jordan nowhere makes clear just how he went about deciding that six preachers were Puritans on the basis of the internal evidence in their sermons. G. E. Aylmer suspects that he classified as "Puritan" all "strongly protestant religious impulses,"[5] and I am inclined to agree when I find quotations from Humphrey Sydenham (p. 185) and Henry Hammond (p. 205) included among many references to undoubted Puritans (e.g., Thomas Gataker, Thomas Watson, Richard Harris, Arthur Hildersam, Laurence Chaderton, etc.). In the footnotes, Jordan identified Bruno Ryves and several others as Anglicans (pp. 190, 191, 203), but not Sydenham and Hammond. Although he recognizes the essentially Calvinist ethos of the English clergy (at least before Laud), and although he mixes anglican with puritan quotations to demonstrate the frequency with which the duty of charity was urged, he nevertheless continues to assert that "the great strength of the charitable impulse" was Puritan. His contention seems to rest on two bodies of evidence: (1) an analysis of funeral sermons (pp. 215–28), and (2) the disproportionately large charitable role undertaken by the

4. Jordan, *Philanthropy in England*, pp. 49, 20, 197. For Coleman's critique, see *Economic History Review*, 2d ser. 13 (1960–61): 113–15. For Everitt's, ibid., 15 (1962–63):376–77, cf. p. 547. For Sanderson on social justice and Puritans on "spiritual charity," see chap. 5 above.

5. Aylmer in *Economic History Review*, 2d ser. 15 (1962–63): 156–57. For a good analysis of the strengths and weaknesses of Jordan's book, see Charles Wilson, *England's Apprenticeship*, pp. 120–22, and his review in *EHR*, 75 (1960):685–87.

merchant elites of London, Bristol, and other commercial centers. For the first, he cites a number of funeral sermons in which the puritan merchant, gentleman, or peer is being lavishly praised for his works of charity. For example, Edmund Calamy is quoted as praising the deceased Earl of Warwick for having been "merciful and charitable to the poor members of Jesus Christ," and for protecting and supporting godly preachers (p. 221). But, as we have seen, when Puritans spoke of "the poor members of Jesus Christ" they often meant individuals who had been truly humbled for sin, regardless of their income. In any case, it would be easy to find just as many anglican funeral sermons which gave a high place to charity. For example, Farindon said of the anglican merchant, Sir George Whitmore, that his life had been such that on his way to heaven "there were no cries of orphans, no tears of the widow, no loud complaints of the oppressed, to disquiet him in his passage." Testimony in his favor was supplied by "the mouths of the poor, which he so often filled." He had in his will "bequeathed a legacy . . . to every prison and to many parishes within this city."[6]

The example of Whitmore raises a question about Jordan's second support for his view that the enormous increase in charitable bequests was essentially Puritan. Whitmore was no Puritan; he was a staunch Anglican and Royalist.[7] There is no doubt that many merchants were Puritan, but neither is there any doubt that many were not (as readers of Dr. Pearl's *London and the Outbreak of the Puritan Revolution* are fully aware). There may not be enough information about the religious inclinations of merchants who made sizable charitable bequests to allow a breakdown of Jordan's totals into anglican and puritan categories. But without such a breakdown it seems unfair to give so much credit to the Puritans when many Anglicans are also represented in these totals.

The same tendency to attribute primarily to the Puritans what seems on closer examination to be just as much a feature of Anglicanism is seen in Christopher Hill's *Society and Puritanism in Pre-Revolutionary England* (pp. 287–92). In his chapter "The Poor and the Parish," he illustrates "the new attitude towards charity," but

6. Farindon, 1:212–13. For other examples of anglican funeral sermons in which charity is praised, see Byam, pp. 238–39; Taylor, 6:563–65, 1:23.
7. Pearl, pp. 305–06.

quotes Anglicans as often as Puritans. Hill suggests at the end of his book that this charity was one of the attitudes that Puritanism contributed to English society—i.e., that it was a legacy which remained after the death of the political potency of the movement. But it seems at least arguable, even on the basis of the evidence he cites, that this new attitude toward charity was part of the changing English Protestant ethos all along, not a return to the main line from a puritan shunt. Running throughout this often fascinating book is a basic problem; although Hill professes to be interested in what he calls "the main stream of puritan thought, . . . associated with men like Perkins, Bownde, Preston, Sibbes, Thomas Taylor, William Gouge, Thomas Goodwin, Richard Baxter," his argument rests almost as heavily upon quotations from such Anglicans as Sanderson, Barrow, Donne, Hales, Fuller, and Joseph Hall as it does on the puritan sources (p. 29). The reader is not always warned when an Anglican is being used to make a point about the Puritans.[8] Students must be alert to the sort of argument which begins with the assertion that the reasons for "the new attitude" toward poor relief lay "deep in Protestant theology" (p. 271), and ends with the conclusion that this was part of "the social content of Puritan doctrine" which after 1660 "was ultimately accepted outside the ranks of the Nonconformists and even by the apparently triumphant Church of England" (pp. 506–507).

It might be suggested, at least tentatively, that the many trusts set up to provide schools, colleges, scholarships, almshouses, lectureships, stocks of raw materials for the poor to work, etc. were the result of the application of the Calvinist notion of stewardship to changing social and economic conditions. This "new charity" was therefore the product of ideas which were not the exclusive or even primary property of Anglicans or Puritans, but grew out of the heritage which they shared. Puritans urged proper stewardship of wealth and expected that the charitable institutions which emerged would aid in the shaping of a "godly commonwealth" in their sense. Anglicans gave in much the same way and expected instead the

8. For criticism of Hill's method in his essay on "William Perkins and the Poor" in *Puritanism and Revolution,* see Laura O'Connell, "Social Perceptions in Elizabethan Best-Sellers and Popular Drama, 1558–1603." Ph.D. dissertation, Yale, 1974. p. 124n.

preservation of the social and religious order they knew. Both regarded charity as one of the touchstones of true faith. Puritans, however, valued gifts which were in accord with their conception of First Table duties, whereas Anglicans rejected such "partiality" and "singularity" in favor of a more catholic generosity.

BIBLIOGRAPHY

REFERENCE AND BIBLIOGRAPHICAL AIDS

Abbott, Wilbur Cortez. *Bibliography of Oliver Cromwell: A List of Printed Materials.* Cambridge, Mass.: Harvard University Press, 1929.

Arber, Edward, ed. *A Transcript of Registers of the Company of Stationers, 1554–1640.* 5 vols. London, private printing, 1875–94, reprinted 1950.

Brunton, Douglas, and Pennington, Donald H. *Members of the Long Parliament.* London: Allen and Unwin, 1954.

Bush, Douglas. *English Literature in the Earlier Seventeenth Century, 1600–1660.* 2d ed. rev. New York: Oxford University Press, 1962.

Corbett, Margery, and Norton, Michael. *Engraving in England in the Sixteenth and Seventeenth Centuries.* Cambridge: At the University Press, 1964.

Cross, Frank L., and Livingstone, E. A., eds. *The Oxford Dictionary of the Christian Church.* 2d ed. rev. New York: Oxford University Press, 1974.

Davies, Godfrey, ed. *Bibliography of British History, Stuart Period, 1603–1714.* 2d ed. rev. by Mary Frear Keeler. Oxford: At the Clarendon Press, 1970.

Fortescue, G. K., ed. *Catalogue of the Pamphlets, Books, Newspapers and Manuscripts Relating to the Civil War, the Commonwealth, and Restoration Collected by George Thomason, 1640–1661.* 2 vols. London, 1908.

Foster, Joseph, ed. *Alumni Oxonienses.* 4 vols. Oxford, 1891–92.

Keeler, Mary Frear. *The Long Parliament: A Biographical Study of Its Members, 1640–41.* Philadelphia: American Philosophical Society, 1954.

Matthews, A. G. *Calamy Revised.* Oxford: At the Clarendon Press, 1934.

—. *Walker Revised.* Oxford: At the Clarendon Press, 1948.

Plomer, Henry R., ed. *A Dictionary of the Booksellers Who Were at Work in England, Scotland and Ireland from 1641 to 1667.* London: Bibliographical Society, 1907.

Pollard, A. W., and Redgrave, G. R., comps. *A Short-Title Catalogue of Books Printed in England, Scotland, and Ireland and of English Books Printed Abroad, 1475–1640.* London: Bibliographical Society, 1946.

Stephen, Sir Leslie, and Lee, Sir Stephen, eds. *The Dictionary of National Biography.* 22 vols. 1885–1901. Reprint. London: Oxford University Press, 1967–68.

Venn, J., and Venn, J. A., comps. *Alumni Cantabrigiensis.* Part 1 (to 1751). 4 vols. Cambridge: At the University Press, 1922–27.

276 BIBLIOGRAPHY

Wing, Donald, comp. *Short-Title Catalogue of Books Printed in England, Scotland, Ireland, Wales and British America and of English Books Printed in Other Countries, 1641–1700.* Vol. 1. 2d ed. rev. New York: Modern Language Association, 1972.

——. *Short-Title Catalogue of Books Printed in England, Scotland, Ireland, Wales and British America and of English Books Printed in Other Countries.* Vols. 2 and 3. New York: Columbia University Press, 1948–51.

Wood, Anthony à. *Athenae Oxonienses: An Exact History of All the Writers and Bishops Who Have Their Education in the Most Famous and Ancient University of Oxford, from 1500 to 1690. To Which Are Added the Fasti or Annals of the Said University, For the Same Time.* Edited by Philip Bliss. 4 vols. London: C. and J. Rivington, 1813–20.

PRIMARY SOURCES

An Account given to the Parliament by the Ministers sent by them to Oxford. London, 1647.

Ash, Simeon. *The Best Refuge for the Most Oppressed.* London, 1642.

Ashton, Robert, ed. *James I By His Contemporaries.* London: Hutchinson, 1969.

Baker, Sir Richard. *An Apologie For Lay-Mens Writing in Divinity.* London, 1641.

——. *Meditations and Motives for Prayer Upon the Seven Dayes of the Weeke.* London, 1642.

——. *A Chronicle of the Kings of England.* London. 1679.

——. *Meditations and Disquisitions upon the First Psalm; the Penitential Psalms; and Seven Consolatory Psalms.* Edited by A. B. Grosart. London: Charles Higham, 1882.

Benbrigge, John. *Christ Above All Exalted.* London, 1645.

——. *Gods Fury, Englands Fire.* London, 1646.

——. *Usura Accommodata.* London, 1646.

Bolton, Robert, *Instructions for a right comforting Afflicted Consciences.* 2d ed. London, 1635.

——. *Works.* 4 vols. London, 1641.

——. *A Cordiall for a fainting Christian.* London, 1644.

Bramhall, John. *Works.* 5 vols. Library of Anglo-Catholic Theology. Oxford, 1842–45.

Brooks, Thomas. *Works.* 4 vols. Nichol's Series of Standard Divines, Puritan Period. Edinburgh, 1866.

Burges, Cornelius. *The First Sermon.* London, 1641.

——. *Another Sermon.* London, 1641.

——. *Two Sermons Preached to the Honourable House of Commons.* London, 1645.

Bunyan, John. *Christian Behaviour.* London, 1663.

Burroughs, Jeremiah. *Sions Joy.* London, 1641.

———. *Irenicum To The Lovers of Truth and Peace.* London, 1646.

Burton, Henry. *The Seven Vials.* London, 1628.

———. *A Most Godly Sermon Preached at St. Albons in Woodstreet.* London, 1641.

Byam, Henry. *Thirteen Sermons.* London, 1675.

Calamy, Edmund. *Englands Looking-Glasse.* London, 1642.

———. *Englands Antidote, Against the Plague of Civil Warre.* London, 1645.

———. *An Indictment Against England.* London, 1645.

Calder, Isabel M., ed. *Activities of the Puritan Faction of the Church of England.* 1625–33. London: S.P.C.K., 1957.

Calvin, John. *Institutes of the Christian Religion.* Edited by John T. McNeill and translated by Ford Lewis Battles. 2 vols. Library of Christian Classics XX. Philadelphia: Westminster Press, 1960.

Cardwell, Edward, ed. *Documentary Annals of the Reformed Church of England.* 2 vols. 1844. Reprint. Ridgewood, N. J.: Gregg Press, 1966.

Cary, Henry, ed. *Memorials of the Great Civil War in England from 1646 to 1652.* 2 vols. London: Henry Colburn, 1842.

Caryl, Joseph. *Davids Prayer for Solomon.* London, 1643.

———. *The Nature, Solemnity, Grounds, Property, and Benefits of a Sacred Covenant.* London, 1643.

———. *An Exposition With Practicall Observations Upon the Three First Chapters of the Book of Job.* London, 1647.

———. *An Exposition with Practicall Observations Continued upon the Fifteenth, Sixteenth and Seventeenth Chapters of the Book of Job.* London, 1653.

———. *An Exposition with Practicall Observations Continued upon the Eighteenth, Nineteenth, Twentieth, and Twenty-one Chapters of the Book of Job.* London, 1653.

———. *An Exposition with Practicall Observations Continued upon the Twenty-second, Twenty-third, Twenty-fourth, Twenth-fifth, and Twenty-sixth Chapters of the Book of Job.* London, 1655.

———. *An Exposition with Practicall Observations Continued upon the Twenty-seventh, the Twenty-eighth, and Twenty-ninth Chapters of the Book of Job.* London, 1657.

———. *An Exposition with Practicall Observations Continued upon the Thirty-second, the Thirty-third and the Thirty-fourth Chapters of the Book of Job.* London 1661.

———. *An Exposition with Practicall Observations Continued upon the Thirty-eighth, Thirty-ninth, Fortieth, Forty-first, and Forty-second Chapters of the Book of Job.* London, 1666.

———. *An Exposition with Practicall Observations Continued upon the Eighth, Ninth and Tenth Chapters of the Book of Job.* Preface dated January 12, 1646. London, 1669.

———. *An Exposition with Practicall Observations Continued upon the Fourth, Fifth,*

Sixth and Seventh Chapters of the Book of Job. Preface dated April 28, 1645. London, 1671.

Casaubon, Meric. *The Originall Cause of Temporall Evils.* London, 1645.

Case, Thomas. *Two Sermons Lately Preached at Westminster.* 2d ed. London, 1642.

—. *The Root of Apostacy and Fountain of true Fortitude.* London, 1644.

—. *Spirituall Whordome Discovered.* London, 1647.

—. *Correction, Instruction: or, a Treatise of Afflictions.* London, 1652.

Cawdrey, Daniel. *The Inconsistencie of the Independent Way.* London, 1642.

Chandos, John, ed. *In God's Name: Examples of Preaching in England from the Act of Supremacy to the Act of Uniformity, 1534–1662.* Indianapolis, Ind.: Bobbs-Merrill Co., 1971.

[Charles I]. *Eikon Basilike.* Edited by Philip A. Knachel. Ithaca, N. Y.: Cornell University Press, 1966.

Chillingworth, William. *Works.* 3 vols. 1838. Reprint. New York: AMS Press, 1972.

Clarke, Samuel. *The Saints Nose-gay.* London, 1642.

—. *A Mirrour or Looking-Glasse.* Vol. 2. London, 1671.

Clifford, Anne. *The Diary of the Lady Anne Clifford.* Intro. by V. Sackville-West. London: William Heinemann, 1923.

Coachman, Robert. *The Cry of a Stone.* London, 1642.

Cosin, John. *A Collection of Private Devotions.* Edited by P. G. Stanwood. Oxford: At the Clarendon Press, 1967.

Cragg, Gerald R., ed. *The Cambridge Platonists.* Library of Protestant Thought. New York: Oxford University Press, 1968.

Cromwell, Oliver. *The Writings and Speeches of Oliver Cromwell.* Edited by Wilbur Cortez Abbott. 4 vols. Cambridge, Mass.: Harvard University Press, 1937.

—. *The Letters and Speeches of Oliver Cromwell with Elucidations by Thomas Carlyle.* Edited by S. C. Lomas. London: Methuen, 1904.

—. *Oliver Cromwell's Letters and Speeches.* Edited by Thomas Carlyle. 2 vols. Carlyle's Complete Works, IX and X. New York: John W. Lovell Company, n. d.

Cudworth, Ralph. *A Sermon Preached Before the House of Commons, March 31, 1647.* Series 3 (Philosophy), vol. 2. New York: The Facsimile Text Society, 1930.

D[oolittle], T[homas]. *Rebukes for Sin By God's Burning Anger.* London, 1667.

Doolittle, Thomas. *A Spiritual Antidote Against Sinful Contagion.* 2d ed., corr. London, 1667.

Evelyn, John. *Diary and Correspondence.* Edited by William Bray. London: George Routledge and Sons, n.d.

Falkland, Viscount (Sir Lucius Cary). *His Discourse of Infallibility.* London, 1651.

Farindon, Anthony. *The Sermons of the Reverend Anthony Farindon.* 4 vols. Prefixed by a life of Farindon by Thomas Jackson. London: William Tegg and Co., 1849.

Fenner, William. *A Treatise of the Affections: or, the Soules Pulse.* London, 1642.

——. *The Souls Looking-Glasse.* Cambridge, 1643.

Ferne, Henry. *A Sermon Preached Before His Majesty at Newport in the Isle of Wight.* London, 1649.

——. *Certain Considerations of present Concernment.* London, 1653.

Gardiner, Samuel Rawson. *The Constitutional Documents of the Puritan Revolution, 1652–1660.* 3rd ed. rev. Oxford: At the Clarendon Press, 1962.

Gardiner, Stephen. *The Letters of Stephen Gardiner.* Edited by James Arthur Muller. Cambridge: At the University Press, 1933.

Gatford, Lionel. *Englands Complaint.* London, 1648.

Gauden, John. *The Love of Truth and Peace.* London, 1641.

——. *Three Sermons Preached upon Severall Publicke Occasions.* London, 1642.

Gell, Robert. *Stella Nova.* London, 1649.

——. *Noah's Flood Returning.* London, 1655.

Goodwin, Thomas. *The Tryall of A Christians Growth.* London, 1641.

—— *The Works of Thomas Goodwin.* 11 vols. Nichol's Series of Standard Divines, Puritan Period. Edinburgh, 1861–65.

Gouge, William. *Gods Three Arrowes: Plague, Famine, Sword.* London, 1631.

——. *The Saints Support.* London, 1642.

——. *Mercies Memoriall.* London, 1645.

——. *The Progresse of Divine Providence.* London, 1645.

——. *The Saints Sacrifice.* Edinburgh, 1868.

Grant, John. *Gods Deliverance of Man by Prayer.* London, 1642.

Great Brittaines Distractions. London, 1642.

Hales, John. *The Works of the Ever Memorable Mr. John Hales of Eaton.* 3 vols. 1765. Reprint (3 vols. in 2). New York: AMS Press, 1971.

Hall, George. *Gods Appearing For the Tribe of Levi.* London, 1655.

——. *A Fast-Sermon Preached to the House of Lords.* London, 1666.

Hall, Joseph. *Contemplations on the Historical Passages of the Old and New Testaments.* 2 vols. London, 1825.

——. *The Works.* Edited by Philip Wynter. 10 vols. Oxford, 1863.

Hammond, Henry. *A Practical Catechism.* 14th ed. London, 1700.

——. *A Paraphrase and Annotations Upon all the Books of the New Testament.* 7th ed., corr. London, 1702.

——. *The Miscellaneous Theological Works.* Vol. 3. 3rd ed. Library of Anglo-Catholic Theology. Oxford, 1850.

Harrison, James. Notes on his sermons taken by members of Sir Thomas Barrington's family, Hatfield Broad Oak, Essex. Essex Record Office Barrington MSS/D/DBa/F5/2.

Harwood, Richard. *King Davids Sanctuary.* Oxford, 1644.

—. *The Loyall Subject's Retiring-Roome*. Oxford, 1645.

Hill, Thomas. *The Trade of Truth Advanced*. London, 1642.

Hodges, Thomas. *A Glimpse of Gods Glory*. London, 1642.

Hooke, William. *New Englands Teares, For Old Englands Feares*. London, 1641.

Hooker, Thomas. *The Christians Two Chiefe Lessons*. London, 1640.

—. *Heautonaparnumenos: or, a Treatise of Self-Denyall*. London, 1646.

—. *Redemption: Three Sermons (1637–1656)*. Edited by Everett H. Emerson. Gainesville, Fla.: Scholars' Facsimiles and Reprints, 1956.

Hubbard, Benjamin. *Sermo Secularis*. London, 1648.

Hyde, Edward. *The Mystery of Christ in Us*. London, 1651.

—. *A Christian Legacy*. Oxford, 1657.

Hyde, Sir Edward (Earl of Clarendon). "Contemplations and Reflections Upon the Psalms of David." In *A Collection of Several Tracts of the Right Honourable Earl of Clarendon*. London, 1727.

Kem, Samuel. *An Olive Branch Found after a Storme*. London, 1647.

Knappen, M.M., ed. *Two Elizabethan Puritan Diaries*. 1933. Reprint. Gloucester, Mass.: Peter Smith, 1966.

Knyvett, Sir Thomas. *The Knyvett Letters (1620–1644)*. Transcribed and edited by Bertram Schofield. London: Constable and Co., 1949.

Laud, William. *Sermons Preached by William Laud*. Edited by J. W. Hatherell. London, 1829.

Leighton, Robert. *The Works*. London, 1860.

Lockyer, Nicholas. *Baulme for Bleeding England and Ireland*. London, 1644.

Love, Christopher. *Mr. Love His Funeral Sermon*. London, 1651.

—. *Two Speeches*. London, 1651.

—. *The Whole Tryall of Mr. Christopher Love*. London, 1660.

Marshall, Stephen. *A Sermon Preached*. London, 1641.

—. *A Peace Offering to God*. London, 1641.

[Mayne, Jasper]. *A Sermon Concerning Unity and Agreement*. Oxford, 1646.

Mocket, Thomas. *The Churches Troubles and Deliverance*. London, 1642.

Montagu, Richard. *Appello Caesarem*. London, 1625.

More, Henry. *Enthusiasmus Triumphatus*. London, 1662. Los Angeles, Calif.: The Augustan Reprint Society, 1966.

More, Paul Elmer, and Cross, Frank Leslie, eds. *Anglicanism*. London: S.P.C.K., 1962.

Morley, George. *A Modest Advertisement*. London, 1641.

—. *Several Treatises*. London, 1683.

Newcomen, Matthew. *The Craft and Cruelty of the Churches Adversaries*. London, 1643.

Nuttall, Geoffrey F., ed. *Letters of John Pinney, 1679–1699*. Oxford: Oxford University Press, 1939.

Owen, John. *The Works.* Vol. 8. Edited by William H. Goold. 1850. Reprint. London: The Banner of Truth Trust, 1967.

Panzani, Gregorio. *The Memoirs of Gregorio Panzani.* Collected by Joseph Berington. 1793. Reprint. Farnborough, Hampshire, England: Gregg Press, 1970.

Perkins, William. *Works.* 3 vols. Cambridge, 1613.

Petition . . . praying for the establishment of Presbyterian Church government and discipline. Broadside. B. M. Press-mark 669.f.10(37). London, 1645.

Pierce, Thomas. *Philallēlia, or The Grand Characteristick Whereby a Man May Be Known To Be Christ's Disciple.* London, 1658.

—. *A Collection of Sermons Upon Several Occasions.* Oxford, 1671.

[Pierse, William]. *A Sermon Preached at the Tower, February 20, 1641.* London, 1641.

A Pious and Seasonable Perswasive To the Sonnes of Zion. Broadside. B. M. Press-mark 669.f.10(118). London, 1647.

Prall, Stuart E., ed. *The Puritan Revolution: A Documentary History.* Garden City, N. Y.: Doubleday and Co., 1968.

Preston, John. *Breast-Plate of Faith and Love.* London, 1631.

—. *Sermons Preached Before his Majestie.* London, 1631.

—. *Life Eternall.* 3rd ed., corr. London, 1632.

—. *Cuppe of Blessing.* London, 1633.

Prothero, G. W., ed. *Select Statutes and Other Constitutional Documents Illustrative of the Reigns of Elizabeth and James I.* 4th ed. Oxford: At the Clarendon Press, 1965.

Reynolds, Edward. *Israels Petition in Time of Trouble.* London, 1642.

Rous, John. *The Diary of John Rous.* Edited by Mary Anne Everett Green. Camden Society Publications, no. 66. London: The Camden Society, 1856.

Sanderson, Robert. *Sermons.* 2 vols. London: Thomas Arnold, 1841.

Saye and Sele, Viscount (William Fiennes). *A Speech of the Right Honorable the Lord Viscount Say and Sele.* London, 1642.

Sheldon, Gilbert. *Davids Deliverance and Thanksgiving.* London, 1660.

Sibbes, Richard. *The Saints Cordialls.* London, 1637.

—. *A Consolatory Letter To An afflicted Conscience.* London, 1641.

—. *The Complete Works.* 7 vols. Nichol's Series of Standard Divines, Puritan Period. London, 1862–64.

Skippon, Philip. *A Salve For Every Sore.* London, 1643.

Sparke, Edward. *Scintilla Altaris.* London, 1652.

[Sparke, Michael]. *Crumms of Comfort.* London, 1632.

—. *Crumms of Comfort: The Second Part to the Grones of the Spirit in Prayers.* London, 1652.

—. *A Second Beacon Fired by Scintilla*. London, 1652.

Sparrow, Anthony. *A Rationale upon the Book of Common-Prayer of the Church of England*. London, 1668.

The Speeches and Prayers of Some of the late King's Judges. London, 1660.

S.P. of Cambridge. *A Brief Account of the New Sect of Latitudinarians*. Preface signed June 12, 1662. London, 1669.

Stampe, William. *A Sermon Preached before His Majestie at Christ-Church in Oxford*. Oxford, 1643.

—. *A Treatise of Spiritual Infatuation*. The Hague, 1650.

Sydenham, Humphrey. *The Rich Mans Warning-Peece*. London, 1630.

—. *The Royall Passing-Bell*. London, 1630.

—. *The Waters of Marah and Meribah*. London, 1630.

—. *Five Sermons*. London, 1637.

—. *Sermons upon Solemne Occasions*. London, 1637.

Taylor, Jeremy. *The Whole Works*. Edited by Reginald Heber. 15 vols. London, 1822.

Trinterud, Leonard J., ed. *Elizabethan Puritanism. A Library of Protestant Thought*. New York: Oxford University Press, 1971.

Tuckney, Anthony. *Forty Sermons Upon Several Occasions*. London, 1676.

Ussher, James. *The Principles of Christian Religion*. 7th ed., corr. London, 1678.

W[ard], R[ichard]. *The Anatomy of Warre*. London, n.d.

—. *Jehoshaphats Going Forth to Battell with the Wicked*. London, n.d.

Watson, Thomas. *A Body of Divinity*. 1692. Reprint. Rev. ed. London: The Banner of Truth Trust, 1965.

Wenlock, John. *The Humble Declaration of John Wenlock*. London, 1662.

Whichcote, Benjamin. *Works*. 4 vols. Aberdeen, 1751.

White, John. *A Speech of Mr. John White*. London, 1641.

—. *Mr. Whites Speech in Parliament on Monday, the 17th of January*. London, 1642.

—. *The First Century of Scandalous, Malignant Priests, Made and Admitted into Benefices by the Prelates*. London, 1643.

Winthrop, John. *Winthrop Papers*. 1929. Reissue of vols. 1 and 2. New York: Russell and Russell, 1968.

Woodhouse, A. S. P., ed. *Puritanism and Liberty*. London: J. M. Dent and Sons, 1966.

Wotton, Sir Henry. *Reliquiae Wottonianae*. 3rd ed., with additions. London, 1672.

—. *The Life and Letters of Sir Henry Wotton*. Edited by Logan Pearsall Smith. 2 vols. Oxford: At the Clarendon Press, 1907.

SECONDARY SOURCES

Allen, J. W. *English Political Thought, 1603–60*. Vol. 1. London: Methuen, 1938.

Allison, Charles F. *The Rise of Moralism: The Proclamation of the Gospel from Hooker to Baxter*. London: S.P.C.K., 1966.

Bangs, Carl. *Arminius: A Study in the Dutch Reformation*. Nashville, Tenn. and New York: Abingdon Press, 1971.

Barnes, Thomas G. *Somerset, 1625–1640: A County's Government During the "Personal Rule"*. Cambridge, Mass.: Harvard University Press, 1961.

Bosher, Robert S. *The Making of the Restoration Settlement: The Influence of the Laudians, 1649–1662*. Reprint, with slight revision. London: Adam and Charles Black, 1957.

Brauer, Jerald C. "Reflections on the Nature of English Puritanism." *Church History* 23 (1954): 99–108.

Breen, Timothy H. "The Non-Existent Controversy: Puritan and Anglican Attitudes on Work and Wealth, 1600–1640." *Church History* 25 (1966): 273–87.

Breslow, Marvin Arthur. *A Mirror of England: English Puritan Views of Foreign Nations, 1618–1640*. Harvard Historical Studies, 84. Cambridge, Mass.: Harvard University Press, 1970.

Bridenbaugh, Carl. *Vexed and Troubled Englishmen, 1590–1642*. New York: Oxford University Press, 1968.

Capp, Bernard S. *The Fifth Monarchy Men: A Study in Seventeenth-Century English Millenarianism*. Totowa, N.J.: Rowman and Littlefield, 1972.

Caspari, Fritz. *Humanism and the Social Order in Tudor England*. Chicago: University of Chicago Press, 1954.

Cassan, S. H. *Lives of the Bishops of Bath and Wells*. London: C. and J. Rivington, 1829.

Clark, Sir George. *The Later Stuarts, 1660–1714*. 2d ed. London: Oxford University Press, 1965.

Cohn. Norman. *The Pursuit of the Millennium: Revolutionary Millenarians and Mystical Anarchists of the Middle Ages*. Revised and expanded edition. New York: Oxford University Press, Galaxy Book, 1970.

Colie, Rosalie L. *Light and Enlightenment: A Study of the Cambridge Platonists and the Dutch Arminians*. Cambridge: At the University Press, 1957.

Collinson, Patrick. "John Field and Elizabethan Puritanism." In S. T. Bindoff, Joel Hurstfield, and C. H. Williams, eds. *Elizabethan Government and Society*, pp. 127–62. London: University of London, Athlone Press, 1961.

——. "The Beginnings of English Sabbatarianism." In *Studies in Church History*, edited by C. W. Dugmore and C. Duggan, vol. 1, pp. 207–21. London: Nelson, 1964.

——. *A Mirror of Elizabethan Puritanism: The Life and Letters of "Godly Master Dering."* Friends of Dr. Williams's Library, Seventeenth Lecture, 1963. London: Dr. William's Trust, 1964.

——. *The Elizabethan Puritan Movement.* Berkeley and Los Angeles: University of California Press, 1967.

Coolidge, John S. *The Pauline Renaissance in England: Puritanism and the Bible.* Oxford: At the Clarendon Press, 1970.

Cragg, Gerald R. *From Puritanism to the Age of Reason: A Study of Changes in Religious Thought Within the Church of England, 1660–1770.* Cambridge: At the University Press, 1966.

——. *Puritanism in the Period of the Great Persecution, 1660–1688.* Cambridge: At the University Press, 1957.

Cross, Claire. *The Royal Supremacy in the Elizabethan Church.* Historical Problems: Studies and Documents, no. 8, edited by G. R. Elton. New York: Barnes and Noble, 1969.

Curtis, Mark H. *Oxford and Cambridge in Transition, 1558–1642.* London: Oxford University Press, 1959.

Daly, J. W. "John Bramhall and the Theoretical Problems of Royalist Moderation." *Journal of British Studies* 11 (1971): 26–44.

Davies, Godfrey. *The Early Stuarts, 1603–1660.* 2d ed. London: Oxford University Press, 1963.

Davies, Horton. *Worship and Theology in England From Cranmer to Hooker, 1534–1603.* Princeton: Princeton University Press, 1970.

Dickens, A. G. *The English Reformation.* London: B. T. Batsford, 1964.

——. *Thomas Cromwell and the English Reformation.* New York: Harper and Row, Perennial Library, 1969.

Elson, James Hinsdale. *John Hales of Eton.* New York: King's Crown Press, 1948.

Elton, G. R., ed. *The Tudor Constitution: Documents and Commentary.* Cambridge: At the University Press, 1960.

Emerson, Everett H. *English Puritanism from John Hooper to John Milton* Durham, N.C.: Duke University Press, 1968.

Eusden, John D. *Puritans, Lawyers and Politics in Early Seventeenth-Century England.* 1958. Reprint. Hamden, Conn.: Archon Books, 1968.

Firth, Charles Harding. *Oliver Cromwell and the Rule of the Puritans in England.* London: Putnam, 1947.

Fussner, F. Smith. *Tudor History and Historians.* New York: Basic Books, 1970.

Gardiner, Samuel Rawson. *History of the Great Civil War, 1642–1649.* 4 vols. London: Longmans, Green, 1897–98.

—. *History of England from the Accession of James I to the Outbreak of the Civil War, 1603–1642.* 10 vols. London: Longmans, Green, 1899.

George, Charles H., and George, Katherine. *The Protestant Mind of the English Reformation, 1570–1640.* Princeton: Princeton University Press, 1961.

George, Charles H. "A Social Interpretation of English Puritanism." *Journal of Modern History* 25 (1953):327–42.

—. "Puritanism as History and Historiography." *Past and Present,* no. 41 (December, 1968), pp. 77–104.

Gerth, H. H., and Mills, C. Wright, eds. *From Max Weber: Essays in Sociology.* New York: Oxford University Press, Galaxy Books, 1958.

Greene, Robert A., and MacCullum, Hugh, eds. *An Elegant and Learned Discourse of the Light of Nature* by Nathanael Culverwell. Toronto: Toronto University Press, 1970.

Grierson, H. J. C. *Cross Currents in English Literature of the Seventeenth Century.* Baltimore, Md.: Penguin Books, 1966.

Griffin, Martin I. J., Jr. "Latitudinarians in the Seventeenth-Century Church of England." Ph.D. dissertation, Yale University, 1962.

Hall, Basil. "Puritanism: The Problem of Definition." In *Studies in Church History,* edited by G. J. Cuming, vol. 2, pp. 283–96. London: Nelson, 1965.

—. "The Genevan Tradition." *Journal of Ecclesiastical History* 20 (1969): 111–16.

Haller, William. *The Rise of Puritanism.* New York: Columbia University Press, 1938.

—. *Liberty and Reformation in the Puritan Revolution.* New York: Columbia University Press, 1963.

—. *The Elect Nation.* New York: Harper and Row, 1963.

Hardacre, Paul H. *The Royalists During the Puritan Revolution.* The Hague: Martinus Nijhoff, 1956.

Harrison, A. W. *Arminianism.* London: Duckworth, 1937.

Hexter, J. H. *The Reign of King Pym.* Harvard Historical Studies, 48. 1941. Reprint. Cambridge, Mass.: Harvard University Press, 1961.

—. *Reappraisals in History.* London: Longmans, 1962.

—. "The Loom of Language and the Fabric of Imperatives: The Case of *Il Principe* and *Utopia.*" *American Historical Review* 59 (1964):945–68.

—. "The English Aristocracy, Its Crises, and the English Revolution, 1558–1660." *Journal of British Studies* 8 (1968):22–78.

—. *Doing History.* Bloomington, Ind.: Indiana University Press, 1971.

Hill, Christopher. *Society and Puritanism in Pre-Revolutionary England*. London: Mercury Books, 1966.

—. *Puritanism and Revolution*. New York: Schocken Books, 1967.

—. *Economic Problems of the Church from Archbishop Whitgift to the Long Parliament*. 1956. Reprint, with corrections. Oxford: At the Clarendon Press, 1968.

—. *Antichrist in Seventeenth-Century England*. London: Oxford University Press, 1971.

—. *The World Turned Upside Down: Radical Ideas During the English Revolution*. New York: Viking Press, 1972.

Hudson, Winthrop S. "Denominationalism as a Basis for Ecumenicity: A Seventeenth-Century Conception." *Church History* 24 (1955): 32–50.

Ives, E. W., ed. *The English Revolution, 1600–1660*. London: Edward Arnold, 1968.

Jones, Whitney R. D. *The Tudor Commonwealth, 1529–1559*. London: University of London, Athlone Press, 1970.

Jordan, Wilbur Kitchener. *Philanthropy in England, 1480–1660: A Study of the Changing Pattern of English Social Aspirations*. London: George Allen and Unwin, 1959.

—. *The Development of Religious Toleration in England from the Accession of James I to the Convention of the Long Parliament (1603–1640)*. 1936. Reprint. Gloucester, Mass.: Peter Smith, 1965.

—. *The Development of Religious Toleration in England from the Convention of the Long Parliament to the Restoration, 1640–1660*. 1938. Reprint. Gloucester, Mass.: Peter Smith, 1965.

—. *The Development of Religious Toleration in England: Attainment of the Theory and Accommodations in Thought and Institutions*. 1940. Reprint. Gloucester, Mass.: Peter Smith, 1965.

Judson, Margaret Atwood. *The Crisis of the Constitution: An Essay in Constitutional and Political Thought in England, 1603–1645*. 1949. Reprint. New York: Octagon Books, 1964.

Kenyon, J. P., ed. *The Stuart Constitution: Documents and Commentary*. Cambridge: At the University Press, 1966.

Ketton-Cremer, R. W. *Norfolk in the Civil War*. Hamden, Conn.: Archon Books, 1970.

Kingston, Alfred. *East Anglia and the Great Civil War*. London: Elliot Stock, 1902.

Knappen, M. M. *Tudor Puritanism: A Chapter in the History of Idealism*. Chicago: University of Chicago Press, Phoenix Books, 1965.

Knox, R. Buick. *James Ussher, Archbishop of Armagh*. Cardiff: University of Wales Press, 1967.

Lamont, William M. *Marginal Prynne, 1600–1669.* London: Routledge and Kegan Paul, 1963.

—. *Godly Rule: Politics and Religion, 1603–1660.* London: Macmillan, 1969.

—. "Puritanism in History and Historiography: Some Further Thoughts." *Past and Present,* no. 44 (August, 1969), pp. 133–46.

Lasky, Melvin J. "The Birth of a Metaphor: On the Origins of Utopia and Revolution (II)." *Encounter,* March 1970, pp. 30–42.

Little, David. *Religion, Order and Law: A Study in Pre-Revolutionary England.* New York: Harper and Row, 1969.

Liu, Tai. *Discord in Zion: The Puritan Divines and the Puritan Revolution, 1640–1660.* International Archives of the History of Ideas, no. 61. The Hague: Martinus Nijhoff, 1973.

Lovatt, Roger. "The *Imitation of Christ* in Late Medieval England." *Transactions of the Royal Historical Society,* 5th series 18 (1968): 97–121.

McAdoo, H. R. *The Structure of Caroline Moral Theology.* New York: Longmans, 1949.

—. *The Spirit of Anglicanism.* London: Adam and Charles Black, 1965.

MacCaffrey, Wallace. *The Shaping of the Elizabethan Regime.* Princeton: Princeton University Press, 1968.

McConica, James K. *English Humanists and Reformation Politics.* Oxford: At the Clarendon Press, 1965.

McGrath, Patrick. *Papists and Puritans Under Elizabeth I.* London: Blandford Press, 1967.

McNeill, John T. *A History of the Cure of Souls.* London: S. C. M. Press, 1952.

Manning, Roger B. *Religion and Society in Elizabethan Sussex: A Study of the Enforcement of the Religious Settlement, 1558–1603.* Leicester: Leicester University Press, 1969.

—. "The Crisis of Episcopal Authority During the Reign of Elizabeth I." *Journal of British Studies* 11 (1971): 1–25.

Mattingly, Garrett. *The Armada.* Boston: Houghton Mifflin, 1959.

Micklem, Nathaniel, ed. *Christian Worship.* Oxford: At the Clarendon Press, 1936.

Miller, Perry. *Orthodoxy in Massachusetts, 1630–1650.* Cambridge, Mass.: Harvard University Press, 1933.

—. "The Marrow of Puritan Divinity." *Publications of the Colonial Society of Massachusetts* 32 (1937): 247–300.

—. *The New England Mind: The Seventeenth Century.* 1939. Reprint with a new preface. Boston: Beacon Press, 1961.

Mitchell, William Fraser. *English Pulpit Oratory from Andrewes to Tillotson.* 1932. Reprint. New York: Russell and Russell, 1962.

Morgan, Edmund S. *The Puritan Dilemma: The Story of John Winthrop.* Boston: Little, Brown, 1958.

—. *Visible Saints: The History of a Puritan Idea.* Ithaca, N.Y.: Cornell University Press, 1965.

—. *Puritan Political Ideas, 1558–1794.* Indianapolis, Ind.: Bobbs-Merrill, 1965.

—. *The Puritan Family.* New York: Harper and Row, 1966.

—. *Roger Williams: The Church and the State.* New York: Harcourt, Brace and World, 1967.

Morgan, Irvonwy. *Prince Charles's Puritan Chaplain.* London: George Allen and Unwin, 1957.

Morris, Christopher. *Political Thought in England: Tyndale to Hooker.* Home University Library of Modern Knowledge, no. 225. London: Oxford University Press, 1953.

Mosse, George L. "Puritan Political Thought and the 'Cases of Conscience.' " *Church History* 23 (1954): 109–17.

Neal, Daniel. *The History of the Puritans.* 2 vols. New York: Harper and Brothers, 1843.

New, John F. H. *Anglican and Puritan: The Basis of Their Opposition, 1558–1640.* Stanford, Calif.: Stanford University Press, 1964.

—. "Oliver Cromwell and the Paradoxes of Puritanism." *Journal of British Studies* 4 (1965): 53–59.

—. "The Whitgift-Cartwright Controversy." *Archiv für Reformationsgeschichte* 59 (1969): 203–11.

Nobbs, Douglas. *Theocracy and Toleration: A Study of the Disputes in Dutch Calvinism from 1600 to 1650.* Cambridge: At the University Press, 1938.

Nuttall, Geoffrey F. *The Holy Spirit in Puritan Faith and Experience.* Oxford: Basil Blackwell, 1946.

—. *Visible Saints: The Congregational Way, 1640–1660.* Oxford: Basil Blackwell, 1957.

—. *Richard Baxter.* Edinburgh: Nelson, 1965.

Ogg, David. *England in the Reign of Charles II.* 2d ed. London: Oxford University Press, 1956.

O'Malley, John. "Erasmus and Luther, Continuity and Discontinuity As Key to Their Conflict." *Sixteenth Century Journal* 5 (1974): 47–65.

Orr, Robert R. *Reason and Authority: The Thought of William Chillingworth.* Oxford: At the Clarendon Press, 1967.

Packer, John William. *The Transformation of Anglicanism, 1643–1660: With Special Reference to Henry Hammond.* Manchester: The University Press, 1969.

Parker, Theodore M. "Arminianism and Laudianism in Seventeenth-Century England." In *Studies in Church History,* vol. 1, edited by C. W. Dugmore and Charles Duggan, pp. 20–34. London: Nelson, 1964.

Parry, R. H., ed. *The English Civil War and After, 1642–1658*. Berkeley and Los Angeles: University of California Press, 1970.

Paul, Robert S. *The Lord Protector: Religion and Politics in the Life of Oliver Cromwell*. London: Lutterworth, 1955.

Pearl, Valerie. *London and the Outbreak of the Puritan Revolution*. London: Oxford University Press, 1964.

Pettit, Norman. *The Heart Prepared: Grace and Conversion in Puritan Spiritual Life*. Yale Publications in American Studies, 11. New Haven, Conn.: Yale University Press, 1966.

Phillips, John. *The Reformation of Images: Destruction of Art in England, 1535–1660*. Berkeley and Los Angeles: University of California Press, 1973.

Plumb, John H. *The Growth of Political Stability in England, 1675–1725*. Harmondsworth, Middlesex, England: Penguin Books, 1969.

Porter, H. C. *Reformation and Reaction in Tudor Cambridge*. 1958. Reprint with new preface. Hamden, Conn.: Archon Books, 1972.

Richardson, Caroline Francis. *English Preachers and Preaching, 1640–1670*. New York: Macmillan, 1928.

Richardson, R. C. *Puritanism in North-west England: A Regional Study of the Diocese of Chester to 1642*. Totowa, N. J.: Rowman and Littlefield, 1972.

—. "Puritanism and the Ecclesiastical Authorities: The Case of the Diocese of Chester." In *Politics, Religion and the English Civil War*, edited by Brian Manning, pp. 3–33. New York: St. Martin's Press, 1973.

Ridley, Jasper. *Thomas Cranmer*. Oxford: At the Clarendon Press, 1962.

Rogers, Philip G. *The Fifth Monarchy Men*. London: Oxford University Press, 1966.

Roots, Ivan. *Commonwealth and Protectorate: The English Civil War and Its Aftermath*. Fabric of British History. New York: Schocken Books, 1966.

Roushaw, Walter C. "Notes from the Act Books of the Archdeaconry Court of Lewes." *Sussex Archaeological Collections* 49 (1906): 47–65.

Rupp, Gordon. "Patterns of Salvation in the First Age of the Reformation." *Archiv für Reformationsgeschichte* 57 (1966): 52–66.

Russell, Conrad. *The Crisis of Parliaments: English History, 1509–1660*. Shorter Oxford History of the Modern World. London: Oxford University Press, 1971.

Russell, Conrad, ed. *The Origins of the English Civil War*. New York: Harper and Row, Barnes and Noble Import Division, 1973.

Sasek, Lawrence A. *The Literary Temper of the English Puritans*. Baton Rouge, La.: Louisiana State University Press, 1961.

Scarisbrick, J. J. *Henry VIII*. Berkeley and Los Angeles: University of California Press, 1970.

Schaff, Philip, ed. *The Creeds of Christendom*. 3 vols. New York: Harper, 1887.

Schlatter, Richard. *Richard Baxter and Puritan Politics*. New Brunswick, N. J.: Rutgers University Press, 1957.

Schwartz, Hillel. "Arminianism and the English Parliament, 1624–1629." *Journal of British Studies* 12 (1973): 41–68.

Seaver, Paul S. *The Puritan Lectureships: The Politics of Religious Dissent, 1560–1662*. Stanford, Calif.: Stanford University Press, 1970.

Shapiro, Barbara. *John Wilkins, 1614–1672: An Intellectual Biography*. Berkeley and Los Angeles: University of California Press, 1969.

Sharrock, Roger. *John Bunyan*. 1954. Reprint. New York: St. Martin's Press, 1968.

Shipps, Kenneth W. "Lay Patronage of East Anglian Puritan Clerics in Pre-Revolutionary East Anglia." Ph.D. dissertation, Yale University, 1971.

Simpson, Alan. *Puritanism in Old and New England*. Chicago: University of Chicago Press, Phoenix Books, 1961.

Slavin, Arthur J., ed. *Humanism, Reform and Reformation in England*. Major Issues in History. New York: John Wiley and Sons, 1969.

Solt, Leo F. *Saints in Arms: Puritanism and Democracy in Cromwell's Army*. Stanford, Calif.: Stanford University Press, 1959.

Stearns, Raymond Phineas. *The Strenuous Puritan: Hugh Peters, 1598–1660*. Urbana, Ill.: University of Illinois Press, 1954.

Stearns, Raymond Phineas, and Brawner, David Holmes. "New England Church 'Relations' and Continuity in Early Congregational History." *Proceedings of the American Antiquarian Society*, New Series, 75 (1965): 13–45.

Stewart, Byron S. "The Cult of the Royal Martyr." *Church History* 38 (1969): 175–200.

Stoeffler, F. Ernest. *The Rise of Evangelical Pietism*. Studies in the History of Religion, no. 9. Leiden: E. J. Brill, 1965.

Stone, Lawrence. *An Elizabethan: Sir Horatio Palavicino*. Oxford: At the Clarendon Press, 1956.

Stranks, C. J. *Anglican Devotion*. London: S. C. M. Press, 1961.

Sydenham, G. F. *The History of the Sydenham Family*. East Molesey, Surrey: E. Dwelly, 1928.

Tatham, G. B. *The Puritans in Power*. Cambridge: At the University Press, 1913.

Thomas, Keith. *Religion and the Decline of Magic*. New York: Charles Scribner's Sons, 1971.

Thomas-Stanford, Charles Giesler. *Sussex in the Great Civil War and the Interregnum, 1642–1660*. London: Chiswick Press, 1910.

Toon, Peter, ed. *Puritans, the Millennium and the Future of Israel: Puritan Eschatology, 1600 to 1660*. Cambridge: James Clarke and Co., 1970.

Trevor-Roper, Hugh R. *Archbishop Laud, 1573–1645*. 2d ed. London: Macmillan, 1965.

—. *The Crisis of the Seventeenth Century*. 1956. Reprint. New York: Harper and Row, 1968.

Trinterud, Leonard J. "The Origins of Puritanism." *Church History* 20 (1951): 37–57.

Tuck, Richard, "*Power* and *Authority* in Seventeenth-Century England." *Historical Journal* 17 (1974):43–61.

Tuveson, Ernest Lee. *Millennium and Utopia: A Study in the Background of the Idea of Progress*. 1949. Reprint with new preface. New York: Harper and Row, 1964.

Underdown, David. *Pride's Purge: Politics in the Puritan Revolution*. Oxford: At the Clarendon Press, 1971.

Van Beek, M. *An Enquiry into Puritan Vocabulary*. Groningen: Wolters-Noordhoff, 1969.

Walzer, Michael. *The Revolution of the Saints*. Cambridge, Mass.: Harvard University Press, 1965.

Watkins, Owen C. *The Puritan Experience: Studies in Spiritual Autobiography*. New York: Schocken Books, 1972.

Webber, Joan. *The Eloquent "I": Style and Self in Seventeenth-Century Prose*. Madison, Wis.: University of Wisconsin, Press, 1968.

Wedgwood, Cicely Veronica. *Thomas Wentworth, First Earl of Strafford, 1593–1641*. London: Jonathan Cape, 1964.

—. *The Life of Cromwell*. New York: Collins, 1966.

—. *The Trial of Charles I*. London: Collins, 1967.

—. *The King's Peace, 1637–1641*. London: Collins, 1966.

—. *The King's War, 1641–1647*. London: Collins, 1966.

—. "Charles I: the Case for the Execution." In *Charles I*. Historical Association Pamphlet G.11. London: Historical Association, 1967.

Welsby, Paul A. *George Abbot: the Unwanted Archbishop, 1562–1633*. London: S.P.C.K., 1962.

Willson, David Harris. *King James VI and I*. London: Jonathan Cape, 1966.

Wilson, Charles. *England's Apprenticeship, 1603–1673*. Social and Economic History of England, edited by Asa Briggs. London: Longmans, 1965.

Wilson, John F. *Pulpit in Parliament: Puritanism during the English Civil Wars, 1640–1648*. Princeton, N.J.: Princeton University Press, 1969.

Wormald, Brian H. G. *Clarendon: Politics, Historiography and Religion, 1640–1660*. Cambridge: At the University Press, 1964.

Yule, George. *The Independents in the English Civil War*. Cambridge: At the University Press, 1958.

Zagorin, Perez. *The Court and the Country: The Beginnings of the English Revolution*. New York: Atheneum, 1971.

Zeeveld, W. Gordon. *Foundations of Tudor Policy*. Cambridge, Mass.: Harvard University Press, 1948.

INDEX

Abbot, George, 74–75
Absalom, 159. *See also* David
"Additions of men." *See* Adiaphora
Adiaphora, 95–97, 154, 218, 219; Puritans on, 20, 83–88 passim, 128, 242, 261, 262; defined, 73, 74. *See also* Idolatry; Mixtures of religion
Affliction: triumph through, 16; comfort in, 16, 42–44, 55, 236; response to, 16, 113; necessity of, 17, 18, 52–53, 140; explanations for, 17–18; cause of, 20–25, 125; message of, 25–38; God's Second Book, 32; imagery of, 33–35, 47–51 passim; interpretation of, 35–38; appropriate to sins, 36–37, 40–41; use of, 38–54; results of, 39–40, 46–47, 51–54, 64, 79–80; limits on, 41–42; cure of, 54–67
Allison, Charles F., 3*n*
Ames, William, 132*n*
Anabaptism, 2, 160, 175*n*, 187, 214
Anglicanism, bibliography of, 267–68
Anglicans: defined, 10–11; on the church, 11, 94–95, 144, 146; on conversion, 55–63 passim, 231–34; on the will, 70, 104, 108, 209; on the Two Tables, 95, 106, 148, 226, 253; on obedience, 100–01, 143–44, 151, 152; on salvation, 103–05, 152; on imitation of Christ, 107–13 passim, 152; on peace, 129, 166–68, 169–70; on disobedience, 134, 139, 146–52 passim, 159–60; on the godly ruler, 144; on Fifth Commandment, 148; on unity, 152–61; on trial of doctrine, 157–59; on Puritan brotherhood, 173–74; on the community of saints, 204; on the doctrine of merit, 209; on charity, 209–34; on faction, 213–21 passim; on scope of the brotherhood, 221; on ideal Christian, 233–34, 253; and Puritans com-

pared, 244–45; on order, 246; pessimistic expectations, 256–58
Antinomianism, 2, 57
Appello Caesarem, 152, 173. *See also* Montagu, Richard
Arminianism, 2, 10, 76, 155, 174*n*
Arminians, 63*n*, 73, 75
Arminius, 59, 103, 104*n*
Ash, Simeon, 19, 50–51, 83
Ashburnham, Sussex, 13
Atkins, Thomas, 83
Aylett, Robert, 78, 79*n*
Axtell, Colonel Daniel, 133, 187

Baker, Sir Richard, 45–46; on affliction, 23, 39, 43–44; identified, 23*n*; on conversion, 58; on foreign policy, 76; on obedience, 118; on charity, 192; on discipline, 198; on proselytizing, 200; on lay divinity, 200; on brotherhood, 203–04, 206
Bancroft, Richard, 11, 106*n*, 179*n*
Baptists, 175*n*, 187. *See also* Anabaptists
Barnes, Thomas G., 80*n*, 239
Bastwick, John, 79*n*
Baxter, Richard, 3, 4*n*, 148*n*, 183*n*
Benbrigge, John, 13, 257–58; on affliction, 21, 41, 125; identified, 22*n*; on personal reformation, 29; on conversion, 62; on idolatry, 72*n*; on Sabbath, 84; on adiaphora, 85; on formal professors, 85; on preaching, 85; on Two Tables, 92–93; on obedience, 125; on boutefeux, 134; on peace, 137*n*; on brethren, 183; on the poor, 191; on proselytizing, 199
Bernardiston, Sir Nathaniel, 33, 239
Bolton, Robert: on foreign policy, 75; on causes of strife, 138; on brotherhood, 182, 205–06; rebutting hypocrisy charge, 188; on charity, 195; on prayer, 201

294

INDEX